Sexuality, Citizenship and Belonging

This book brings together a diverse range of critical interventions in sexuality and gender studies and seeks to encourage new ways of thinking about the connections and tensions between sexual politics, citizenship and belonging. The book is organised around three interlinked thematic areas, focusing on sexual citizenship, nationalism and international borders (Part 1), sexuality and 'race' (Part 2) and sexuality and religion (Part 3). In revisiting notions of sexual citizenship and belonging, contributors engage with topical debates about 'sexual nationalism' or the construction of Western/European nations as exceptional in terms of attitudes towards sexual and gender equality vis-à-vis an uncivilised, racialised 'Other'.

The collection explores macro-level perspectives by attending to the geopolitical and socio-legal structures within which competing claims to citizenship and belonging are played out; at the same time, micro-level perspectives are utilised to explore the interplay between sexuality and 'race', nation, ethnicity and religious identities. Geographically, the collection has ı prevalently European focus, yet contributions explore a range of trans-ational spatial dimensions that exceed the boundaries of 'Europe' and of uropean nation-states.

ancesca Stella is a Research Fellow in Sociology at the School of Social ∃ Political Sciences, University of Glasgow.

tte Taylor is Professor of Education at the University of Strathclyde.

ey Reynolds is Professor of Social Sciences at the University of nwich.

ne Rogers is a Principal Lecturer in Sociology at London South Bank ˙sity.

Routledge Advances in Critical Diversities

Series Editors: Yvette Taylor and Sally Hines

1 **Sexuality, Citizenship and Belonging**
Trans-National and Intersectional Perspectives
Edited by Francesca Stella, Yvette Taylor, Tracey Reynolds and Antoine Rogers

Sexuality, Citizenship and Belonging
Trans-National and Intersectional Perspectives

Edited by Francesca Stella, Yvette Taylor, Tracey Reynolds and Antoine Rogers

NEW YORK AND LONDON

First published 2016
by Routledge
711 Third Avenue, New York, NY 10017

and by Routledge
2 Park Square, Milton Park, Abingdon, Oxon OX14 4RN

Routledge is an imprint of the Taylor & Francis Group, an informa business

© 2016 Taylor & Francis

The right of the editors to be identified as the authors of the editorial
material, and of the authors for their individual chapters, has been asserted
in accordance with sections 77 and 78 of the Copyright, Designs and Patents
Act 1988.

All rights reserved. No part of this book may be reprinted or reproduced or
utilised in any form or by any electronic, mechanical, or other means, now
known or hereafter invented, including photocopying and recording, or in any
information storage or retrieval system, without permission in writing from
the publishers.

Trademark notice: Product or corporate names may be trademarks or
registered trademarks, and are used only for identification and explanation
without intent to infringe.

Library of Congress Cataloging-in-Publication Data
Sexuality, citizenship and belonging : trans-national and intersectional
    perspectives / edited by Francesca Stella, Yvette Taylor, Tracey Reynolds
    and Antoine Rogers.
       pages cm.—(Routledge advances in critical diversities ; 1)
    Includes bibliographical references and index.
   1. Sexual minorities. 2. Sexual orientation. 3. Sex discrimination.
4. Citizenship. 5. Nationalism. 6. Human rights. I. Stella, Francesca,
1975– editor.
    HQ73.S52 2016
    306.76—dc23   2015027615

ISBN: 978-1-138-80504-0 (hbk)
ISBN: 978-1-315-75256-3 (ebk)

Typeset in Sabon
by Apex CoVantage, LLC

Contents

List of Figures	vii
Acknowledgements	viii

Introduction FRANCESCA STELLA, YVETTE TAYLOR, TRACEY REYNOLDS AND ANTOINE ROGERS	1

PART I
Sexual Nationalisms and the Boundaries of Sexual Citizenship

1 **Sexual Citizenship, Nationalism and Biopolitics in Putin's Russia** FRANCESCA STELLA AND NADYA NARTOVA	17
2 **Sexuality, Citizenship and Migration: The Irish Queer Diaspora in London** RÓISÍN RYAN-FLOOD	37
3 **Narrativising One's Sexuality/Gender: Neo-Liberal Humanitarianism and the Right of Asylum** CALOGERO GIAMETTA	55
4 **The New Trans-National Politics of LGBT Human Rights in the Commonwealth: What Can UK NGOs Learn from the Global South?** MATTHEW WAITES	73

PART II
Racialised Subjects and Feminist/Queer Solidarities

5 **Black Mammy and Company: Exploring Constructions of Black Womanhood in Britain** TRACEY REYNOLDS	95

vi *Contents*

6 Activism through Identities: Building Shared Alliances against Homophobia and Racism in Palermo   112
MARIA LIVIA ALGA

7 What Does a 'Genuine Lesbian' Look Like?: Intersections of Sexuality and 'Race' in Manchester's Gay Village and in the UK Asylum System   131
NINA HELD

8 'Time After Time': Gay Conditionality, Colonial Temporality and *Āzādī*   149
TARA ATLURI

PART III
Sexuality, Religion and Belonging

9 Creating Citizens, Constructing Religion, Configuring Gender: Intersectional Sites, Scripts and Sticking Points   165
YVETTE TAYLOR AND RIA SNOWDON

10 Changing Churches: Sexuality, Difference, Power   183
SAVITRI HENSMAN

11 Counter-Normative Identities: Religious Young Adults Subverting Sexual Norms   199
SARAH-JANE PAGE

12 Angels and the Dragon King's Daughter: Gender and Sexuality in Western Buddhist New Religious Movements   218
SALLY R. MUNT AND SHARON E. SMITH

Contributors   245
Index   251

Figures

12.1	Religion's positioning in relation to gender from Woodhead (2007: 670, used with permission).	222
12.2	The Dragon King's daughter (East Asian depiction).	232
12.3	The Dragon King's daughter offers a jewel to Buddha.	233
12.4	Vijayatara/Sharon Smith (1962–2011).	239

Acknowledgements

Thanks to all the contributors for their efforts and patience.

Chapter 12 was previously published as Munt, S.R. and Smith, S.E. (2010) 'Angels and the Dragon King's Daughter: Gender, Sexuality in Western Buddhist New Religious Movements', *Theology and Sexuality* 16(3): 229–258. Maney Publishing. www.maneyonline.com/tas. http://essential. metapress.com/content/122845/. The article is reprinted by kind permission of Maney Publishing.

Introduction

Francesca Stella, Yvette Taylor, Tracey Reynolds and Antoine Rogers

This volume brings together a diverse range of critical interventions within the interdisciplinary field of sexuality and gender studies. The collection as a whole explores topical and emergent debates within the field and seeks to encourage new ways of thinking about the connections and tensions between sexual politics, citizenship, multiple identifications and belonging. We focus here in particular on three interlinked thematic areas that we believe deserve particular attention: sexuality in relation to citizenship, nationalism and international borders; sexuality and 'race'; and sexuality and religion. The choice of these thematic foci is partly a reflection of personal and political concerns which are important to each of the co-editors (see e.g. Reynolds 2001, 2005; Rogers 2012, 2015; Stella 2007, 2013, 2014; Taylor et al. 2010; Taylor and Snowdon 2014). It was also inspired, however, by ongoing and often heated debates around 'sexual nationalisms', which have been particularly prominent in queer and feminist circles at least since the publication of Puar's *Terrorist Assemblages* (Puar 2007) and have been variously articulated as 'homonationalism' (Puar 2007) or 'femonationalism' (Farris 2012). In revisiting debates around sexual citizenship and belonging, our contributors engage more or less explicitly with these perspectives. It has been argued that changes in sexual and intimate lives across the globe have led to the progressive democratisation of sexual relations and the trans-national mainstreaming of notions of gender and sexual equality (Giddens 1992; Weeks 2007). These perspectives, however, have been challenged by research highlighting persistent disparities in gender and sexuality equality across nation-states (Stychin 2003; Roseneil, Halsaa and Sumer 2012), conservative backlashes against the globalisation of sexual and reproductive rights (Waites and Kollman 2009; Stella and Nartova, this volume) and enduring inequalities and tensions within the diverse communities ostensibly represented by LGBT and feminist politics (Taylor et al. 2010; Lutz et al. 2011).

Critical of triumphalist narratives of global progress in the field of sexual and reproductive rights, 'sexual nationalism' perspectives have instead highlighted how gender and sexual equality are often deployed 'in the invention of a civilized, mature Europe and its irrational, perverse, barbaric Others'

2 Francesca Stella et al.

(Petzen 2012). Fitfully for a collection which is part of the 'Advances in Critical Diversities' series, our intention is not to dismiss the significance of sexual and gender equality, the difference it makes to people's lives and the ongoing political struggles associated with them. Instead, our aim is to foreground persistent tensions, discomforts and inequalities within feminist and LGBT/queer politics, for example, around the co-optation of sexual and reproductive rights into Orientalist, neocolonial, racist and antireligious discourses (Fassin 2010) or the mainstreaming of the language of diversity in feminist and LGBT politics in ways that often contribute to mask and maintain white middle-class privilege (Ward 2008). Foregrounding tensions does not mean throwing the baby away with the bath water: it means shifting the focus from 'the world we have won' (Weeks 2007) to other important struggles that intersect, sometimes uneasily, with those around gender and sexual equality. Others before us have passionately engaged in, and contributed to, these debates, and we recognise our debt in particular to US Black feminists and to the concept and politics of intersectionality. Intersectional perspectives foreground how oppression is institutionalised and experienced around different configurations of 'race', gender, class, sexuality, age and able-bodiedness and also help us to imagine and sustain solidarities across these boundaries (hooks 1981; Lorde 1984; Crenshaw 1989). We also wish to acknowledge the legacies of now more established academics whose work on sexuality and gender was initially pioneering and lacked institutional support and in whose footsteps we tread, even as we take aspects of their work as points of departure and contestation (McIntosh 1986; Plummer 1975; Pateman 1988; Jackson, 1999; Weeks 2007). We are also indebted to activists, academics and activist scholars who have highlighted enduring and painful absences around 'race', ethnicity, migration and religion in these legacies, particularly in a UK and European context where there has arguably been a more marked reluctance to engage with these issues than, for example, in the US (see for example Luibhéid and Cantú 2005; Kuntsman and Miyake 2008; Ahmed 2011; Hariwatorn 2012;).

The geographic focus of this collection is admittedly Eurocentric: with the exception of Atluri, who explores sexual politics in contemporary India, the chapters focus on the UK, Russia, Ireland and Italy. The collection, however, does not comprise a range of national case studies or foreground a comparative perspective, a format common in edited books on social movements and LGBT and women's rights (Kelly and Breslin 2010; Tremblay, Paternotte and Johnson 2011; Roseneil, Halsaa and Sumer 2012; Kollman 2013; Ayoub and Paternotte 2014). Instead, the contributions explore a range of trans-national spatial dimensions that exceed the boundaries of the nation-state and of 'Europe': they consider, for example, links between Britain as a former imperial power and its former colonies (Waites, Atluri); the construction of a European 'core' and its 'peripheries' in discourses on sexual and reproductive rights (Stella and Nartova, Alga); or forms of belonging shaped by migration from within and outside 'fortress Europe' (Ryan-Flood, Giametta, Alga, Held). Thus the edited collection

Introduction 3

explores macro-level perspectives by attending to the broader geopolitical and socio-legal structures within which competing claims to citizenship and belonging are played out; at the same time, micro-level perspectives are utilised to explore the interplay between sexuality and 'race', nation, ethnicity and religious identities, both in individuals' lived experiences and in activism and forms of collective belonging (see chapters by Reynolds, Held, Ryan-Flood, Taylor and Snowdon, Page, Munt and Smith, Hensman).

Indeed, despite its apparent emphasis on 'nation', the notion of 'sexual nationalism' is conceptually useful to open up the map and to go beyond the nation-state and beyond methodological nationalism by connecting different geographical scales: the global, the regional, the national, the local and the body (Colpani and Habed 2014). Puar defines homonationalism as 'an analytical category deployed to understand and historicise how and why a nation's "gay-friendly" status has become desirable' as a marker of progress, modernity and civilisation' (Puar 2013: 336). This status, evidenced by policy and legislation designed to recognise same-sex coupledom and to protect LGBT citizens from discrimination and violence, has been widely celebrated as a progressive development. The symbolic inclusion of non-heterosexual and gender-nonconforming individuals into the citizenry is a relatively new phenomenon, particularly visible in (although not confined to) the 'Western' world (Tremblay, Paternotte and Johnson 2011). Yet Puar (2007, 2013) argues that the selective inclusion of queer bodies as worthy of state protection is often acquired at the expense of the racialised 'Other'. Internationally, LGBT rights become a badge of national pride for many Western countries, while being used on a symbolic level as a marker of progress which distinguishes the 'civilised' Global North from the 'uncivilised' South (and, within Europe, to mark the 'modern' West/North from its Eastern and Southern 'homophobic' peripheries). Domestically, the new recognition of LGBT rights is paralleled by the problematisation of racialised ethnic communities, for example, Muslim populations, imagined as the 'culturally other' and inherently homophobic. However, debates about 'sexual exceptionalism' are neither confined to LGBT rights nor are they new: the deployment of sexuality and gender in the construction of specific 'geographies of perversion and desire' can be traced back to European colonial history, whereby modern, civilised 'Western' sexualities were pitted against perverse and exotic sexual 'Others' (Stoler 1995; Bleys 1996; Binnie 2004). This legacy continues as constructions of 'Europeanness' and of 'progressive' national identities within Europe continue to deploy discourses of 'civilisation' which increasingly hinge on values such as gender equality, sexual liberalisation and secularism as core values (Fassin 2010). These discourses are deployed internationally to justify or curtail military or humanitarian intervention (e.g. the liberation of women from the yoke of patriarchy offered as an argument for US intervention in Afghanistan, UK aid to certain African countries being made conditional on the decriminalisation of homosexuality; see Allison 2013, Waites and Atluri, this volume). 'Sexual exceptionalism' is also deployed in the

4 *Francesca Stella et al.*

pervasive political obsession with immigration to 'fortress Europe' and to specific European states, where, for example radicalised migrant women are portrayed as victims of their own (sexist and homophobic) culture (Farris 2012; Bracke 2012).

* * * * *

The first section of the book, 'Sexual Nationalisms and the Boundaries of Sexual Citizenship', explores national and trans-national dimensions of sexual citizenship and its politics. Despite the projection of 'sexual democracy' as a European value to be mainstreamed across the continent (Fassin 2010; Ayoub and Paternotte 2014), legal and policy recognition of gender equality and LGBT rights remains uneven across different European counties (see for example Trappolin et al. 2012; ILGA-Europe 2015). Colpani and Habed (2014) observe a tendency in analyses of 'sexual nationalisms' in Europe to take Northern European states, where elusive notions of gender equality and sexual diversity are hailed as national values, as paradigmatic of Europe as a whole. This ignores the fact that 'homonationalist imaginaries and practices operate simultaneously, if not contradictorily, in different European locations', and erases from the map the sexual nationalisms of many parts of Southern and Central and Eastern Europe, which are often constructed in opposition to 'European' values. Indeed, Francesca Stella and Nadya Nartova (chapter 1) argue that homonationalism is an unsuitable conceptual framework to understand the politicisation of gender and sexuality as a marker of national identity in Russia, a nation very much positioned on the periphery of Europe. Drawing on a careful discourse analysis of media, policy and legal documents, they consider how restrictions on citizens' sexual and reproductive rights are justified in the name of the national interest and in explicit opposition to European notions of 'sexual democracy'; they also highlight how family and demographic policies are deployed in the construction of ideals of nation and national belonging, which are both sexualised and gendered. They propose Foucault's notion of biopower, a technology of power concerned with the social and biological control of populations (Foucault 1978/1998, 1997/2004), as a more productive concept to understand the workings of Russian sexual nationalism.

The following two chapters explore the boundaries of sexual citizenship from the point of view of two very different groups of migrants in the UK: LGBT Irish migrants (Róisín Ryan-Flood, chapter 2) and LGBT asylum seekers (Calogero Giametta, chapter 3). The relationship between trans-national queer migration and sexual citizenship rights remains poorly understood, and both chapters highlight the complexities of migrants' motivations, circumstances and positionalities. Róisín Ryan-Flood's chapter is based on interviews with LGBT Irish migrants in London, whose experiences are contextualised within the broader history of Irish migration to the UK. She highlights how, for LGBT Irish migrants, economic motives are often intertwined with the search of a more tolerant and supportive social climate; thus she argues that 'theorising sexuality and migration separately offers only a partial and determinist understanding of the experiences of queer migrants'. She also shows that LGBT migrants' experiences illuminate changes over time in both British and Irish sexual citizenship regimes and explores the impact of migration on the formation of Irish queer subjectivities and on relationships with family 'back home'. Calogero Giametta considers the paradoxical position occupied by asylum claimants who seek protection from persecution on the grounds of sexuality and gender identity in the UK, recently ranked the most progressive European country in terms of legislation and policies concerning LGBT rights (ILGA-Europe 2015). Yet legal protection is not automatically extended to LGBT asylum claimants: in the UK as well as in other European countries, asylum is increasingly seen as a system threatening the success of 'managed' migration (Squire 2009), and the legitimacy and credibility of asylum claimants is a priori doubted and scrutinised (Cowen et al. 2011). Despite a humanitarian 'moral attachment to the principle of asylum' (Squire 2009: 5) as a marker of moral superiority compared to refugee producing states, in practice, asylum is increasingly framed as a security issue needing intensified surveillance and policing. Drawing on interviews with LGBT asylum claimants and refugees on their experience of the asylum system, Calogero Giametta analyses the biographical narratives they are compelled to produce, prompted and assisted by state institutions as well as by humanitarian bodies (i.e. immigration lawyers, refugee NGOs) whose aim is to protect them. Thus the process of certifying the credibility of their narratives acts as a 'biographical border' (Mai 2014) between the threat of deportation and the safety of recognition.

The final chapter in this section, by Matthew Waites, also explores the paradoxes of humanitarianism, albeit from a different angle. The chapter examines the activities of London-based NGOs focused on the promotion of LGBT human rights in the Commonwealth of Nations, an organisation comprising 53 member states, for the most part territories of the former British Empire. The chapter compares the activities and approaches of four London-based LGBT NGOs working trans-nationally. Matthew Waites explores the power relations and tensions arising from UK-based NGOs utilising the Commonwealth as a 'political opportunity structure' (Kitschelt 1986). He shows that, while their activities are well intentioned and in many ways beneficial, these organisations act with limited understanding of the national contexts they purport to influence and often do not seem alive to the hierarchies of privilege around 'race' and class within their own structure. Their engagement with the experience of LGBT organisations operating locally, and their ability to learn from their experiences and perspectives, has thus far been very limited. Indeed, London-based trans-national LGBT organisations have tended to privilege a single-issue approach to human rights rather than considering postcolonial and intersectional perspectives.

6   *Francesca Stella et al.*

The second section of the book, 'Racialised Subjects and Feminist/Queer Solidarities', explores the intersections between racialised/postcolonial subjects and sexuality/gender, both in terms of lived experiences and of political activism. Recent work has proposed that the image of Europe or of the national community as exceptionally progressive with regards to sexual and gender equality hinges on binary notions of civilisation/barbarity and enlightenment/darkness, often rooted in histories of slavery and colonialism. For example, the mythology of 'sexual exceptionalism' echoes in historical work on modern American sexualities, which has shown how both constructs of 'deviant' homosexuality and of 'normal' heterosexuality were underpinned by understanding of 'whiteness' as the invisible norm (Bleys 1996; Carter 2007). Sexual exceptionalism has historically been deployed to racialise the ethnic and religious 'Other', and this continues to be the case in contemporary societies (Puar 2007; Fassin 2010; Ahmed 2011; Hariwatorn 2012). Yet uncomfortable silences continue to surround 'race' in sexualities and gender studies, as well as in feminist and queer activism (Reynolds 2001, 2005; Kuntsman and Miyake 2008; Rahman 2010; Ahmed 2011; Rogers 2012, 2015). Lutz et al. (2011) suggest that this is perhaps less the case in the US than in Europe: while in the US race equality is associated with the civil rights movement and the pivotal role African-Americans played within it, in Europe 'race' retains uncomfortable associations with theories of white racial supremacy based on notions of race as a 'natural', biological fact, theories used in the not too distant past to justify colonial domination and exploitation, as well as genocide outside and within Europe itself (see e.g. Lutz et al. 2011 on the problematic connotations of the term *Rasse* in German-speaking countries). The contributions in this section engage with 'race' as an analytical category in order to illuminate the workings of institutional racism, racial prejudice and colonial histories. Yet challenging racism involves not only understanding how processes of racialisation affect black people's lived experiences but also scrutinising 'whiteness' as a relational but invisible backdrop.

The section is opened by Tracey Reynolds's chapter, which explores constructions of black womanhood in the UK. She argues that there is political value in using the term 'black women' as a means to challenge and resist racism, even as it conflates differences around ethnicity, geographical positioning (Global North/South) and citizenship status, as well as class, generation and sexuality. Against the depoliticised use of intersectionality (Erel et al. 2010), she also argues for the need to trace it back to its origins in Black feminist theory, as a way to foreground the importance of racial oppression in black women's lives and make their voices heard. Reynolds shows how black women continue to be positioned as the racialised other by white majority society, a construction underpinned by a denigrating mythology about black women's sexuality. She identifies in the figures of the Black Mammy, the 'Welfare' Mum, the Jezebel and the Matriarch the main dominant stereotypical representations of black women's sexualities and shows how they are constructed as either hypersexual (Jezebel, the 'Welfare'

Mum), asexual (the Black Mammy) or threatening and emasculating (the Matriarch). She then analyses in more detail the figure of the Black Mammy to illustrate how racialised images of black women's sexuality continue to influence policies and social attitudes in the UK and the implications these images and discourses have on black women's everyday lives.

Maria Livia Alga's contribution explores the possibilities for building alliances across antihomophobic and antiracist movements in Italy as a way to transcend single-issue identity politics and challenge homonormative notions of 'sexual democracy' as a distinctively 'white/European' value (Fassin 2010). Drawing on ethnographic fieldwork conducted in Palermo, capital of the autonomous region of Sicily, the chapter contextualises the research within the specific geopolitical space of Italy and Sicily. As one of the southern frontiers of 'fortress Europe', Italy plays an important part in policing and controlling migration, particularly non-white migration from Africa and the Middle East. Non-EU migrants are increasingly portrayed as a threat to European security, economic prosperity and values (including values of sexual and gender equality). At the same time, lack of recognition of LGBT rights in policy and legislation positions Italy as a 'ghost sexual democracy' compared to other European countries. Thus homonationalism does not occur as a discourse affirming the superiority of Italian national laws vis-à-vis other 'homophobic' cultures; rather, it features in demands towards greater recognition of LGBT rights as a process which would make Italy truly 'European'. The shared marginality experienced by racialised migrants and LGBT citizens in Italy, Alga argues, creates spaces for solidarities across antiracist and LGBT activism in the Palermo-based women's group *La migration*. Echoing Waites (this volume), Alga explores the potential as well as the complexities and tensions of intersectional politics and solidarities.

The following chapter, by Nina Held, takes us from Palermo, Sicily to Manchester, England, widely regarded as one of the most gay-friendly cities in the UK owing to the presence of a very visible gay scene ('the Gay Village') in its city centre. Echoing Reynolds and Alga (this volume), Held explores the exclusionary repercussions of discourses which construct the homosexual other as white and the racialised other as straight (Puar 2008). Drawing on ethnographic fieldwork, the chapter examines the racialisation of lesbian spaces in the Village, showing how publicity, door policies and other practices affect how certain bodies are mis/recognised as 'lesbian'. In the second part of the chapter, Held shows how assumptions about the 'genuine' lesbian body affect not only non-white women's experiences of the Village but also those of women claiming asylum in the UK on the grounds of their sexuality. Like Giametta (this volume), Held shows how proving the credibility of one's story is a crucial criterion in obtaining refugee status; yet credibility is often assessed on the basis of living a 'Western' lesbian lifestyle, including its public expression, regardless of whether this is actually feasible or imaginable in women's countries of origin. Thus both scene spaces and

8 Francesca Stella et al.

the asylum system in Britain reproduce normative racialised notions of the 'genuine lesbian'.

The last contribution to this section, by Tara Atluri, draws on ethnographic fieldwork conducted in New Delhi, India and discusses how the legacies of British colonialism continue to shape queer and feminist politics in India. Atluri focuses on three important moments in recent sexual politics struggles: the proposal by British Prime Minister David Cameron to make aid to 'developing countries' dependent on their respect of LGBT rights (2011) ; the street protests against government complacency in acting to stop sexual violence against women, following the high profile 2012 Delhi gang rape case; and the protests following the 2013 reinstatement of Section 377 of the Indian Penal Code, criminalising consensual same-sex practices and introduced during British colonial rule and temporarily repealed in 2009 on grounds of violating the Indian constitution. Atluri shows how these moments are connected and argues that feminists and queer activism in India should be understood in relation to neocolonial attempts to speak on behalf of the 'Global South' (see also Waites, this volume). Rather than assessing their efforts against ethnocentric measures of progress based on notions of 'sexual democracy' (Fassin 2010), Atluri contends that they should be understood in their own terms, as articulated outside the grammar of 'Western' political subjectivities and rights-based activism.

The third and final section of the collection explores the intersections between sexuality, religion and belonging. 'Sexual democracy' has often been linked to secularisation and the declining influence of religious institutions in Western societies (Hunt and Yip 2012; Nynäs and Yip 2012). Indeed, both feminism and gay liberation have mostly regarded religion as 'an intrinsically constraining and restrictive force, policing gendered and sexual subjectivities and practices' (Nynäs and Yip 2012: 9). While the tension between sexual liberalism and religious norms continues to be a site of contestation, increasingly heated public debates on the role of religion in Western democracies have generally focused on the danger posed by religious 'Others' (El-Tayeb 2012; Haritaworn 2012). LGBT rights and women's sexual rights feature prominently in debates about the backlash against multiculturalism in religiously diverse societies: against the backdrop of the 'war on terror' and the rise of Islamophobia across Europe, much of this work has focused on the cultural racism experienced by Muslims (Mepschen, Duyvendak and Tonkens 2010; El-Tayeb 2012; Haritaworn 2012). The representation of Muslims as 'traditional', sexist and homophobic is 'cast within Orientalist narratives that underwrite the superiority of European secular modernity' (Mepschen, Duyvendak and Tonkens 2010: 963). Rather than explicitly focusing on the religious 'Other', contributions to this volume foreground new research agendas focused on 'vernacular religion' (Lassander 2012) and explore the intersection between sexuality and religion through an examination of everyday practices and identifications. This research challenges the assumption that religious beliefs are incompatible with non-reproductive and non-heteronormative sexual practices and identities, while foregrounding tensions between institutionalised religion, individual practices and interpretations and collective contestations around sexual and reproductive rights within religious communities (Nynäs and Yip 2012; Yip and Page 2013; Taylor and Snowdon 2014).

The first chapter in the section, by Yvette Taylor and Ria Snowdon, is a case study exploration of young Christian lesbians' experiences in the UK. The chapter draws on interview data collected for a broader study on British queer-identified religious youth involved in the Metropolitan Community Church (MCC), founded in, for and by the LGBT community. While young people are typically assumed to be uninterested in religion and their voices are thus often marginalised within religious communities, the chapter's exploration of Christian young lesbians' experiences foregrounds religious organisations, practices and spaces as deeply gendered and sexualised. The authors examine women's interactions with role models and mentors who are meant to make space for them within religious communities; they highlight how role models are often experienced by young women as reproducing gendered and heteronormative hierarchies, as well as familial discourses, and show how these perceptions shape young women's religious subjectivities and their engagements with religious spaces. Young lesbians' experiences of participation in religious communities are carefully framed as taking place during a time when debates on religion and sexuality were highly visible in the public arena, through contestations over same-sex marriage and the ordination of female bishops in the Church of England.

Public debates on sexuality and religion are the focus of a reflexive piece by Savitri Hensman, a UK-based Christian and lesbian activist who has been involved in activism seeking greater equality for LGBTQI people in church and society and challenging 'top-down', hierarchical models. Hensman reflects on her position as both an 'insider' (as a member of the Church of England and as a lesbian campaigner) and an 'outsider' within these campaigns (as a minority ethnic woman and as someone who has a more detached perspective on what is happening in non-Anglican Christian communities). Hensman argues that, although churches are often portrayed as monolithic, hierarchical institutions, the term 'church' in the Christian tradition originally referred to a fellowship of people. This leaves room for members of various churches to question dominant discourses on same-sex relationships and gender equality; indeed these debates have always been part of various churches' theological traditions. While there are indeed power imbalances in faith communities, these may be actively contested by drawing on religious beliefs and not just on secular influences. Over the years, gradual shifts in thinking among ordinary members of the church as well as its clergy have allowed the revisiting of seemingly established gender and sexual norms.

The next chapter, by Sarah-Jane Page, explores how religious British young people negotiate sexual norms. Page draws on interview data with

10 *Francesca Stella et al.*

both heterosexual and LGBT-identified young people, who come from a variety of religious backgrounds (Buddhist, Christian, Hindu, Jewish, Muslim, Sikh or a combination of these). Page shows how young people's choices around sexuality continue to be made within regulatory frames; *contra* the widespread perception of religion as a sexually illiberal sphere, she argues that young people draw on both religious and secular scripts in making sense of, and navigating, sexual norms and that the regulation of sexuality should not solely be associated with religious frameworks. Young people's experiences are shaped by dominant discourses within youth culture portraying sex as an imperative aspect of young people's lives, promoting pleasure-seeking hedonism and problematising stable couple relationships. The majority of young people involved in the study endorsed monogamous relationships, while being negative about celibacy (variously understood as temporarily refraining from sex or longer-term abstinence). Yet Page shows how a minority of young people within her sample supported either celibacy or non-monogamy and in doing so they utilised religious scripts as a resource in negotiating sexual norms and carving out their own sexual practices and identities.

Sally Munt and Sharon Smith's chapter continues the exploration of gender and sexual norms and focuses on two Buddhist organisations with the largest following in the UK. Buddhism is here explored as a new religious movement, which emerged as an alternative form of spirituality to the mainstream religions in Western societies (typically various Christian denominations). Drawing on interview data with members of two Western Buddhist organisations, Munt and Smith explore their interpretations and constructs of gender and sexuality; they also tease out how the latter intersect with queer identifications and (to a lesser extent) with ethnicity and 'race'. They outline dominant constructs of gender and sexuality in different Buddhist traditions, noting that they tend to be androcentric, while at the same time problematising sexual activity per se (regardless of the gender of the partners involved). While in some contexts Buddhist traditions have accommodated gender variation and same-sex relations (particularly between men), findings suggest that the Western Buddhist movements explored are perceived as highly heteronormative, yet these norms continue to be contested by their members; indeed, members subtly challenge and subvert hegemonising attempts to use traditional symbolic language (e.g. women as 'angels'). Buddhism appears a welcoming space for those traditionally marginalised on account of their gender or sexuality, because it privileges individual subjectivity and experience over doctrine or tradition, although within it white middle-class identity positions remain dominant.

In revisiting notions of sexual citizenship and belonging through the prisms of nationalism, 'race' and religion, contributors to this volume foreground tensions as well as common ground and encourage critical, yet constructive approaches to issues of equality and diversity. In bringing together trans-national and intersectional perspectives, we seek to give

Introduction 11

depth to seemingly abstract notions of citizenship and two-dimensional categories of 'social divisions' by contextualising them in time and space, while also teasing out how macro-level social change at the levels of geo-political and socio-legal structures is experienced, interpreted and supported or resisted by diverse subjects. This can hopefully go some way towards challenging the Orientalism and racism of Cold War–era 'Three Worlds' ideology, which still informs the way we associate 'postcoloniality with a bounded space called the Third World and postsocialism with the Second World' (Chari and Verdery 2009: 12). Our hope is that combining trans-national and intersectional perspectives can help us imagine a different world.

BIBLIOGRAPHY

Ahmed, S. (2011) 'Problematic Proximities: Or Why Critiques of Gay Imperialism Matter', *Feminist Legal Studies* 19: 119–132.

Allison, K. (2013) 'American Occidentalism and the Agential Muslim Woman', *Review of International Studies* 39(3): 665–684.

Ayoub, P. and Paternotte, D. (eds.) (2014) *LGBT Activism and the Making of Europe: A Rainbow Europe*. Basingstoke: Palgrave.

Binnie, J. (2004) *The Globalization of Sexuality*. London: Sage.

Bleys, R. C. (1996) *The Geography of Perversion: Male-to-Male Sexual Behaviour Outside the West and the Ethnographic Imagination, 1750–1918*. London: Cassell.

Bracke, S. (2012) 'From "Saving Women" to "Saving Gays": Rescue Narratives and Their Dis/Continuities', *European Journal of Women's Studies* 19(2): 237–252.

Carter, J. B. (2007) *The Heart of Whiteness: Normal Sexuality and Race in America, 1880–1940*. Durham: Duke University Press.

Chari, S. and Verdery, K. (2009) 'Thinking between the Posts: Postcolonialism, Postsocialism, and Ethnography after the Cold War', *Comparative Studies in Society and History* 51(1): 6–34.

Colpani, G. and Habed, A. J. (2014) 'In Europe Its Different: Homonationalism and Peripheral Desires for Europe', in Ayoub, P. and Paternotte, D. (eds.) *LGBT Activism and the Making of Europe: A Rainbow Europe*. Basingstoke: Palgrave, 73–94.

Cowen, T., Stella, F., Magahy, K., Strauss, K. and Morton, J. (2011) *Sanctuary, Safety and Solidarity. LGBT Asylum Seekers in Scotland*. A report by Equality Network, BEMIS (Black and Ethnic Minorities Infrastructure in Scotland) and GRAMnet. Glasgow: University of Glasgow.

Crenshaw, K. (1989) 'Demarginalizing the Intersection of Race and Sex: A Black Feminist Critique of Antidiscrimination Doctrine, Feminist Theory and Antiracist Politics', *The University of Chicago Legal Forum* 139: 139–168.

El-Tayeb, F. (2012) ' "Gays Who Cannot Properly be Gay": Queer Muslims in the Neoliberal European City', *European Journal of Women's Studies* 19(1): 79–95.

Erel, U., Harotaworn, J., Gutierrez-Rodrigues, E. and Klesse, K. (2010) 'On the Depoliticisation of Intersectionality Talk. Conceptualising Multiple Oppressions in Critical Sexuality Studies', in Taylor, Y., Hines, S. and Casey, M. (eds.) *Theorizing Intersectionality and Sexuality*. Basingstoke: Palgrave, 56–77.

Farris, S. (2012) 'Femonationalism and the "Regular" Army of Labour Called Migrant Women', *History of the Present* 2(2): 184–199.

12 *Francesca Stella et al.*

Fassin, E. (2010) 'National Identities and Transnational Intimacies: Sexual Democracy and the Politics of Immigration in Europe', *Public Culture* 22(3): 507–529.

Foucault, M. (1978/1998) *The History of Sexuality. Vol. I: The Will to Knowledge.* London: Penguin.

Foucault, M. (1997/2004) *Society Must be Defended. Lectures at the Collège de France, 1975–96.* Penguin: London.

Giddens, A. (1992) *The Transformation of Intimacy: Sexuality, Love and Eroticism in Modern Societies.* Cambridge: Polity Press.

Haritaworn, J. (ed) (2012) 'Women's Rights, Gay Rights and Anti-Muslim Racism in Europe', Special Section in *European Journal of Women's Studies* 19(1/2): 73–78.

hooks, b. (1981) *Ain't I a Woman: Black Women and Feminism.* London: Pluto Press.

ILGA-Europe. (2015) 'Rainbow Europe 2015'. Available at http://www.ilga-europe. org/resources/rainbow-europe/2015, last accessed 22 June 2015.

Hunt, S. and Yip, A. (eds.) (2012) *The Ashgate Research Companion to Contemporary Religion and Sexuality.* Farnham: Ashgate.

Jackson, S. (1999) *Heterosexuality in Question.* London: Sage.

Kelly, S. and Breslin, J. (eds.) (2010) *Women's Rights in the Middle East and North Africa: Progress Amid Resistance.* London: Rowman & Littlefield.

Kitschelt, H. (1986) 'Political Opportunity Structures and Political Protest: Anti-Nuclear Movements in Four Democracies', *British Journal of Political Science* 16(1): 57–85.

Kollman, K. (2013) *The Same-sex Unions Revolution in Western Democracies: International Norms and Domestic Policy Change.* Manchester: Manchester University Press.

Kuntsman, A. and E. Miyake (eds.) (2008) *Out of Place: Interrogating Silences in Queerness/Raciality.* York, England: Raw Nerve Books.

Lassander, M. (2012) 'Grappling with Liquid Modernity: Investigating Postsecular Religion', in Nynäs, P., Lassander, M. and Utriainen, T. (eds.) *Postsecular Society.* London: Transaction Publishers, 239–267.

Lorde, A. (1984) *Sister Outsider. Essays and Speeches.* Trumansburg, NY: Crossing Press.

Luibhéid, E. and Cantú, L. (eds.) (2005) *Queer Migrations: Sexuality, U.S. Citizenship, and Border Crossings.* Minneapolis: University of Minnesota Press.

Lutz, H., Herrera Vivar, M. T. and Supik, L. (2011) *Framing Intersectionality: Debates on a multi-Faceted Concept in Gender Studies.* Farnham: Ashgate.

Mai, N. (2014) 'Between Embodied Cosmopolitanism and Sexual Humanitarianism: The Fractal Mobilities and Subjectivities of Migrants Working in the Sex Industry', in Baby-Collins, V. and Anteby, L. (eds.) *Borders, Mobilities and Migrations. Perspectives from the Mediterranean in the 21st Century.* Brussels: Peter Lang, 175–192.

McIntosh, M. (1986) 'The Homosexual Role', *Social Problems* 16(2):182–192.

Mepschen, P., Duyvendak, J. W. and Tonkens, E. H. (2010) 'Sexual Politics, Orientalism and Multicultural Citizenship in the Netherlands', *Sociology* 44(5): 962–979.

Nynäs, P. and Yip, A. (2012) *Religion, Gender and Sexuality in Everyday Life.* Farnham: Ashgate.

Pateman, C. (1988) *The Sexual Contract.* Cambridge: Polity Press.

Petzen, J. (2012) 'Contesting Europe: A Call for an Anti-Modern Sexual Politics', *European Journal of Women's Studies* 19(1): 97–114.

Plummer, K. (1975) *Sexual Stigma: An Interactionist Account.* London: Routledge.

Puar, J. K. (2007) *Terrorist Assemblages: Homonationalism in Queer Times.* Durham: Duke University Press.

Puar, J. K. (2008) 'Q&A with Jasbir Puar', *Darkmatter*, 3. Available at http://www.darkmatter101.org/site/2008/05/02/qa-with-jasbir-puar/, last accessed 28 February 2014.

Puar, J. K. (2013) 'Rethinking Homonationalism', *International Journal of Middle East Studies* 45: 336–339.

Rahman, M. (2010) 'Queer as Intersectionality: Theorising Gay Muslim Identities', *Sociology* 44(5): 1–18.

Reynolds, T. A. (2001) 'Black Mothering, Paid Work and Identity', *Ethnic and Racial Studies* 24(6): 1046–1064.

Reynolds, T. A. (2005) *Caribbean Mothers: Identity and Experience in the U.K.* London: Tufnell Press.

Rogers, A. (2012) ' "In This our Lives": Invisibility and Black British Gay Identity', in Rivers, I. and Ward, R. (eds.) *Out of the Ordinary: Representations of LGBT Lives*. Cambridge: Cambridge Scholars Publishing, 43–60.

Rogers, A. (2014) 'Crossing Deep Waters: Transatlantic Reflections Black Gay Men and Journeys influenced by "In the Life" ', in Fullwood, S. and Stephens, C. (eds.) *Black Gay Genius: Answering Joseph Beam's Call*. New York: Vintage Entity Press, 43–60.

Roseneil, S., Halsaa, B. and Sumer, S. (eds.) (2012) *Remaking Citizenship in Multicultural Europe: Women's Movements, Gender and Diversity*. Basingstoke: Palgrave.

Squire, V. (2009) *The Exclusionary Politics of Asylum*. Basingstoke: Palgrave.

Stella, F. (2007) 'The Right to be Different? Sexual Citizenship and Its Politics in Post-Soviet Russia', in Kay, R. (ed.) *Gender, Equality and Difference during and after State Socialism*. Basingstoke: Palgrave, 146–166.

Stella, F. (2013) 'Queer Space, Pride and Shame in Moscow', *Slavic Review* 72(2): 458–480.

Stella, F. (2014) *Lesbian Lives in Soviet and Post-Soviet Russia: Post/Socialism and Gendered Sexualities*. Palgrave: Basingstoke.

Stoler, A. L. (1995) *Race and the Education of Desire: Foucault's History of Sexuality and the Colonial Order of Things*. Durham: Duke University Press.

Stychin, C. F. (2003) *Governing Sexuality: The Changing Politics of Citizenship and Law Reform*. Oxford: Hart.

Taylor, Y., Hines, S. and Casey, M. (eds.) (2010) *Theorizing Intersectionality and Sexuality*. Basingstoke: Palgrave.

Taylor, Y. and Snowdon, R. (eds.) (2014) *Queering Religion, Religious Queers*. London: Routledge.

Trappolin, L., Gasparini, A. and Wintermute, R. (eds.) (2012) *Confronting Homophobia in Europe: Social and Legal Perspectives*. Oxford: Hart Publishing.

Tremblay, M., Paternotte, D. and Johnson, C. (eds.) (2011) *The Lesbian and Gay Movement and the State: Comparative Insights into a Transformed Relationship*. Farnham: Ashgate.

Waites, M. and Kollman, K. (eds.) (2009) Special Issue on the Global Politics of Lesbian, Gay, Bisexual and Transgender Human Rights. *Contemporary Politics* 15(1): 1–17.

Ward, J. (2008) *Respectably Queer: Diversity Culture in LGBT Activist Organizations*. Nashville: Vanderbilt University Press.

Weeks, J. (2007) *The World We Have Won: The Remaking of Erotic and Intimate Life*. London: Routledge.

Yip, A. K. T. and Page, S. (2013) *Religious and Sexual Identities: A Multi-faith Exploration of Young Adults*, Farnham: Ashgate.

Part I

Sexual Nationalisms and the Boundaries of Sexual Citizenship

1 Sexual Citizenship, Nationalism and Biopolitics in Putin's Russia

Francesca Stella and Nadya Nartova

INTRODUCTION

Since the mid-2000s, sexual and reproductive rights have become increasingly politicised in Russian society (Zdravomyslova 2009; Rivkin-Fisch 2006, 2013; Stella 2007, 2013; Temikina 2013). This politicisation has occurred both from above, as a result of the introduction of new legislation and social policy restricting sexual and reproductive rights and from below, as laws and policies are debated and contested by activists and ordinary citizens. A substantial amount of international media coverage and academic analysis has focused on the introduction of the infamous 'gay propaganda' laws and discussed the ambiguous impact of global LGBT solidarities on the Russian domestic context (Stella 2013; Kondakov 2014; Wilkinson 2014). However, an exclusive focus on LGBT rights overlooks the fact that recent restrictions on sexual and reproductive rights affect other social groups (particularly women). This chapter explores the relationship between sexuality and nationalism in the Russian context. We consider how restrictions on citizens' sexual and reproductive rights are justified in the name of the national interest and how family and demographic policies are deployed in the construction of ideals of nation and national belonging, which are both sexualised and gendered. We draw on Foucault's concept of biopower as a technology of power specific to modern nation-states, which is concerned with the control of social and biological processes at the level of the population (Foucault 1978/1998, 1997/2004).

Our discussion of sexual nationalism in Russia is based on discourse analysis of official documents and media sources. Official documents comprise the text of new laws concerning sexual and reproductive rights introduced in 2011–2013, as well as official commentaries on the rationale and intended effects of the legislation. Media sources include articles and opinion pieces published in the Russian daily newspaper *Rossiiskaia Gazeta* (RG) from January 2011 until December 2013, a period marked by heated political debate on new legislation and policy concerning sexual and reproductive rights (notably restriction on access to abortion and the introduction of the 'gay propaganda' laws) and a heightened politicisation of sexuality in the

18   *Francesca Stella and Nadya Nartova*

public sphere. RG is the official mouthpiece of the Russian government. As well as articles and opinion pieces, RG publishes official statements and documents issued by the government and state bodies, including the text of newly approved federal laws and presidential decrees.[1] Relevant articles were retrieved through keyword searches on RG's online archive.[2]

SEXUALITY, BIOPOLITICS AND THE 'NATIONAL INTEREST' IN RUSSIA

A substantial body of recently published work has explored the links between sexuality, normativity and nationalism (Puar 2007; Fassin 2010; Kulpa 2011; Farris 2012). Puar's concept of homonationalism has been particularly influential in work focused on societies where non-heterosexual citizens, traditionally cast as outlaws and perverts, have been recently more fully included into the citizenry as worthy of legal protection from discrimination and violence. Puar and others have argued that this inclusion is selective and often reinforces new social divisions, as the new legitimisation of same-sex relations is often paralleled by the othering and demonisation of racialised ethnic communities, assumed to come from deeply homophobic cultures and to be unable to embrace sexual diversity and respect for LGBT rights as a newly shared national value (Puar 2007; Fassin 2010). Drawing explicitly on Puar's work, Farris (2012) argues that in Western societies—increasingly dependent on a migrant workforce to perform domestic and care work—migrant women are portrayed as oppressed 'victims of their own culture', in need of being rescued. Amidst demands that migrants should integrate and adopt the national cultural values of the host society, gender equality is mobilised as a distinctive 'national' value by an odd coalition of (sometimes accidental) bedfellows, ranging from feminist movements, to neo-liberal government, to nationalist and overtly xenophobic parties. Internationally, gender and LGBT equality are increasingly upheld as a paradigmatic 'European' value by some states and supranational institutions such as the EU and have been instrumentally used to reinforce notions of a 'progressive' west and a 'conservative' east (Binnie 2004; Fassin 2010; Farris 2012).

Less attention, however, has been given in recent work to other articulations of sexuality and nationalism, which, unlike homonationalism or femonationalism, do not hinge on liberal attitudes towards sexual and reproductive rights as a defining feature of national identity but emphasise 'traditional' family values, gender roles and sexual norms. In this chapter, we seek to understand how discourses about the national interest, national identity and patriotism in contemporary Russia promote a specific brand of sexual conservativism as a shared value, as well as specific sexual and gender normativities which are constructed as 'traditionally Russian'. As Billig (1995) argues, the pervasive yet taken for granted and hidden nature of everyday, 'banal nationalism' makes it a very powerful ideology. It should

Sexual Citizenship, Nationalism and Biopolitics in Putin's Russia 19

be pointed out, however, that soul-searching over national identity has been very prominent in the Russian Federation as a nationalising state, which emerged in 1991 from the breakup of the Soviet Union and the demise of state socialism. Indeed, as Gal and Kligman (2000) point out, debates on gender relations and sexuality have been central to the renegotiation of national identity across the postsocialist region more generally. It is common for analyses of Russian nationalism to focus on its most extreme manifestations (the 'red-brown' threat), or to brand Kremlin-backed patriotism as fascist. As Laruelle (2009) perceptively notes, however, nationalist rhetoric has become prominent across the political spectrum in contemporary Russia and is used by extremist movements, populist protest parties and mainstream political parties alike, albeit with different nuances and aims. Indeed, Laruelle (2009) argues that nationalism is the ideological matrix of United Russia, the current ruling party closely associated with three-time president Vladimir Putin. Ever since the late1990s, the ruling political elites have sought to appropriate the narrative of national unity and national interest in order to create order, build consensus and strengthen their dwindling legitimacy in a deeply divided society, fraught with gaping social inequalities and interethnic tensions, and United Russia has promoted itself as the party of national reconciliation. We understand nationalism as a strategy deployed to deal with symbolic conflicts of interests and to establish and naturalise a normative set of beliefs and values around sexuality, family and intimate life; through our analysis of legislation and government media sources, we focus on the hegemonic sexual nationalism of the political elites. It should be noted that political pluralism has been systematically eroded in Russia over the last 15 years,[3] and in this context, politically hegemonic discourses about national values and sexual morality have a particularly strong normative force.

Concerns about national population decline and strategies to reverse this trend have featured prominently in Russian political discourse, significantly impacting on debates on sexual and reproductive rights. Since the mid-2000s, 'national priority projects' became prominent in the agenda of the ruling party and of expert think tanks such as the Institute of Contemporary Development (INSOR) (Laruelle 2009: 137–138).[4] INSOR currently lists five national priorities, including health, education, housing, agriculture and demographic sustainability. Indeed, demographic sustainability has been considered a priority policy area by the Russian government since the mid-2000s. Deep anxieties about Russia's demographic crisis and its impact on the nation's future stemmed from the steep population decline experienced by the newly independent country as the population fell from 148.5 million in 1993 to 142 in 2007; very high mortality rates (particularly among working-age men) consistently exceeded falling birth rates and could not be offset by net migration (United Nations Development Programme Russia 2008).[5] As Yuval-Davis (1997: 29) points out, in some forms of nationalist discourse, population is seen as a source of collective wealth

20   Francesca Stella and Nadya Nartova

and power, and the future of 'nation' is seen as dependent on its continuous growth. The discourse of 'people as power' is dominant in contemporary Russia, amidst concerns about the implications of Russia's demographic crisis for the country's economic development and international geopolitical standing (Snarskaia 2009). The problem of population as an object of political economy and state administration is, according to Foucault, central to modern forms of government:

> [. . .] population comes to appear above all else as the ultimate end of government. In contrast to sovereignty, government has as its purpose not the act of government itself, but the welfare of the population, the improvement of its condition, the increase of its wealth, longevity, health, and so on; and the means the government uses to attain these ends are themselves all, in some sense, immanent to the population; it is the population itself on which government will act either directly, through large-scale campaigns, or indirectly, through techniques that will make possible, without the full awareness of the people, the stimulation of birth rates, the directing of the flow of population into certain regions or activities, and so on.
>
> (Foucault 1978/2001: 216–217)

Foucault's notions of biopower and biopolitics are helpful in trying to unpack the relationship between power/knowledge, sexuality and the nation as an imagined community (Anderson 1983). Foucault defines biopower as the power over life exercised at the level of the (nation) state: with the onset of modernity, the realm of the biological and of the sexual, once the domain of religious morality in feudal societies, 'came under state control' (Foucault 1997/2004: 240). This reflects a more general process of rationalisation and centralisation, as the state became an instrument of national unification. Biopower is, according to Foucault, a technology of power specific to modern nation-states; whereas in feudal societies sovereign power translated into the king or queen's right to make die or let live, biopower concerns social and biological processes at the level of the population, and its essence can be encapsulated in the right to make live or let die. A related concept used by Foucault is biopolitics, or a mode of governance that 'deals with the population as a political problem, as a problem that is at once scientific and political, as a biological problem and as a power's problem' (Foucault 1997/2004: 245). Biopolitics finds expression in 'an explosion of numerous and diverse techniques for achieving the subjugations of bodies and the control of populations' (Foucault 1978/1998: 140) and is concerned with issues such as the birth rate, reproduction, the mortality rate, public hygiene, social medicine and the urban environment. Although Foucault was writing about biopolitics as a phenomenon and a mode of governance specific to Western modernity, we draw on some of his insights to reflect on how, in contemporary Russia, policies and legislation restricting sexual

Sexual Citizenship, Nationalism and Biopolitics in Putin's Russia   21

and reproductive rights are justified in the name of national values and of the national interest, thereby naturalising normative discourses about sexual morality, family and intimate life. Indeed, population growth and the well-being of the nation are explicitly linked to fertility and family values in two white papers [Russian: *Kontseptsii*, literally 'Concepts'] issued by the Russian government, the *Concept on the Demographic Policy of the Russian Federation until 2025* (CDP 2007) and the *Concept on State Family Policy* (CFP 2013). The two white papers set out government policy priorities and preferences, which are reflected in new policies and legislation in the areas of reproductive health and family policy. Two of the six key aims of CDP concerned support for families and for 'traditional' family values: the growth of the birth rate on account of the birth of a second child or subsequent children in families, and the strengthening of the family as an institution (CDP 2007). The notion that family policies are key to the success of demographic policies and that both hinge on the preservation of 'traditional' family values is articulated even more explicitly in the Concept on Family Policy (CFP 2013), which explicitly references CDP and defines the family as 'the foundation of Russian society'.

Among family values worthy of state protection, CFP explicitly mentions marriage, understood 'solely as the union between a man and a woman [. . .] and undertaken by the spouses with the aim of perpetuating their kin, birth and joint upbringing of children' (CFP 2013), although Russian law does not explicitly define 'marriage' or 'family' as the union between two differently gendered heterosexual individuals (Gorbachev 2014: 91). The case made in CFP for traditional family values is both pragmatic and ideological. Pragmatically, heterosexual nuclear families are presented as both more fertile and as a better environment for children's upbringing than other types of households. CFP notes that divorce and birth outside of wedlock are very common in Russia and estimates that one out of every third child is born into a single-parent family. However the document emphasises that birth rates among married women are higher and that children from single-parent families lack a model of 'harmonious relations between a man and a woman on which they can orient themselves in future' (CFP 2013). Ideologically, CFP states that 'for almost a thousand years', a family with many children and with different generations living under the same roof has been a part of Russia's traditions; however, the 'social engineering' that followed the 1917 Russian Revolution dealt a blow to Russia's traditional family values by giving legal recognition to de facto relationships and by legalising abortion. CFP emphasises the biological and symbolic continuity between kin and nation and explicitly advocates a return to spiritual and family values grounded in Russia's prerevolutionary past:

> Russian Orthodoxy strengthens the spiritual maintenance of kin and family. The family is not only the communion of two spouses, parents and children, but also a spiritual unit, a 'little church'. This approach to

22 Francesca Stella and Nadya Nartova

the institution of the family allows us to emphasise not the private side of family problems, but rather to see family in the context of the society out of which it grows.

(CFP 2013)

The reference to Russian Orthodoxy reflects its growing influence in Russian political and social life and its symbolic use as a marker of national identity by the political elites. Indeed, prominent politicians such as Elena Mizulina, head of the Committee on Family, Women and Children and main author of CFP; Dmitrii Medvedev, former president and current prime minister of the Russian Federation; and Vitalii Milonov, the author of the 2012 'gay propaganda law' for the city of Saint Petersburg have publicly declared their orthodox faith and advocated a greater role for religious values in Russian society.

In the reminder of the article, we explore how moral discourses about sexual and reproductive behaviour are legitimised in the name of the nation and naturalised through references to the biologising ideas of the nation as an extension of blood-based kinship (Anderson 1983; Rivkin-Fish 2006). We analyse legislation restricting sexual and reproductive rights and coverage of related issues in the government newspaper *Rossiiskaia Gazeta*. We aim to tease out how the naturalisation of values rooted in an imagined national tradition produces new normativities which are deeply gendered and sexualised.

WOMEN'S REPRODUCTIVE RIGHTS

In the summer of 2011, MP Valerii Draganov submitted a draft bill on abortion to State Duma, the Russian Federal Parliament. The bill stipulated, among other things, that: 1) abortion for married women should only be conducted with the written consent of their husband; 2) abortion during the first 12 weeks of pregnancy should be conducted no sooner than 48 hours after a woman's medical examination; 3) before signing a consent form for surgical abortion, a woman is required to undergo the following procedures: visualisation of the foetus by means of ultrasound, listening to the foetal heartbeat (after six weeks' gestation), consultation with a psychologist and/ or a social worker 'during which the right to refuse abortion is explained'; and 4) physicians have the right to refuse to perform an abortion for religious or other beliefs (Draganov and Gerasimova 2011). The explanatory note to the bill linked the demographic crisis to the high number of abortions; this, Draganov argued, reflects

[. . .] the imperfection of Russian legislation, its inconsistency with Russian traditions. [Current] Russian abortion legislation is based on the principle of freedom of reproductive choice and the protection of the

Sexual Citizenship, Nationalism and Biopolitics in Putin's Russia 23

mother's reproductive health. This approach, based on the freedom of reproductive choice, goes against traditional Christian values and leads to the spiritual and moral degradation of the Russian people.

(Draganov 2011)

Consistently high abortion rates in Russia, the highest in Europe, have long been a cause for concern among health professionals. During the Soviet period, abortion was one of the main means of birth control, as contraceptives were unavailable or unreliable, and their use was either not promoted or discouraged by health professionals. This legacy still shapes attitudes to birth control: amidst resistance to the introduction of sex education and moral panics about the commodification of sexuality, the use of contraceptives remains comparatively low, whilst abortion rates, albeit much lower than in the Soviet period, remain very high (Sankevich 2009: 140; Zdravomyslova 2009). It is worth noting, however, that Draganov's draft bill presented a distinctive pro-life argument. First, restrictions on abortion were argued on moral grounds, invoking national traditions and values. Second, the proposal called for an amendment of the existing law on the protection of *children's rights* and other legislation aimed to strengthen the *right to life* (Draganov and Gerasimova 2011). A number of provisions from Draganov's draft bill were eventually included in the federal law 'On the fundamental healthcare principles in the Russian Federation' (N323–FZ). However, concerns for women's sexual and reproductive health were rarely foregrounded by those supporting restrictions on abortion.

Although Draganov's proposal caused widespread debate and resistance among gender studies researchers, feminist activists, health practitioners and women in general (Rivkin-Fish 2013: 574–577), the State Duma approved law N323–FZ. The new law restricted free access to abortion by establishing a mandatory 'week of silence' from 7 days to 48 hours between the visit to a medical facility and the termination of pregnancy, depending on gestational age (N323-FZ, art.56). Postponing abortion surgery was explicitly aimed at reducing the number of abortions, as the coverage of the issue in RG makes clear:

[P]rovisions are made to reduce the number of abortions. Women will be given a minimum of 2 days to think about their decision.

(Zykova 2012)

Postponing abortion surgery was not justified on medical grounds; rather, it was meant to provide a period for reflection when a woman can reconsider her decision independently or through external influence. Health Minister Veronika Skvortsova quoted the decline in the number of abortion as evidence that the new policies, including the provision of counselling services for pregnant women, were working. She did not respond to criticisms

24   *Francesca Stella and Nadya Nartova*

about the additional pressures put on women to reconsider their decision under the new system:

> The set of measures on protection of motherhood and childhood had a positive effect. Counselling services for pregnant women, including those who find themselves in difficult situations, were set up, resulting in a 53.9 thousand decline in the number of abortions.
>
> (Gritsiuk 2013)

Whilst up to the twelfth week of pregnancy abortion can be performed solely on the request of the pregnant woman, for the past several decades, Russian legislation has also allowed abortion up to the twenty-second week of pregnancy for medical reasons or difficult personal circumstances. However, over the last ten years, access to abortion within the second trimester of pregnancy on the grounds of so-called social reasons has also been drastically limited. Whilst 1996 legislation specified 13 such 'social reasons' (RF Government Decree N. 567, 1996), by 2003 these had been reduced to four: deprivation or restriction of parental rights, pregnancy resulting from rape, pregnancy whilst serving time in prison and the woman's husband having a type I–II disability or dying during pregnancy (RF Government Decree N. 485, 2003). In February 2012, this list was further reduced, and abortion in the second trimester is currently only permitted for pregnancies resulting from rape (RF Government Decree N. 98, 2012). Another important change in the legal regulation of abortion concerns the right of the doctor to refuse to perform medical 'termination of pregnancy if it does not directly threaten the patient's life and health of others' (N323-FZ, art.70, item 3). Thus abortion is no longer considered a moral choice only for the patient but also for the doctor (Zdravomyslova 2009).

The new abortion legislation was not intended to protect women's reproductive rights or health; rather, it was conceived as a measure to boost the birth rate. The legislation focuses on hindering access to surgical abortion and discursively constructs individual socio-economic reasons for terminating a pregnancy as unjustifiable. At the same time, measures to prevent abortion are directed primarily towards already pregnant women, not towards promoting contraception and sex education. Russian demographers have argued that these measures reinforce the misplaced idea, widespread among ordinary Russians and policymakers alike, that 'birth control is synonymous with birth reduction, and access to contraception allegedly leads to birth rate decrease and depopulation' (Sakevich and Denisov 2011). Indeed, despite the recent commitment to invest in counselling services for pregnant women, the provision of family planning facilities and information on birth control was curtailed or neglected for years. Most programmes set up in post-Soviet Russia to increase awareness of sexual and reproductive health were discontinued, and family planning centres created in the 1990s were closed due to the lack of funding (Sakevich and Denisov 2011; Temkina

Sexual Citizenship, Nationalism and Biopolitics in Putin's Russia 25

2013). Anna Temkina's study shows that doctors and gynaecologists in municipal hospitals are aware of the importance of discussing contraception with women. However, they do not have sufficient time for it in their daily practice, which is now aimed at preparing women for pregnancy; a shift has been stimulated by a pay increase for practitioners working in prenatal care:

> While supporting the idea of 'family planning', in practice they [doctors] redefine it as 'pregnancy planning', meaning primarily preparing women for pregnancy. In the area of reproduction, birth rate increase and the preferential treatment of pregnant women are the biopolitical priority for the state, which is reflected in the institutional rules of medical facilities, while contraception issues in interactions with medical personnel are given much less attention.
>
> (Temkina, 2013: 20)

In public debate, health care issues in the context of reproductive health are primarily associated with the availability and quality of obstetrics care, as well as ease of access to it, particularly for women living in rural areas:

> If a woman gives birth once in her life, she can just endure it, live through this horror of having to travel many miles and just forget about it; but what if she thinks about giving birth more than once? Each subsequent childbirth occurs quicker, and it is important for her to have a hospital nearby.
>
> (Trukhanova 2012)

Desired developments in reproductive medicine are constructed primarily as the improvement of obstetric, gynaecological and paediatric care. Access to information about contraception and safer sex practices, however, are either ignored or opposed on the grounds that they stimulate hedonistic attitudes towards sex.

The debate on sexual and reproductive rights is also linked to new normative discourses about the ideal family. Providing support for a 'model' family in order to stimulate the national birth rate has becoming a state policy priority since the introduction of the 'mother's capital' scheme in 2007. The scheme provides financial incentives to families who give birth or adopt a second or third child; although it was later renamed 'family capital', the expectation is that the funds should be administered by, and directly benefit, women, thus reinforcing the notion of women's primary roles as mothers and carers. Indeed, the fund can only be spent on housing improvement, children's education or to boost a working mother's pension fund (as a way to 'compensate' women for lower achievements in paid work owing to time spent on domestic unpaid labour) (Borodzina et al. 2012). The scheme, explicitly couched in pronatalist terms, strengthens the idea that a woman is a mother first and foremost and that she gains moral legitimacy and social

26 Francesca Stella and Nadya Nartova

status from motherhood. Indeed, despite the fact that in most dual-parent families both partners work, current policies are underpinned by the assumption that the care of children, especially young ones, should be carried out by the mother. Critics of the 'family capital' and related policies have pointed out that the financial support provided via the scheme is too limited to make a difference, particularly for poorer families (Borodzina et al. 2012). Moreover, financial support is mostly directed at individual families rather than being invested in developing adequate structures to support women in managing work and family responsibilities, such as affordable childcare facilities; this disadvantages women on the labour market (Chernova 2013).

The debates surrounding the 'family capital' scheme and other measures aimed at supporting working families explicitly promote a normative model of family, childbirth and motherhood: a dual-parent family formed of a heterosexual couple with two or more children. Alternative choices, such as, for example, single motherhood, are problematised because of the potential inability of single mothers to meet state-set reproductive targets:

> Let's start with the fact that single women will not give birth to more than one child,—director of the Institute for Demographic Research Igor Beloborodov explains his point of view.—Of course, there are single mothers who have two and even three children, but as a rule, single mothers only have one child.
>
> (Vladykina 2011)

Delayed childbearing is not seen as a modern demographic trend associated with, among other things, women's increased autonomy and career choices but as a consequence of their selfish, immoral behaviour. RG references the expert opinion of specialists such as Irina Soldatova, Moscow chief neonatologist and deputy chief physician of the Filatov Children's Clinical Hospital:

> These things are so popular nowadays: changing sexual partners, frequent abortions, a carefree attitude to your own health, when everything is allowed: you can smoke, drink, choose to have children some time later—nothing good will come out of this. There are inexorable statistics—the majority of premature infants are born from first-time mothers who are over 30 years old. Maybe it sounds trivial, but believe me, it is important: we sometimes have to pay through the nose for our lack of spirituality.
>
> (Krasnopol'skaia 2013a)

'Lack of spirituality' as a cause of reproductive problems is also raised in relation to assisted reproductive technology (ART):

> It is no secret that many modern women prefer to think of children after . . . they have already had a lot of abortions and contracted different

Sexual Citizenship, Nationalism and Biopolitics in Putin's Russia   27

diseases—including sexually transmitted ones—changed sexual partners several times, and so on.

(Krasnopol'skaia 2013b)

ART use is associated with the consequences of the 'wrong' sexual behaviour and is not seen as an independent reproductive strategy (e.g. choosing donor and surrogate programmes). Only heterosexual couples desperately wanting to have children and having fertility problems are portrayed as having relatively legitimate access to ART in RG:

> If the decision to hire a surrogate mother is serious and carefully thought through, and all parties are satisfied, then it is very good that there is such a possibility. A wanted and loved baby is born. People who have a yearned-for child, and have to turn to surrogate mothers but not on a whim, usually make good parents because they really do want this child.
>
> (TSENZURY.NET 2013)

Although allowances are made for heterosexual couples with fertility problems, RG generally upholds the idea that 'it's [sexually] healthy young people who should give birth to children' (TSENZURY.NET 2013). Thus despite the fact that Russia has one of the most liberal ART legislations and that it is increasing government financial support for IVF protocols (Nartova 2008; Brednikova, Nartova and Tkach 2009), everyday moral regulation is embedded in the discourse of the nuclear heterosexual family and of 'proper' motherhood (Tkach 2013).

We argue that the spectrum of reproductive rights in modern Russia has been restricted to the right to give birth, disavowing the right to abortion and neglecting the right to birth control, sexual health and sex education. Underpinned by demographic objectives and by the political will to promote specific models of family and intimate life, recent policies and legislation prioritise the 'national interest' and the idea of 'people as power'. In their explicit attempt to optimise Russian women's reproductive capabilities, they reinforce the notion of women as the reproducers of the nation (and implicitly as second-class workers) and of womanhood as 'naturally' rooted in heterosexual motherhood.

THE 'GAY PROPAGANDA' LAW

On 27 March 2012, the Legislative Assembly of the Novosibirsk Region approved a law banning the 'propaganda' of homosexuality among minors. Novosibirsk joined a growing list of regional and city administrations across Russia in approving legislation banning the promotion of homosexuality to minors. The list included Ryazan (2006), Arkhangel'sk (2011), Kostroma (2012) and, most notably, Saint Petersburg city, where the law had been

28 Francesca Stella and Nadya Nartova

introduced only a few weeks earlier than in the Novosibirsk region. The introduction of the law in Saint Petersburg was particularly controversial and unexpected, since the city had a reputation for being the most gay-friendly in Russia and for having a very active LGBT community.

The introduction of the 'gay propaganda' law in Saint Petersburg and Novosibirsk marked a turning point, as the debate began to shift from the regional to the federal level. Indeed, in an official letter to the speaker of the State Duma, the Novosibirsk Legislative Assembly officially proposed extending the ban on 'gay propaganda' to the whole of the Russian Federation, by amending the existing Code for Administrative Offences (*Zakonodatel'noe Sobranie Novosibirskoi Oblasti* 2012). The accompanying note explained the rationale of the proposal:

> The propaganda of homosexuality has acquired a wide resonance in contemporary Russia. This propaganda is conducted both through the media and through the active organising of social demonstrations, which promote homosexuality as normal behaviour. This is especially harmful for children and young people, who are not yet able to critically assess the onslaught of information that befalls them every day. As a consequence, it is necessary to protect the new generations from the influence of homosexual propaganda.
>
> (Moroz 2012)

The draft bill 'On the introduction of amendments in the Code of the Russian Federation on administrative offences' proposed the introduction of fines for private citizens, officials and legal entities. The explanatory note clarifies that the law would punish the promotion of homosexuality to *minors* and not a person's homosexual orientation per se, therefore not falling foul of constitutional guarantees of protection from discrimination and freedom of expression (Moroz 2012). The emphasis is very much on the pernicious effect that exposure to same-sex relations can have on children and young people: indeed, the draft bill was subsequently modified and debated in the Russian Duma as project N44554–6-FZ, proposing amendments to the existing federal law 'On defending children from information harmful for their health and development' (N124-FZ), and other legislative acts aimed at defending children from information 'promoting the negation of traditional family values'. Indeed, in debates on the 'gay propaganda' law, anxieties over the relatively new visibility of same-sex relations in Russian society are articulated in relation to the future of the nation, embodied by children and young people. A renewed commitment to the protection of children and adolescents is central to both the Concept on Family Policy (CFP 2013) and to the National Strategy to Act in the Interest of Children (RF Presidential Decree N. 761, 2012). Both highlight concerns about the falling number of children and young people in the country, as well as their healthy upbringing and development. Significantly, after the approval of the

Sexual Citizenship, Nationalism and Biopolitics in Putin's Russia 29

'gay propaganda law', the Russian government imposed temporary restrictions on the international adoption of Russian children in countries where same-sex unions are legally recognised (N167-FZ). The final version of the law, incorporated into the amended Family Law of the Russian Federation as Article 127, excludes spouses in a gay marriage or civil partnership, as well as single people from countries where same-sex unions are recognised, from becoming adoptive or foster parents of Russian children (SKRF 2014). An explanatory note states that adopted children had to be protected 'from possible unwanted influence, such as artificial forcing of non-traditional sexual behaviour and the suffering, complexes and stresses that, according to psychological studies, are often experienced by children raised in same-sex families' (Vneseny Izmeneniia 2013). Thus non-heterosexual citizens, both in Russia and abroad, are constructed as both morally deviant (and therefore as a negative influence on children and young people) and as unfit, and biologically unable, to parent.

The 'gay propaganda law' was eventually approved by an overwhelming majority of MPs and signed into law in June 2013 (N135-FZ). As critics have pointed out, the term 'propaganda' is legally ill defined; nonetheless, the scope of what can potentially be punished as 'propaganda' is very broad. It includes any public discussion of same-sex relations (restricting, among others, the activities of school teachers and LGBT organisations), as well as representations of same-sex relations in the media and the Internet.[6] 'Propaganda' is defined as the 'dissemination of information among minors' whose aim is 'forming non-traditional sexual arrangements, making non-traditional sexual relationships look attractive, perversely presenting traditional and non-traditional sexual relations as socially equal', or creating an interest in 'non-traditional' sexual relations (N135-FZ). Thus the law restricts sexual citizenship for non-heterosexuals to the private sphere.

Both in the debates on the 'gay propaganda' law and in RG's coverage of LGBT issues, same-sex sexualities are constructed as the 'Other' to Russian national traditions and family values. Indeed, whilst the original draft bill referred to the 'propaganda of homosexuality', subsequent drafts debated in the State Duma refer to the 'propaganda of non-traditional sexual relations' (Gorbachev 2014; Kondakov 2014). In Russia, 'non-traditional' immediately evokes the association with same-sex relationships; indeed, the term 'non-traditional sexual orientation' has been commonly used in Russia since the 1990s to refer to male homosexuality, lesbianism and bisexuality. Moreover, as Gorbachev (2014) perceptively notes, previous regional 'propaganda' legislation had reinforced the dichotomy between 'traditional' (heterosexual) family relations and same-sex sexualities (or, in some formulations, a range of non-normative sexual and gender practices variously named as homosexuality, *muzhelozhestvo*,[7]bisexuality, transgenderism and paedophilia). Thus heterosexuality is normalised as 'natural' and 'traditional' through its association with reproduction, whilst same-sex relations are othered through their association with nonreproductive sex and deviance.

30 Francesca Stella and Nadya Nartova

The meaning of national 'traditional family relations' is also buttressed in relation to what is 'non-traditional', foreign and alien through the pages of *Rossiiskaia Gazeta*, often by juxtaposing Russia to a sexually and morally decadent Europe. Indeed, most of RG's articles focusing on LGBT issues discuss other European countries rather than the domestic context and the introduction of the 'gay propaganda' laws. Between December 2012 and December 2013, RG published 17 full-length features by its Paris correspondent, Viacheslav Prokof'ev. The articles discuss in detail the controversies surrounding the introduction of gay marriage in different parts of Europe, focusing mostly on France. The importance of 'Europe' as a point of reference and contestation is apparent in other articles that mention LGBT issues only in passing; in these articles, European liberalism is equated to political correctness gone mad and criticised for being imposed on sovereign states through institutions, such as the European Court of Human Rights, and for going against prevailing local customs and sensibilities (see for example Iamshanov 2011). Furthermore, 'European' values of gender equality, respect for minority groups and sexual democracy are presented not only in opposition to Russian ones but as majorly controversial in Europe itself. The coverage of gay marriage in France is a case in point: the introduction of gay marriage is portrayed as very divisive and controversial, as evidenced by the large-scale street protests and the refusal of some French mayors to officiate gay marriages on the grounds of 'freedom of conscience'. The coverage is very heavily skewed, as the views presented almost invariably belong to the anti-gay marriage campaign, and the tone of the articles clearly indicates the author's support for the anti-gay marriage camp. For example, a very lengthy article on the controversies around gay marriage in France and Britain concludes that gay marriage is a threat to the institution of marriage and family, as well as a threat to the moral fabric of society (Prokof'ev 2012). The titles of some of the articles also make the author's stance on the issue clear (for example, 'Europe: the Rape of the Family'; 'Marriage Has Lost Its Orientation', Prokof'ev 2012, 2013). Furthermore, both in France and elsewhere in Europe, the anti-gay marriage camp is portrayed as reflecting the 'commonsense' majority opinion. An article on the referendum on gay marriage in Croatia, which saw a landslide victory of the 'no' vote, applauds Croatians' resistance to EU norms:

> Croatians refused to be like everyone else in the EU. Croatians were not afraid of being the black sheep of the EU. At a time when same-sex couples parade triumphantly across Western European countries, Croatia dared to say 'no'.
>
> (Vorob'ev 2013)

The prominence given to gay marriage abroad contrasts with the much slimmer volume of articles about LGBT issues in Russia itself, which unsurprisingly focus on the 'gay propaganda' laws. There is a noticeable change of

Sexual Citizenship, Nationalism and Biopolitics in Putin's Russia   31

tone between the first two articles on the proposed introduction of the law in Saint Petersburg and subsequent coverage related to the Saint Petersburg and federal laws. In early coverage, the Saint Petersburg law is described as controversial (*skandal'nyi*) and is jokingly referred to as the 'don't say gay' law; the features focus on the criticisms surrounding the introduction of the law (Golubkova 2012a, 2012b). Subsequent articles, however, discursively legitimise the law by quoting the opinions of the city's inhabitants supporting the law (Tsikler and Golubkova 2012) and by referring to the ruling of the Russian Supreme Court, which deemed that the law was not discriminatory and did not violate the Russian constitution (Kozlova 2012). This corroborates the view that the law seriously hinders any criticism and open debate about the law itself (Gorbachev, 2014).

Indeed, in RG there is no open debate of the federal law at all. In the run-up to the first Duma debate on the federal law (January 2013), RG was silent on the issue except for a brief reference to it in an interview with Prime Minister Medvedev, who suggested that the law may not be necessary, as moral issues are not always best regulated by the law (Kuz'min 2012). An opinion piece published in early June 2013, just a few days before the law was approved upon second and third reading by the State Duma, speculated that the progress of the law had been hampered because of pressures from Western 'pro-homosexual oriented elites', whilst also pointing out how controversial the support for LGBT rights remains in most of Europe. The article also emphasised that the majority of the Russian population is 'traditionally oriented' and mostly opposed to gay marriage and that the propaganda law would enhance social cohesion in Russian society (Kasatonova 2013). A subsequent article published after the approval of the law portrayed the latter very much as a triumph of national unity and consensus. Entitled 'Laws Greeted by 'Bravo!'', the article emphasised that the law had been approved by a majority of 436 MPs in favour to 1 abstained. The article also pointed out that, despite unauthorised protests in Moscow, the law enjoyed extraordinary popular support:

> By the evening, when the Duma had already voted in favour of both laws [. . .] the supporters of traditional family values came back. The head of the committee on family, women and children Elena Mizulina and her colleagues, who successfully led the draft law on the ban of gay propaganda, were met with applause and approving remarks. The crowd addressed one of the MPs with the cry of 'bravo'! The MPs could not remember a comparable expression of appreciation for their legislative work.
>
> (Shkel' 2013)

Thus the 'gay propaganda' law is presented as the triumph of the 'commonsense' majority view and of traditional national values. Subsequent coverage of LGBT issues focus on the outcry generated by the law outside of Russia:

32 *Francesca Stella and Nadya Nartova*

calls to boycott Russian vodka and the 2014 Sochi Olympics, gestures of solidarity with the Russian LGBT community by foreign athletes competing at the 2013 World Athletic Championships in Moscow and criticisms of a Russian athlete who publicly supported the law. Criticism from abroad, however, is dismissed as an example of political correctness gone mad or as politically motivated, once more reinforcing the symbolic and moral distance between 'European' sexual democracy and Russian national traditions and values.

CONCLUSIONS

In Putin's Russia, restrictions on sexual and reproductive rights are justified on both pragmatic and ideological grounds. On a practical level, they are advocated in the name of the national interest and of the state's biopolitical aims of increasing the population and improving its health. Restrictions on abortion are intended to boost the birth rate and optimise women's reproductive capabilities; the 'gay propaganda' law is meant to contribute to the healthy psychological and moral development of Russia's younger generations by strengthening 'traditional' family values. On an ideological level, these restrictions construct specific models of motherhood, relationships and family as legitimate and 'traditionally' Russian. Pragmatic reasons and moral values are deeply intertwined, particularly in the case of reproductive rights: pronatalist policies deploy pro-life rhetoric and construct motherhood as simultaneously a moral issue, a patriotic duty and as a public concern. Importantly, the meaning of Russian 'traditional values' is constructed in opposition to European 'sexual democracy' (Fassin 2010), particularly in relation to same-sex relationships.

Internationally, Russia increasingly presents itself on the international stage as a stronghold of social conservatism and the defender of traditional family values (Wilkinson 2014), whilst domestically, these very values are deployed to shore up specific notions about Russian national identity. A vision of the Russian nation as an 'imagined community' built on tradition and biological kinship promotes specific sexual and gender normativities. Women are valued first and foremost as reproducers of the nation, although not all models of motherhood and family relationships are equally legitimised. Non-heterosexual citizens are constructed as deviant both because of their polluting effect on young people and as unfit parents.

NOTES

1 http://www.rg.ru/about.html.
2 Over four hundred articles were retrieved through keyword searches. Keywords utilised were: gender, abortion, to give birth, sex, gay, lesbian, homosexual, same-sex love [*odnopolaia liubov'*], sexual orientation, sexual relationships, family values, traditional family, reproductive rights.

Sexual Citizenship, Nationalism and Biopolitics in Putin's Russia   33

3 United Russia, purposefully created as a presidential party and to remain in power over the long term, has dominated Russian electoral politics and state institutions since it was created in 2001.
4 INSOR was created in March 2008 and originally overseen by then First Deputy Prime Minister Dmitry Medvedev, see http://www.insor-russia.ru/en/_about_us/history.
5 An in-depth discussion of the reasons behind Russia's demographic crisis is beyond the scope of this chapter. The socio-economic upheavals that followed Russia's 'transition' to market capitalism, high levels of poverty and the downsizing and partial monetisation of the country's welfare system are widely considered important factors behind declining public health indicators and high mortality rates, although historical demographic imbalances also play a role (Field 2000; United Nations Development Programme Russia 2008). Russian demographers have debated the relative impact on population decline of mortality rates (very high by European standards) and declining birth rates (broadly in line with European trends and reflecting a combination of economic and socio-cultural factors, such as changing patterns of marriage and cohabitation, delayed childbearing). They have generally been critical of the Russian government's emphasis on boosting the birth rates as a key measure to solve the demographic crisis vis-à-vis the neglect of measures to tackle mortality and poor public health indicators (United Nations Development Programme Russia 2008).
6 Article 6.21 has been compared to infamous UK Section 2A of the 1988 Local Government Act, which forbade teaching in schools about homosexuality as a 'pretended family relation'. Whilst the UK law only concerned the activities of local authorities (and particularly educational settings), the implications of article 6.21 are much broader. Russian citizens, public officials and registered organisations are liable to fines or (in the case of organisations) can be sanctioned to stop operations for up to 90 days; however, even harsher penalties are contemplated for the propaganda of 'non-traditional relations' in the media or on the Internet. Moreover, the law specifies that non-Russian citizens (foreigners or stateless subjects) are subject to fines or can jailed for up to 15 days and subsequently deported if found guilty.
7 The literal meaning is 'a man lying with a man'. This was the term used in Soviet legislation criminalising consensual relations between men.

BIBLIOGRAPHY

Policy and Legislative Documents:

CDP (2007) *Kontseptsiia Demograficheskoi Politiki Rossiskoi Federatsii na period do 2015*. Available at http://demoscope.ru/weekly/knigi/koncepciya/koncepciya25.html, last accessed 10 June 2014.

CFP (2013) *Kontseptsiia Gosudarsvennoi Semeinoi Politiki Rossiiskoi Federatsii na Period do 2025 Goda (Obshchestvennyi Proekt)*. Available at http://www.komitet2–6.km.duma.gov.ru/site.xp/050049124053056052.html, last accessed 10 June 2014.

Draganov, V. (2011) 'Poiasnitel'naia Zapiska k Proektu (575934–5) Federanl'nogo Zakona "O Vnesenii Izmenenii v Federal'nti Zakon 'Ob Osnovnykh Garantiiakh Prav Rebenka v Rossiiskoi Federatsii' i Otdel'nye Zakonodatel'nye Akty Rossiiskoi Federatsii v Tseliakh Usileniia Garantii Prava na Zhizn' " ', 7 July 2011. Available at http://asozd2.duma.gov.ru/main.nsf/%28SpravkaNew%29?OpenAgent&RN=575934–5&02, last accessed 12 June 2014.

34 Francesca Stella and Nadya Nartova

Draganov, V. and Gerasimova, N. (2011) 'Zakonoproekt 575934–5 "O Vnesenii Izmenenii v Federal'nti Zakon 'Ob Osnovnykh Garantiiakh Prav Rebenka v Rossiiskoi Federatsii' i Otdel'nye Zakonodatel'nye Akty Rossiiskoi Federatsii v Tseliakh Usileniia Garantii Prava na Zhizn' " ', 7 July 2011. Available at http://asozd2.duma.gov.ru/main.nsf/%28SpravkaNew%29?OpenAgent&RN=575934–5&02, last accessed 12 June 2014.

Federal Law N124-FZ 'Ob Osnovnykh Garantiiakh Prav Rebenka v Rossiiskoi Federatsii', 24 July 1998.

Federal Law N323-FZ 'Ob Osnovakh Okhrany Zdorov'ia Grazhdan v Rossiiskoi Federatsii', 21 November 2011.

Federal Law N135-FZ 'O vnesenii Izmenenii v Stat'iu 5 Federal'nogo Zakona "O Zashchite Detei ot Informatsii, Prichiniaiushchei Vred ikh Zdorov'iu i Razvitiiu" i Otdel'nye Zakonodatel'nye Akty Rossiiskoi Federatsii v Tseliakh Zashchity Detei ot Informatsii, Propaganduiushchei Otritsanie Traditionnykh Semeinykh Tsennostei', 29 June 2013.

Federal Law N167-FZ, 'O Vnesenii Izmenenii v Otdel'nye Zakonodatel'nye Akty Rossiiskoi Federatsii po Voprosam Ustroistva Detei-Sirot I Detei, Ostavshikhsia Bez Popecheniia Roditelei', 2 July 2013.

Federal Draft Law N44554–6-FZ, 'O Vnesenii Izmenenii v Stat'iu 5 Federal'nogo Zakona "O Zashchite Detei ot Informatsii, Prichiniaiushchei Vred ikh Zdorov'iu i Razvitiiu'. Available at http://asozd2.duma.gov.ru/main.nsf/(Spravka)?Open Agent&RN=44554–6, last accessed 12 June 2014.

Moroz, I. (2012) 'O Proekte Federal'nogo Zakona "O Vnesenii Izmenenii v Kodeks Rossiiskoi Federatsii ob Administrativnykh Pravonarushenii', 27 March 2012. Available at http://asozd2.duma.gov.ru/main.nsf/(Spravka)?OpenAgent&RN=44554–6, last accessed 12 June 2014.

RF Government Decree N. 485, 'O Perechne Sotsial'nykh Pokazanii Dlia Isskustvennogo Preryvaniia Beremennosti', 1 August 2003.

RF Government Decree N. 567, 'Ob Utverzhdenii Perechnia Sotsialnykh Pokazanii Dlia Iskusstvennogo Preryvaniia Beremennosti', 8 May 1996.

RF Government Decree N98, 'O Sotial'nom pokazanii dlia Isskusstvennogo Preryvaniia Beremennosti', 6 February 2012.

RF Presidential Decree N.761, 'On the National Strategy to Act in the Interest of Children, 2012–2017', 1 June 2012.

Semeinyi Kodeks Rossiiskoi Federatsii (2014), current edition (4 November 2014).

'Vneseny Izmeneniia v Zakonodatel'stvo po Voprosam Ustroistva Detei-Sirot I Detei, Ostavshikhsia Bez Popecheniia Roditelei', 2013. Available at http://www.kremlin.ru/news/18459.

Articles from Rossiiskaia Gazeta:

Golubkova, M. (2012a) 'Ne Govori Gei', RG No 53(5726), 12.03.2012.

Golubkova, M. (2012b) 'Sud'i na Nikh Net', RG No 78 (5751), 10.04.2012.

Gritsiuk, M. (2013) 'Podvergli analizu', RG No 111 (6087), 27.05.2013.

Iamshanov, B. (2011) 'Sami s Sudami', RG No 167(5543), 02.08.2011.

Kasatonova, O. (2013) 'S Ogliadkoi na Evropu', No 122(6098), 07.06.2013.

Kozlova, N. (2012) 'Gei, Slaviane', RG No 228(5901), 04.10.2012.

Krasnopol'skaia, I. (2013a) '400 Grammov Zhizni', RG No 104 (6080), 17.05.2013.

Krasnopol'skaia, I. (2013b) 'Liubov' v Probirke', RG No 241 (6217), 25.10.2013.

Kuz'min, V. (2012) 'Fakty o Vlasti', RG No 284(5957), 10.12.2012.

Prokof'ev, V. (2012) 'Evropa: Pokhishcheniie Sem'i', RG No 284(5957), 10.12.2012

Prokof'ev, V. (2013) 'Brak Poterial Orientatsiiu', RG. No 78(6054), 11.04.2013.

Shkel', T. (2013) 'Zakon pod "Bravo!" ', RG No 125(6101), 13.06.2013.

Sexual Citizenship, Nationalism and Biopolitics in Putin's Russia 35

Trukhanova, E. (2012) 'Bunt Beremennykh', RG No 298 (5971), 26.12.2012.
TSENZURY.NET (2013), RG No 236 (6212), 21.10.2013.
Tsikler, E. and Golubkova, M. (2012) 'Potushchili Goluboi Ogonek', RG No 154 (5827), 09.07.2012.
Vladykina, T. (2011) 'Mamapapa', RG No 125 (5501), 10.06.2011.
Vorob'ev, V. (2013) 'Odopolye Braki Zabrakovali', RG No 272(6248), 03.12.2013.
Zakatova, A. (2011) 'Imeesh Pravo', RG No 244(5620), 31.10.2011.
Zakonodatel'noe Sobranie Novosibiirskoi Oblasti (2012), RG online edition, www.rg.ru/2012/03/29/proekt-anons.html
Zykova, T. (2012) 'Chelovecheskii Kapital', RG No 1 (5674), 10.01.2012.

Secondary Literature:

Anderson, B. (1983) *Imagined Communities: Reflections on the Origin and Spread of Nationalism*. London: Verso.
Billig, M. (1995) *Banal Nationalism*. London: Sage.
Binnie, J. (2004) *The Globalization of Sexuality*. London: Sage.
Borodzina, E., Zdravomyslova, E. and Temkina, A. (2012) 'Materinskii Kapital: Sotsial'naia Politika I Strategii Semei', *Demoskop Weekly* N. 495–496, 23 January–5 February.
Brednikova, O., Nartova, N., and Tkach, O. (2009) 'Assisted Reproduction in Russia: Legal Regulations and Public Debates', in de Jong, W. and Tkach, O. (eds.) *Making Bodies, Persons and Families. Normalising Reproductive Technologies in Russia, Switzerland and Germany*. Berlin: LIT Verlag, 43–55.
Chernova, Zh. (2013) *Sem'ia kak Politicheskii Vopros: Gosudarstvennyi Proekt i Praktiki Privatnosti*. Saint Petersburg: Evropeiskii Universitet v Sankt-Peterburge.
Farris, S. (2012) 'Femonationalism and the "Regular" Army of Labor Called Migrant Women', *History of the Present* 2(2): 184–199.
Fassin, E. (2010) 'National Identities and Transnational Intimacies: Sexual Democracy and the Politics of Immigration in Europe', *Public Culture* 22(3): 507–529.
Field, G. (2000) 'The Health and Demographic Crisis in post-Soviet Russia: A Two-Phase Development', in Field, G. and Twigg, J. (eds.) *Russia's Torn Safety Nets: Health and Social Welfare during the Transition*. Basingstoke: Palgrave, 11–42.
Foucault, M. (1978/1998) *The History of Sexuality. Vol. I: The Will to Knowledge*. London: Penguin.
Foucault, M. (1978/2001) 'Governmentality', in Faubion, J.D. (ed.) *Essential Works of Foucault, 1954–1984: Power (Vol. 3)*. Penguin: London, 201–222.
Foucault, M. (1997/2004) *Society Must be Defended. Lectures at the Collège de France, 1975–96*. Penguin: London.
Gal, S. and Kligman, G. (2000) *The Politics of Gender after Socialism: A Comparative-Historical Essay*. Princeton, NJ: Princeton University Press.
Gorbachev, N. (2014) 'Proizvodstvo Normativnosti v Diskurse Zapreta "Propagandy Gomoseksualizma"', in Kondakov, A. (ed.) *Na Perepute. Metodologiia, Teoriia i Praktika LGBT i Kvir-Issledovanii. Sbornik Stat'ei*. Saint Petersburg: Tsentr Nezavisimykh Sotsiologicheskikh Issledovanii, 86–100.
Kondakov, A. (ed) (2014) *Na Perepute. Metodologiia, Teoriia i Praktika LGBT I Kvir-Issledovaniii. Sbornik Stat'ei*. Saint Petersburg: Tsentr Nezavisimykh Sotsiologicheskikh Issledovanii.
Kulpa, R. (2011) 'Nations and Sexuality—"West" and "East"', in Kulpa, R. and Mizielińska, J. (eds.) *De-Centering Western Sexualities. Central and East European Perspectives*. Farnham: Ashgate, 43–62.

36 Francesca Stella and Nadya Nartova

Laruelle, M. (2009) *In the Name of the Nation: Nationalism and Politics in Contemporary Russia*. Basingstoke: Palgrave Macmillan.

Nartova, N. (2008) ' "Kto Komu Mat'?" Problematizatsiia Surrogatnogo Materinstva v Diskurse SMI", in Saralieva, Z. Kh. (ed.) *Semia i Semeinye Otnosheniia: Sovremennoe Sostoianie i Tendentsii Razvitiia*. Nizhnyi Novgorod: NISOTS, 146–148.

Puar, J. K. (2007) *Terrorist Assemblages: Homonationalism in Queer Times*. Durham: Duke University Press.

Rivkin-Fish, M. (2006) 'From "Demographic Crisis" to "Dying Nation": The Politics of Language and Reproduction in Russia', in Goscilo, H. and Lanoux, A. (eds.), *Gender and National Identity in Twentieth-century Russian Culture*. DeKalb, IL: Northern Illinois University Press, 151–173.

Rivkin-Fish, M. (2013) 'Conceptualizing Feminist Strategies for Russian Reproductive Politics: Abortion, Surrogate Motherhood, and Family Support after Socialism', *Signs: Journal of Women in Culture and Society* 38(3): 569–594.

Sakevich, V., and Denisov, B. (2011) 'Pereidet Li Rossiia k Planirovaniiu Sem'i?', *Demoscope Weekly* N.465–466, 2–20 May 2011.

Sankevich, V. (2009) 'Problema aborta v sovremmennoi Rossiii', in Zdravomyslova, E. and Temkina, A. (eds.) *Zdorov'e i Doverie. Gendernyi Podkhod k Reproduktivnoi Meditsine*. Saint Petersburg: Evropeiskii Universitet v Sankt-Peterburge, 136–154.

Snarskaia, O. (2009) 'Seksual'noe Obrazovanie Kak Sfera Proizvodstva Gendernykh Razlichii I Konstruktirovaniia Predstavlenii o Natsii', in Zdravomyslova, E. and Temkina, A. (eds.) *Zdorov'e i Doverie. Gendernyi Podkhod k Reproduktivnoi Meditsine*. Saint Petersburg: Evropeiskii Universitet v Sankt-Peterburge, 51–89.

Stella, F. (2007) 'The Right to Be Different? Sexual Citizenship and Its Politics in Post-Soviet Russia', in Kay, R. (ed.) *Gender, Equality and Difference during and after State Socialism*. Basingstoke: Palgrave, 146–166.

Stella, F. (2013) 'Queer Space, Pride and Shame in Moscow', *Slavic Review* 72(3): 458–480.

Temkina, A. (2013) 'Sovety Ginekologov o Kontratseptsii i Planirovanii Beremennosti v Kontekste Sovremennoi Biopolitiki v Rossii', *Zhurnal Issledovanii Sotsial'noi Politiki* 11(1): 7–24.

Tkach, O. (2013) ' "Napolovinu Rodnye?" Problematizatsiia Rodstva i Sem'I v Gazetsnykh Publikatsiiakh o Vspomogatel'nykh Reproduktivnykh Tekhnologiiakh', *Zhurnal Issledovanii Sotsial'nykh Politiki* 11(1): 49–68.

United Nations Development Programme Russia (2008) *National Human Development Report—Russian Federation. Russia Facing Demographic Challenges*. Moscow: UNDP Russia. Available at http://hdr.undp.org/sites/default/files/nhdr_russia_2008_eng.pdf, last accessed 31.8.215.

Wilkinson, C. (2014) 'Putting "Traditional Values" into Practice: The Rise and Contestation of Anti-Homopropaganda Laws in Russia', *Journal of Human Rights* 13(3): 363–379.

Yuval-Davis, N. (1997) *Gender and Nation*. London: Sage.

Zdravomyslova, E. (2009) 'Gendernoe Grazhdanstvo i Abortnaia Kul'tura', in Zdravomyslova, E. and Temkina, A. (eds.) *Zdorov'e i Doverie. Gendernyi Podkhod k Reproduktivnoi Meditsine*. Saint Petersburg: Evropeiskii Universitet v Sankt-Peterburge, 108–135.

2 Sexuality, Citizenship and Migration
The Irish Queer Diaspora in London

Róisín Ryan-Flood

INTRODUCTION

This chapter will draw on research that examined the experiences of Irish lesbian, gay, bisexual and transgendered (LGBT) people living in London. Various writers have noted the appeal of global cities to LGBT people. Metropolitan centres are associated with tolerance of sexual diversity and established queer communities. There is a long history of Irish migration to the UK, particularly London. This has coincided historically with many Irish LGBT people feeling compelled to emigrate in search of a more tolerant and supportive social climate. The study explores Irish queer migrants' reasons for moving to London and their experiences there. Research questions address notions of home, identity, belonging, familial relationships and subjectivity. The ways in which identities become circulated in global contexts and are rearticulated, as well as the significance of migration in the formation of Irish queer subjectivities, are examined. By exploring the relationship between sexuality, ethnicity and migration, the study attempts to uncover the ways in which contemporary sexual citizenship, migration and queer imaginaries of the metropolis are mutually implicated in complex ways. The chapter considers some of the implications of the research findings for wider theories of sexual citizenship.

Research on sexualities has too often overlooked the significance of 'race' and ethnicity, while work on diasporic communities has similarly neglected the importance of sexuality to migration and diaspora (e.g. Brah 2005). This intersection of sexuality, ethnicity and diaspora is perhaps most poignantly highlighted in the case of the annual St. Patrick's Day parade in New York. In 1993, the US Supreme Court upheld a decision to exclude the Irish Lesbian and Gay Organisation (ILGO) from participating in New York's annual parade. The justification for this ruling relied on the construction of Irishness as inherently heterosexual. Interestingly, this decision contrasts with the welcome participation of lesbian, gay, bisexual and transgendered (LGBT) community floats in St. Patrick's Day parades in Ireland itself. Or, as Axel (2002: 426) writes in his essay 'The Diasporic Imaginary', 'rather than conceiving of the homeland as something that creates the diaspora, it may be more productive to consider the diaspora as something that

38   Róisín Ryan-Flood

creates the homeland'. The exclusion of lesbian and gay migrants from the celebrations in New York illuminates how the boundaries of 'the nation' are firmly demarcated along heteronormative lines within Irish American nationalism. It also highlights the potential role of the state in the regulation of diasporic identities (Munt and O'Donnell 2007). This example further reveals the importance of inflecting understandings of migrant communities with a critical analysis of sexuality and identity.

This chapter will explore the intersections of sexuality, migration and the city. It will be argued that theorising sexuality and migration separately offers only a partial and determinist understanding of the experiences of queer migrants. An exploration of Irish LGBT migrants' experiences also illuminates changes across time in LGBT politics and rights both in Ireland and the UK. Those experiences also illustrate important shifts in family relationships across generations, with younger people far more accepting of LGBT family members. The chapter draws on original empirical research carried out in 2008–2009 with Irish lesbian, gay, bisexual and transgendered migrants living in London.

Contextualising Sexuality, Migration and the City

Sexuality and migration have been largely theorised in relation to the significance of the city in queer imaginaries. Young (1990: 241) argues in favour of a city that recognises diversity, does not suppress difference and oppress others but is 'open to unassimilated otherness'. This association of metropolitan cities with greater tolerance and acceptance of difference is acknowledged by Weston's (1998) classic essay, where she argues that the anonymity offered by urban environments makes them a better place to live a lesbian or gay lifestyle compared to rural society, which offers less privacy. Weston goes so far as to suggest that the symbolic contrast offered by the urban/rural dichotomy is crucial to making sense of lesbian and gay identities, being central to the organisation of many 'coming out' stories in which sexual dissidents migrate from the country to the city to escape prejudice and to forge their own identities. Certainly, many authors have documented the greater visibility of gay men (and to a lesser extent, lesbians) within metropolitan cities. It has been argued that this reflects not simply greater tolerance of LGBT identities but also an assertion of the right to public space on the part of sexual dissidents (Browne et al. 2009). Every year in late June, Queer Pride parades take place in many major cities around the globe. The function of these parades is to express a call for LGBT rights and to celebrate queer identities but also to expose the extent to which public space is normatively coded as heterosexual.

So how is queer sexuality expressed spatially? The Castro District in San Francisco, USA, is perhaps one of the most famous lesbian and gay neighbourhoods in the world. Its reputation as a gay-friendly area began in the 1950s. Many servicemen departed for and returned from overseas duties from the port of San Francisco, which was also where dishonourable discharges

Sexuality, Citizenship and Migration   39

from the navy were often carried out; many servicemen were discharged for engaging in same-sex relations. Those leaving or dismissed from the services often remained in the city and established networks among themselves. California had relatively liberal state laws on homosexuality, and San Francisco became associated with tolerance and difference, including sexual diversity. This reputation attracted LGBT migrants from other parts of the country. In the 1970s, the Castro District emerged as a gay-friendly neighbourhood. This was initially an area of cheap housing, but as some of the more affluent gay men moved into the neighbourhood and commercial services catering to them appeared, they gradually displaced long-term ethnic minority residents (as well as poorer lesbians and gay men), gentrifying the area. Knopp (1998: 159) observes that 'the forging of identities through the economic and political colonisation of territorial spaces (and the related creation of gay-identified places) is much facilitated by class, racial and gender privilege'. Although lesbians, like gay men, have also established supportive spaces within urban environments, these spaces have typically been less fixed and more ephemeral—for example, a women's night once a month, rather than a specific women's bar. Adler and Brenner (1992) suggest that this is because, like heterosexual women, lesbians have less financial resources and also because the threat of male violence makes them more reluctant to establish an overt presence in the landscape. Rothenburg (1995) argued that lesbian spaces were more politically rather than commercially oriented compared to gay male spaces and also that lesbians tended to create residential rather than commercial spaces.[1] Houlbrook (2006) finds similar developments in the early establishment of London as a queer-friendly city in his work focusing on the post-First World War period until the 1950s. It was not until after the decriminalisation of homosexuality in 1961 that a queer presence gradually began to become more visible, however. Now the annual LGBT Pride Parade in London attracts visitors from around the world. Gay-friendly commercial districts such as Soho enhance its reputation for queer community and acceptance, although of course it must be noted that numerous authors have highlighted the exclusionary practices that occur on the gay scene in relation to class and race (e.g. Binnie 2011; Taylor 2011). In England and Wales, civil partnership for same-sex couples was introduced in 2004, with same-sex marriage becoming available in 2014. More recently, the Internet has come to play a significant role in both facilitating LGBT community and undermining the need for separate spaces (Mowlabocus 2007).

In terms of LGBT migration, Binnie (2004: 95) makes the cautionary point that 'it is not simply the case that queers migrate to somewhere where they may benefit from greater state protection and enjoy more rights and entitlements'. In the case of LGBT diaspora, movement across borders is assumed to be unproblematic, yet there are very real obstacles and barriers to such movement, including heteronormative and homophobic policies, as well as the economic and emotional costs of migration. This chapter will explore these points in more depth in relation to the Irish LGBT diaspora.

40 Róisín Ryan-Flood

The Irish Queer Diaspora

The notion of diaspora is central to understandings of globalisation and processes of social change. A substantial body of work exists that explore the Irish diaspora (Gray 2004; Nash 2002, 2004, 2005; Bielenberg 2013). Over seventy million people worldwide claim an Irish identity but only five million live in Ireland (Walter 2001). Research on the Irish diaspora has contributed to theoretical work on whiteness, gender and postcolonialism (Hickman 2002; Ryan 2007). However, the importance of sexuality to processes of migration, belonging and identity in the Irish diaspora remains a significant omission within the wider literature and indeed much of the literature on migration more generally. As already outlined, various authors have noted the links between lesbian and gay sexuality and migration to urban areas. Metropolitan environments are associated with a more visible queer community and greater tolerance of sexual diversity (Weston 1998). Binnie (2004) suggests that the desire among sexual dissidents to migrate may be born out of a fear of persecution. London is often cited as a popular destination for LGBT migrants, due to the existence of commercial districts catering to a queer client base (e.g. Soho) and established queer communities. The appeal of London for Irish queer migrants is accompanied by a tradition of emigration from Ireland to Britain—particularly London—for improved employment prospects. Both factors contribute to Irish LGBT people moving to London.

However, Ireland has changed enormously in recent years in the wake of the economic transformation and collapse associated with the rise and fall of the Celtic Tiger. At the same time, there are more images of lesbian and gay Irish people in the British media, such as chat show host Graham Norton or Anna Nolan and Brian Dowling from Big Brother. This raises questions about how LGBT emigrants' ways of relating to Ireland and life in the UK, and their notions of home and belonging, may also change. Researchers in Ireland have noted the significance of Irish queer migrants achieving visibility abroad for reconsidering conceptualisations of Irishness and contributing to the development of a more tolerant social climate within Ireland (Bowyer 2004). Much work remains to be done to uncover the ways in which sexuality shapes migration processes. How does identity become reconfigured among Irish LGBT migrants? Have shifts in Anglo-Irish relations and social changes in Ireland affected their experiences in Britain? What constraints and possibilities are afforded to Irish LGBT migrants living in London?

Sexual Citizenship in Ireland

The referendum on making marriage a gender neutral category that was held in May 2015 in the Republic of Ireland was supported with a resounding yes. Perhaps no single event so clearly signifies the extraordinary transformation

Sexuality, Citizenship and Migration 41

in gay rights that has taken place there within the past two decades. Homosexuality was only decriminalised in Ireland in 1993 (although it was not prosecuted under this law for decades prior to decriminalisation). At the time of the research (2008–2009), no possibility of civil partnership existed in the Republic of Ireland, although this was subsequently introduced in 2011. Following the 2015 referendum, marriage will be open to both gay and heterosexual couples. The 22 years between these two pivotal changes in Irish law with regard to sexual equality reflect a period of dramatic change in attitudes towards gay rights in Ireland. This is attributed to several factors: the declining power of the Catholic Church in Ireland during the same period; a changed political climate in Ireland where citizenship rights were increasingly contested in relation to intimate life (for example, also in relation to divorce and abortion); and trans-national debates about sexuality, rights and citizenship (Ryan, F. 2014). The economic transformation associated with the Celtic Tiger and wave of inward migration are also associated with opening up debates about change and diversity within contemporary Irish society (Ryan, P. 2014). At the time of the research and continuing today, there was substantial visibility in relation to Irish queer identities in media, culture and politics (Ryan-Flood 2014). The UK has also witnessed dramatic changes in equality and sexual citizenship within a similar period. Participants' experiences of Ireland were therefore variable depending on their generation and the point at which they moved to London. The relationship between sexual dissidence and emigration was explored in the project.

The Irish LGBT diaspora in London, like other queer diasporas, contributes to debates about shifting dimensions of globalisation, identity and politics. Gopinath (2003: 209), for example, argues that a queer South Asian diasporic geography rewrites colonial constructions that depict Asian sexualities as less 'developed' than their Western counterparts, an assumption that is also present in trans-national LGBT movements. Queer diaspora further challenges nationalist narratives that imagine and consolidate the nation in terms of organic heterosexuality.

Puar (2007: 172) explores how awareness of homophobia has become incorporated in a limited sense within US nationalist ideologies. She argues that in a US context, 'configurations of sexuality, race, gender, nation, class, and ethnicity are realigning in relation to contemporary forces of securitization, counterterrorism, and nationalism'. This means that a limited form of what she terms 'homonationalism' becomes incorporated into the national imaginary, in which queer migrants are liberated from their homophobic cultures of origin, thus 'positing queer as an exemplary or liberatory site devoid of nationalist impulses, an exceptionalism that narrates queerness as emulating the highest transgressive potential of diaspora'.

A study of the queer Irish diaspora contests understandings of Irishness within discourses 'at home' and abroad. However, this research does not begin with the assumption that Irish LGBT migrants' move from Ireland

42 Róisín Ryan-Flood

to London represents a linear shift from repression to 'freedom', as this would potentially erase the complexity of their experiences. As Luibhéid (2005) notes, migration rarely represents a clear-cut resolution to difficulties faced by LGBT people. Other barriers are inextricable from global histories of imperialism and colonialism. The difficulties traditionally faced by Irish migrants in Britain include social disadvantage, discrimination and related issues such as homelessness, poor health and mortality rates (Hickman and Walter 1997; Parekh 2000). The changing context for sexual citizenship within Ireland and the UK, as well as Anglo-Irish relations also has implications for theorising the queer Irish diasporic experience in London.

THE RESEARCH PROJECT

The data collection process involved semi-structured in-depth interviews with 40 Irish LGBT participants (20 women and 20 men) and three focus group discussions (consisting of six members each). Participants' ages ranged from 22–80 years. The average age was 32 years. The time spent living in London ranged from 2 years to 66 years, with a mean of 10 years, capturing different moments of migration and of being Irish in Britain. Participants were from a range of backgrounds; half were from rural Ireland, the remainder from towns or cities. Most described themselves as middle class, with 15 describing their backgrounds as working class. Some of these considered themselves to now be middle class. Most lived in suburban London. A small number of participants (n = 6) were from Northern Ireland.

This project had explored a number of issues concerning processes of 'home', identity and belonging among Irish queer migrants. A central theme concerned their relationships with families of origin and how coming out and migration affected this. The research also explored reasons for migration. Participants were asked about their experiences of being Irish in London. In addition, participants were asked about LGBT life in London and what possibilities and constraints were afforded by life in the metropolis.

SEXUAL CITIZENSHIP AND THE POLITICS OF MIGRATION

Although the academic literature on LGBT identities and urban migration tends to present sexuality as a sole determining factor in migration paths and choices, this research indicates that LGBT migration must be situated within wider histories and contexts of migration. For example, participants who moved to London during the 1980s indicated that they would have been forced to emigrate irrespective of their sexuality, given the prevailing economic conditions in Ireland at that time. This suggests that the literature on sexuality, migration and citizenship needs to situate theories within

Sexuality, Citizenship and Migration   43

wider frameworks that encompass cultural and economic specificity. Similarly, however, a critical engagement with sexual identity would displace the heteronormativity of much migration theory.

> I left Ireland in a period when emigration was an accepted reality for almost everyone. [. . .] In 1983 when I left school, the country was in a very, very deeply entrenched recession [. . .] you know if you didn't work for the civil service or [. . .] there was actually really nothing and a huge level of unemployment. So [. . .] I think going to university on some level was part of that . . . an introduction to the process of emigration.
>
> —Connor, 42-year-old Irish man

> Well, first of all [. . .] I left Ireland, in '91 because for one there was no work back then. So it was quite difficult, as in, to be on the dole for the rest of your life, it was just a horrible situation. I was made redundant and it was really hard to get another job and that particular time, you had like forty people going for like a job making burgers in McDonalds. So it was [. . .] really difficult like to get another job and I was on the dole I think about six months at that stage. And, I said that's it, I had enough, I'm going for work, but I also went for other reasons as in, family and the way I was being treated by family and also of the way I was treated really since I was young, as in I was sick of being called queer and all of that like.
>
> —Donal, 38-year-old Irish man

In the excerpts from Connor and Donal, they explain their decision to emigrate in terms of prevailing economic conditions within Ireland and the opportunities for employment offered in London. Donal also refers to the significance of London as presenting the possibility of freedom from harassment and homophobia. Other participants similarly referenced London as a place where they could 'be themselves'. Even when they initially moved to London for other reasons or were unaware of their sexuality, life in London provided them with more opportunities to explore their sexual identity:

> I can't say that I went to London with the view in mind of exploring my sexuality or saying I can't explore it but now that I look back on it there was no way I could've, it was a great decision for me. [. . .] What I mean about that is when I was in secondary school I was quite a good student and [. . .] there was a lot of [. . .] expectation that I would do very well in University and actually I was sick of actually being academic that's it and not exploring at all sexuality, social life to the way my peers were. So I know that that affected my mood at the time and made me quite reckless and a bit wayward cause I had no interest cause I was sick of

44 Róisín Ryan-Flood

just pursuing that area of my life, but it's only in hindsight I was completely unaware that that was going on at the time I think.

—Julie, 30-year-old Irish woman

The usual difficulties facing migrants were experienced by participants in this study, such as vulnerability in the absence of familial networks and support. However, in many cases they were exacerbated through homophobic exclusions, such as homophobia in the workplace. Legal protection against homophobic discrimination in employment was introduced in Ireland in 1997, six years before it was finally introduced in the UK in 2003. Other difficulties experienced by long-term residents in London included lack of legal protection for cohabiting partners prior to the introduction of civil partnerships in 2004. The significant legal changes introduced since the turn of the millennium regarding partnership and employment had a clear impact on participants' lives, many of whom had moved there prior to these changes. However, even when participants were able to avail themselves of these possibilities, particular vulnerabilities remained. The taking up of new possibilities, such as civil partnership, was also not always straightforward. For example, one participant moved to London in order to have a civil partnership with his Latin American partner:

Basically because there's no civil partnership [in Ireland], there's no rule that I could bring him into the country because he's from South America. [. . .] We came to London and we met up with an immigration lawyer whom we had a really bad experience with. [. . .] One of the requirements for Paulo [partner] entering the country was he could only do it from Uruguay, so basically he went home for what we thought was gonna be a two month stint and it turned into eleven months that we were separated so I was here on my own—and he was at home obviously with his family but that was tough in itself you know so we've kind of fought a lot to, we fought the system basically to stay together, you know.

—Cormac, 35-year-old Irish gay man

Cormac gave up a well-paying job in Ireland in order to work in menial employment in London. Unfortunately, he and his partner suffered at the hands of an unscrupulous lawyer and were forced to live in different countries for eleven months, as well as losing a substantial amount of money. This highlights Binnie's (2004) argument that even when legislative provisions and support are in place, the process of migration is not straightforward for queer migrants. More information and support is needed for LGBT migrants to London about rights and services, particularly in the context of new forms of citizenship, such as civil partnership or same-sex marriage.

One participant moved to London to escape domestic violence from his brother. He had previously lived in England but returned to Ireland to care

Sexuality, Citizenship and Migration   45

for an ill parent, so he lived in his parents' home. He was repeatedly subjected to violent attacks by his homophobic brother and got a restraining order against him. Unfortunately, the judge for the case required his mother to testify against the brother, which she refused to do as she would not interfere in the conflict between her sons:

> Last July I just had enough and I was attacked again, was after being through the court systems over in Dublin. That was after being to the police, I had no support off the police, unless I had a safety injunction put in order. And I went to court, I had, all I can describe as some homophobic twat of a judge basically that wasn't taking up for me in any way at all like, and I had to put my case across pretty well [. . .] towards a violent blaggard really of a brother. [. . .] He gave me a pardon order for three months and [. . .] if I wanted to extend that pardon order, which I did, I had to get my mother to come in cause it was her house that I lived in and this is where he lived as well. And I tried to explain to him at the time that I can't, cause my mother won't take sides. And then, after the three months she wouldn't support me and it went back to normal then and it was a free for all again and [. . .] that's how I ended up then just coming back to London. I had a good job at home, I had a car, I had everything like, do you know what I mean, I left everything even in the house behind me, I think I just threw two pairs of jeans, a few tops and, uh, some shoes basically. And I just took my bank card, so that's everything that meant a lot to me like sentimental and everything. And I got out of it. And my face was like all punched up like and it was Turlough [friend] that put me up and I stayed with him for ten weeks and then I got in touch with an organisation here that it's the only one in Europe and they actually have a, it's like a safe house for gay men that have suffered domestic violence and are fleeing domestic violence. And I was lucky enough that I went for an interview with them and I explained the whole situation and then we did two weeks of that, that was in the end of September so [in] October I moved into to the safe house and I've been there ever since.
>
> —Seán, 38-year-old Irish gay man

As the case of Seán highlights, LGBT migrants can emigrate for a range of reasons, including escaping from homophobic harassment and violence. The refuge that he refers to offered a much needed service. Refuges for victims of domestic violence are typically underfunded and under-resourced, and it is extremely rare for one to offer its services to gay male victims (Donovan and Hester 2010, 2011).

Sexual citizenship for LGBT migrants encompasses recognition of same-sex relationships, intimate violence and also gender transitions. Tauches (2011) points out that for transgendered people, documents hold a particular significance as they document and endorse new or old gender

46 Róisín Ryan-Flood

identities. This research included one interview with a transman, who was thinking of applying for a British passport, as this would allow him to have his male gender identity represented on his passport (a possibility that was not available in Ireland).

> I changed my name officially two years ago [. . .] and I'm considering getting a British passport in July, I'll have been here five years and will have full residency so can get a British passport then because under the Gender Recognition Act I can have my new name which is official in the UK on my driver's licence so on and so forth'.
> —John, 32-year-old Irish transman

In all of the migrant stories outlined here, visibility and sexual citizenship played an important role. London offered the freedom to explore their identity in a more tolerant climate. In some cases, it also presented them with important rights, such as civil partnership (facilitating a partner's visa), gender recognition and a refuge from domestic violence. While economic prospects were a key factor influencing migration and should not be treated as less relevant than sexual identity, these narratives do nonetheless highlight the importance of sexuality as a category of analysis in migration research.

CHANGING IRELAND, CHANGING IRISHNESS: CROSS-GENERATIONAL DIFFERENCES

A number of cross-generational differences emerged in the research. By 'cross-generational', I mean across age differences among participants, since all participants in the study were first-generation Irish in London. These differences reflected diverse temporalities concerning: tolerance and diversity within Ireland itself, as well as differing contexts for migration from Ireland and of being Irish in England. There was a clear awareness that Ireland had undergone significant changes in recent decades. The experiences of more recent migrants contrasted sharply with those of previous generations. Contemporary Ireland was seen as far more tolerant and diverse than in previous years. This is not to say that younger, recent migrants had not experienced difficulties within Ireland. Nonetheless, the increased visibility of LGBT people in popular culture and the media, as well as their inclusion in the equalities agenda within Ireland has clearly had an impact on their experiences and ability to be open about life with family and friends within Ireland. At the same time, migration could offer greater freedom and privacy to explore their sexual identity.

Another key difference concerned the experiences of being Irish in England. While those who emigrated prior to the mid-1990s often vividly described incidents of anti-Irishness in London, the experiences of more recent migrants reflect changes in Anglo-Irish relations and the rise of the

Celtic Tiger economy. Thus it could be suggested that constructions of Irishness in Britain may have changed. The economic transformation in Ireland in the 1990s resulted in a new wave of immigration to Ireland, traditionally a country of outward migration. In this research, emigrants from Ireland during this period were more likely to be in search of wider job opportunities and the possibility for progress and promotion, as opposed to migration on the grounds of economic necessity. Class seemed to be significant in exposure to anti-Irishness and the degree to which it occurred.

Developments in the peace process in Northern Ireland and changes in community relations following the 7/7 bombings also suggest that the tensions around terrorism that have traditionally been experienced by Irish communities in Britain have now been displaced onto Muslim communities. Participants often pointed to parallels with earlier Irish experiences in England and contemporary Muslim experiences. This perhaps calls for a reconceptualisation of Irishness in Britain or at least that contemporary Irish experiences should be explored further.

The research project included a small number of participants from Northern Ireland. Their interviews were particularly fascinating and illuminating about the ways in which sexual identity and citizenship were informed by the Troubles. These included: accounts of homophobic verbal harassment by British troops in the north towards young Catholic men, cross-community romantic relationships and cross-community and cross-border dialogue among lesbian and gay people. One example of homophobic harassment arose during an interview in relation to the detainment of a participant, Tadhg, during his youth when living in Belfast at the time of internment in the early 1970s. He was among a group of young Catholic men rounded up and detained at the local police station. Tadhg describes his shock when subjected to homophobic verbal abuse. He wondered initially how the soldiers were aware of his gay identity, which was a secret at that time, but later came to realise that they were making disparaging remarks of this kind partly because he had long blond hair:

> I mean my hair was long and was blond, I was [. . .] insulted being called a fucking queer and all kinds of things and I thought to myself how do they know but they didn't know it was just a way of abusing you, I could've been anything.
>
> —Tadhg, 52-year-old Irish gay man

This presents an interesting example of hegemonic masculinity intersecting with ethnicity, sexuality and citizenship. As a working-class Catholic young man during a period of heightened tension in the Troubles, Tadhg was subjected to homophobic harassment (despite not being openly or obviously gay) by British soldiers in Northern Ireland.

Cross-community relationships faced particular difficulties and exclusions. Tadhg, for example, also talked about his first love, a young Protestant

48 *Róisín Ryan-Flood*

man he met at work. They were never open about their relationship but came under criticism from colleagues for being so friendly with one another, which eventually led to them breaking up. Overall, however, the interview narratives suggested that the gay community was a positive resource for people from different ethnic communities in the north, as well as different sides of the border, to meet and interact, an interesting facet of the Irish experience in relation to conflict and dialogue. Duggan (2012) has argued that in Northern Ireland, sectarian divisions resulted in a climate of social conservatism that led to homophobia becoming an integral part of community politics and identity formation. Decades of political instability in the region led to the marginalisation of rights for lesbians and gay men. However, in more recent years the peace process has facilitated the growth of a more inclusive equality politics which has gradually improved the context for LGBT rights in Northern Ireland.

RECONCEPTUALISING QUEER KINSHIP

The research also examined dimensions of identity, belonging and difference by exploring participants' narratives of home and kinship. As Fortier (2003) points out, 'home' is a contested concept for many LGBT people, who may face rejection from families of origin. Weston (1997) argues that LGBT communities have a distinctive approach to kinship that is characterised by choice, rather than 'blood ties'. Many LGBT people are excluded or alienated from the families in which they grew up, so they create new family networks, or 'elective families', consisting of friends, lovers and ex-lovers. The project explored participants' relationships with family in Ireland, including the extent to which they are 'out' to their families and the impact of this.

Plummer (2010) notes the significance of 'generational narratives', which he defines as 'perspectives or standpoints on social worlds' (2010: 171). As he points out, sexual life stories 'change over age and time' (2010: 167). Similarly, there have been significant shifts in sexual citizenship in Ireland in recent years. These are reflected in greater political and social equality, as well as far greater visibility, for lesbian, gay, bisexual and transgendered people in Ireland than ever before. These changes in sexual citizenship also impacted family relationships. In the case of the Irish participants in this research, family relationships were generally better with younger generations. This included participants who were themselves younger, as well as older participants' relationships with nephews and nieces compared to older family members, reflecting a great tolerance of sexual diversity among younger generations.

Bell and Binnie (2000) have been critical of family-based approaches to sexual citizenship. They argue that a theoretical and empirical concern with partnership and marriage limits understandings of queer experiences and subjectivities to a heteronormative framework. Halberstam (2003,

Sexuality, Citizenship and Migration   49

2005) suggests that queer time and space in fact develop in opposition to the heteronormative life cycle. Queer kinship therefore presents alternative temporalities: 'Queer uses of time and space develop in opposition to the institutions of family, heterosexuality, and reproduction, and queer subcultures develop as alternatives to kinship-based notions of community' (2003: 1). Halberstam highlights the potential for queer spaces to provide an alternative to a heteronormative life-course model. She also provides a critique of the heteronormative aspects of parenthood politics. However, her argument creates a dichotomy between the apparent subversions of queer communities on the one hand and heteronormativity of parenthood on the other. This perspective creates an assimilation/transgression dichotomy, which reduces the complexities of queer kinship and places a higher value on queer subversions. Elsewhere I have argued that rather than simply assessing the extent to which, for example, lesbian parents subvert or reinforce social norms, a more productive approach is to consider the consequences for those who make choices beyond conventional heteronormativity and how they negotiate this (Ryan-Flood 2009).

Butler (2002) expresses a reservation towards familial developments in sexual citizenship. While acknowledging the significance of marriage and parenting rights for the everyday lives of many LGBT people, she also suggests that this recent legislative trend has problematic implications for queer kinship imaginaries. Becoming incorporated into the institution of marriage, for example, potentially inhibits queer imaginaries, rendering alternative relationship forms unimaginable so that 'The life of sexuality, kinship and community that becomes unthinkable within the terms of these norms constitutes the lost horizon of radical sexual politics and we find our way "politically" in the wake of the ungrievable' (2002: 40). These various arguments present a cautionary or even critical note towards developments in sexual citizenship for the radical potential of queer kinship. By acknowledging that developments in sexual citizenship have led to improved bonds between LGBT people and their families of origin compared to previous generations, my aim here is not to suggest that queer kinship is now simply incorporated within heteronormative parameters. Rather, I want to consider the implications of these shifts in the wider political and social landscape for theorising LGBT family experiences in a way that includes relationships with parents and siblings. I also argue that an assimilation/transgression dichotomy is inadequate for understanding queer kinship.

A striking feature of interview narratives were the lengths to which participants attempted to continue to sustain relationships with their families in Ireland, even in the face of hostility towards coming out. The extent to which participants engaged in 'emotional labour' (Hochschild 1983) in their efforts to reach out to families, communicate and be involved in their lives was a recurrent aspect of interview accounts. This often involved a considerable degree of patience and understanding that it took their families time to get used to the idea of having a gay family member. It was also the case that

50 *Róisín Ryan-Flood*

participants had to stand up for themselves in the face of family discomfort around their sexuality.

For example, although not religious herself, Sorcha always returned to Ireland for family events, such as her younger siblings' confirmations. This willingness to participate in events that were important within her family was taken for granted, at the same time she had to be patient with her parents' struggles around accepting her sexuality:

> I think that they struggled with [. . .] what people's perception of me and therefore the family would be, so I think they were quite conflicted and so it was it was difficult for me at times. But once I'd sort of come out to myself [. . .] and was okay with it myself I was quite [. . .] determined I think and basically fairly confident about it and didn't really take any crap. And there was one point when [. . .] my brother was having his confirmation and my mum decided I think because my dad had been talking to her that my partner shouldn't be invited and so that was a big, that was a big upheaval [. . .] but I think also it was the point where she realised that actually this is not a phase, it's me and its' not gonna go away. [. . .] And I said to her at that point, you know, if this happens again if you're not going to invite my partner then don't invite me cause I'm not gonna come. [. . .] So, I think from that point onwards, you know, my mum got it pretty straight in her head at that point that, you know, this is how it's gonna be so she'd better get used to it.
>
> —Sorcha, 26

Participants often described their parents' concern about other people in the local community discovering their gay child's sexual identity. This concern with the 'image' of the family within the locality is not exclusive to Ireland, but it is not something that has been addressed in any depth within wider literature about gay migrants returning home to visit. In these instances, their family member's life in London was seen to create a suitable compromise between their freedom to live a gay life, while still retaining a sense of secrecy within the wider community (but not their immediate family) when returning home. For example, Orla describes her coming out experience with her parents on a weekend visit home:

> Mum was saying oh you're just an embarrassment to the family and who all knows and do your friends [. . .] know cause then they're going to tell their families and everyone's gonna know and [. . .] they were just so embarrassed and I was like well [. . .] not nobody knows and it's fine [. . .] it'll stay in London obviously it will not come back and [. . .] my dad said okay, that'll be an agreement as long as you keep 'your problem' he kept saying, in London and I said that's fine, so that was kind of where they left it.
>
> —Orla, 26

It is hopefully the case that the result of the marriage referendum in Ireland in 2015 will help parents of gay children to feel reassured that their wider community will be more accepting. In Orla's case, like many participants, her siblings defended her to their parents and helped facilitate her parents' gradual acceptance of her sexuality. This reflected a wider generational shift in attitudes towards LGBT rights in Ireland, whereby younger people are far more tolerant and supportive of LGBT people compared to older generations (Ryan, P. 2014; Ryan-Flood 2014).

Theories of queer kinship (e.g. Weston 1998; Weeks et al. 2001) tend to emphasise the ways in which LGBT people may experience alienation from families of origin. However, this research suggests that it may be necessary to reconceptualise our understandings of queer kinship. The efforts to continue to maintain connections with families of origin may reflect shifts in openness towards having a gay child or sibling, as well as a growing self-confidence on the part of LGBT people to expect and demand support from their families.

The narrative of 'families we choose' and the decentralisation of blood ties implied is perhaps also becoming more illustrative of families more generally, with the increase in blended families, for example, as well as many migrants, of course. These findings are relevant, not just for Irish families but for all families who have a lesbian/gay/bisexual family member. They also suggest that scholars could consider shifting the emphasis on conflict, stress and difficulty surrounding LGBT people's relationships with parents and siblings and acknowledge the positive efforts made by LGBT people to maintain family relationships. These efforts include keeping open channels of communication, as well as considerable forgiveness work in the face of homophobic responses to disclosures of their sexuality.

Recognition of this attempt to retain connection with families of origin would require recasting families with a gay family member as 'lucky' in relation to the commitment to dialogue and forgive within the context of LGBT people's family connections (see also Ryan-Flood 2014 for further discussion of kinship discourses among Irish LGBT migrants).

CONCLUSIONS: QUEERING DIASPORA

Rather than present a notion of 'queer/LGBT diaspora' in an essentialising way as a distinct monolithic group, this research has alternatively sought to queer the concepts of diaspora and migration. The notion of 'queer diaspora' could too easily be understood as a homogeneous category, without acknowledgement of diversity among migrants. The experiences of participants in this research, for example, varied across generation. Temporality was significant in terms of the shifting context for sexual citizenship both where they came from (Ireland) and where they moved to (the UK). This chapter has sought to integrate a critical awareness of queer identities into

52 Róisín Ryan-Flood

Irish diasporic scholarship. The analysis presented here suggests that without an understanding of sexual diversity, any work on diaspora and migration will be incomplete. However, the experiences of queer migrants do not simply form a homogenous category. Critically inflecting migration studies with an understanding of sexual diversity facilitates deeper understandings of processes of migration, belonging, identity and place.

The May 2015 referendum in Ireland fundamentally changed the context for LGBT politics in Ireland. With a significant majority, people voted in support of same-sex marriage. This reflected an enormous shift in attitudes to LGBT rights. It is also the case that the Irish diaspora played a high-profile role in the campaign for equality. Media in Ireland and internationally noted the 'home to vote' campaign, whereby Irish people who had moved abroad within the previous 18 months were eligible to return to vote and many of them did so with the explicit intention of voting yes. This campaign was clearly visible on social media, including Twitter and Facebook. It was also a statement reflecting the continued engagement of the Irish diaspora with Irish politics at home, and it was seen to play an important role in promoting the yes campaign. This reflects the role of the diaspora in both national imaginaries and practical political engagement.

Finally, the research interviews and findings affirmed the importance of documenting queer histories. Participants talked of wanting to 'tell their stories' and having a sense that they were absent from wider discussions of the Irish experience of Britain and migration more generally. The narratives that were uncovered in the research suggest that exploring minority histories can be illuminating not just in terms of the minority groups themselves but also the assumptions underpinning wider theory and research. Uncovering the life narratives of Irish LGBT migrants allows for more nuanced accounts of the Irish diaspora and rectifies the heteronormative focus of much previous writing and research within migration. It also illuminates the importance of understandings of ethnicity, postcolonialism and place to work on sexual citizenship.

NOTE

1 The association of urban spaces with a more gay-friendly environment is accompanied by a view of rural areas as less supportive of sexual difference. Phillips and Watt (2000) argue that sexualities and sexual discourses, both hegemonic and emancipatory, have traditionally been structured around centres and margins. This can be seen clearly with Foucault's work, where the history of sexuality has a hidden geography: the legal, medical, religious and other institutions, which discursively constitute and regulate sexualities, are concentrated in geographical and political centres (i.e. metropolitan centres). Metropolitan cities are seen as the centre of the regulation and liberation of sexualities. This has led to the empirical neglect of in-between spaces on the margins of sexual geography. They argue that 'de-centring sexualities charts an ambivalent politics, marked both by danger and power, in a post-liberatory politics which does not simply shadow hegemonic sexualities' (Phillips and

Watt 2000: 16). In other words, de-centring sexualities from metropolitan centres can be critically transformative. This is an important point, yet it is also the case that more work needs to be carried out on both urban and rural spaces in relation to queer identities and histories.

BIBLIOGRAPHY

Adler, S. and Brenner, J. (1992) 'Gender and Space: Lesbians and Gay Men in the City', *International Journal of Urban and Regional Research* 16(1): 24–34.

Axel, B. (2002) 'The Diasporic Imaginary', *Public Culture* 14(2): 411–428.

Bell, D. and Binnie, J. (2000) *The Sexual Citizen*. Cambridge: Polity Press.

Bielenberg, A. (2013) *The Irish Diaspora*. London: Routledge.

Binnie, J. (2004) *The Globalization of Sexuality*. London: Routledge.

Binnie, J. (2011) 'Class, Sexuality and Space: A Comment', *Sexualities* 14(1): 21–26.

Bowyer, S. (2004) 'Lesbian and Gay Visibility and Changing Social Relations'. Unpublished PhD thesis, Department of Anthropology, University of Manchester.

Brah, A. (2005). *Cartographies of Diaspora: Contesting Identities*. London: Routledge.

Browne, K., Lim, J. and Brown, G. (eds.) (2009) *Geographies of Sexualities: Theory, Practices and Politics*. London: Ashgate.

Butler, J. (2002) 'Is Kinship Always Already Heterosexual?' *Differences: A Journal of Feminist Cultural Studies* 13(1): 14–44.

Donovan, C. and Hester, M. (2010) ' "I Hate the Word Victim": An Exploration of Recognition of Domestic Violence in Same-sex Relationships', *Social Policy and Society* 9(2): 279–289.

Donovan, C. and Hester, M. (2011) 'Seeking Help from the Enemy: Help-Seeking Strategies of Those in Same-sex Relationships Who Have Experienced Domestic Abuse', *Child and Family Law Quarterly* 23(1): 26–40.

Duggan, M. (2012) *Queering Conflict: Examining Lesbian and Gay Experiences of Homophobia in Northern Ireland*. Farnham: Ashgate.

Fortier, A. (2003) 'Making Home: Queer Migrations and Motions of Attachment', in Ahmed, S. et al. (eds.) *Uprootings/Regroundings*. Oxford: Berg, 115–135.

Giffney, N. and Shildrick, M. (2013) *Theory on the Edge: Irish Studies and the Politics of Sexual Difference*. Basingstoke: Palgrave MacMillan.

Gopinath, G. (2003) 'Nostalgia, Desire, Diaspora: South Asian Sexualities in Motion', in Corber, R. J. and Valocchi, S. (eds.) *Queer Studies: An Interdisciplinary Reader*. Oxford: Blackwell, 206–218.

Gray, B. (2004) *Women and the Irish Diaspora*. London: Routledge.

Halberstam, J. (2003) 'The Brandon Teena Archive', in Corber, R. J. and Valocchi, S. (eds.) *Queer Studies: An Interdisciplinary Reader*. Oxford: Blackwell Publishing, 159–169.

Halberstam, J. (2005) *In a Queer Time and Place: Transgender Bodies, Subcultural Lives*. New York: New York University Press.

Hickman, M. (2002) ' "Locating" The Irish Diaspora', *Irish Journal of Sociology* 11(2): 8–26.

Hickman, M. and Walter, B. (1997) *Discrimination and the Irish Community in Britain*. London: Commission for Racial Equality.

Hochschild, A. (1983) *The Managed Heart: The Commercialization of Human Feeling*. California: University of California Press.

Houlbrook, M. (2006) *Queer London: Perils and Pleasures in the Sexual Metropolis, 1918–1957*. Chicago, IL: University of Chicago Press.

Knopp, L. (1998) 'Sexuality and Urban Space: Gay Male Identity Politics in the United States, the United Kingdom and Australia', in Fincher, R. and Jacobs, J. (eds.) *Cities of Difference*. London: Guilford Press.

54 Róisín Ryan-Flood

Luibhéid, E. (2005) 'Introduction: Queering Migration and Citizenship', in Luibhéid, E. and Cantú Jr., L. (eds.) *Queer Migrations: Sexuality, U.S. Citizenship and Border Crossings*. Minnesota: University of Minnesota Press, ix–xlvi.

Mowlabocus, S. (2007) 'Gaydar: Gay Men and the Pornification of Everyday Life', in Paasonen, S. (ed.) *Pornification: Sex and Sexuality in Media Culture*. Oxford: Berg, 61–72.

Munt, S. and O'Donnell, K. (2007) 'Pride and Prejudice: Legalising Compulsory Heterosexuality in New York's Annual St. Patrick's Day Parades', *Space and Culture* 10(1): 94–114.

Nash, C. (2002) 'Genealogical Identities', *Environment and Planning D: Society and Space* 20(1): 27–52.

Nash, C. (2004) 'Genetic Kinship', *Cultural Studies* 18(1): 1–34.

Nash, C. (2005) 'Geographies of Relatedness', *Transactions of the Institute of British Geographers* 30(4): 449–462.

Nash, C. (2008) *Of Irish Descent: Origin Stories, Genealogy and the Politics of Belonging*. Syracuse: Syracuse University Press.

Parekh, B. (2000) *Report of the Commission on the Future of Multi-Ethnic Britain*. London: Runnymede Trust.

Phillips, R., Watt, D. and Shuttleton, D. (eds.) *Decentring Sexualities: Politics and Representations Beyond the Metropolis*. London: Routledge.

Plummer, K. (2010) 'Generational Sexualities, Subterranean Traditions and the Haunting of Sexual Worlds', *Symbolic Interaction* 33(2): 163–190.

Puar, J. (2007) *Terrorist Assemblages*. North Carolina: Duke University Press.

Rothenburg, T. (1995) 'And She Told Two Friends: Lesbians Creating Urban Social Space', in Bell, D. and Valentine, G. (eds) *Mapping Desire: Geographies of Sexualities*. London: Routledge.

Ryan, L. (2007) 'Migrant Women, Social Networks and Motherhood: The Experiences of Irish Nurses in Britain', *Sociology* 41(2): 295–312.

Ryan, F. (2014) '"We'll Have What They're Having": Sexual Minorities and the Law in the Republic of Ireland', in Leane, M. and Kiely, E. (eds.) *Sexualities and Irish Society: A Reader*. Dublin: Orpen Press, 55–100.

Ryan, P. (2014) 'The Pursuit of Gay and Lesbian Sexual Citizenship Rights, 1980–2011', in Leane, M. and Kiely, E. (eds.) *Sexualities and Irish Society: A Reader*. Dublin: Orpen Press, 101–126.

Ryan-Flood, R. (2009) *Lesbian Motherhood: Gender, Families and Sexual Citizenship*. Basingstoke: Palgrave MacMillan.

Ryan-Flood, R. (2014) 'Staying Connected: Irish Lesbian and Gay Narratives of Family', in Connolly, L. (ed.) *The 'Irish' Family*. London: Routledge, 173–187.

Tauches, K. (2011) 'Transgendering: Challenging the "Normal"', in Seidman, S., Fischer, N. and Meeks, C. (eds.) *Introducing the New Sexuality Studies* (2nd edition). London: Routledge, 134–139.

Taylor, Y. (2011) 'Sexualities and Class', *Sexualities* 14(1): 3–11.

Walter, B. (2001) *Outsiders Inside: Whiteness, Place and Irish Women*. London: Routledge.

Weeks, J., Heaphy, B. and Donovan, C. (2001) *Same Sex Intimacies: Families of Choice and Other Life Experiments*. London: Routledge.

Weston, K. (1997) *Families We Choose: Lesbians, Gays, Kinship*. New York: Columbia University Press.

Weston, K. (1998) *Long Slow Burn: Sexuality and Social Science*. London: Routledge.

Young, I. M. (1990) *Justice and the Politics of Difference*. Princeton: Princeton University Press.

3 Narrativising One's Sexuality/Gender
Neo-Liberal Humanitarianism and the Right of Asylum

Calogero Giametta

INTRODUCTION

In neo-liberal democracies, *gender* and *sexuality* can provide people with the opportunity of asking for social and legal protection. Within the global legal-political framework, gender became a legitimate rights-claiming object at the end of the 1980s; this at the time reflected the novel focus of international human rights law and NGOs on women's rights and violence against women (Ticktin 2006). Sexuality and gender identity, in turn, have attracted humanitarian attention only very recently. Today sexuality and gender-based right claims[1] can be enacted by people claiming asylum in the Global North. Within the institutional settings defining the refugee-granting context, asylum seekers confront the legal interface, making their stories intelligible through intimate presentations of the self. In this chapter, I contend that in the process of certifying their sexuality and gender-based claims, asylum claimants' autobiographical presentations are limited by a specific vocabulary established by the current humanitarian apparatus. Therefore, I here focus on how humanitarian *mentality* enters the politics of asylum, that is, the decision-making process structures, procedures, practices and discourses of support when sexuality/gender are put under legal scrutiny.

I elaborate on data emerging from an extensive body of research,[2] including stories from people who use sexuality/gender to claim protection in the context of the current British migration regime. I draw from my ethnography, primarily with sexual/gender minority asylum claimants and refugees in the UK but also within various legal firms and a refugee support organisation. I use respondents' accounts to address some salient issues with regards to how the right to asylum is granted and how the discourse on social protection is articulated under neo-liberal governance—where asylum still features as a central institution in the system of international protection. This, in turn, leads me to consider whether social protection can ever exist without having to submit to the filtering logic of migrant populations' control; that is, granting rights to the few and denying the same to the majority. With this in mind, I attempt to problematise the discourses and practices defined not only by the state and immigration institutions but also by those legal

56   Calogero Giametta

and humanitarian bodies (i.e. immigration legal practitioners and refugee NGOs), whose aim is to protect these populations.

In the first part of the chapter, I focus on the emerging humanitarian moral economy when sexuality/gender becomes a rights-claiming object in current migration regimes. In the second part, I concentrate on two important themes pertaining to the refugee-granting process, namely the asylum institutions' search for truth and the rights claimant's search for freedom. Throughout the chapter, I attempt to elaborate on the theoretical work of some critics of humanitarianism and to bring those considerations close to the analysis of respondents' lived experiences of asylum. Respondents' accounts highlight what is at stake with the emergence of what Nicola Mai names humanitarian 'biographical borders' (2014). In the final part of the chapter, I reflect on the term *borders*, bearing in mind that these are not metaphorical frontiers, rather material and tangible limitations that shape people's migratory experiences and future life plans.

FROM PROTECTION TO CONTROL AND THE POLITICS OF HUMANITARIANISM

Sexuality and Gender in Humanitarian Discourses and Practices

At present, many political movements join forces with the politics of humanitarianism, creating a context where morals-centred discourses are strongly embedded into mainstream politics (Ticktin 2011). Didier Fassin (2012) has recently introduced the phrase 'humanitarian government' to designate the deployment of moral sentiments in contemporary geo/global politics. In Fassin's formulation, government is understood in a Foucaultian sense, namely, 'government of the living'; that is 'the set of procedures established and actions conducted in order to manage, regulate, and support the existence of human beings: government includes but exceeds the intervention of the state, local administrations, international bodies, and political institutions more generally' (Fassin 2012: 1). This is the notion of governmentality that Foucault used to grasp the features of the shaping of individual and collective conduct, which did not emerge from the state but rather from non-state apparatuses (Foucault 1980).

In his book *Humanitarian Reason* (2012), Fassin critically explores what happens when moral sentiments enter the field of the political. By moral sentiments he describes 'the emotions that direct our attention to the suffering of others and make us want to remedy them' (2012:1). Fassin builds on the question of morality in the political present and identifies a humanitarian reason that influences the domestic policies at home and individual reactions and state interventions triggered by the 'distant suffering' (Boltanski 1999) of vulnerable others in poverty-stricken countries. For the purposes of this chapter, I am interested in examining whether one can evidence the claim that an emerging humanitarian moral economy (Fassin and Rechtman

Narrativising One's Sexuality/Gender   57

2009, 2012; Pandolfi, 2011; Ticktin 2006, 2011) impacts on immigration policies within the state when sexuality and gender become political objects that mobilise sentiments. It is to this point that I will now turn my attention.

Nicola Mai (2014) argues that moral panics target in particular those migrants who use sexuality and gender as the objects of their rights claims. For instance, the moral panic about the extent of trafficking in the sex industry and the presence of 'bogus' sexual/gender minority refugees triggers affective responses within neo-liberal governance in the form of humanitarian interventions. Within this moral economy, oftentimes asylum and social protection are granted on the basis of stereotypical understandings of victimhood, gender relations and sexuality. This occurs in the certification processes of the credibility of rights claimants' sexuality/gender in the asylum process and the credibility of victimhood for those migrant sex workers who have been subjected to trafficking. The stereotyping form of affective governance to which these migrants are exposed gives rise to 'sexual humanitarianism' (Mai 2014). Mai argues that the political use of individual 'emergencies' based on sexuality and gender is a legitimating tool for the control of undesirable migrant groups.

> Sexual humanitarianism operates by containing through social interventions the mobility of migrant groups that are strategically essentialized and othered as 'pure' victims of sexual oppression and exploitation. As migrants' nuanced understandings and experiences of ambivalence, vulnerability and resilience are obfuscated, only a minority of them receives appropriate support through sexual humanitarian social interventions. Such interventions tend to exacerbate, rather than reduce, migrants' vulnerability to exploitation as they are vehicle for enforcing restrictive migration laws and lead to deportation.
>
> (2014: 176–177)

Sexual humanitarianism works through the set of discourses and practices of various actors (governmental, non-governmental and academic). Its raison d'être is in the imperative of intervening to end the suffering to which sexual/gender minorities and other forms of *sexual/gender-subalternised Others* are subjected. The *subalternised Others* phrase aims to stress the contingent conditions of subalternity that emerge within the specific contexts in which non-heteronormative individuals live—both where they come from and where they move to. I privilege using this expression rather than the term 'subaltern', as it focuses on the process that these subjects go through. In so doing, I attempt to shift the emphasis from identity to process[3] (Giametta, forthcoming). Further, my challenging the subaltern-as-identity category is also in line with Gayatri C. Spivak's recent speculations on subalternity, defining it as a 'position without identity' (2013: 431).

One fundamental problem pertaining to humanitarian logic is that it posits the suffering body as a common denominator of the human condition

58   Calogero Giametta

(i.e. we all, as human beings, share the vulnerability of our bodies). This shared human characteristic can easily be used to produce the figure of the quintessential victim,[4] deemed worthy of recognition in the forms of rights and protection (e.g. refugee status). Yet would the person who does not possess the characteristics that make up a quintessential victim be allocated protection? Here one can start noting that the discourse of victimisation—for example, of certain sexual-subalternised Others in the asylum system—can easily be transformed into an active mode of migrants' exclusion.

Returning to my ethnography, I found that during the certification process, the sexual/gender minority refugees were often asked to think and articulate 'how they felt' when something had happened to them. Lawyers, aid groups, individual support workers and other humanitarian operators with whom they came into contact stressed the importance to focus on their 'internal feelings' to present their cases in an effective way. The requirement of this type of emotional testimony generates a context where it is *how* one is able to articulate one's story rather than *what* has happened to them which grants them rights. As already mentioned, in this sense, humanitarianism acts as a borders' filter in the politics of migration control; namely, it chooses exceptional individuals and excludes the rest (Ticktin 2006). Here the perversity of the logic is apparent; namely, the sudden shift from a discourse of social protection to the practice of border control.

Under the current biopolitical order, sexuality/gender, in particular, has come to be a problematic object within the politics of migration because of how the facile victimisation of *some* rights claimants is all too often used as a way to mistrusting *many*. Further, in sexuality/gender-based asylum claims. the autobiographical narratives elicited in the process are uniquely intimate (it is *this* intimacy that distinguishes them from asylum claims lodged on other bases). Here the migration institutions go deep into people's subjectivities to access and question the authenticity of their stories. In this process, the danger of psychologising claimants' accounts tends to increase compared with asylum claims outside the realm of sexuality/gender. The 'how they felt' criteria in judging the veracity of someone's sexual/gender history and orientation seems to suggest that there is a right and a wrong way to *feel* things (to feel violence, for instance).

If a migrant claims the right to protection as a sexual/gender minority individual, she or he has to adopt a recognisable script that will give her or him more chances to obtain the right to remain in the country. Within a context marked by the sharing of one's intimate life on the part of the claimant, protection is easily denied and becomes dependent on the ability of the rights claimant to appear credible. The psychologised testimony of suffering that characterises the path to validation (as a refugee) must inspire participation of others into the suffering of the asylum claimant. Thus what story or what storyteller will be more or less believable? Julia O'Connell Davidson, in her analysis of the language of trafficking and modern slavery in sex work, suggests that 'human agency is typically read through the lens of gender and age, women and children (especially those working in prostitution) are much more likely to be described as victims of trafficking than adult men' (2013: 6). In a similar fashion, I noted that gender, age, class alongside sexuality were all important components in constructing a credible presentation of the self during the refugee-granting process.

However, I noted that one is not granted refugee status only if one presents oneself as an absolute victim but also when managing to skilfully articulate one's story of suffering. In fact, those people who appear to possess clear signs of agency are not automatically excluded from the realm of protection. At times, they can better manage to trigger an empathic atmosphere when facing the adjudicators insofar as they are perceived to be *proximate* subjects and therefore more relatable. I observed that some respondents—those who had a good education and came from a middle-class background—could strategically draw on the set of knowledge and behaviours they carried to produce a 'credible' presentation of the self. In the refugee determination process, it appeared clear that these embodied signifiers of social privilege, or lack thereof, may provide the claimant with more or less chances to be believed. Asylum seekers being adjudicated are not immune to the judgement of the type of signifiers that they manage to mobilise. How they look, where they come from and how they speak also give authority and credibility to their stories.

TRUTH IN EXCHANGE FOR *FREEDOM*

The Making of the File: Building the 'Good File'

Throughout the verification process of sexuality/gender-based claims, the asylum claimant must tell his or her story to Home Office officials, the lawyers, the judges and the support organisations. The asylum process involves an initial interview called a 'screening interview' to be followed by a 'substantive interview', where applicants describe to the case owner what has happened to them and what it is they fear in their countries. After the screening interview, some claimants are taken to immigration removal centres, where their applications are 'fast tracked'. In this case, they are held in detention whilst decisions are made on their applications.

In the asylum process, great emphasis is placed on building up a 'file' on the part of the claimant. The file includes the written story, stating the reasons behind the necessity of seeking asylum and the accompanying evidence that goes with it, such as photographic material, letters, official documents and so on. When building up a file, claimants need to focus on their past lived experiences in their own countries, which must uncover sentiments of fear and suffering. Compelled to adhere to scripts of victimhood and

60 Calogero Giametta

suffering, during the ethnography, refugees often told me about *their* suffering when internalising their 'official' story:

> The process leaves you like a shell of who you are. Before the process I never questioned the love that my parents had for me. I believed that being homosexual wasn't right, and then you come here and it takes everything you believe in away from you! There was a time I became so indecisive that I would even go to the market to buy food, I would stand by the vegetables stand and I couldn't decide which veggie to buy. 'Cos the whole basis on which I make decisions had been taken completely away from me that I couldn't decide any longer about anything. Even very simple decisions.
>
> (Jamaican lesbian refugee, 46 years old)

Building up a file requires legal advice. Since 2014, this has become more of an issue, as the government budget for legal aid has been severely cut; therefore, there is less availability of free legal support for asylum claimants.[5] Yet people need to contact a lawyer before lodging a claim. Many respondents told me that given the complexity of the certification process, receiving legal advice should be an imperative for all asylum claimants:

> To build my file I had to bring evidence. So for example I had to tell them where the hospital where I was admitted in Pakistan exactly was. They would ask me: 'what was the name of the doctor? How did the building look like?' They google mapped the location, they found out the hospital, the doctor. These kinds of minor things as well they want to see that. The solicitor did that in front of me. She took all the links and the details of the doctor, who was a psychiatrist who ended up in jail by the way. So they went through all those details.
>
> (Pakistani gay refugee, 26 years old)

> In these cases you see how important the role of the solicitor is. The Home Office they say that you should claim asylum at the airport! I don't think that that's right cos you don't know, you just arrive in a new country, you need to build up your case, you need to be relaxed, to have a solicitor. The solicitor is very important I think that he's the backbone of your case. Without the solicitor it's too risky.
>
> (Pakistani gay asylum claimant, 24 years old)

In building up their files with the help of legal representatives and advice workers, those whose voices are authoritative, claimants have to show that they have come to the UK to be safe. Most importantly, however, sexual/gender minority asylum seekers have to prove their 'difference' (pertaining to their sexuality/gender) and the danger to which such difference can expose them. Often, the only way of 'proving' this is through their personal statement, as nobody else knows about their sexuality. This is a paradoxical situation where the claimant's only evidence is her or his testimony, yet the asylum seeker's word is structurally mistrusted (Giametta forthcoming). Throughout my research, it appeared obvious that adjudicators often adopt a strategic scepticism. They seem to strategically choose not to believe, and in so doing, they deny rights. In this process, there seems to be a constant tension between not believing and denying an event or an identification.

The Paradox of (Crafting) Genuineness

The current migration regime in the UK is defined by proactive forms of containment and management of migrants' numbers (Geiger and Pecoud 2010, 2012). As such, across current political discourses defining Western European migration regimes, the word of the asylum seeker is fundamentally mistrusted (Fassin 2012). Paradoxically, in the UK, sexuality and gender identity have become a legitimate terrain for claiming rights and refugee status. However, as policy emphasises the containment of migrants' numbers, the sexual/gender minority migrant asking for protection becomes an unwelcomed object of scrutiny for the Home Office.

In my ethnography with sexual/gender minority claimants, I noted that the experiences of lesbian, gay, bisexual and trans* asylum seekers have some specificities that differ from other asylum claimants' in that, very often, they do not have support from their families or ethnic minority social networks (90 per cent of the studied group of 60 people), and they have grown to feel ashamed of who they are as well as of what has happened to them. Moreover, they have to prove their sexual orientation to UK authorities, and in so doing, they feel the pressure of having to externalise very intimate narratives about their past experiences and emotions—the type of information that other asylum seekers are not necessarily forced to disclose. But it is noteworthy that in Britain *all* asylum seekers, sexual/gender minority or not, are subject to political and media stigmatisation and procedural mistrust by often being described as 'bogus'; that is, economic migrants in disguise lying about their 'true' reasons for migrating. It is in such a climate of institutional scepticism that the asylum claimant faces the legal structures of the receiving society.

Throughout the refugee-granting process, the claimant is required to affirm and 'prove' his or her sexuality or gender. At times the statement that the claimant produces about him or herself gives enough proof to the adjudicators. More often, they require additional material evidence and witnesses' statements as necessary proof. All the evidence collated has to finally satisfy the requirements of the Home Office caseworkers or immigration judges. Yet what are the Home Office or the immigration courts looking for to deliberate whether a sexual/gender subjectivity is authentic or not? The truth-finding mechanisms focus on the applicant's body and psyche (McGhee 2000). To be sure, in this process, there is a clear problem with

62 Calogero Giametta

enactments of gayness (O'Leary 2008) which do not reflect the repertoires of LGBT identifications and lifestyles expected in the West. In this context, one can readily note how the narrative for articulating the self becomes extremely narrow for the claimant, imposing rigid biographical borders on the subject. One must tell the story about one's sexuality/gender, but it has to be coherent and has to be told in a 'convincing' way to be deemed credible. Paradoxically, truth is recognised when skilfully produced and rehearsed. A subject forms through the telling of a story at a certain time and in a certain context (Butler 1993). Thus the telling of the story of the asylum claimant provides the setting in which he or she can shape himself or herself as a particular subject, clearly there are strategic choices to be made here in terms of disclosing or silencing parts of one's life—what one chooses to tell and what one chooses to retain. Although lawyers and organisations may inform these choices, it is ultimately the claimant who needs to perform them in front of the Home Office (at least during the initial phase of the process).

In the asylum process, the ethical request that the granting system seems to address to the rights claimant is 'you give us "the (absolute) Truth" we give you "freedom from the risk of harm"'. I have already gestured towards the issue of *whose truths* the claimant must provide; now I want to turn the attention to the question of what freedoms can one hope for. Let us look more closely at some issues in relation to the neo-liberal notion of freedom for sexual/gender minorities during (and after) the refugee-granting process.

THE SEARCH FOR FREEDOM

Challenging Freedom Ideals

Claiming asylum is a highly atomising process where the claimant must go through the ordeal of telling and proving the truth of his or her gender/sexuality. One has to uncover a detailed biography to be granted the right to remain in the country. Once the story told has been certified by the decision makers, the asylum seeker is expected to prepare himself/herself to become an autonomous subject in the new democratic society. In this context, one's path to 'freedom' comes at a high price. In fact, whilst expressing their desire to be safe and free in the country of arrival, a linear narrative of passage from uncivilisation (characterising their *irrational* home countries) to a *rationally* chosen emancipation (unproblematically inscribed into the present history of modern neo-liberal democracies) was often imposed on the subject formation processes of the asylum seekers and refugees I studied. The metanarrative of progress underpinning the asylum system (Giametta 2014) draws an imagined neat trajectory that goes from claimants' past oppressions to their present liberation. This obfuscates the complexities and precariousness of their present living circumstances.

In a research with Bolivian migrant workers in the garment sector in Argentina and Brazil, Bastia and McGrath (2011) aimed to trouble the dichotomy between rational/irrational choice-making that defines the constitutive divide between the neo-liberal subject (construed as rational) and the migrant of the Global South (construed as irrational). In fact, in this compelling ethnography, they noted that their studied migrant group often accepted very exploitative working conditions after rationally evaluating their past lives and choosing to focus on the possibility of a better future to come. Following their accounts with regards to the temporal dimension of migratory trajectories, they claim that for their research respondents 'the future is only important to the extent that it provides the means for the realisation of one's aspirations (Bastia and McGrath 2011: 11). In this process, normally the present is less important than the future, which often means that a present characterised by abusive working relationships with employers is accepted, because it is seen to be conducive to providing them with possibilities of better lives (for them and their families). In my research, I observed that respondents also tended to focus on the future rather than on the precariousness of their material living conditions in the present. At the level of their biographical presentations, this was a commonly adopted strategy. However, when talking to respondents who had already been granted refugee status,[6] I noted that they often commented more willingly on their present living conditions, expressing disillusionment about their futures in the UK.

In the context of the institution of asylum, freedom is equivalent to living a life free from persecution, or from the fear of being persecuted, on the grounds of one's nationality, political opinion, ethnicity, religion and membership to a particular social group (Article 1 of the Geneva Convention, International Committee of the Red Cross 19, International Committee of the Red Cross 1949). Seeking freedom from the fear of being persecuted on the grounds of one's gender and sexual non-normativity is a novel development in the history of asylum. The search for such freedom is cast as a basic human right and must be granted to whoever lives under the threat of harm and persecution. Searching for such freedom is first cast as an inalienable right and second as a rational choice that the individual takes to minimise risks and to live as a self-determined, autonomous subject. Thus it is clear that this search for freedom is in line with the foundational narrative of the Western sovereign individual. 'The sovereign individuals of liberal thought have the right to liberty and equality' (O'Connell Davidson 2013). Indeed, rationality is embedded in the formation of neo-liberal European citizenship, and it supports the hierarchies of mobility and civilisation that define modernity.

The paradoxical logic of asylum consists in offering freedom from persecution and simultaneously establishing a process of control that explicitly restrains people's sense of being free as well as their physical freedoms. This is achieved through i) the prohibition to work, for the asylum claimant, in the first twelve months after lodging an asylum claim, ii) the practice of detention in immigration removal centres and iii) the

64   *Calogero Giametta*

impossibility to return to one's country whilst a claim is being adjudicated, and if refugee status is granted. In this context, obtaining a certain freedom, namely the freedom not to be persecuted in the past, triggers a series of new unfreedoms in the present that shape the future of the refugees.

People who lodge their asylum claims are not allowed to work, and the risk of poverty, destitution and marginalisation are ever present. The inability to work[7] had a huge impact on many respondents' everyday lives. The lack of work can lead to depression and it affects people's aspirations, hopes and plans for the future. The lack of a working routine is very often described as debilitating:

> I applied for asylum 2 and half years ago, since I have done my interview I haven't had any response from them (Home Office). And it's ridiculous 'cos I am not allowed to work, even though I am eligible to go to university 'cos of this paperwork and lack of money I can't go to uni . . . The government gives me 35 pounds a week so I can't socialize. They also gave me accommodation—now I am sharing a room with a straight guy and it's horrible. I don't wanna complain though 'cos I don't wanna risk losing my accommodation.
> (Bangladeshi asylum seeker, 27 years old)

> (. . .) During the day, 'cos I don't work, I stay at home or I go to the library and use the computer, read books, I just keep myself busy . . . The support has been good. But as I said I am waiting for more than 2 years now. It's affecting my mental health. 'Cos I am not working I cant socialize with people and I don't wanna rely on people.
> (Ugandan asylum seeker, 29 years old)

The vast majority of respondents revealed that they came to the UK because they wanted to feel *safe* and *free*. In their search for safety and freedom, respondents found a system that does not believe them and that makes it very hard for them to feel that they can belong to British society. Alongside the issue of work, a major obstacle restricting people's freedom is the fear of being detained, removed or deported. One of the issues that repeatedly emerged in my ethnography when talking to those with experiences of detention was the feeling of being unsafe as they were often 'put together with everyone else, with a lot of people from your community', as one respondent put it. Sharing a room with a person from one's own nationality/ethnic background is perceived to be a constant risk. Respondents said that they were forced to keep quiet and lie about the reasons of their claims, having to make up convoluted stories in order not to be recognised as sexual Others. This fear leads to feelings of extreme isolation in the confined space of the detention centre. In the words of Bashir,

Narrativising One's Sexuality/Gender 65

a Pakistani gay man who had been detained in the Harmondsworth centre near Heathrow:

> I was lying. I was telling them (other detainees) they caught me from somewhere—that it was a misunderstanding. You have to deny all the time. I went to the manager of the detention center and I told him that I was feeling very alone. He was nice to me, we went to a room and he told me that he knew, and that I shouldn't be afraid of telling him who I was. I only told him that I was feeling alone and he introduced me to a Venezuelan couple, two guys. They were also pretending to be straight. I went to talk to them, and I told them: 'I am the same as you'. At the beginning one of them was rude to me but the other one said: 'come! You're my sister'. Then they were released after 2 days, I felt so sad again.
>
> (Pakistani gay asylum seeker, 28 years old)

Although there are various ways in which people recognise each other and break the silence that marks their identities, there is always fear of opening up to the wrong person. The speech act of 'coming out' (Harvey 1997), or more likely to be outed, within the space of detention is an extremely problematic event. On the one hand, the individual is eager to share his or her story with someone who can be trusted without fear of repercussions, on the other, there is a common acknowledgement that when one's difference is enunciated, one becomes exposed to high risk of abuse, and there is no escape in confinement, neither physical nor mental.

Lastly, many respondents questioned the notion that winning an asylum claim leads to gaining freedom.

> The moment I applied for asylum I felt that I no longer belonged to me. After the papers you are not free. I need the protection because I am this and I knew that some of the onus would be on me to prove that I am this. But you become non-existent. It narrows down all of who you are in this small narrative, there is no space to contextualise anything and nothing else matters apart from that story, that written statement.
>
> (Jamaican lesbian refugee, 46 years old)

> Being told by an external authority that you can't go back to your country is terrible psychologically. It's not that I could have gone anyway, but being mandated by an external authority that you can' t go . . . that stays with you. It has an impact on your life, in fact, even though I can't live in my country that doesn't mean that I don't want to go there every now and then. So the idea that if I can't live somewhere I can never go there at all it's just horrible.
>
> (Algerian gay refugee, 37 years old)

66   *Calogero Giametta*

In expressing frustration about the inquisitive nature of the asylum procedures and helplessness at being unable to return to one's own country, the urgent question emerging from these excerpts is: what does it mean to be free for a refugee? The neo-liberal political rhetoric about freedom and autonomy are interestingly put under scrutiny by some observations respondents provided throughout the study:

> The real journey starts after getting the status. You face a lot of problems and you feel lonelier 'cos you have left your country, the organisations are not there anymore (how long are they staying with you?), many communities won't accept you, if you wanna find a proper job they can and ask you if you've lived in this country for 5 years.
>
> (Pakistani gay refugee, 32 years old)

> (. . .) So *what is freedom?* Freedom is being lonely, freedom is that you can't get a proper job 'cos you haven't lived in this country for 5 years? Freedom is not being accepted in your British-Asian gay community? It's been 3 years now and I don't have an English friend. Giving you a status and putting you to work somewhere very nasty like a chicken shop, do you call that freedom? That's not life to me. I didn't come here to work in a chicken shop and end up alone. Is that freedom? *Is that what I have to pay for my freedom?*
>
> (Same respondent as presented earlier, emphasis mine)

Discussing the concepts of truth and freedom by using the ethnographic data is vital to highlight the contradictions of the workings of the asylum system; namely, the conditional provision of protection resting upon *filtering* institutions. Indeed, the system keeps raising difficult frontiers to overcome for this migrant group, which contribute to materially limiting their freedoms in their quotidian lives. Problematising the notion of achieving freedom for the asylum seeker in the democratic North leads to critically positioning humanitarian practices and discourses. After all, guaranteeing freedom to a self-determined subject is one of the main triggers for humanitarian action. Yet the humanitarian discourse in relation to asylum is a very fragile façade that easily crumbles when one analyses the system of protection for people claiming asylum. Routinely, claimants are inherently perceived to be 'economic' migrants rather than 'genuine' refugees, not allowed to work or detained in immigration removal centres on the grounds of the risk of absconding. It is politically important in all of these instances to question where the humanity of humanitarianism is to be found.

BIOGRAPHY VERSUS EVIDENCE: EMBODIED BORDERS

Whether seeking support for producing their narratives or not, sexual and gender minority asylum claimants are exposed to the scrutiny of the law

Narrativising One's Sexuality/Gender 67

and border institutions. It was clear from my ethnography that when claimants obtain support they very often think that they would not have made it through the process had they not received help from organisations. The support given is often translated by the recipients into a capacity of 'building up'. As explored earlier in the text, the expression of building up is used in relation to one's case, one's confidence and self-presentation within institutional settings:

> Both organizations and solicitors are important help! I really think that people who are helped by organizations have more chances, even mentally they are stronger, emotionally they have built up confidence 'cos of the organization. They build up, not only your case, but also your confidence. They're there for you! They build your confidence just by giving you a hug, they take you out, you go to these events, you do theatre, you do activities, you know, emotionally they support you . . . You give them a call anytime, for instance I was homeless and the support worker was literally calling me every minute and she was telling me that nobody in Britain can live in the streets, she was saying that that won't happen to me and she was there for me. They are very important, they do everything!
>
> (Iranian gay refugee, 30 years old)

> I think that going to support organizations is not about winning your case. I think that that is up to you; how you present your case, how you present yourself and your case in front of the Home Office people. I think these kind of organizations give you more confidence, 'cos you need confidence to go and talk at the Home Office, it's not a nice place to go. At least they prepare you and give you confidence, and tell you what is the right thing to do, and how to represent yourself.
>
> (Algerian lesbian refugee, 31 years old)

The importance of gaining confidence and feeling prepared to speak to the Home Office is a recurrent theme amongst the narratives of those using the services of support organisations. Indeed, when facing the Home Office, respondents realise that they are confronted with a system that fundamentally does not believe them. Here they are situated vis-à-vis institutional scepticism. During an interview, a Jamaican respondent told me:

> I speak English, and damn well! (smile), but during the interview at the UKBA I said 'next door' instead of 'around the block'. And this was perceived as a lie and it questioned my whole story! This made me realize how easy it is for people to be disbelieved. There is a complete lack of sensitivity to the different uses of English and the culture where you are coming from.
>
> (Jamaican lesbian refugee, 35 years old)

68 *Calogero Giametta*

Very often, respondents had to 'prove' their sexual orientation or gender to someone (an officer or a judge) who would question their credibility at every step of the process. Throughout this chapter, I have argued that the process of certification of the credibility of migrants' suffering—being both supported and controlled—acts as 'a biographical border between deportation and recognition' (Mai 2014) of their rights. As in the respondent's case mentioned earlier, when the sexual/gender minority asylum seeker lodges a claim, the biographical border materialises in the telling of her life narrative. As already discussed, the claimant's biography acquires salience in the process of certification. Yet the requirement for a 'true'—logical, credible, plausible and so forth—biographical narration, in turn, triggers more constraining borders that unavoidably make the teller reveal just as much as confuse her or his experiences. Often respondents expressed awareness of the limits of *what* they could say and *how* they should say something in their demands for justice via acknowledging the limitations of the judicial system itself.

> Every story is a story, but you can tell it from a particular angle, and none of it is untrue! So what was a loving and caring action from your parent suddenly is now abuse. And your own childhood is destroyed in one interview. Then you go home and start thinking: is this true? Does it mean that if my parents did that to me they didn't love me? So, then you're given a piece of paper and they seem to tell you: 'go on live your life!'
>
> (Nigerian lesbian refugee, 37 years old)

> When I realised that I couldn't go back it was hard . . . you know. I was living in Pakistan for 20 and past years, so I have some great memories as well. I still miss my country, not everything is horrible there.
>
> (Pakistani gay refugee, 35 years old)

The life fragments that one needs to remember, reconstruct and articulate are framed by the necessity of fitting them into a coherent account. Throughout the asylum certification process, there exists a tension between the biographical narrative (the story that one tells) and the factual knowledge, or hard evidence, that one is able to produce and assemble to confront the Home Office and the immigration tribunals. The biographical borders work at their best when the narrative that the asylum claimants write and tell is the only evidence they have when presenting their cases. These borders are triggered in the process of certification and contribute to essentialise the sexual/gender minority claimant, who often struggles to vocalise an unvoiced history of the self.

> I know that people add spices on their stories, just to make it more interesting and tragic. For me, I was pretty confident . . . I was pretty fine 'cos I knew I didn't have to make things up! I was told from certain

Narrativising One's Sexuality/Gender 69

people to spice it up a bit, you know, but it wasn't appropriate for me. For example, they told me: 'if you have been harmed just include that you've been raped as well, it'd make it stronger'. You know what I mean? There are some people who do that, not a lot, but there are some. They go through a lot to get this, I don't even blame them. You know . . . everybody wants a better future, they are so much under pressure, they are so scared and they have no choice, sometimes they do it. But in my case, it wasn't appropriate. In my case I had enough evidence.

(Pakistani gay refugee, 27 years old)

Following the circulation of rumours amongst asylum claimants—the hearsay, as described earlier, it is easy for someone in the asylum process to start thinking that one's story has to necessarily overcome the suffering of other claimants in order to be successful. Thus the focus on one's gender and sexuality-based victimhood seems to become the most effective discursive strategy for the individual to claim the right of asylum. Humanitarian reason supports the notion that the *showing* of suffering is the most potent way for a rights claimant to be considered as deserving of state protection. Here it appears clear that the management of migration is influenced by humanitarian governmentality, according to which some migrants become more deserving than others to be granted protection and rights on the basis of their suffering or, more precisely, of how they show it. This logic inevitably creates a perverse ranking system amongst migrants—a sort of hierarchy of suffering that determines one's future in the country of destination.

CONCLUSIONS

Oftentimes asylum and social protection appear to be granted on the basis of stereotypical understandings of victimhood in relation to gender and sexuality. Sexual humanitarianism effectively acts as a filter, therefore those who are able to present their stories of sexual/gender-based violence in a convincing and compassion-triggering manner may be granted asylum and those who do not, or cannot, are far more likely to be excluded. The neo-liberal humanitarian epistemology perceives the world, its heterogeneity and its growing inequalities, in terms of a unified humanity, which is opposed to absolute victims to be cared for. In our humanitarian present (Weizman 2011), one learns to trust and empathise with images and stories of absolute victims (Hesford 2011). This sensibility misrecognises the broad range of people's different needs and material living conditions. In the context of asylum, this leaves very little space for those who present themselves as non-absolute victims, unless they manage to mobilise the right social signifiers (i.e. class) and provide proficient performances of self-narration likely to make their stories recognised and validated. The issue remains for those who do not either fall under the category of the quintessential victim or

70 Calogero Giametta

do not appear to be worthy of trust to the Home Office caseworkers and immigration judges.

It remains important to keep questioning how the human category is used in humanitarian discourses. This is a crucial exercise in that it opens up more critical debates regarding problematic categories, such as 'the racialised victim' 'the vulnerable Other' or the 'the sexual victim'. These categories of social protection reify violence by glorifying suffering (Arendt 1951, Fassin 2012). At present, what we see is that these very humanist-centred inquiries of human suffering contribute to producing, or reinforcing, conditions of subalternity. Thus very easily, sexual-subalternised Others become easily trapped in restrictive performances in relation to how they can claim a right to be protected—or their victimisation is instrumentally used to exclude others.

The intrinsic inclusion/exclusion dichotomy that characterises the long route to accessing citizenship rights is not a new logic. In fact, it is only reinforced, and not created, by humanitarian reason. Migrants' subjectivities are heterogeneous and what sexual humanitarianism does to the subjects in need of protection is to assemble them together under the badge of the absolute victim. Thus the claimants' heterogeneity is lost when they are perceived to be a homogeneous social category. Producing the depoliticising archetype of *refugee suffering* as univocal is therefore analytically disingenuous and politically dangerous.

NOTES

1 When using the term 'gender' in the text, I specifically refer to 'gender identity'. My focus is on lesbian, gay, bisexual and trans* people claiming the right of asylum on the grounds of their sexual orientations and gender identity. Throughout the chapter, I use the phrase 'sexual/gender minorities' to refer to the research participants. Indeed, despite its critical implications about notions of fixity of a majority/minority logic, 'sexual/gender minority' still seems more fitting to capture respondents' self-understandings and self-narrations than categories, such as 'gay' or 'lesbian'.

2 The study on which the chapter is based examines the lived experiences of migrants claiming asylum in the UK. I conducted ethnography over a two-year time period with 60 sexual/gender minority asylum seekers and refugees, mostly based in the London. The age of the sample ranged from 23 to 60 years old, half identified as women and half as men. The main countries of origin were Uganda, Pakistan, Bangladesh, and Jamaica. The ethnographic data discussed here emerges from semi-structured interviews and participatory activities with an equal number of asylum seekers and refugees. In the analysis I also draw on the ethnographic material produced by the research project I am currently involved in. The project Embodied Mediterranean Borders: Problematizing Sexual Humanitarianism through Experimental Filmmaking is based at the LAMES of Aix-Marseille University, directed by Professor Nicola Mai and funded by the A*MIDEX Aix-Marseille University Foundation.

3 In her book *Erotic Justice* (2005), Ratna Kapur uses the analytical phrase 'sexual subalterns', but she is attentive to clarify that the 'sexual subaltern' is a

Narrativising One's Sexuality/Gender   71

discursive device to bring together the range of sexual Others within contemporary India. She adds that she does not intend to 'suggest(ing) that it is either a homogenised or stable category. The location of the sexual subaltern in post-colonial India is complex, at times contradictory, and not invoked exclusively as an identity of resistance to dominant sexual categories' (2005: 69). When formulating the expression sexual-subalternized Others, I considered Kapur's critical position towards the term that she used in her book.

4 The current humanitarian epistemology in the neo-liberal West presents us with decontextualized images of quintessential victims through scientific, journalistic, as well as fictional representations of victim avatars. These figures are marked by passivity, trauma (or post-traumatic stress disorder) and irrationality. Passivity and trauma are perhaps categories that have been more obviously attached to the migrant/victim figure, yet as I will discuss later in the text, 'irrationality' is an equally important term to unpack. One needs to think about how, when expressing rational choice-making, migrants are readily denounced as calculating economic migrants who are not deserving of state protection.

5 Law firms had to drastically reduce the number of hours that they could dedicate to working on an asylum claim (this emerged from many conversations with solicitors and barristers specializing on immigration cases in London, UK).

6 It is important here to draw a difference between the asylum claimant, still going through the process and waiting for a decision on his or her case, and the refugee who supposedly has already been provided with the tools to integrate into mainstream society.

7 In the UK, an asylum claimant is not allowed to work for the first 12 months after applying for asylum. Asylum seekers are eligible to receive a voucher of circa 35 pounds per week.

BIBLIOGRAPHY

Arendt, H. (1951) *The Origins of Totalitarianism*. New York: HBJ Book.

Bastia, T. and McGrath, S. (2011) 'Temporality, Migration and Unfree Labour: Migrant Garment Workers'. Working Paper No. 6, Manchester Papers in Political Economy. Manchester: University of Manchester.

Boltanski, L. (1999) *Distant Suffering: Morality, Media and Politics*. Cambridge University Press.

Butler, J. (1993) *Bodies That Matter: On the Discursive Limits of Sex*. London and New York: Routledge.

Fassin, D. (2012) *Humanitarian Reason. A Moral History of the Present*. Berkeley: University of California Press.

Fassin, D. and Rechtman, R. (2009) *The Empire of Trauma: An Inquiry into the Condition of Victimhood*. Princeton: Princeton University Press.

Foucault, M. (1980) *Power/Knowledge: Selected Interviews and Other Writings, 1972–1977*. New York: Pantheon Books.

Harvey, K. (1997) 'Everybody Loves a Lover. Gay Men, Straight Men and the Problem of Lexical Choice', in Harvey K. and Shalom C. (eds.) *Language and Desire: Encoding Sex, Romance, and Intimacy*. London: Routledge, 60–82.

Hesford, W. (2011) *Spectacular Rhetorics: Human Rights Visions, Recognitions, Feminisms*. Durham and London: Duke University Press.

International Committee of the Red Cross (1949) *Geneva Convention Relative to the Protection of Civilian Persons in Time of War (Fourth Geneva Convention)*, 12 August 1949. Available at: http://www.refworld.org/docid/3ae6b36d2.html, last accessed 20 March 2015.

72 Calogero Giametta

Kapur, R. (2005) *Erotic Justice: Law and the New Politics of Postcolonialism.* Glasshouse Press: Cavendish Publishers

Mai, N. (2014) 'Between Embodied Cosmopolitanism and Sexual Humanitarianism: The Fractal Mobilities and Subjectivities of Migrants Working in the Sex Industry', in Baby-Collins, V. and Anteby, L. (eds.) *Borders, Mobilities and Migrations, Perspectives from the Mediterranean in the 21st Century.* Brussels: Peter Lang, 175–192.

Geiger, M. and Pecoud, A. (2010) *The Politics of International Migration Management.* Basingstoke: Palgrave Macmillan.

Geiger, M. and Pecoud, A. (2012) *Disciplining the Transnational Mobility of People.* Basingstoke: Palgrave Macmillan.

Giametta, C. (2014) 'Rescued' Subjects: The Question of Agency and Religiosity for Non-heteronormative Asylum Seekers in the UK, *Sexualities* 17: 5–6, 583–599.

Giametta, C. (forthcoming) *The Sexual Politics of Asylum.* New York: Routledge.

McGhee, D. (2000) 'Accessing Homosexuality: Truth, Evidence and the Legal Practices for Determining Refugee Status—the Case of Ioan Vraciu', *Body & Society* 6(1): 29–50.

O'Connell Davidson, J. (2013) Troubling Freedom: Migration, Debt, and Modern Slavery, *Migration Studies* 1(2): 176–195.

O'Leary, B. (2008) 'We Cannot Claim Any Particular Knowledge of the Ways of Homosexuals, Still Less of Iranian Homosexuals . . .: The Particular Problems Facing Those Who Seek Asylum on the Basis of Their Sexual Identity', *Feminist Legal Studies* 16(1): 87–95.

Pandolfi, M. (2011) 'Humanitarianism and Its Discontents', in Bornstein, E. and Redfield, P. (eds.) *Forces of Compassion between Politics and Ethics: The Anthropology of Global Humanitarianism.* Santa Fe: School for Advanced Research Press, 227–248.

Spivak, C. G. (2013) *An Aesthetic Education in the Era of Globalization.* Cambridge and London: Harvard University Press.

Ticktin, M. (2006) 'Where Ethics and Politics Meet: The Violence of Humanitarianism in France', *American Ethnologist* 33(1): 33–49.

Ticktin, M. (2011) 'The Gendered Human of Humanitarianism: Medicalizing and Politicizing Sexual Violence', *Gender and History* 23(2): 250–265.

Weizman, E. (2011) *The Least of All Possible Evils: Humanitarian Violence from Arendt to Gaza.* London: Verso.

4 The New Trans-National Politics of LGBT Human Rights in the Commonwealth
What Can UK NGOs Learn from the Global South?

Matthew Waites

In recent years, a significant new social phenomenon has emerged in global sexual politics, which can be identified here as 'the new London-based trans-national politics of LGBT[1] human rights'. This has consisted primarily of the appearance of new non-governmental organisations (NGOs) working internationally, specifically the Kaleidoscope Trust, the Human Dignity Trust and the Peter Tatchell Foundation, all formed in 2011; and it also includes the development of the national organisation Stonewall into increasing international activity. These organisations have, in particular, sought to foreground and utilise the Commonwealth of Nations—the intergovernmental organisation which emerged from the former British Empire—as a 'political opportunity structure' (Kitschelt 1986) for claiming human rights. The task addressed in this chapter is the examination of how this trans-national political activity emerging from the UK can be analysed and evaluated through learning from struggles in formerly colonised states worldwide.

In light of postcolonial studies of Orientalism and prevailing discourses (Said 1978), recent critical debates have grappled with the problematic power of Western societies in the contestation of LGBT human rights. Much debate has focused on Jasbir Puar's (2007) conception of 'homonationalisms', whereby many Western nationalisms are argued to endorse human rights related to same-sex sexualities, while remaining problematic in relation to racism, 'development' and imperialism. Others influenced by this have raised concerns about 'homocolonialism' as 'the deployment of LGBTIQ rights and visibility to stigmatise non-Western cultures' (Rahman 2014: 6)—suggesting the need to contextualise invocations of human rights. Hence this chapter presents analysis of NGO approaches in 'the new London-based trans-national politics of LGBT human rights', then draws contrasts with findings from previous cross-national comparative analysis of struggles for decriminalisation and human rights (Lennox and Waites 2013a). This process is conducted through a critical sociological analysis concerned with multiple forms of power and inequality and yields findings about what might be learned in the Global North from movements and

74　*Matthew Waites*

conflicts in the Global South (defined later)—particularly for UK-based LGBT trans-national activism.

The chapter seeks to develop research on the global politics of LGBT human rights (Kollman and Waites 2009) by offering an original comparison between UK-based LGBT NGOs working trans-nationally and analysis of their approaches. It takes the following structure. The first section, 'Human Rights, Sexual Orientation and Gender Identity in the Commonwealth', introduces the Commonwealth and summarises existing comparative research on human rights, sexual orientation and gender identity in the Commonwealth context. The second section, 'The New London-Based Transnational Politics of LGBT Human Rights', starts by outlining existing global LGBT activism before focusing on analysis of NGO activity in London from 2011. The third section, 'Learning from the Global South', brings the two previous sections together, comparing findings from national studies across the Commonwealth to the policies and practices of UK-based NGOs in the context of postcolonial perspectives. The conclusion then reflects on what this analysis implies for debates over the global politics of LGBT human rights.

HUMAN RIGHTS, SEXUAL ORIENTATION AND GENDER IDENTITY IN THE COMMONWEALTH

The Universal Declaration of Human Rights made by states of the United Nations in 1948 marked the founding of the global human rights system. But only later, particularly from the 1980s, did international human rights become identified as a medium to contest the social status of same-sex sexualities and, subsequently, gender identity, leading to a 'human rights turn' by LGBT movements and ongoing conflicts (Kollman and Waites 2009: 4). This took shape partly through global power relations structured by imperialism and colonialism, and critical analyses of sexualities and gender have drawn attention to ways in which those relations are important to understanding human rights claims in particular contexts (Binnie 2004). Meanwhile, the sociology of human rights increasingly highlights how selective representations of human rights are mobilised by various actors (Hynes et al. 2012). These themes are useful to keep in mind while approaching the Commonwealth as an international organisation with an imperial history and the records of its member states.

The modern Commonwealth emerged from 1949 out of the British Commonwealth of Nations, which existed within the Empire from 1931, and is sometimes known as the Commonwealth of Nations to distinguish it from the Commonwealth of Independent States emerging from the former Soviet Union. Given the history, the current intergovernmental organisation needs to be understood in the contexts of racism, colonialism and imperialism. These include the history of slavery in the British Empire (Morgan 2008)

The New Trans-National Politics of LGBT Human Rights 75

and imperial violence and genocides, recognised, for example, by Stephen Howe (2012: 703–704).

Significantly, the Commonwealth was late to becoming a 'human rights' organisation. In its major statement of principles the *Singapore Declaration* of 1971, reference to 'equal rights' appeared but only explicitly with respect to issues of 'race, colour, creed or political belief' (Commonwealth Heads of Government 1971). Only in the Harare Commonwealth Declaration of 1991 did reference to 'fundamental human rights' appear (Commonwealth Heads of Government 1991).

An Eminent Persons Group established at the Commonwealth Heads of Government Meeting in Trinidad and Tobago in 2009 recommended that human rights become more institutionalised (Eminent Persons Group 2011; Commonwealth Secretariat 2014). Human rights were subsequently entrenched in the Charter of the Commonwealth created in 2013 (Commonwealth 2013). It is significant that 'sexual orientation' and 'gender identity' are still not explicitly mentioned, although it is possible to argue that these are encompassed by 'other grounds'.

Commonwealth Secretary-General Kamalesh Sharma only began speaking out against 'discrimination on grounds of sexual orientation' from 2011 (Lennox and Waites 2013b: 35). It is also noteworthy that on 19 December 2012, foreign ministers of all Commonwealth states adopted recommendation 60 of the Eminent Persons Group report, which states that:

> Heads of Government should take steps to encourage the repeal of discriminatory laws that impede the effective response of CW countries to the HIV/AIDS epidemic [. . .].
>
> (Eminent Persons Group 2011: 102)

However, governments have discretion in defining discriminatory laws (Kaleidoscope 2014a: 11); clearly, change overall remains very limited.

Comparative research on experiences in Commonwealth states was initiated in the volume *Human Rights, Sexual Orientation and Gender Identity in the Commonwealth: Struggles for Decriminalisation and Change*, published from the Institute of Commonwealth Studies (Lennox and Waites 2013a). The book focused on 54 (now 53) Commonwealth states, of which 42 criminalised same-sex behaviour, representing more than half of the states in the world to do so—with most such criminal laws having been introduced by the British, others revising and partially replicating imperial statutes. The first quantitative analysis of legal change in all Commonwealth states is offered and national case study chapters covering sixteen states by academics and activists which were used for comparative analysis (Lennox and Waites 2013b, 2013c). UK-based NGO Kaleidoscope Trust notably drew upon this in its report *Speaking Out* (Kaleidoscope Trust 2014a: 9–14).

The British Empire's criminalisation of same-sex behaviour had initially been analysed in the Human Rights Watch report *This Alien Legacy*

(Human Rights Watch 2008; an abridged version was reprinted in the Commonwealth volume: Lennox and Waites 2013a). Criminalisation began with the Indian Penal Code created in 1860, in which Section 377 infamously defined 'unnatural offences' to include 'carnal intercourse against the order of nature with any man, woman or animal' (Waites 2010). The focus on penetration reflected the character of laws prohibiting buggery in the United Kingdom. However, following creation of the offence of 'gross indecency' in the UK via the Criminal Law Amendment Act 1885, potentially encompassing all male same-sex sexual activity, colonial criminalisation similarly widened. The offence of 'gross indecency' between men was introduced across much of the Empire, beginning in the Sudan in 1899. In some later contexts, including African states, indecency laws were formulated as gender neutral. Some form of criminalisation for some or all same-sex sexual behaviour was enacted in most of the imperial realm and remains.

However, after the modern Commonwealth emerged, it can also be noted that the United Kingdom was the first state to instigate decriminalisation—though initially only in England and Wales in 1967, only later in Scotland in 1981 and in Northern Ireland in 1982 (Waites 2013). The starting point was the Wolfenden Report—formally the report of the Committee on Homosexual Offences and Prostitution (1957), a joint departmental committee of the British government. Led by Sir John Wolfenden and constituted of medical and social authorities, the report made the groundbreaking recommendation that a 'homosexual act' in private, between consenting adults aged over 21, should not be a criminal offence. There followed a decade of lobbying by groups, including the Homosexual Law Reform Society, leading to the partial decriminalisation in England and Wales (Waites 2013). Further decriminalisations occurred gradually in Commonwealth states, though typically partial, especially with respect to unequal age of consent laws: Canada in 1969, Australian federal states from 1972, Malta (1973), New Zealand (1986), The Bahamas (1991), Cyprus (1998), South Africa (1998), Vanuatu (2007), India (2009, reversed in 2013), Fiji (2010) (Lennox and Waites 2013b).

It is useful to consider how this chronology of decriminalisation has related to the Global North and Global South. Here the need for a social rather than purely geographical definition is apparent, yet definitions remain contested. The most widely used definition refers to the Human Development Index (HDI) of the United Nations Human Development Programme (2014), from which the 49 states categorised as having 'Very High Human Development' are often framed as 'Global North' in policy discussion. In the 2014 Human Development Report, rankings for Commonwealth states which have experienced decriminalisation are: Australia (2), New Zealand (7), Canada (8), UK (14), Cyprus (32), Malta (39), Bahamas (51), Fiji (88), South Africa (118), Vanuatu (131) and India (135). So the first six of these states including Malta could be categorised as 'Global North', and there is a pattern of association between high development and early decriminalisation.

The New Trans-National Politics of LGBT Human Rights   77

However, it is important to problematise normative conceptions of 'development' and engage more critical definitions of the Global South as 'a place that is less a place [. . .] than a condition' (Lopez 2007: v). Relationships to colonialism and racism are usefully highlighted by this approach, which also implies attention to how these have shaped contextually specific forms of gender and sexuality. Even where a state-based analysis is necessary, an approach influenced by this is preferable and should also distinguish Malta, which benefited economically from colonial trade and experienced limited racism towards the Maltese ethnic majority, from the Bahamas, which can be seen as more clearly on the periphery and subject to racism. From such a perspective more focused on colonial power, it can still be argued that the first five Commonwealth states to decriminalise were in the Global North.

The first decriminalisation to take place in the Global South was in the Bahamas in 1991. Further decriminalisations in the South have been rare: South Africa in 1998; Vanuatu in 2007; India in 2009, followed by recriminalisation in 2013; and Fiji in 2010 (after a suspension from the Commonwealth had already begun, running until 2014). It has been argued that these decriminalisations are particularly significant to study for developing strategies to win rights across the Commonwealth (Lennox and Waites 2013c).

The relationship of gender identity issues to the Commonwealth context is much less clear than for sexual orientation, given the history of imperial criminalisation of same-sex behaviour. However, the International Lesbian Gay, Bisexual, Trans and Intersex Association (ILGA) report *State-Sponsored Homophobia* does cover laws relating to transgender experience (Itaborahy 2012). Generally, Commonwealth states do poorly relative to all states globally. Reasons require further analysis, but it seems that states which move to non-discrimination with respect to sexual orientation are likely to be more liberal, and to consider progressive reform (see Lennox and Waites 2013b, 2013c). What is clear is that the criminalisation of same-sex sexual behaviour not only affects certain transgender people directly, particularly where they are perceived to be in a same-sex relationship, it also has considerable indirect effects. For example, police harassment of people invoking prohibitions on 'unnatural offences' can be used to threaten hijra people—a cultural group often described as a third gender, outside the dominant gender binary in South Asian states (Baudh 2013).

In the following section, I turn to explore recent UK-based attempts to address all of these issues.

THE NEW LONDON-BASED TRANS-NATIONAL
POLITICS OF LGBT HUMAN RIGHTS

The emergence of a 'new London-based trans-national politics of LGBT human rights' has become apparent as a feature of trans-national social relations over the past five years. This has consisted primarily of the appearance of

78   *Matthew Waites*

new non-governmental organisations (NGOs), specifically the Kaleidoscope Trust, the Human Dignity Trust and the Peter Tatchell Foundation, all formed in 2011; and it has also involved Stonewall's development into greater international activity. While appreciating there are wider forms of trans-national political activity by LGBT people and allies from the UK, outside London and often online, this focus reflects an emphasis on the central significance of the NGOs mentioned. To understand the significance of this social formation in trans-national politics first requires a brief overview of global LGBT organising as context, after which it is possible to examine each of the NGOs mentioned in turn, including indicative comments on the racial/ethnic and class characteristics of their leaderships. Regarding research methods, data used has been selected from the websites of the organisations after several readings between January 2014 and March 2015, for content from 2011.

At a global level, the oldest and most globally representative LGBT organisation is ILGA, formed as the International Gay Association in 1978, now the International Lesbian, Gay, Bisexual, Trans and Intersex Association(Power 1991; ILGA, 2015). This organisation was founded in the UK by Europeans and has been influenced by gay liberationism, later human rights and broader analysis of inequalities (Paternotte 2014). ILGA was joined in 1990 by the International Gay and Lesbian Human Rights Commission (IGLHRC, 2015), based in the United States, contrasting with ILGA's European origins. IGLHRC contrasts to ILGA in key respects: its focus was human rights rather than broader inequalities and liberation; it also had less emphasis on national representation and participatory democracy (Thoreson 2014).

While ILGA and IGLHRC have been most prominent, a number of other organisations can be mentioned. ARC-International was created in Canada in 2003 to work on sexual orientation, gender identity and human rights; it is the longest-standing organisation in Geneva to lobby the United Nations. Coalition of African Lesbians is just one alternative trans-national example originating in the Global South. Also important are leading international human rights organisations which have LGBT programmes, particularly Human Rights Watch and Amnesty International. All these 'social movement organisations' play a key role in representing the trans-national LGBT 'social movement' and form a 'social network' (Melucci 1996). All of this pre-existed the new London-based NGOs, which can now be discussed.

In the United Kingdom, the most prominent and well-funded national organisation is Stonewall (2015a), working on lesbian, gay and bisexual issues—adding transgender only from 2014, although earlier in Stonewall Scotland. However, Stonewall chose for a long time to limit its international work, discussed later (Stonewall 2015b). It was in this context from 2011, after approaches to Stonewall on international issues were not satisfied, that other organisations were created.

The most significant new organisation to appear in London was the Kaleidoscope Trust, prominently launched at the UK parliament in 2011

The New Trans-National Politics of LGBT Human Rights 79

and becoming a registered charity from 2012 (Kaleidoscope Trust 2014b). Its founding document stated the aim to 'promote diversity and respect for all regardless of sexual orientation', also stating it would deploy resources in relation to 'gender identity' (Kaleidoscope Trust 2011: 3), but the organisation has since become more consistently 'LGBT', with specific policies referring to 'LGBTI' from 2014 (Kaleidoscope 2014a: 9). Stated objectives included 'capacity building' in various countries, 'network development', 'opinion forming' and 'international lobbying and dialogue' (Kaleidoscope Trust 2011: 3).

Kaleidoscope was conceived and led by Lance Price, who formerly worked in the Labour Party as a special adviser to Prime Minister Tony Blair, and was well-connected in Westminster. Hence the initial leadership did not emerge from established LGBT activist networks, but it was formed from the circles of political elites with related contacts, suggesting a mainstream orientation and lack of international LGBT relations. Statements of support at its inception came from Prime Minister David Cameron, Labour Leader Ed Miliband and Liberal Democrat Leader Nick Clegg.

The place of gender identity in Kaleidoscope's initial aims was somewhat secondary to sexual orientation. The leading individuals who initially created and led this small organisation—with only two full-time paid staff by 201 were white, although the board had some ethnic diversity, and Siddarth Deva became Acting Chair in 2014. Probably more importantly, the organisation's website initially gave little information on how it would achieve representation of, or work with, existing activist groups in different states and regions. This contrasted with the institutionalised practices of representation in ILGA. Kaleidoscope's emergence was thus indicative of the need to develop new forms of trans-national working (Lennox and Waites 2013b: 39).

Kaleidoscope's approach emphasising human rights, and particularly the value of contesting these in the Commonwealth, was captured in its report *Speaking Out: The Rights of LGBTI Citizens from across the Commonwealth* (Kaleidoscope Trust 2014a). The 'Introduction' by Chair Purna Sen, formerly Head of Human Rights at the Commonwealth Secretariat, argues that LGBTI people across the world 'are demanding . . . their rights . . . are protected under the law' (Kaleidoscope Trust 2014a). The report provides a 'platform' for 'contributors from across the Commonwealth' (p.10). However, in Sen's 'Introduction' and the opening chapter (pp. 9–13), Kaleidoscope can be seen—in a sociological light (Hynes et al. 2012: 10)—to enact a subtle interpretation of the 'voices of LGBTI citizens'. Claims are made such as that 'The demands of LGBTI people in the Commonwealth are [. . .] to be included in what the Commonwealth itself says it believes in [human rights]' (ibid.). The emphasis is on people's support for the moral universalism of human rights as principle, without distinguishing the issue of who is to claim those rights within states and when. This has the effect of obfuscating the differential processes of claiming which are in fact taking place.

80   *Matthew Waites*

By contrast, research evidence from LGBT social movement studies led by Currier (2009) in Namibia and Jjuuko (2013) in Uganda, present a different picture, echoing studies in the sociology of human rights (Hynes et al. 2012). The academic research shows that in practice movements in most contexts have made selective and delimited claims for specific human rights, according to strategic priorities—what Jjuuko (2013) calls an 'incremental approach'. This is not surprising, since this was certainly also the case in the United Kingdom, where, for example, an equal age of consent was claimed before same-sex adoption (Waites 2005). These variable subnational processes of rights-claiming relate to Kate Nash's distinction between top-down 'global constitutionalist' and bottom-up 'subaltern cosmopolitan' understandings of how human rights can and should emerge (Nash 2012). Yet this tension between international moral universalism simultaneously claiming all rights and selective local/national political strategies is not recognised or addressed in the discourse of Kaleidoscope.

The figure of Kaleidoscope's Chair Purna Sen is a key example of an individual from the Commonwealth Secretariat, as an organisation still somewhat infused with colonial attitudes, who came to occupy a key position in UK LGBT organising. Her arrival with wide and intersectional human rights expertise, and as a South Asian woman from an Indian family, brought change to the leadership's previous narrower LGBT rights focus. As argued elsewhere, however, this can be conceptualised with reference to the sociology of elites, whereby the circulation of elites allows for a few talented members of ethnic minorities to achieve meritocratic advancement within networks of postcolonial governance (Mills 1956; Waites 2015). This affected how the Commonwealth's value as a political opportunity structure has been positively evaluated by UK-based LGBT NGOs, despite limited explicit attention to developing postcolonial strategies for North/South alliance building.

A second new London-based non-governmental organisation to emerge in 2011, also launched at the UK parliament, was the Human Dignity Trust (2014a). The Trust began as a UK company limited by guarantee and gained charitable status in 2014. As clearly stated at the top of its website's homepage, the focus is 'Decriminalising Homosexuality by Upholding International Law'—hence it is concerned only with sexual orientation, not gender identity as such, and with decriminalisation rather than wider human rights struggles (Human Dignity Trust 2014a). In light of social constructionist, bisexual and queer theories of sexualities, the Trust's tendency to conflate sexual orientation with homosexuality and heterosexuality is unhelpful (Lennox and Waites 2013b: 40).

The organisation defines itself as a network to mobilise lawyers and law firms to provide assistance to local groups challenging criminalisation—this is offered 'pro bono' ('for the public good', on a voluntary or reduced fee basis). The Trust's formation was led by Chief Executive Jonathan Cooper, who was awarded the Order of the British Empire (OBE) for human rights

The New Trans-National Politics of LGBT Human Rights   81

work in 2007. Although the chief executive is white, the Trust has involved black barristers such as Philip Dayle who initially worked with J-Flag in Jamaica. The Trust is explicit concerning its limited political remit: 'The Trust does not campaign. We seek clarification of the law through test case litigation' (Human Dignity Trust 2014b). It states a commitment to only bring a case or to intervene if acting in consultation with local groups (Lennox and Waites 2013b: 40). However, while its first engagement in Belize proceeded with agreement of the litigant Caleb Orozco of the United Belize Advocacy Movement (UNIBAM), Caribbean activist Colin Robinson argued there was a lack of engagement with the regional Caribbean Vulnerable Communities coalition and its pre-existing strategy (Lennox and Waites 2013b: 41–42).

A third new organisation formed in London in 2011 was the Peter Tatchell Foundation (2014a). This grew out of Peter Tatchell's long-standing activism since involvement in the Gay Liberation Front in the early 1970s and particularly with Outrage! as a radical direct action group from the early 1990s (Lucas 1998), together with other collective campaigns and individual work (Tatchell 2014). The Foundation's aims are clearly focused on human rights, in some contrast to the wider politics of equality, social justice and liberation, which Tatchell has campaigned for:

> The aims and objectives of the PTF are to raise awareness, understanding, protection and implementation of human rights in the UK and worldwide.
>
> (Peter Tatchell Foundation 2014b)

Hence formation of the Foundation was significant as part of a wider focusing on human rights in London-based trans-national LGBT campaigning; indeed, Tatchell collaborated with Sen on Commonwealth lobbying from 2009 (Waites 2015). However, criticisms have sometimes been made of Peter Tatchell's work, for example, from African LGBTI Human Rights Defenders (2007) who found his initiatives insensitive to their contexts (Tauqir et al. 2011; Long 2015). Hence the institutionalisation of his activism, with growing resources and support from a board (apparently all white in March 2015), posed questions about who was to be represented.

Returning to Stonewall, particularly since 2014, there has been increasing involvement in international activity, after earlier reticence partly related to problems of white leadership. By March 2015, two black individuals, Phyll Opoku-Gyimah and Sheldon Mills, were among the senior team of ten. The organisation's international campaigning is framed with reference to human rights rather than more expansive equality politics; it supports 'LGBT human rights defenders around the world' (Stonewall 2015b). International Officer Jasmine O'Connor has played a key role. Stonewall hosts learning exchange visits for national LGBT groups worldwide, thus facilitating capacity building. When new Chief Executive Ruth Hunt replaced Ben Summerskill from 28 July 2014, a greater focus on international issues

82 *Matthew Waites*

was clear in opening comments, and in 2014–2015, one of six key priorities was 'Our friends abroad' (Stonewall 2015c). Hunt's ascendance posed questions about whether Stonewall might occupy international territory previously covered by other organisations, which remains unclear.

However, by March 2015, the international web pages still focused on providing information, largely via links to ILGA and other organisations. There were only specific briefings on two states—India and Russia—plus web pages on Uganda, Nigeria and Brunei. Kollman (2014) has noted Stonewall's lack of reference to European examples in policy papers on partnership laws; its publications, research and consultations still do not focus on international issues.

To summarise this section, the emergence in 2011 of three new London-based NGOs focused on LGBT human rights (only sexual orientation for Human Dignity Trust) marked a development of international significance. This needs to be conceptualised as an institutionalised social network and also as having characteristics of a social movement (Melucci 1996). The next section will elaborate key findings from comparative research on movements in different states, discussing what these imply for the London-based trans-national politics of LGBT human rights.

LEARNING FROM THE GLOBAL SOUTH

Key findings from existing cross-national comparative analysis (Lennox and Waites 2013b) can usefully be summarised in relation to six themes. For each theme, these findings will be compared to the existing practices of London-based NGOs. Hence new analysis can suggest how Global South activist experiences and analyses might better inform UK LGBT NGOs.

1. Decriminalisation is not always the top priority.

The first key finding is that 'decriminalisation' is not always the first priority of movements. This is particularly clear from the Caribbean, where in Trinidad and Tobago the key NGO Coalition Advocating Inclusion of Sexual Orientation (CAISO) has explicitly prioritised issues of hate crime and violence ahead of decriminalisation in its approaches to the national government (Gaskins 2013). It also emerges from South Asia, where interviews with activists in Pakistan, Bangladesh and Sri Lanka find that criminal law prohibiting same-sex sexual behaviour has been more rarely invoked in legal practice than in India, and even police threats to use such laws have been infrequent—with other laws more frequently used (Baudh 2013). Hence the connection between decriminalisation campaigns and lived experiences is far from straightforward; sexual health promotion or anti-violence work often have greater immediacy.

This clearly contrasts with substantial aspects of the London-based trans-national politics of LGBT human rights as it emerged with an emphasis on decriminalisation. In particular, the Human Dignity Trust is solely focused on decriminalisation through law. However, while decriminalisation

The New Trans-National Politics of LGBT Human Rights   83

is central for Kaleidoscope, the Peter Tatchell Foundation and Stonewall, they also have had broader human rights approaches. Nevertheless, there has been a considerable emphasis on lobbying for legal changes relative to broader activist movement-building strategies being adopted by NGOs like CAISO.

2. Decriminalisation need not derive from global constitutionalism.

A second central finding from previous comparative analysis is that decriminalisation has not only occurred through reference to international law or human rights as defined by the United Nations. This emerges from Gaskins' (2013) groundbreaking study of the Bahamas, the first Commonwealth state to see a decriminalisation in the Global South. He finds that the Bahamas decriminalisation in 1991 was not the result of a mass movement but occurred after a change of view to endorse the right to privacy by Attorney General Paul Adderley, who crucially made reference to this right in the national constitution (Gaskins 2013: 442). There does not appear a process in which human rights as defined by the United Nations were invoked legally or politically. What Gaskins account interestingly suggests is that the right to privacy in the national constitution was invoked without reference to other specific rights; hence as elsewhere, reformers do not always invoke all human rights together as an indivisible package.

As previously mentioned, British sociologist of human rights Kate Nash has characterised a certain understanding of human rights as developing through 'global constitutionalism'; that is, through international law and global human rights discourses, particularly from the United Nations (Nash 2012). The Bahamas case stands as an empirical refutation of such assumptions. This problematises assumptions which have been pervasive throughout the London-based trans-national politics of LGBT human rights: that reference to human rights as defined by the UN must be central in legal and political activity. This is evidently in tension with the Human Dignity Trust's definitive focus on trans-national legal work, also an empirical corrective to the way that Kaleidoscope Trust (2014a) and Peter Tatchell Foundation (2014a) tend to presume that human rights defined by the UN are always the appropriate frame to invoke rather than national constitutions. The Bahamas case suggests that national politics can work, so global or North/South international work may sometimes need to focus on supporting national responses. Relatedly, a need to avoid conflation between supranational and global emerges from attention to the Caribbean Vulnerable Communities coalition as a regional network, which activist Colin Robinson emphasises has international strategies (Gaskins 2013; Lennox and Waites 2013a; Caribbean Vulnerable Communities 2014).

3. Human rights can be won without a narrowly defined movement.

A third central finding from comparative analysis is that movements have not always needed to utilise narrow definitions of 'gay and lesbian'

84 Matthew Waites

identity in order to win decriminalisations or human rights, as Western scholarship has sometimes implied (Adam, Duyvendak and Krouwel 1998; Tremblay, Paternotte and Johnson 2011). Generally, there is a need to understand the diversity of genders and sexualities that exist within different local, national and regional cultural contexts and to interpret struggles in that light (Lennox and Waites, 2013b: 8–10, 2013c: 508–514). In particular, the India case shows that the Voices Against 377 coalition was explicitly and self-consciously 'queer', deploying that category in its central campaigning documents to include the vast range of relevant sexual and gender identities and experiences, including 'hijra' and 'kothi' (Waites 2010; Baudh 2013).

This contrasts with much of the London-based trans-national politics. Again divergence from the Human Dignity Trust (2014a) is most clear; the Trust advocates decriminalisation of 'homosexuality', repeating the Wolfenden Report's conflation of acts and identities, while rendering invisible bisexual and queer experiences. However, there is also a clear difference with the Kaleidoscope Trust and its initial aim focused on sexual orientation, and treatment of gender identity as somewhat secondary (Kaleidoscope Trust 2011). Although Kaleidoscope moved to a more consistent emphasis on lesbian, gay bisexual and transgender (LGBT) human rights, and recently LGBTI on occasion (Kaleidoscope Trust 2014a), this still represents a use of Western identity categories. Meanwhile, Stonewall, having initially been 'lesbian and gay', had become 'lesbian, gay and bisexual' by 2011 but only added transgender work in 2014 (Topping 2014a). The Peter Tatchell Foundation (2014) has a broad approach, often LGBT or LGBTI, sometimes venturing to be queer.

4. Avoid linkage of LGBT human rights to cuts to development aid.

A fourth central point to emerge from comparative analysis was an opposition from activists in African states to linkages being made by Northern governments between development aid provision and LGBT human rights. This opposition was stated clearly by leading Ugandan activist Adrian Jjuuko (2013) and by activist Undule Mwakasungula (2013) from Malawi, who commented:

> In recent years we have seen how some donors, such as the British, have been threatening aid cuts if countries like Malawi do not decriminalise homosexuality. Unfortunately, such approaches are counterproductive as they evoke memories of imperial control.
>
> (Mwakasungula 2013: 366)

This was in contrast to earlier comments of Peter Tatchell, who in 2008 called for the US State Department to link rights and aid (Tatchell 2008). In 2009, he commented regarding Malawi that there should be 'no blank cheque' for countries that 'violate human rights' and that if

The New Trans-National Politics of LGBT Human Rights   85

diplomacy failed, 'the UK should reconsider its aid and trade agreements with Malawi' (Scotsman 2009). Prime Minister David Cameron subsequently proposed, 'We want to see countries that receive our aid adhering to proper human rights, and that includes how people treat gay and lesbian people . . . British aid should have more strings attached' (Long 2011; Lennox and Waites 2013b: 36–37). This was an approach lacking subtlety or strategy. Following a statement by African social justice activists opposing this linkage (reproduced in Tatchell 2011), Tatchell changed position in November 2011 to propose 'switching' aid: 'donor countries should divert their aid money from human rights abusing governments and redirect it to grassroots, community-based humanitarian projects' (Tatchell 2011). Other NGOs, such as Kaleidoscope and Human Dignity Trust, did not take a stance linking human rights to aid. In 2014, Kaleidoscope hosted a seminar with the Overseas Development Institute which shifted talk of cuts towards possible targeting of aid.

5. Engage with religious traditions and beliefs.

A fifth finding was the importance of engaging with religious frameworks of belief, traditions and cultures. This emerges most clearly in work of Shah (2013) on Malaysia, although it is also clear in Baudh's (2013) discussion of Islam in Pakistan and Bangladesh, and in Ward's (2013) work on Uganda and South Africa. Shah argues that engagement with religious beliefs is essential in Malaysia as a 'Muslim-majority state', particularly since both of the main political parties are Islamic. He argues that winning 'acceptance' of the existence of people with same-sex desire is an important starting point and notes some Muslim religious experts internationally who see same-sex love as compatible with Islam.

By contrast, London-based NGOs such as Kaleidoscope and Stonewall generally do not propose ways to positively utilise religious traditions. Peter Tatchell has been recently criticised for ill-conceived forms of activism, including a placard stating 'Islam Nazis behead and burn queers' in 1994, though he argues this should be interpreted in the context of demonstrating against the radical group Hizb ut-Tahrir (Tatchell 2012; Hizb ut-Tahrir 2015). While Tatchell (2012) argues that he has been equally critical of other religions, his criticisms of 'Islamic fundamentalists' have been perceived as problematic by critics, such as Puar (2007: 17–22), although his 2014 move to become patron of anti-hate crime Muslim NGO Tell Mama seems constructive (Pink Paper 2014).

6. Understand human rights struggles in a broader intersectional politics.

A sixth, final and centrally important theme is the value of understanding how human rights can be established within the context of a broader hegemony—a term describing a political and cultural formation, from

86 Matthew Waites

Marxist Antonio Gramsci. This theme emerges in South Africa, where the African National Congress formed a hegemonic project coming out of the apartheid era in which principles of equality and human rights became central (da Costa Santos 2013; Lennox and Waites 2013c: 524). Hence while most ANC supporters did not engage with sexual orientation before apartheid came to an end, the movement's ethos of equality provided the political opportunity structure in which key movement leaders, including Mandela, felt able to make South Africa the first state to place 'sexual orientation' in its Bill of Rights, within the new constitution of the 'rainbow nation'.

The lesson here is about how struggles in relation to sexual orientation and gender identity take place in the context of wider struggles for social justice and human rights along multiple axes of inequality. What is striking, however, is that the London-based trans-national politics has tended to adopt the character of single-issue identity politics, claiming LGBT human rights. In Kaleidoscope, discourse initially could have been more sensitive to postcolonial dynamics or 'intersectional' strategies (Crenshaw 1989; Waites 2015). In 2013, its website proclaimed 'we're telling the Commonwealth' to support 'LGBT human rights', as if a UK-based NGO should be able to 'tell' the Commonwealth what to do, and as if the Commonwealth—with its London-based secretariat—did not remain an organisation considerably shaped by colonialism. The Queen remaining Head of the Commonwealth is still a substantial problem, especially as the only signatory of the 2013 Charter. There is a need for UK-based NGOs to more explicitly and consistently refer to other human rights, such as in relation to racial discrimination and religion, in order to convince that they support human rights per se rather than only for LGBT people (Waites 2015). More explicitly decolonising and intersectional human rights discourse is needed, as in our recent *Statement* of the LGBTI Human Rights in the Commonwealth conference (2014) in Glasgow.

Frustratingly, despite sustained collaborative work on developing a postcolonial and intersectional framing in this *Statement*—between Kaleidoscope, Glasgow Human Rights Network, Equality Network and others—it is noticeable that Kaleidoscope's subsequent approach shows limited signs of change. The Commonwealth Equality Network of over 30 human rights NGOs, instigated by Kaleidoscope, wrote to the Commonwealth Secretary-General in March 2015, selectively quoting the Glasgow *Statement* in calling on the Commonwealth to act on LGBT rights. Yet it does so without making any similar mention of rights on racism and religion or suggestions about how this could be done in a postcolonially sensitised manner (Commonwealth Equality Network 2015).

CONCLUSION

This chapter has analysed four organisations working on LGBT human rights, using six themes to compare experiences of LGBT movements

The New Trans-National Politics of LGBT Human Rights 87

worldwide to the recent practices of those NGOs. What emerges is a clear sense that the new London-based politics of LGBT human rights still has much to learn from subnational, national and regional LGBT movements in the Global South. Given that the UK-based organisations formed in 2011 show no sign of having conducted or published any reviews of what could be learned from existing LGBT organising globally before they commenced work, this is hardly surprising—instead, these organisations have been learning on the job. No evidence appeared that existing global or trans-national NGOs, such as ILGA, IGLHRC, ARC-International or Coalition of African Lesbians, were asked for advice or guidance, which certainly seems to speak of confidence and power in London, and a feeling of being at the centre of the world. The leadership of UK-based LGBT NGOs has tended to come from the circles of political elites, disproportionately from white, middle-class sections of the population, and while the desire to act internationally for human rights has usually been well-intentioned and achieved much that is beneficial, the willingness to act with limited contextual understanding—particularly to invoke the Commonwealth from the north without southern leadership (Waites 2015)—does somewhat reflect experiences of privilege.

Certainly the organisations in London are not very similar, and to group them together as a single phenomenon has analytical limitations. However, it is fair to speak of the London-based NGOs as having certain shared tendencies and characteristics. I have highlighted six tendencies as follows. First, a tendency to privilege decriminalisation of same-sex sexual behaviour in law relative to wider struggles for the social realisation of human rights. Second, a tendency to assume a global constitutionalist model of human rights whereby change occurs top-down, through international law and global deployment of UN human rights discourse. Third, a tendency to use narrow and Western-originating identity frames such, as homosexual or, more usually, 'LGBT' rather than more queer and open framings. Fourth, a tendency towards sympathy for linkage of UK-development aid to the achievement of LGBT human rights in other states, initially via threats of cuts, more recently via suggested targeting. Fifth, lack of positive engagement with religious discourses and traditions, though with a few signs of change. Sixth, a tendency to approach LGBT human rights as a single issue rather than adopt a broader intersectional, multidimensional and anticolonial human rights politics or via broader strategising over cultural conflicts and the contestation of hegemony. This list of themes is intended to be suggestive rather than definitive; and it is crucial to emphasise that the extent to which any particular organisation corresponds to these varies.

There is ongoing contact of all the groups with southern activists; the questions which remain concern the forms, degrees and depth of engagement and crucially how engagement is constrained within overall conceptual framings. In particular, a human rights universalist framing strategy is widely used, but there is no consistent sense of these NGOs espousing or

88 *Matthew Waites*

enacting intersectional and postcolonial framings and strategies. The issue of the global distribution of money is also noticeably missing; each organisation's website invites online donations via debit or credit card, but an appeal for funds from Ugandan NGOs in 2014 made by Kasha Jacqueline Nabagesera did not appear prominently on the any of the four UK NGO websites. Hence the analysis suggests the need for a more critical approach to resources, as well as discourses in the development of trans-national politics.

ACKNOWLEDGEMENT

Thank you to the editors who provided very helpful and insightful review comments.

NOTE

1 LGBT refers to lesbian, gay, bisexual and transgender and is used here since this has been the predominant frame used by NGOs since 2011 (see discussion). It is recognised, however, that LGBTI—including intersex—is increasingly used (Kaleidoscope 2014: 9; LGBTI Human Rights in the Commonwealth conference 2014).

BIBLIOGRAPHY

Adam, B. D., Duyvendak, J. W. and Krouwel, A. (1998) *The Global Emergence of Gay and Lesbian Politics: National Imprints of a Worldwide Movement*. Philadelphia, PA: Temple University Press.

African LGBTI Human Rights Defenders. (2007) 'African LGBTI Human Rights Defenders Warn Public Against Participation in Campaigns Concerning LGBTI Issues in Africa Led by Peter Tatchell and Outrage!'. Available at http://www.indymedia.org.uk/en/2007/02/361469.html, last accessed 1 September 2014.

Baudh, S. (2013) 'Decriminalisation of Consensual Same-Sex Sexual Acts in the South Asian Commonwealth: Struggles in Contexts', in Lennox, C. and Waites, M. (eds.) *Human Rights, Sexual Orientation and Gender Identity in the Commonwealth: Struggles for Decriminalisation and Change*. London: School of Advanced Study, University of London, 287–312. Available at http://commonwealth.sas.ac.uk/publications/house-publications/lgbt-rights-commonwealth, last accessed 10 August 2014.

Binnie, J. (2004) *The Globalization of Sexuality*. London: Sage.

Caribbean Vulnerable Communities. (2014) *Caribbean Vulnerable Communities*. Available at http://cvccoalition.org/, last accessed 1 September 2014.

Committee on Homosexual Offences and Prostitution. (1957) *Report of the Committee on Homosexual Offences and Prostitution*, Cmnd. 247. London: HMSO.

Commonwealth. (2013) *Charter of the Commonwealth*. Available at http://thecommonwealth.org/sites/default/files/page/documents/CharteroftheCommonwealth.pdf, last accessed 10 August 2014.

Commonwealth Equality Network. (2015) 'Open Letter to Kamalesh Sharma', 9 March 2015. Available at http://kaleidoscopetrust.com/usr/library/documents/

The New Trans-National Politics of LGBT Human Rights 89

main/open-letter-to-commonwealth-secretary-general.pdf, last accessed 31 March 2015.

Commonwealth Heads of Government. (1971) *Singapore Declaration of Commonwealth Principles*. Available at http://thecommonwealth.org/sites/default/files/history-items/documents/Singapore%20Declaration.pdf, last accessed 10 August 2014.

Commonwealth Heads of Government. (1991) *Harare Commonwealth Declaration*. Available at http://secretariat.thecommonwealth.org/shared_asp_files/GFSR.asp?NodeID=141095, last accessed 10 August 2014.

Commonwealth Secretariat. (2014) *Eminent Persons Group*. Available at http://secretariat.thecommonwealth.org/subhomepage/228488/home/, last accessed 31 August 2014.

Crenshaw, K. (1989) 'Demarginalizing the Intersection of Race and Sex: A Black Feminist Critique of Antidiscrimination Doctrine, Feminist Theory and Antiracist Politics', *University of Chicago Legal Forum* 140: 139–167.

Currier, A. (2009) 'Deferral of Legal Tactics: A Global LGBT Social Movement Organization's Perspective', in Barclay, S., Bernstein, M. and Marshall, A.-M. (eds.) *Queer Mobilizations: LGBT Activists Confront the Law*. New York: New York University Press, 21–37.

da Costa Santos, G. G. (2013) 'Decriminalising Homosexuality in Africa: Lessons from the South African Experience', in Lennox, C. and Waites, M. (eds.) *Human Rights, Sexual Orientation and Gender Identity in the Commonwealth: Struggles for Decriminalisation and Change*. London: School of Advanced Study, University of London, 313–338. Available at http://commonwealth.sas.ac.uk/publications/house-publications/lgbt-rights-commonwealth, last accessed 10 August 2014.

Eminent Persons Group. (2011) *A Commonwealth of the People: Time for Urgent Reform—the Report of the Eminent Persons Group to the Commonwealth Heads of Government*. London: Commonwealth Secretariat.

Gaskins Jr., J. (2013) ' "Buggery" and the Commonwealth Caribbean: A Comparative Examination of the Bahamas, Jamaica and Trinidad and Tobago', in Lennox, C. and Waites, M. (eds.) *Human Rights, Sexual Orientation and Gender Identity in the Commonwealth: Struggles for Decriminalisation and Change*. London: School of Advanced Study, University of London, 429–454. Available at http://commonwealth.sas.ac.uk/publications/house-publications/lgbt-rights-commonwealth, last accessed 10 August 2014.

Hizb ut-Tahrir. (2015) *Hizb ut-Tahrir*. Available at http://www.hizb.org.uk/, last accessed 5 June 2015.

Howe, S. (2012) 'British Worlds, Settler Worlds, World Systems and Killing Fields', *Journal of Imperial and Commonwealth History* 40(4): 691–725.

Human Dignity Trust. (2014a) 'Human Dignity Trust: Decriminalising Homosexuality by Upholding International Law'. Available at http://www.humandignitytrust.org/, last accessed 1 September 2014.

Human Dignity Trust. (2014b) 'About Us'. Available at http://www.humandignitytrust.org/pages/ABOUT%20US, last accessed 1 September 2014.

Human Rights Watch. (2008) *This Alien Legacy: The Origins of 'Sodomy' Laws in British Colonialism*. New York: Human Rights Watch. Available at http://www.hrw.org/reports/2008/12/17/alien-legacy-0, last accessed 30 November 2012.

Hynes, P., Lamb, M., Short, D. and Waites, M. (2012) *The Sociology of Human Rights*. Special Issue: The Sociology of Human Rights, *Sociology* 46(5).

ILGA. (2015) *ILGA*. Available at http://ilga.org/, last accessed 5 June 2015.

IGLHRC. (2015) *IGLHRC*. Available at http://iglhrc.org/, last accessed 5 June 2015.

Itaborahy, L. P. (2012) *State-Sponsored Homophobia: A World Survey of Laws Criminalising Same-Sex Sexual Acts between Consenting Adults*. Available at http://ilga.org/ilga/en/article/1161, last accessed 11 March 2013.

90 *Matthew Waites*

Jjuuko, A. (2013) 'The Incremental Approach: Uganda's Struggle for the Decriminalization of Homosexuality', in Lennox, C. and Waites, M. (eds.) *Human Rights, Sexual Orientation and Gender Identity in the Commonwealth: Struggles for Decriminalisation and Change*. London: School of Advanced Study, University of London, 381–408. Available at http://commonwealth.sas.ac.uk/publications/house-publications/lgbt-rights-commonwealth, last accessed 10 August 2014.

Kaleidoscope Trust. (2011) *Kaleidoscope International Diversity Trust*. September, available at http://www.kaleidoscopetrust.com/PDFs/Kaleidoscope%20aims%20and%20beliefs.pdf, last accessed 7 Dec. 2012.

Kaleidoscope Trust. (2014a) *Speaking Out: The Rights of LGBTI citizens from across the Commonwealth*. London: Kaleidoscope Trust. Available at http://kaleidoscopetrust.com/speaking-out, last accessed 10 August 2014.

Kaleidoscope Trust. (2014b) *Kaleidoscope Trust*. Available at http://kaleidoscopetrust.com/, last accessed 1 September 2014.

Kitschelt, H. (1986) 'Political Opportunity Structures and Political Protest: Anti-Nuclear Movements in Four Democracies', *British Journal of Political Science* 16(1): 57–85.

Kollman, K. (2014) 'Deploying Europe: The Creation of Discursive Imperatives for Same-Sex Unions', in Ayoub, P. and Paternotte, D. (eds.) *LGBT Activism and the Making of Europe: A Rainbow Europe?* Houndmills: Palgrave Macmillan, 97–118.

Kollman, K. and Waites, M. (eds.) (2009) *The Global Politics of LGBT Human Rights*, special issue, *Contemporary Politics* 15(1).

Lennox, C. and Waites, M. (eds.) (2013a) *Human Rights, Sexual Orientation and Gender Identity in the Commonwealth: Struggles for Decriminalisation and Change*. London: School of Advanced Study, University of London. Available at http://commonwealth.sas.ac.uk/publications/house-publications/lgbt-rights-commonwealth, last accessed 10 August 2014.

Lennox, C. and Waites, M. (2013b) 'Human Rights, Sexual Orientation and Gender Identity in the Commonwealth: From History and Law to Developing Activism and Transnational Dialogues', in Lennox, C. and Waites, M. (eds.) *Human Rights, Sexual Orientation and Gender Identity in the Commonwealth: Struggles for Decriminalisation and Change*. London: School of Advanced Study, University of London, 1–59. Available at http://commonwealth.sas.ac.uk/publications/house-publications/lgbt-rights-commonwealth, last accessed 10 August 2014.

Lennox, C. and Waites, M. (2013c) 'Conclusion. Comparative Analysis of Decriminalisation and Change across the Commonwealth: Understanding Contexts and Discerning Strategies', in Lennox, C. and Waites, M. (eds.) *Human Rights, Sexual Orientation and Gender Identity in the Commonwealth: Struggles for Decriminalisation and Change*. London: School of Advanced Study, University of London, 507–547. Available at http://commonwealth.sas.ac.uk/publications/house-publications/lgbt-rights-commonwealth, last accessed 10 August 2014.

LGBTI Human Rights in the Commonwealth conference. (2014) *LGBTI Human Rights in the Commonwealth Conference Statement on Nelson Mandela International Day 18 July 2014*. Available at http://www.gla.ac.uk/research/az/glasgowhumanrightsnetwork/lgbtihrc/, last accessed 31 August 2014.

Long, S. (2011) 'African Activists on Human Rights and Aid', 31 October. Available at http://paper-bird.net/2011/10/31/african-activists-on-human-rights-and-aid/, last accessed 5 March 2015.

Long, S. (2015) 'Help I'm Being Persecuted: Hypocrisy and Free Speech', 19 February. Available at http://paper-bird.net/2015/02/19/hypocrisy-and-free-speech/, last accessed 5 March 2015.

Lopéz, A. J. (2007) 'Introduction: The (Post) Global South', *The Global South* 1(1&2): 1–11.

The New Trans-National Politics of LGBT Human Rights 91

Lucas, I. (1998) *Outrage! An Oral History*. London: Continuum.

Melucci, A. (1996) *Challenging Codes: Collective Action in the Information Age*. Cambridge: Cambridge University Press.

Mills, C. W. (1956) *The Power Elite*. New York: Oxford University Press.

Morgan, K. (2008) *Slavery and the British Empire: From Africa to America*. Oxford: Oxford University Press.

Mwakasungula, U. (2013) 'The LGBT Situation in Malawi: An Activist Perspective', in Lennox, C. and Waites, M. (eds.) *Human Rights, Sexual Orientation and Gender Identity in the Commonwealth: Struggles for Decriminalisation and Change*. London: School of Advanced Study, University of London, 359–379. Available at http://commonwealth.sas.ac.uk/publications/house-publications/lgbt-rights-commonwealth, last accessed 10 August 2014.

Nash, K. (2012) 'Human Rights, Movements and Law: On Not Researching Legitimacy'. Special Issue: The Sociology of Human Rights, *Sociology*, 46(5):797–812.

Paternotte, D. (2014) 'The International (Lesbian and) Gay Association and the Question of Paedophilia: Tracking the Demise of Gay Liberation Ideals', *Sexualities*, 17(1–2):121–138.

Peter Tatchell Foundation. (2014a) *Peter Tatchell Foundation: Speaking Out for Human Rights*. Available at http://www.petertatchellfoundation.org/, last accessed 1 September 2014.

Peter Tatchell Foundation. (2014b) 'About Us'. Available at http://www.petertatc hellfoundation.org/about, last accessed 1 September 2014.

Pink Paper. (2014) 'Peter Tatchell Becomes a Patron of Anti-Hate Crime Muslim Campaign Group', March 20, 2014. Available at http://www.pinknews. co.uk/2014/03/20/peter-tatchell-becomes-patron-anti-hate-crime-muslim-campaign-group/, last accessed 1 September 2014.

Power, L. (1991) 'The International Lesbian and Gay Association', *Feminist Review* 39:172–173.

Puar, J. (2007) *Terrorist Assemblages: Homonationalism in Queer Times*. Durham, NC: Duke University Press.

Rahman, M. (2014) *Homosexualities, Muslim Cultures and Modernity*. Houndmills: Palgrave Macmillan.

Said, E. (1978) *Orientalism*. London: Routledge and Kegan Paul.

Scotsman. (2009) 'Scotland Is Urged to Act after Malawi Police Arrest Gay Couple for Marrying', 29 December. Available at http://www.scotsman.com/news/world/scotland-is-urged-to-act-after-malawi-police-arrest-gay-couple-for-marrying-1-784104, last accessed 25 May 2015.

Shah, S. (2013) 'The Malaysian Dilemma: Negotiating Sexual Diversity in a Muslim-Majority Commonwealth State', in Lennox, C. and Waites, M. (eds.) *Human Rights, Sexual Orientation and Gender Identity in the Commonwealth: Struggles for Decriminalisation and Change*. London: School of Advanced Study, University of London, 262–285. Available at http://commonwealth.sas.ac.uk/publications/house-publications/lgbt-rights-commonwealth, last accessed 10 August 2014.

Stonewall. (2015a) *Stonewall*. Available at http://www.stonewall.org.uk/, last accessed 5 June 2015.

Stonewall. (2015b) 'Stonewall's International Campaign'. Available at http://www.stonewall.org.uk/what_we_do/stonewalls_international_campaign/default.asp, last accessed 5 March 2015.

Stonewall. (2015c) 'Stonewall's Key Priorities 2014/15'. Available at http://www.stonewall.org.uk/about_us/2534.asp, last accessed 9 March 2015.

Tatchell, P. (2008) 'No US Aid for Anti-Gay Regimes', 21 July. Available at http://www.petertatchell.net/international/united_states/nousaidforantigayregimes.htm, last accessed 20 May 2015.

92   *Matthew Waites*

Tatchell, P. (2011) 'UK: Don't Cut Aid Over Human Rights Abuses, Switch It'. 1 November. Available at http://petertatchellfoundation.org/general/uk-don-t-cut-aid-over-human-rights-abuses-switch-it, last accessed 20 May 2015.

Tatchell, P. (2012) 'Cameron Urged to Repeal Insults Ban', 30 August. Available at http://www.petertatchellfoundation.org/free-speech/cameron-urged-repeal-insults-ban, last accessed 9 March 2015.

Tatchell, P. (2014) *Peter Tatchell: Human Rights, Democracy, Global Justice, LGBTI Freedom*. Available at http://www.petertatchellfoundation.org/, last accessed 1 September 2014.

Tauqir, T., Petzen, J., Haritaworn, J., Ekine, S., Bracke, S., Lamble, S., Jivraj, S. and Douglas, S. (2011) 'Queer Anti-Racist Activism and Strategies of Critique: A Roundtable Discussion', *Feminist Legal Studies* 19(2): 169–191.

Thoreson, R. (2014) *Transnational LGBT Activism*. Minneapolis: University of Minnesota Press.

Topping, A. (2014) 'Stonewall Chief Ruth Hunt: We Will Do More to Promote Transgender Rights', *The Guardian*, 28 July. Available at http://www.theguardian.com/world/2014/jul/28/stonewall-ruth-hunt-promote-transgender-rights, last accessed 1 September 2014.

Tremblay, M., Paternotte, D. and Johnson, C. (eds.) (2011) *The Gay and Lesbian Movement and the State: Comparative Insights into a Transformed Relationship*. Farnham: Ashgate.

United Nations Human Development Programme (2014) *Human Development Report. Sustaining Human Progress: Reducing Vulnerabilities and Building Resilience* (New York: United Nations Development Programme). Available at: http://hdr.undp.org/sites/default/files/hdr14-report-en-1.pdf, last accessed 24 September 2015.

Waites, M. (2005) 'The Fixity of Sexual Identities in the Public Sphere: Biomedical Knowledge, Liberalism and the Heterosexual/Homosexual Binary in Late Modernity', *Sexualities* 8(5): 539–569.

Waites, M. (2010) 'Human Rights, Sexual Orientation and the Generation of Childhoods: Analysing the Partial Decriminalisation of "Unnatural Offences" in India', in Hynes, P., Lamb, M., Short, D. and Waites, M. (eds.) Special Issue: Sociology and Human Rights: New Engagements, *International Journal of Human Rights* 14(6): 971–993.

Waites, M. (2013) 'United Kingdom: Confronting Criminal Histories and Theorising Decriminalisation and Governmentality', in Lennox, C. and Waites, M. (eds.) *Human Rights, Sexual Orientation and Gender Identity in the Commonwealth: Struggles for Decriminalisation and Change*. London: School of Advanced Study, University of London, 145–181. Available at http://commonwealth.sas.ac.uk/publications/house-publications/lgbt-rights-commonwealth, last accessed 10 August 2014.

Waites, M. (2015) 'Claiming LGBTI Human Rights in the Commonwealth after Empire', *Discover Society* 16, 3 January.

Ward, K. (2013) 'Religious Institutions and Actors and Religious Attitudes to Homosexual Rights: South Africa and Uganda', in Lennox, C. and Waites, M. (eds.) *Human Rights, Sexual Orientation and Gender Identity in the Commonwealth: Struggles for Decriminalisation and Change*. London: School of Advanced Study, University of London, 409–427. Available at http://commonwealth.sas.ac.uk/publications/house-publications/lgbt-rights-commonwealth, last accessed 10 August 2014.

Part II
Racialised Subjects and Feminist/Queer Solidarities

5 *Black Mammy* and Company
Exploring Constructions of Black Womanhood[1] in Britain

Tracey Reynolds

INTRODUCTION

In contemporary Britain anchored by racialised and gendered discourses of the nation and national belonging (Erel 2015), key constructions of black womanhood *have been* mobilised to legitimise gender and racialised 'otherness'. Within this article, the key constructions specifically highlighted are the *Black Mammy, Dominating Matriarch, 'Baby Mother'* and the *Jezebel.* At the root of these images, there exists a complex and denigrating mythology about black women's sexuality. In this chapter, I explore how sexuality provides an important starting point for understanding and contextualising black women's experiences. The fact that these images maintain a long-lasting appeal is because they provide ideological justification for the persistent racial and gender oppression experienced by black women. These images also mask the structural arrangements that maintain systemic racial inequality, which result in black women being blamed for their 'failed' gender performances rather than the broader systems and structures of inequality that persist in society (Hill-Collins 2004). Black feminist theory, and its approach to intersectionality, has been pivotal to understanding the way in which structural power determines black women's societal position as 'other' or 'different'. I therefore draw on an intersectional approach to identify the extent to which issues of sexuality and sexual identity act as markers of being non-normative, deviant and 'pathological' for Black women, specifically those of African and Caribbean parentage or heritage.

BLACK FEMINIST THEORY AND THE POLITICS OF INTERSECTIONALITY

By using the terms 'black womanhood' and 'B/black women', I am consciously presenting an essentialised and homogenised construct of Black women that actively conflates and collapses differences between the women, including social class, generational divisions, sexual identity, ethnic identity, differences between women who were born in the Global North or

96 Tracey Reynolds

migrated from the Global South.[2] Arguably, however, there is political value to be gained by using this term. This is because, irrespective of the differences and diversity existing between the women, as a collective they continue to be positioned, constructed and understood as racialised selves by a white-majority society. As Black feminist theory has shown, there is a history and legacy of Black women across different times, spaces and contexts collectively organising around this term in order to subvert and resist racial and gender oppression. A critical project of Black feminism has been to chart the story of raced and gendered domination of Black and other ethnicised women across the differing cultural, social, political and historical landscapes (McKittrick 2006). Through a 'process of quilting a genealogical narrative of other ways of knowing' (Mirza 2009: 2), fragments of memory are collected that link the past to the present (Flannery 2001). As a Black feminist researcher, I am also engaged in this quilting process. For example, central to this chapter is an exploration of black women's sexual identity by connecting strands and threads of narratives on black women's experiences. These narratives draw from several empirical-based projects exploring the everyday lives of black women in Britain and, importantly, position black women's voices at the centre of analysis. Although each of these projects does not explicitly focus on black women's sexuality, the viewpoints expressed by these women were in most instances imbued with private, cultural and public beliefs about gender, race and sexuality. The first study, which began my academic career, explored the mothering practices of black women living in London—as well as several other cities in Britain (Birmingham, Manchester and Huddersfield)—to identify the cultural strategies these mothers engaged in order to develop a critical consciousness about 'race' in their children's lives (Reynolds 2005). A second and closely related project investigated black women's community activism in contemporary Britain; it explored how women collectively organised within their communities to respond to the daily challenges of racism (Reynolds 2003). A third study explored the way in which trans-national and diasporic social capital networks informed identity construction among young black women (as well as men) (Reynolds 2008). My current study introduces a cross-cultural dimension, investigating how 'race' and ethnic identity are implicated in the citizenship practices of black and other ethnicised mothers, who are also newly arrived migrants to the UK[3] (Erel and Reynolds 2014). An overarching ambition with these various projects focused on black women has been to raise awareness and understanding of the diverse and complex ways that black women respond to, resist and protect themselves against the generally negative way in which they are portrayed in public debates and political commentary alike.

A Black feminist theoretical approach provides an analytical framework in which to focus on the power relations and intersecting systems which normalise a hierarchy of privilege. It allows for a reconsideration of social structural inequalities resulting from intersections of race, class, gender and sexual identities. Black feminism also provides an oppositional discourse

Black Mammy *and Company*   97

within social theory for the purposes of political empowerment and social justice (Hill-Collins 1991). In doing so, it allows scholars and policymakers to recognise the limitations of White feminist theorising and also 'race' (male-dominated) discourses in understanding the experiences of Black women in Britain today. A clear example of this can be seen in the unspoken whiteness at the centre of feminist analyses actively challenging neo-liberal debates in family policy around individualism, choice and citizen responsibility. In the critiques of these policies, particularly those judging the way in which the success and failures of children are blamed on individual parents, their styles, values and practices, the issue of 'race' and racism and the ways these work to entrench structural inequalities and systems of privilege, is by and large overlooked in discussions. Instead, feminist critiques within this field have foregrounded gender and social class inequality (see e.g. Gillies 2011; Jensen and Tyler 2012). Yet we are witnessing a return to the racialisation of deficit mothering that is often coded and goes unnoticed. For example, in the aftermath of the 2011 riots, which spread from London to other towns and cities across England, it was observed that narratives of race and racism were implicated and embedded in the cultural commentary. So, for example, words such as 'gang cultures', 'uncivilised', 'intellectually underdeveloped' and animalistic terms such as 'savage wild' and 'feral youths' acted as coded words to denote 'race' and the 'racial inferiority' of black individuals. At various points in history, such terms have been drawn upon to represent pathological constructions of black family life and related understandings of black feminine identities and also black masculine identities. Consequently, this coded narrative means that 'overt racialisation is not required for meaning' (Lewis 2005: 553).

Black feminist theory provides a framework to interpret and raise awareness of such coded narratives, which typically operate in everyday discourses around family, community and intimate lives. As an oppositional standpoint, Black feminist theory is unique in creating a specialised knowledge produced by Black women and clarifying a particular standpoint about them. Knowledge production is also grounded in the critical analysis of their lives (Griffin 1996). This therefore involves an 'interpretation of Black women's experiences by those who participate in them' (Hill-Collins 1990: 15). Black feminism similarly valorises a discourse of global connection among Black women, which is formed on notions of a collective history involving racial struggle, suffering and marginalisation (Mama 1995, Mirza 1997). Using this collective definition of black womanhood, some of the earlier writings by Black feminist scholars during the 1970s and 1980s identified the legacy of 'triple oppression' formed around race, gender and class subjugation (Carby 1982; Amos and Parmar 1984). This discourse of 'triple oppression' creating a collective history has been widely criticised as being an outmoded way of contextualising Black women's lives (Mirza 1997, 2014). Yet the notion of shared struggle, pain and marginalisation experienced by Black women in differing cultural and historical contexts is still very central to

98 *Tracey Reynolds*

debates. For example, an examination of Black women's status in the British labour market revealed a historical and continued experience of discrimination and disadvantage in the workplace on account of their subordinated race and gender status (Clarke and Drinkwater 2007; Yeandle et al. 2013). I have argued elsewhere that black (i.e. African-Caribbean) women's experience in the UK labour market today is a direct outcome of slavery and British colonialism, which positions them as source of cheap, flexible and disposable labour (Reynolds 2001). The experience of collective struggle by these women is revealed in the way that black women, alongside other ethnicised migrant women, continue to collectively mobilise themselves at national and local levels in order to confront this and respond to discrimination and disadvantage in the workplace (Reynolds 2002, 2005; Erel and Reynolds 2014).

As more and more studies emerge on understanding and documenting black women's experiences, it is becoming increasingly apparent that to speak and make claims of a Black women's knowledge presents some interesting dilemmas. For an increased availability of knowledge means that it reinforces Black women's status as objects of investigation as opposed to subjects of investigation. Indeed, Patricia Hill-Collins (1997) suggests that a process of 'knowing without knowing' occurs whereby more powerful groups in society who have a particular interest in understanding the lives of Black women can voyeuristically observe these women from a distance and without them ever having to personally communicate or critically engage with them. Critical analysis by White feminists of their own racial and gendered privileged lives is also avoided. For Black women, however, their subordinate racial and gender location means that they cannot afford to view other social groups 'from a distance', because any understanding of their own lives is relational and contingent upon their status as the racial and gender 'other'. This leaves them vulnerable and open to exploitation, because their accounts can be appropriated and commoditised by more dominant groups in society in order to benefit their own self-serving interests.

Another consequence of Black women's greater opportunity to define and name their experiences, and to have these experiences reach a wider public audience, is that some areas of social life become the dominant narrative of Black womanhood, whilst other areas get silenced. The latter is particularly true with regards to issues of black women's sexuality. Within academic scholarship, there are few accounts by black women about their intimate and sexual lives, despite such stories about black women being all around us. Other silences have been in suitably connecting and intersecting the experiences of black heterosexual and lesbian, bisexual and trans women. Research exploring this has highlighted the risks and fears associated with black women speaking up about this issue, outside of the semi-safe space of fictional narratives, because of the way in which the white (male and female) and Western interpretative lens can easily distort their stories, thus confirming the negative stereotypes and representations of them, which are so omnipresent in society (Wilkins 2012).

Black Mammy *and Company* 99

The term 'intersectionality', a concept introduced by black female scholar Kim Crenshaw (1991) in the USA has been a particularly useful concept to trouble some of these silences and invisibilities within black women's narratives. Intersectionality focuses on the way 'race' and ethnicity intersect and overlap with gender, class and sexuality to create gender and racialised inequality that is felt universally by all women of colour but at the same time is culturally and historically specific. As a concept, it removes some of the critique about essentialising Black women's experiences by recognising that different people experience different social structural oppressions. Yet these systems of power (racial, economic, social, cultural) interlock to cause unequal relations in society. Despite the recent proliferation of scholarship on intersectionality, few studies have focused on theorising this complexity, taking into account what McCall (2005: 1780) says is 'the potential for both multiple and conflicting experiences of subordination and power' and also the multiple and conflicting dimensions of inequality. The way this term is being increasingly used across many disciplines, for example, queer theory, to reframe identities, subjectivities and demarcations is indicative of the way in which intersectionality now operates as an uncritical space in which all marginalised groups and categories are equivalent to each other (Ludvig 2006). The problem with this, however, is that it sometimes obscures any substantive and critical discussion of the uneven power relations that may exist among and between such groups, between, for example, white lesbian and Black heterosexual women (Phoenix and Pattynama 2006). Looking at this within the context of the current backlash against multiculturalism and immigration from the Global South and Eastern Europe across many EU nations, the depoliticisation of intersectionality has also created a situation whereby those who are left out of these spaces—e.g. white, native-born, working class males—now want be included by asserting the right for recognition of what they believe to be their own marginalised culture and identity (Crenshaw 2014).

Yet despite the contested nature of intersectionality as a critical space and the challenges faced by racial-majority communities who can overlook their racial privilege, I would argue that it is still an important analytical tool for black women to critically interrogate the way in which black women's absences/presences and visibility/invisibility occurs in everyday social contexts. This is because it moves Black women's voices and the knowledge that emerges to the centre stage from the margins. It also allows for the creation of an epistemological position and enables Black feminist scholarship to critically explore the interconnectedness of black women's experiences across the myriad of the social fields that they occupy, whilst also recognising how the structural order of gender and race is maintained and reproduced across different generations, nations and cultures (Brah and Phoenix 2004). Thus in using a Black feminist framework, the concept of intersectionality is returned to its origins as an analytical tool intended to explore the intersections of 'race', gender, ethnicity and sexuality by positioning these issues

100 Tracey Reynolds

at the centre of our thinking about our own lives and then to apply this knowledge in an effort to create a society in which all voices are heard and where public policy can be responsive to multiple voices and perspectives.

RACIALISATION OF GENDERED SEXUALISED IDENTITIES

The issue of sexuality provides an important starting point with regards to understanding and situating black women's experiences. This is because I believe that the way in which black women are constructed and positioned in contemporary Britain stems from a complex and denigrating mythology about black women's sexuality. Not only is sexuality central to race, class, and gender meanings, but it is also used to confer citizenship, status and resources on different groups of people and to justify inequalities among them. The societal inequalities that continue to define black women's experiences are predicated on a denigrating mythology that inflicts narrow, pathological and stereotypical images on black women. These can be broadly described as *Black Mammy, Matriarch, Baby Mother* and *Jezebel*, controlling images that seek to depict and reify black women as the sexual other, sexual immoral and sexual deviant. Through these images, black women are either ascribed the status of being hypersexual (e.g. *Jezebel, welfare*) or abnormally asexual and emasculating (e.g. *mammy, matriarch*). Both categories work together in such a way as to prevent black women from occupying a normative and unmarked social position. They are images that are also the result of the historical intersection between socially constructed sexuality and socially constructed race.

Patricia Hill-Collins (1991) makes a compelling case for not viewing constructions of sexuality and race as two separate realms of oppression. She notes how each of these concepts depends on the other for meaning. Sexuality has always been used by those in power to support racism and racial hierarchies. Likewise, racism and racial hierarchies are used to impose, control and limit cultural ideas about normative sexuality and draw boundaries between black and white women (also black men and white men). As a cultural invention, the symbiotic relationship between race and sexuality became most heightened during the era of slavery and colonialism. Yet the remnants of this legacy are clear to see in the present day. The continued sexualisation of race—or as some have argued, the racialisation of sex (Crenshaw 1989; Hill-Collins 2004; Thompkins 2004)—means that aesthetic standards and micro-judgements exist in a myriad of ways to devalue those women socially constructed and positioned as black. In many European states, we see examples of this in the difference afforded to the sexualisation of black and white women's maternity by politicians and the mainstream media. White women with three or more children are typically depicted and valued as asexual, motherly, caring, nurturing and self-sacrificing. The recent increase in migratory movements across

Northern European nations also means that these women are categorised as being 'good citizens', because through their acts of multiple childbearing, they are producing future citizens for the nation (Anthias and Yuval-Davis 1992; Erel 2011). In contrast, however, black women with a similar number of children are popularly cast as highly sexualised figures, selfish, irresponsible and uncaring (Reynolds 1997). In policy terms, their acts of multiple childbearing are deemed to produce the 'wrong' type of future citizens. They are structurally positioned as 'outsiders' to the nation and a threat to the stability, identity cohesiveness and security of the nation-state (Erel and Reynolds 2014). Their maternity must be constrained and limited. We saw examples of this in Britain during the 1970s–1980s whereby black women became targets of specific social welfare polices concerned with restricting or enforcing the sterilisation of mothers through the use of the drug Depo-Provera, with disproportionate numbers of black women given this drug (Mirza 1997).

The issue of maternity for black women is also strongly associated with heightened sexuality and sexual desire in a way that simply does not exist for white women, irrespective of their class location. This strong association between sexual desire and maternity is culturally located in the politics of European slavery (Zack 2002). The link between the two is used to deny the existence and possibility of acts of rape and brutal sexual assaults on black female bodies and the recognition of such acts against black women in law and public and private morality. The negative perception and translation of the black female body has continued to make us highly vulnerable to sexual assault in present times.

The issue of sexuality offers Black feminist researchers an important analytic lens for understanding constructions of black womanhood and the multiple levels of oppression and resistance found in these women's lives. As noted by Tricia Rose (2004: 56):

> Sexuality can be defined broadly as attitudes, beliefs, behaviours, and identities associated with sex, pleasure, and desire. Yet, issues related to sexuality are not simply maintained within bodies; they are shaped by and serve a wider social and political terrain.

There is a plethora of research evidence recognising the use of images such as the black mammy and company in the historical demonisation of black female sexuality (Reynolds 1997; Thompkins 2004; West 2008). I shall briefly describe these images to highlight how entrenched ideas about black people, their families and communities grow from them.

The black mammy is generally characterised as loyal, maternal, subservient, compliant, asexual, accepting of the existing status quo and dedicated to the slave family's children, sometimes to the detriment of her own children. The black mammy is one constructed to justify, validate and legitimise an economic system based on slave labour and the reproductive

102 Tracey Reynolds

labour of female slaves. In modern times, however, we have seen different incarnations of the black mammy within Western and US popular culture, with the *Aunt Jemima* as the most clearly identifiable mammy image. The Aunt Jemima character is arguably one of the most dominant stereotypical African-American characters, which originally emerged out of the nineteenth century American-style vaudeville/minstrels shows. This popular figure was later adopted by commercial interests during the 1930s to represent the Aunt Jemima ready-made pancake mix brand. In North America, the UK and Northern Europe, this has been appropriated as a consumer marketing tool in order to sell a particular brand of pancake mixes, syrup and other breakfast products. It has been argued that as a brand its wholesale appeal rests on the continued subtext lurking beneath this image, which elevates and celebrates the master/servant relationship under British plantocracy and colonial societies, whereby everyone 'knew their place' according to racial hierarchy (Reynolds 2001).

Serving as a direct counterpoint to the servile image of the black mammy is the one of the domineering matriarch. This stereotype depicts black women as sexually undesirable, loud, aggressive and the symbolic antithesis of the ladylike status ascribed to 'pure', 'white' women. Sociological studies on 'race' have relied upon this myth to designate black women as the principal cause of the decline of the black family (see for example Dench 1996). When viewed from this viewpoint, she is marked out as keeping black children from achieving their potential and full equality due to her failure to 'keep a man'. She is also unable to maintain a stable heterosexual normative relationship because of her primary decision-making role with the family. Acting as primary financial provider as well as primary caretaker, not only does the domineering matriarch disrupt normative expectations about gendered family roles but she is perceived as displacing men from family life. In modern times, this image has been remade and recast as the angry black woman who is professional, financially independent, educated and single. Within this context, black women's sexuality is indirectly referred to by singling out their supposed lack of sexual desirability and quality to members of the opposite (and same) sex.

If the black mammy and domineering matriarch are categorised as asexual, then the 'welfare mother' or 'baby mother' is characterised as being oversexualised and as recklessly and irresponsibly falling pregnant by as many different fathers as possible to get as much money from them and the welfare state, with little or no concern for her children's care or well-being. Crucially, one of the first earliest policy reports into black families in the US context, the Moynihan Report (1965), alluded to the fact that in 'breeding' multiple children with multiple 'baby fathers', it is her wanton sexuality that is the root cause of poverty within black communities and not wider structural inequalities in society. As we can see, both the baby mother and the domineering matriarch are in different ways responsible for what is perceived as the crisis and breakdown of black families.

Perhaps the most sexualised image, the Jezebel, and more recent configurations, such as the dancehall queen, evokes a more direct and explicit eroticisation and fetishisation of the black female body. This stereotypical image is one linked to sexual promiscuity, an inappropriate display of sexuality and sexual aggressiveness, which brings it into direct contrast to the virtuous Western female heterosexuality. No other figure epitomises the image of sexual deviance better than Saartjie Baartman, the 'Hottentot Venus'.[4] During the early nineteenth century, the display of her colonised body—and most notably the emphasis given to her prominent buttocks and genitalia—served as an important symbol of black women's hypersexuality, reinforcing notions of racial difference between Europeans and African people and Europeans' supposed racial superiority over African people (Hobson 2002; Henderson 2011). It is interesting to see within popular culture today the aesthetic value assigned to aspects of the black female body with, for example, the rise in buttock augmentation surgery.

These prevailing images of black women's sexuality have been an instrumental tool in providing ideological justification of black women's subordinate roles and the continued economic exploitation of these racialised women. We can observe this in the way that throughout history the images have been used as a means to implement and justify continued discrimination, segregation, exploitation (including sexual exploitation) and the vilification of black women. Marshall (2006: 4), for instance, exploring the impact of such myths for black women in the Caribbean context, argues that institutionalisation of myths constitutes a tool of domination that impedes the socio-economic and political advancement of women in the Caribbean region. In the next section, I explore in further detail how the objectification, dehumanisation and relegation of black women as *Mammy, Matriarch, Welfare Mother, and Jezebels* remain similarly embedded in black women's everyday lives in the British context.

THE ENDURING IMPACT OF THE BLACK MAMMY

Black women's labour market position in the global economy, whereby the continued primary status as unpaid/low-paid domestic and care workers serving the global professional elites continues to be the norm, is merely a reinvention of the black mammy figure. First, as a plethora of studies continue to highlight, black and minority ethnic women are disproportionately employed in service sector industries, often as low-paid, casual or self-employed workers (Yeandle et al. 2013). This current period of economic austerity, with cuts to public and service sector jobs actively discriminates against these women. Research undertaken by Runnymede (2011), a UK race equality think tank agency on behalf of British trade union associations Unison, UNITE and TUC, shows a disproportionate increase in black female unemployment in multicultural areas of London, Birmingham and Manchester because public

104   Tracey Reynolds

sector cuts and the casualisation of labour (e.g. workers employed on zero contract hours) within the sector affect the very service industries (central, local government and the voluntary sector) and the very job level (e.g. administrative posts) where black women are concentrated in. Black women are the main or sole economic providers in the majority of black families and therefore these changes to their employment conditions are also adversely affecting the household income of black families (Reynolds 2013).

Second, as research by the Maternity Action (2012) examining the employment experiences of black and minority ethnic newly arrived migrants to the UK from the Global South shows, these women are particularly vulnerable because they have less employment rights compared to other women. Those women working in the 'mammy' roles as cleaners, cooks and unqualified childminders usually have fewer rights in terms of paid maternity leave. As low-paid workers, they have limited financial resources to access differing but expensive types of childcare available for their own children. They often miss out on many health and safety measures designed to protect pregnant women in the workplace. Simply put, these women do not have the legal protection and support available to other women in the workplace (Erel and Reynolds 2014). Feminist scholarship which takes into account globalisation and economic migration of maternal labour shows how family and maternal policies are inextricably linked to migration policies. Studies by Rachel Parreñas (2001, 2005), for example, focus on the care drain affecting countries in the Global South as a result of the increase in female migration and growing demand in care-related jobs in the Global North. This work was important in showing how affluent women of the Global North offload their devalued caring and practical mothering tasks to poorer women from the South who migrate to take up such tasks, whilst these migrant mothers simultaneously devolve their own caring duties to family members or even less fortunate women in their country of origin. It also highlights the public and global nature of seemingly private and local arrangements, such as the hiring of a foreign domestic worker and also the low status and devalued nature of care work worldwide. The research evidence suggests that underlying and providing ideological justification to the devalued and low status of foreign domestic workers providing this caring work is the racialised and gendered construct of the 'black mammy' and with it associated claims of racial difference and hierarchy.

Third, positioning and relating to black women as this image also has additional consequences in terms of accessing health and social welfare services. Health professionals who construct black women as the mammy position view these women as obedient, servile, docile and lacking in intelligence. This has had important implications for black women who internalise this image and may at a subconscious level self-identify in this way when dealing with medical professionals by, for example, never questioning or challenging doctors' prognoses about health conditions. Research evidence indicates that disproportionate numbers of black women are voluntarily agreeing to unnecessary medical procedure, with 40 per cent of black

Black Mammy *and Company* 105

women with fibroids offered hysterectomies as the first type of treatment. In the case of white, middle-class women, other treatments are routinely explored first, with hysterectomies only used as the last option (Pears 2011).

Black women who are highly educated and working in professional occupations are not protected from similarly being constructed and positioned as the 'mammy' figure in the workplace. There is a wealth of research highlighting the increasingly complex and subtle forms of discrimination experienced by these women in the workplace (Bhavnani 1994; Bhopal 2015). This evidence shows that they are less likely to have senior leadership and management roles, but even when they do, they are not perceived as 'true' or 'natural' leaders; and there is the assumption that their appointment is tokenistic, with someone else (typically white, male, middle class) holding the real string of power (Anderson 2013). In a neo-liberal economy that appears to reward and celebrate individualism and self-promotion, our racialised and gendered position makes us even more vulnerable in education and workplace settings. Our very blackness and hypervisibility means that we are always read as embodying and representing 'difference' and belonging to an ethnically/socially diverse group, in a way that is never applied to white women in similar settings (Ahmed 2007). Irrespective of our individual endeavours, black women's location at the intersection of race and gender means that we have awareness and understanding of racial solidarity bond and collective responsibilities to our race—represented in the form of mentor/role model as 'other' and 'community mothers' and a duty of care in our everyday interactions towards those occupying shared structural location and marginalised positions. White female professionals' assumed and unquestioned racial privilege can sometimes reveal itself in casual disregard for others and their needs, especially those working in lower service support and clerical posts. Oftentimes I have observed this causal disregard within the academy revealed in the daily, minutia aspects of working, such as completely ignoring or even acknowledging the (usually black female) cleaner who arrives into their office to tidy away their mess. As Black women we feel a connection to other Black women, recognising that we are bound by the same structural subordinate gendered racialised status, irrespective of any difference in employment status encountered in the workplace setting. Sometimes recognising the needs of others creates cost to ourselves. This is because by doing so black women get cast as the *Mammy* figure in the workplace, encumbered with the caregiver role. Again this can reveal itself in the daily minutia and interactions in the workplace with, for example, the taken-for-granted expectations placed on black female colleagues to be the primary persons to make the tea and coffee for the rest of the colleagues, to organise social gatherings and outings and to act as the 'agony aunts' to those colleagues wanting to discuss their problems. As a result of the caregiving role unquestionably placed on black women professionals in the workplace, many of them struggle to complete functions as a competent professional because they are being overburdened with

106 Tracey Reynolds

additional caregiving duties that are not demanded of other white female and male counterparts (West 2008). The mammy image assigned to black women also contributes to 'role strain' and higher incidence of ill health and mental ill health among black women, which results from balancing multiple roles (West 2008: 287). Of course, many women across ethnic groups face challenge of balancing multiple roles. However, this is enhanced for black women, because not only do their earn less and have lower job status than their white female counterparts, but they are also more likely to be the primary income providers and/or raising their families without economic security or partner support.

What has clearly emerged in my studies of black women is that we are not just passive victims merely accepting of these images but that we are active agents of resistance. We are resisting and subverting these dominant images first by calling attention to the way in which images endure and the negative consequences and social conditions they create for black women and second by challenging these dominant images through their own subjective interpretations of these.

If we again return to focus on the *Jezebel* image, the evidence suggests it shapes constructions of black women's sexuality, including the aesthetic value attached to societal definitions of beauty and concerns about physical features related to hair type, skin colour/complexion and body shape. The construction of black womanhood as ugly and white heterosexual womanhood as beautiful poses a direct threat to black women's self-esteem and positive body image, because they internalise these images, and their perception of beauty and body image become problematic (Weekes 1997). There is also a link between the internalisation of these negative stereotypes and chronic physical and mental ill health (West 2008). The *Jezebel* construct, and related notions of hypersexuality, sexual deviancy and sexual promiscuity, is used to ignore the continued sexual denigration of black women in music videos and to minimise sexual abuse, sexual violence and rape experienced by black women. Policymakers, the media and welfare practitioners also adopt this image to take a victim-blaming approach to the disproportionate increase of sexually transmitted infections and HIV/AIDS among black heterosexual women in Britain.

Yet Black feminist scholars are depicting an understanding of the various ways in which Black women are involved in processes and practices of renaming beauty to broaden and diversify definitions of beauty to encompass skin colour, hair types, body shapes, and they are engaged in creating a healthy sexuality in a society that depicts them as hypersexualised (Okolosie 2013). The dancehall queen, the modern equivalent of the *Jezebel*, provides an example of the way in which black women are subverting images through their own subjective interpretations. The dancehall queen is recast as a celebration of black female sexuality and represents a self-conscious female assertion of control over the representations of their identity (Noble 2000). The dancehall, which operates as a site where women get to perform and play out aspects of their sexuality not ordinarily available to them in the rigid social

Black Mammy *and Company* 107

conventions of the everyday, has its roots in Jamaican reggae culture and music folklore and is a 'liberating space' for black women and a 'paradoxical space' in which race and gender as a marker of sexual identity is allowed to be freely contested and subverted by black women (Cooper 2004: 12).

Black women's location at the intersection of race and gender provides an awareness and understanding of social and collective responsibility for mothering. As a result of this understanding, Black women are able to challenge and subvert the image of the dominating matriarch by showing how, for example, their mothering practices constitute an active engagement and political struggle against racism. In particular, and through the notion of 'community mothering' and 'other mothering', Black feminist scholars highlight how black and ethnicised women regard their parenting as extending beyond the domestic and individualised unit of the family households and individual mother-child relationships towards a more collective action in the public domain (Hill-Collins 1990; Reynolds 2005; Erel and Reynolds 2014).

Through my various studies focused on black women's experiences in Britain and the Caribbean, I have written extensively about community mothering in action—both in terms to the taken-for-granted cultural practices of grandparents and aunts parenting children in their mothers' absences (usually due to internal or outward migration) but also, in the UK context, in the form of black supplementary schools where black female teachers clearly identify their roles as community mothers, nourishing the desire for emancipation education that exists in black communities and ensuring the educational advancement of children attending their schools. However, I was again reminded of importance of 'community mothers' with a study involving women from the Latin American community in a London neighbourhood. These women established a volunteer to represent and advocate on behalf of parents within their community. Thus, for example, these women had the specific responsibility of making sense of bureaucratised and confusing structures of schools, acting as brokers and advocates between parents/teachers, interpreting from English to Spanish and also translating the white colonial heteronormative pedagogy which underpins the national school curriculum. My current project further extends the boundaries of 'community mothering', exploring how black and ethnicised women who are newly arrived migrants from Global South nations enact themselves as citizens. In doing so, these women are disrupting, challenging and potentially extending our understandings of rights and what constitutes citizenship. They are also challenging representations of Black women as 'outsiders' to the British nation-state.

CONCLUSION

The representation and objectification of black women as *Mammy, Matriarch, Welfare Mother* and *Jezebel* exists as a denigrating mythology about black women's sexuality that is mobilised to legitimise black women's

108 Tracey Reynolds

racialised and gendered 'otherness' and to justify their structurally subordinate location in Britain. These images remain embedded in black women's everyday lives, reaffirming their status as 'other' and 'outsider'. There is also evidence to suggest that these images continue to influence social policies and impede the way in which black women understand, articulate and express their sexual identities and relationships. In particular, I have highlighted the *Mammy* and the images of *Jezebel* to illustrate how these asexual and hypersexualised images, which act as the dominant construct of Black womanhood, continue to produce negative consequences for black women in the labour market. Perhaps even more cause for concern is the way these images determine black women's access to health and social welfare services, their treatment at the hands of health professionals and even the health outcomes for black women. Black women's sexuality interweaves with societal structure to determine self-identity. We witness examples of this in the way constructions of black womanhood as ugly and white heterosexual womanhood as beautiful pose a direct threat to black women's self-esteem and positive self-image, because they continue to internalise these negative stereotypes, which can then lead to chronic physical and mental ill health.

In the analysis I have shown how black women are not just passive compliant victims of these images, but they are also active agents of change. In their everyday lived experiences, these women are disrupting, contesting, resisting and subverting these understandings of black women's sexuality by reasserting their own subjective interpretations into the analysis. Central to this activity has been the work of Black feminist scholars, who are utilising Black feminist theorising as an analytical framework to address power relations and their intersecting systems, which normalise a hierarchy of privilege, and the social structural inequalities that result from intersections of race, class, gender and sexuality identities. Black feminism also provides an oppositional discourse within social theory for the purposes of political empowerment and social justice and allows for knowledge of black womanhood to be constructed that gives voice and puts Black women centre stage. Yet even within space, it is clear that certain narratives get brought to the fore —heterosexual motherhood and family are two such examples— whilst other narratives are silenced (for example, black women's expression of sexual desire and also suitably connecting experiences of heterosexual, LBT black women). These latter experiences and narratives of sexuality need to be brought to the fore if we are to challenge and change our notions of race, sexuality and gender in the cultural, political social spheres.

NOTES

    1 In the UK context, the terms 'Black' (upper case) and 'black' (lower case) have undergone considerable change and development since the 1950s. During the 1970s and 1980s, as a term, 'Black' represented an attempt to use this socio-political meaning to unite the victims of racism (whatever the specific

Black Mammy *and Company* 109

gradation of their skin colour or their geographical or ethnic origins) in opposition to its perpetuation and effects. Additionally, there has also been a desire from visible minority ethnic peoples to self-define themselves, including being defined as members of groups distinguished by ethnicity, nationality or religion. In recent years, 'Black' has been used less often in this all-encompassing sense, being replaced by such terms as 'Black and Asian', 'Black and ethnic minority', 'Black/minority ethnic'. Whilst the term is still used in its broad ideological, inclusive sense, for example, with the use of the term 'Black feminism', increasingly 'black' (lower case) is typically being applied to people and communities of African-Caribbean origin/descent. In accordance with this understanding within this article, I interchangeably switch between Black and black, depending on context. For instance, the term 'black womanhood' is used to denote black woman of African and Caribbean heritage or parentage. Whilst the term 'Black feminism' to reflect an ideological frameworks that examine Black women's lives and places gender and class at the centre of analysis.

2   The Global North–South divide is broadly considered a socio-economic and political divide. Generally, definitions of the Global North include North America, Western Europe and developed parts of East Asia. The Global South is made up of Africa, Latin America and developing Asia, including the Middle East.

3   For example, migrant mothers from the Global South and the former Eastern Europe. Migrants from this region are increasingly racialised as 'ethnic' or 'Other' as a result of stringent anti-immigration legislation and rhetoric in policy debates. Newly arrived migrants refers to the category of migrants who have moved to the UK within the past ten years.

4   Saartjie Baartman (more commonly known as Sarah or Sara Baartman) was born in 1789 in the Gamtoos Valley of South Africa. When she was barely in her 20s, an enterprising Scottish doctor named Alexander Dunlop sold her to London, accompanied by a showman named Hendrik Cesars. She spent four years in Britain being exhibited for her large buttocks. After her death in 1825, her body was dissected and then her remains displayed. For more than a century and a half, visitors to the Museum of Man in Paris could view her brain, skeleton and genitalia until she was buried. Since her rise to prominence, Baartman's body has been used to set a borderline between the 'abnormal' African woman and 'normal' Caucasian woman.

BIBLIOGRAPHY

Ahmed, S. (2007) 'The Language of Diversity', *Ethnic and Racial Studies* 30(20): 235–256.

Amos, V. and Parmar, P. (1984) 'Challenging Imperialist Feminism', Special issue on Black feminist perspectives *Feminist Review* 17:3–19.

Anderson, E. (2013) 'The Iconic Ghetto; A Reference Point for the New American', Unpublished keynote address, British Sociological Association Annual Conference, London, 4/4/2013.

Anthias, F. and Yuval-Davis, N. (1992) *Racialised Boundaries: Race, Gender, Colour and the Anti-Racist Struggle*. London: Routledge.

Bhavnani, R. (1994) *Black Women in the Labour Market*, London: Equal Opportunities Commission.

Bhopal, K. (2015) 'The Experiences of Black and Minority Ethnic Academics: Multiple Identities and Career Progression', in Alexander, C. and Arday, J. (eds.) *Aiming Higher Race, Inequality and Diversity in the Academy*. London: Runnymede Trust, 38–40.

Brah, A. and Phoenix, A. (2004). 'Ain't I a Woman? Revising Intersectionality', *Journal of International Women's Studies* 5(3):75–86.

110 Tracey Reynolds

Carby, H. (1982) 'White Woman Listen!: Black Feminism and the Boundaries of Sisterhood', in Centre for Contemporary Cultural Studies (eds.) *The Empire Strikes Back: Race and Racism in 70s Britain*. London: Routledge, 212–235.

Clarke, K. and Drinkwater, S. (2007) *Ethnic Minority in the Labour Market: Dynamics and Diversity*. York: Joseph Rowntree Foundation.

Cooper, C. (2004) *Sound Clash: Jamaican Dancehall Culture at Large*. Basingstoke: Palgrave.

Crenshaw, K. (1989) 'Demarginalising the Intersection of Race and Sex: A Black Feminist Critique of Antidiscrimination Doctrine, Feminist Theory and Antiracist Politics', *University of Chicago Legal Forum* 140: 138–167.

Crenshaw, K. (1991) 'Mapping the Margins: Intersectionality, Identity Politics, and Violence against Women of Color', *Stanford Law Review* 43(6): 1241–1299.

Crenshaw, K. (2014) 'Justice Rising: Moving Intersectionality in the Age of Post Everything'. Public Lecture at the London School of Economics, 24 March.

Dench, G. (1996) *The Place of Men in Changing Family Cultures*. London: Institute of Community Studies.

Erel, U. (2011) 'Reframing Migrant Mothers as Citizens', *Citizenship Studies* 15(6–7): 695–709.

Erel, U. (2015) 'Thinking Migrant Capitals Intersectionally: Using a Biographical Approach', in Ryan, L. Erel, U. and D'angelo, A. (eds.) *Migrant Capital: Network, Identities and Capitals*. London: Palgrave, 18–32.

Erel, U. and Reynolds, T. (2014) 'Black Feminist Theory for Participatory Theatre with Migrant Mothers', *Feminist Review* 108: 106–111.

Flannery, M. (2001) 'Quilting: A Feminist Metaphor for Scientific Inquiry', *Qualitative Enquiry* 17(5): 628–645.

Gillies, V. (2011) 'From Function to Competence: Engaging with the New Politics of Family', *Sociological Research Online* 16(4).

Griffin, C. (1996) 'Experiencing Power: Dimensions of Gender, Race and Class', in Charles, N. (ed.) *Practising Feminism: Identity, Difference and Power*. London: Routledge, 180–201.

Henderson, C. (2011) *Imaging the Black Female Body: Reconciling Image in Print and Visual Culture*. London: Palgrave.

Hill-Collins, P. (1991) *Black Feminist Thought: Knowledge, Consciousness and the Politics of Empowerment*. London: Routledge.

Hill-Collins, P. (1998) *Fighting Words: Black Women in the Search for Justice*. Minneapolis: Minnesota University Press.

Hill-Collins, P. (1991) *Black Feminist Thought: Knowledge, Consciousness and the Politics of Empowerment*. London: Routledge.

Hill-Collins, P. (2004) *Black Sexual Politics: African Americans, Gender and the New Politics of Racism*. New York: Harper Collins.

Hobson, J. (2002) *Venus in the Dark: Blackness and Beauty in Popular Culture*. New York: Routledge.

Jensen, T. and Tyler, I. (2012) 'Austerity-Parenting: New Economies of Parenting-Citizenship', *Studies in the Maternal* 4: 2.

Lewis, G. (2005) 'Welcome to the Margins: Diversity, Tolerance and Policies of Exclusion', *Ethnic and Racial Studies* 28(3): 536–558.

Ludvig, A. (2006) 'Differences between Women? Intersecting Voices in a Female Narrative', *European Journal of Women's Studies* 13: 187–192.

Mama, A. (1995) *Beyond the Mask: Race, Gender and Subjectivity*. London: Routledge.

Marshall, A. L. (2006) 'Jezebel, Soca and Dancehall Divas: the Impact of Images of Femininity upon Social Policies and Gender Relationships in the Carribean', paper presented at the SALISES 7th Annual Conference, Sherbourne Conference Centre, Barbados, 29–31 March 2006.

Maternity Action (2012) 'Maternity Action submission into the Enquiry into Women in the Workplace', December 2012.

Black Mammy *and Company* 111

McCall, L. (2005) 'The Complexity of Intersectionality', *Signs: Journal of Women and Culture* 30(3): 1771–1880.

McKittrick, K. (2006) *Demonic Grounds: Black Women and the Cartographies of Struggle*. Minneapolis: University of Minnesota Press.

Mirza, H. S. (ed.) (1997). *Black British Feminism: A Reader*. London: Routledge.

Mirza, H. S. (2009) Plotting a History: Black and Postcolonial Feminism in 'New Times', *Race Ethnicity and Education* 12(1): 1–10.

Noble, D. (2002) 'Ragga Music: Dis/Respecting Black Women and Dis/Reputable Sexualities', in Hesse, B. (ed.) *Unsettled Multiculturalisms*. London: Routledge, 148–169.

Okolosie, L. (2013) 'Feminisms Must Become Feminisms', *The Guardian*, 9 December 2013.

Parreñas, R. S. (2001) *Servants of Globalization. Women, Migration, and Domestic Work*. Stanford: Stanford University Press.

Parreñas, R. S. (2005) *Children of Global Migration: Transnational Families and Gendered Woes*. Stanford: Stanford University Press.

Pears, E. (2011) 'The Truth about Fibroids'. *The Voice,* 19 July 2011. Available at http://www.voice-online.co.uk/article/truth-about-fibroids, last accessed 30 September 2015.

Phoenix, A., and Pattynama, P. (2006) 'Intersectionality', *European Journal of Women's Studies* 13: 187–192.

Reynolds, T. (1997) '(Mis)Representing the Black (Super)Woman', in Mirza, H. (ed) *Black British Feminism: A Reader*. London: Routledge, 97–112.

Reynolds, T. (2001) 'Black Mothers, Paid Work and Identity', *Journal of Ethnic and Racial Studies* 24(6):1046–1064.

Reynolds, T. (2002) 'Re-thinking a Black Feminist Standpoint', *Journal of Ethnic and Racial Studies* 26(3):591–606.

Reynolds, T. (2003) 'Black to the Community: Black Community Parenting in Britain', *Journal of Community, Work and Family* 6(1):29–41.

Reynolds, T. (2005) *Caribbean Mothering: Identity and Experiences in the UK*. London: Tufnell Press.

Reynolds, T. (2008) 'Ties that Bind: Families, Social Capital and Second-Generation Return Migration'. Working Paper Series, no. 46, Sussex Centre for Migration Research, University of Sussex.

Reynolds, T. (2013) 'Youth Transitions and Wellbeing: The Impact of Austerity on Black Youths Living in Urban "Black Neighbourhoods"', in Helve, H. Evans, K. and Bynner, J. (eds.) *Youth, Work Transitions and Well-being*. London: Tufnell Press, 67–76.

Rose, T. (2004) *Longing to Tell: Black Women talk about Sexuality and Intimacy*. New York: Picador.

Runnymede (2011) *The Equality Deficit*. A day conference organised by the Trade Union Conference, November.

Thompkins, T. (2004) *The Real Black Lives of Strong Black Women: Transcending Myths, Reclaiming Joy*. Chicago: Agate.

Weekes, D. (1997) 'Shades of Blackness: Young Female Constructions of Beauty', in Mirza, H. S. (ed.) *Black British Feminism*. London: Routledge, 113–126.

West, C. M. (2008) 'Mammy, Jezebel, Sapphire, and their Homegirls: Developing an "Oppositional Gaze" Toward the Images of Black Women', in Chrisler, J. Golden, C. and Rozee, P. (eds.) *Lectures on the Psychology of Women*. New York: McGraw Hill, 287–299.

Wilkins, A. (2012) 'Becoming Black Women: Intimate Stories and Intersectional Identities', *Social Psychology Quarterly* 75(2): 173–196.

Yeandle, S., Steill, B. and Buckner, L. (2013) 'Ethnic Minority Women and Access to the Labour Market: A Synthesis Report'. Research Report. Sheffield, Sheffield Hallam University.

Zack, N. (2002) *Philosophy of Science and Race*. London: Routledge.

6 Activism through Identities
Building Shared Alliances against Homophobia and Racism in Palermo

Maria Livia Alga

Palermo, 14 July 2011. I'm driving Sandy home from the celebrations for Palermo's patron saint, *Santa Rosalia*. We waited for the fireworks until midnight, eating traditional street food—snails with garlic—near the waterfront. The crowds are gone now. Sandy lives in Palermo's periphery, where there is little public transport and having a car is almost a necessity. Her parents can't afford one, and usually nobody wants to drive her home, especially at night. But I feel like a big sister.

Riding on my Vespa, we start talking about an event we are organising at the Zabriskie Bar, a local gay-friendly venue, with a group of migrant lesbian friends from LGBT Network,[1] a local organisation. We want to serve traditional Malagasy food prepared by Sandy's mother, who is from Madagascar. "Does your mother know who she's preparing the food for?" I ask Sandy. "Of course she knows", is her reply, "actually she said she's only doing it for the cause, because she's ill and gets tired very easily". Her answer surprises me. I would never ask my mother to prepare her specialties for the LGBT movement knowing that she does not approve of homosexuality. So I ask Sandy whether her parents know she frequents LGBT venues. Half guessing my surprise, she continues:

> Of course they know! My folks are open-minded. They have a European mentality. They kill gay people in Madagascar. Our relatives there would never accept my choice. But those in Europe know that I'm a lesbian, and they're ok with it.

Sandy's mother left her country thirty years ago and has never returned. Even so, according to her she doesn't frequent the Malagasy community in Palermo because, in her opinion, the majority of its members would not approve of her daughter.

Our conversation has taken us from the city centre to the periphery. We've left the smell of the harbour and reached that of uncollected garbage. Cars have dangerously overtaken us along poorly lit, potholed roads, music blasting out of their stereos. When we reach her home, I hug Sandy and start following the road in the opposite direction. Now I'm headed

Activism through Identities   113

from the periphery to the centre, with its affluent residential and commercial districts. I've rented an apartment there for the duration of my fieldwork, even though my family is from Palermo. I notice that there are also heaps of garbage, potholes and cars driving dangerously in this well-to-do part of the city. And yet it's clearly not the same.

* * *

In 2011, I had many important conversations with Sandy along that stretch of road. After living for some time abroad, I came back to Palermo to study the antihomophobic and antiracist movements that developed in the city during the last decade. The study of social movements in the south of Italy is a relatively new field. For a long time, popular theories depicted the area as characterised by the weakness of collective mobilisation and a lack of solidarity and civil society associations or, to use Putnam's (1993) words, as 'uncivic'. According to Banfield (1958), who originally made this argument, the root cause of the area's underdevelopment was the absence of an autonomous public sphere and the privileging of familial and clientelistic affiliations. However, from the mid-1990s, a number of studies (e.g. Floridia and Ramella 1995; Trigilia 1995; Cersosismo and Donzelli 2000) have put forward a more complex interpretation of Southern Italian society, documenting the growth and diversity of cultural associations in the area as an indication of the emergence of new social bonds and the affirmation of citizenship rights. For example, LGBT Network, the local LGBT organisation I had contact with throughout my fieldwork, was founded in Palermo over 30 years ago. It is currently very prominent among local groups promoting human rights. My doctoral research explored new forms of solidarity within and across antihomophobic and antiracist movements in an effort to understand the cultural impact of these mobilisations on the local context.

The periodic rides I took with Sandy allowed me to reflect on the great difference that a few kilometres made, between the city's centre and its periphery. This journey took me from the centre (the Zabriskie Bar and my flat) to the periphery (Sandy's flat) and back. It outlined the everyday geographies of LGBT activists and networks but also their capacity to build links and alliances. This spatial gaze foregrounds the different political positionalities of two activists in Palermo's LGBT movement: I lived in the centre while Sandy lived in the periphery; she was a self-identified lesbian, while other LGBT friends identified me mostly as a heterosexual (I do not define myself as either heterosexual or homosexual). Most of all, we had a different perception of the place we lived in and of the broader context in which, and against which, we fought for our causes.

Born in Palermo to a Malagasy mother and a Ugandan father, Sandy felt that she lived in a 'European' context. In her opinion, Europe symbolised ideals of respect for diversity, tolerance and protection of sexual citizenship rights, which she contrasted strongly to a violent and homophobic Africa.

114 *Maria Livia Alga*

She thus established a dichotomy between those Africans who have adopted a culture that is respectful of diversity, having migrated to Europe, and those who have not embraced these values, having remained in their countries of origin. And yet leaving Africa was not enough to become 'Europeans'. In fact, in the eyes of Sandy and her mother, the Palermo Malagasy community was a menacing stronghold of homophobic culture.

Carnassale has argued that 'to lack a heteronormative sexuality complicates the relationships and loyalty toward the social networks of fellow nationals in the migrant scene' (2013: 83). Sandy's mother's rejection of her community of origin was thus a result of the interstitial positionality adopted by some second-generation lesbians and their families. Various studies have highlighted how LGBT migrants are often faced with an obligatory choice between seemingly mutually exclusive spaces and cultures: the culture of their country of arrival and its LGBT spaces on the one hand and that of their relatives and fellow nationals on the other (ARCI 2008; Lelleri and Pozzoli 2009; Ibry 2012; Carnassale 2013). Often the result is a trajectory of self-exclusion born out of the need to protect oneself. In Sandy's case, this choice was never a neat and definitive one. Indeed, I never witnessed this on the ground. The racism experienced by Sandy, the separation of communities and the lack of collaboration between them produced competing loyalties which were not necessarily irreconcilable. Sometimes, however, the sense of exclusion felt by second-generation migrant lesbians and their families led to binary discourses like Sandy's.

Still, her neat distinction between Europe (Italy, France and Holland, where she had relatives) and Africa (Madagascar and Uganda, where her parents were from) did not fit well with my perception of my hometown, as someone born in Palermo to Sicilian parents. My experience of the city has long since been one of living in a place characterised by a strong sense of homophobia and transphobia, both in institutional and sociocultural terms. Our encounter in a frontier city on the Southern European border, therefore, fragments the idea of a uniformly tolerant continent and raises the question of how our personal histories created differing perceptions of Palermo.

Another element shaped our perceptions: skin colour. The issue of racism in Sicily has had different interpretations. Some authors (e.g. Cole 1997, Cole and Booth 2007) have argued that Sicilians show little sign of racism, because they inhabit a poor region at the centre of the Mediterranean that has historically been characterised by out- and in-migration and cultural exchange. My experience (in the field and as someone born and raised in Sicily) also suggests that the Sicilian public broadly holds a similar view. More recent studies, however, have highlighted specific forms of racism based on class segregation, or the physical separation of different communities and their subordination to one another, rather than on competition for resources (Bartoli 2010). The relationship between Sandy and me, therefore, embodies the meeting of very different Sicilies and offers the possibility of reflecting on the role of activism in the reconfiguration of power and the social order.

Activism through Identities 115

This chapter is divided into three parts. In the first part, I discuss Italy's geopolitical position vis-à-vis the debate on European sexual democracies. Drawing on this debate, in the second part, I analyse various dis/articulations of national belonging and antiracist and LGBT issues. In the third part, I focus on one example of cross-movement coalition between antiracist and antihomophobic activists in Palermo. The chapter is based on fieldwork carried out in Palermo between September 2010 and December 2011. I collected data through a combination of intensive participant observation, action research,[2] informal and voice-recorded interviews. The analysis also uses textual materials that resulted from experimental practices of co- and autoethnography with informants, including their diaries, emails and (naturally occurring) conversations via social networks (Chang 2008; Coia and Taylor 2009; Esteban 2011). My positionality as a researcher was autoethnographic for two reasons: first, because, by conducting research in my hometown, I did 'anthropology at home' and second, because I am an activist in the antiracist and antihomophobic movements I studied. The ethnography thus partly includes autobiographic texts, my own and those of the people who took part in the research. I strive towards a collective narration in which I draw links between the biographies of the people represented in the ethnography and the broader social, geopolitical and historical context. This style of inquiry inevitably reconfigures the categories of subject and object, scientific and non-scientific, rational and emotional in the direction of an engaged feminist anthropology. (Haraway 1988; Chabram 1990; Esteban 2004)

SEXUAL DEMOCRACIES: BOUNDARIES, *CLANDESTINI*[3] AND A GHOST

Some authors (e.g. Fassin 2006; Sabsay 2012; Jaunait, Le Renard and Marteu 2013; Rebucini 2013) argue that a process of sexual democratisation is currently taking place in Europe. The expression 'sexual democracy' refers to the extension of sexual and reproductive rights that has followed the politicisation of questions of gender and sexuality. In particular, this has been prompted by public debates on the (lack of) legal recognition of LGBT couples and families. By using the term 'sexual democracy', Fassin seeks to highlight a change in the definition of the democratic regime, in which a new emphasis is placed on gender and sexuality as a matter of equality. 'The issue here is not that of equality between the races or the classes: republican equality has become equality between the sexes' (Fassin 2006: 127). However, after the 9/11 terrorist attacks, LGBT rights have been deployed as a rhetorical device and as a shorthand for 'European' values. They have been used by institutions, governments and some parts of the LGBT movement to dichotomise and create hierarchies within European society between 'us'—the cultures and states that recognise sexual equality and civil rights

116   *Maria Livia Alga*

for same-sex couples—and 'them'—those that do not. The idea that '[the] homosexual other is white, [while] the racial other is straight' (Puar 2008) demarcates a new space of 'Otherness' that has been created, paradoxically, by the inclusion of certain LGBT subjects in the body of the ('European') nation-state.

The securitisation of borders, both at the national and the European level, is now based on a neo-Orientalist construction of racialised sexualities that reinforces homonationalism and sexual-cultural imperialism. Nations such as Germany, France, Holland and the UK have begun to 'sexualise' their borders, putting in place administrative and juridical regulations inspired by the notion of sexual democracy. Official protocols aimed at policing borders and integrating racial minorities include, ever more frequently, tests to measure the applicant's level of sexism and homophobia, particularly for people of Islamic faith (Haritaworn, Tauquir and Erdem 2008). These institutional practices create a competition between the demands of the LGBT movement and the right to free movement.

However, the sexualisation of 'fortress Europe' should be understood as part of a wider strategy of warding off migrants and making them illegal. As one of Europe's southern borders, Italy plays a crucial role in regulating the arrival of migrants from all over Africa and the Middle East. In 2009 and 2010, the Italian government introduced two new sets of security measures that made it harder to obtain permits of temporary residence. These measures apply both to people from inside and outside the European Union (EU) and introduced the crime of illegal entrance and residence in the Italian territory. They also exacerbated the situation of undocumented migrants, increasing the period of detention in so-called centres of identification to 180 days and forbade migrants from sending money abroad without a permit. Since the introduction of these new measures, the Italian media have taken to using the term *clandestino* obsessively. The term literally means 'clandestine', and conflates all migrants (economic ones, refugees, over-stayers) into a single category that conveys a sense of hidden danger and lack of control.

Italy's geopolitical position is therefore peculiar. The country acts as a territorial border between Europe and Africa and the Middle East with respect to concerns surrounding 'race' and immigration. At the same time, it also represents a symbolic border with regards to sexual rights between western European democracies, and the countries of the Middle East and North Africa. For example, the World Rainbow Map, which charts LGBT rights globally (ILGA 2014), shows a clear divide between western Europe, and South-Eastern Europe and North Africa, with the former being full green (the colour of respect of human rights and equality) and the latter generally yellow or red (the colours of human rights violations and discrimination). The pale green assigned to Italy symbolises its status as a 'ghost sexual democracy',[4] in which LGBT citizens still suffer discrimination and a lack of legal recognition. In the following sections, I will discuss the political possibilities and alliances that Italy's borderline position as a 'ghost sexual

Activism through Identities 117

democracy' creates. In particular, I will show how racial and sexual politics can be jointly articulated and how the struggles of LGBT people and migrants, who live in a shared existential condition of *clandestinità*,[5] or illegality, may become visible in a 'ghost sexual democracy'.

L'ITALIA SONO ANCH'IO[6]: INCLUSION AND CONFLICT AT THE PERIPHERY OF ACTIVISM

Italy currently exhibits different ways of disarticulating antiracism and anti-homophobia. These struggles can be seen as two parallel and competing claims in latent conflict, or as two claims that cross over and support each other notwithstanding their differences. I will analyse first the case of competition: in particular, I examine the ways in which nationalism has become part of discourses on LGBT rights and what kind of tensions this creates with antiracist struggles.

Given Italy's lack of legal recognition of LGBT rights, homonationalism cannot emerge as a discourse that affirms the superiority of the Italian laws vis-à-vis the violent models of other cultures. Homonationalism is found instead in the demands for recognition of LGBT rights (De Vivo 2012). We can see this in the rhetoric of some politicians and social movements (including the LGBT movement), who rely on nationalism in order to promote sexual and gender equality. Nationalism was a recurrent theme, for example, in the 2011 LGBT campaigns to celebrate Italy's 150th anniversary. When the Europride march took place in Rome that year, its organisers created a series of posters showing a cockade with the colours of the Italian flag and the words: 'I am a gay Italian'. The slogan for the International Day against Homophobia was 'Italy is united against homophobia', and another slogan, 'Civilisation: a typical Italian product', appeared on posters that showed same-sex couples kissing in front of a table laid with typical Italian produce, such as Parmesan cheese, Parma ham and red wine.[7] According to De Vivo, these episodes reveal a cultural operation aimed at 'designing new boundaries, a new inside and outside in the popular imagination' (2012: 208). Their aim is to familiarise and domesticate the bodies of LGBT people by promoting an Italian, white, middle-class image that excludes other possible representations not compatible with eating pork and drinking alcohol.

Nationalist arguments in favour of the rights of LGBT people are being promoted not only by the LGBT movement but also by far-right groups. This is evident in a document issued by Casa Pound, a neo-fascist and xenophobic organisation with centres all over Italy, entitled 'Civil Partnerships: Rights and Obligations'. Casa Pound supports the introduction of civil partnerships for same-sex couples: 'Our idea of the state is organic, and thus inclusive, so we cannot tolerate that a considerable section of the population is forced to behave illegally' (Casa Pound 2013). Invoking equality with the rest of the Italian people is a rhetorical device that signals a demand

118 *Maria Livia Alga*

for rights based on nationalist-communitarian ideals. The legitimation of LGBT subjects takes place insofar as these subjects are citizens of the Italian state (Guazzo 2010: 18). Nevertheless, the organisation's support for LGBT rights is partial and opportunistic. Casa Pound, in fact, approves of civil partnerships yet disapproves of the rights of LGBT people to adopt children, maintaining that only one family model exists: the heterosexual nuclear family. At the same time, the group runs an insistent campaign against 'illegal' migrants and the *ius soli* principle, which would grant Italian citizenship to second-generation migrants.

In Puar's formulation (2007), the concept of homonationalism implies that antiracist and antihomophobic claims are in strong competition. Racist statements, or the invisibility of multicultural difference in the campaigns of the mainstream LGBT movement, highlight an aspect of this competition, which is also evident when we analyse antiracist campaigns. This shows that Italy is witnessing simultaneous yet parallel processes of national redefinition brought forward by sexual and ethnic minorities striving for equality and rights.

In 2011, a national campaign called 'I am also Italy' was launched. While this slogan recalled that of the 2011 Rome Europride, it had nothing to do with it. The campaign was promoted by an organisation of migrants and refugees born and/or raised in Italy, called the G2 Network.[8] Its aim was to collect signatures in favour of streamlining the process of granting Italian citizenship and guaranteeing the political participation of migrants through the right to vote. This initiative, while clearly worthwhile, made no mention of issues of gender and sexual orientation. Looking at the everyday politics of activist networks, however, we can see how we are often dealing with unspoken juxtapositions rather than parallel processes, which once voiced tend to generate conflicts.

In 2010, the local LGBT movement organised a sit-in in front of Palermo's prefecture to protest the temporary closure of the Zabriskie Bar, the reasons for which were unclear, and also to protest the latest homophobic comments made by the then prime minister Silvio Berlusconi. Around fifty people gathered around a loudspeaker and distributed leaflets that denounced the homophobic climate of the city and of the nation as a whole. When the sit-in was over, I went for dinner with some friends from the LGBT Network. On our way there, Ana told us about a new set of security measures that had just been approved by the Ministry of the Interior. The measures can be considered part of the drive towards the criminalisation of migrants, as they required both non-EU and EU migrants to demonstrate a series of prerequisites, such as a regular job, a certain level of income and type of accommodation, without which they would be expelled from the country. At a time of deep economic crisis, these criteria were almost impossible to meet, even for Italian citizens, who of course were not subjected to them.

Ana talked about these changes with indignation and anguish. A Romanian, she had lived in Palermo for fifteen years, initially as an undocumented

Activism through Identities 119

immigrant. After obtaining a permit, for years she had to reapply periodically for an extension; this requirement only ceased in 2007 when Romania joined the EU. Though in a better position than many other migrants, her livelihood was decidedly precarious. With the passing of the new law, then, her position was again being put in question. Tiziana, an Italian lesbian activist who was also with us, was surprised by Ana's comments, and asked her: 'So you think this law is wrong? It's meant to force employers to declare the illegal workers they employ. It's done in the workers' interests'.

Ana replied, annoyed: 'This law is just another way to justify the expelling of migrants'.

Oblivious to Ana's personal story, Tiziana went on:

> Personally, I don't want indiscriminate immigration, because I've fought for certain rights. I don't want to keep having to defend the freedoms we have acquired because, say, Muslim people threaten them. If you come to my country you have to respect my laws. I appreciate that there are different traditions that can enrich our lives, but can you tell me what's the positive contribution of *halal* meat, legalised rape, the *burqa* and the *niqab*? If we accept this, sooner or later we will lose fundamental rights like abortion and divorce.

At this point, Ana became visibly distressed and began to talk of leaving. Without specifying exactly what she meant, she said she had 'experienced it on my skin', adding, 'Even though I've been living here for fifteen years, I haven't forgotten my culture, and I don't want to forget it'.

This episode testifies to the lack of articulation between antihomophobic and antiracist issues. It tells of the missed opportunity to generate solidarities and shared protests out of recent events (the closure of a gay-friendly bar, Berlusconi's comments, and the new immigration law). Issues that have not been fully discussed emerge at the margins of the activist scene, creating conflicts and tensions which are never properly addressed. At the official level of press releases and public events, the Palermo LGBT movement supports and promotes the antiracist cause. However, at the level of everyday interaction, there is a lack of attention to issues around 'race' and migration and political will to articulate them. This causes 'race' to be conceived of as an abstract issue, or as a migrants' struggle, which can be supported without ever reflecting on the overall 'whiteness' of the LGBT movement. This problem is made worse by the relaxed stance towards racism held by Sicilians in general, as discussed earlier.

The conversation between Ana and Tiziana was ridden with incomprehension, underscoring the difficulty activists have in confronting each other on the themes of antiracism and sexual rights. While Ana expressed her preoccupation with how new migration policies may affect EU migrants such as her, Tiziana replied on a completely different topic with an Islamophobic argument against opening the borders to Muslim migrants.

120   Maria Livia Alga

Ana's sense of identification with all migrants (including non-EU and Muslim ones) could have been determined by the similarity between the Islamophobic stereotypes used by Tiziana and negative media portrayals of both Romani and Romanian people in Italy. Indeed, since 2007, after a number of cases of violence towards Italian women perpetrated by Romanian men, these men have been consistently been racialised on the basis of their hypersexuality (Bonfiglioli 2010). Crucially, Ana had experienced a similar form of stigma from lesbian women. As she once told me, 'I've often felt a wall in the LGBT community when I said I was Romanian. If I met a girl whom I thought I liked, as soon as I told her my nationality, I could feel the sense of detachment, the refusal of getting to know me'.

The previous examples show that the disjuncture between antiracist and antihomophobic struggles can lead to a perception of a 'false alternative', in the activists' imaginaries, between multiculturalism and sexual democracy (Fassin 2006: 255). To introduce an alternative model, therefore, which intersects antihomophobic and antiracist struggles, we may begin by asking ourselves what value perspectives such as Ana's can have within the LGBT movement. How can these conflicts be managed so that the issue of antiracism transforms the fight against homophobia? There is a need to explore how antiracist themes can become levers to build strategic alliances and points of contact between different groups.

Busarello (2011) argues that the silencing of the racial question within the LGBT movement in Italy, and the ensuing invisibility of non-heterosexual migrant subjectivities, create an important problem in the movement's capacity to build spaces of shared sociability and political action. He furthermore argues that one of the priorities of radical LGBT subjects should be to resist the instrumental use of feminist and LGBT issues for the purposes of state securitisation. The risk is that these issues may be hijacked by legislative initiatives, the true aim of which is not the protection of LGBT people and women but the consolidation of a white and heterosexual virility. In other words, Busarello recognises the importance of contrasting the tendency towards separating LGBT struggles from antiracist demands (Feinberg 2006).

Some activist groups have taken up this call to bridge antihomophobic and antiracist struggles by supporting LGBT asylum claimants through the legal process of applying for refugee status. There are now several lawyers and help centres in the country assisting migrants who apply for asylum on the basis of persecution in relation to sexual orientation or gender identity. These initiatives are undoubtedly of fundamental importance and often yield positive results. However, the issue of asylum can play into the hands of homonationalism. On its own, this kind of approach risks being based on a political strategy of sameness and on a demand for identity that privileges a different sexual orientation over racial difference. The danger is that by focusing on the integration of migrants in the Italian LGBT community, the legal system that regulates migration and asylum is not contested or challenged. Furthermore, immigration officers' decisions are often based

Activism through Identities   121

on stereotypes that force asylum seekers to construct pathological cases of 'exceptional suffering' (ARCI 2008; Ticktin 2011; Giametta, this volume).

From an LGBT perspective, a more radical political stance is that of 'contesting the devices that regulate access to citizenship', both for LGBT people and for migrants, together with 'the conditions for exclusion and inclusion, [and] the thresholds that allow recognition or generate stigma and possibly deportation' (Busarello 2011). Busarello further argues that 'these thresholds are obviously part of a system that is both heteronormative and ethnocentric, or at least propagates a national identity with Islamophobic and racist implications'. This stance involves no longer exclusively asking for citizenship rights and promoting instead more radical struggles that are better able to challenge state-imposed 'conditions of inclusion and exclusion' on a cultural level.

Mindful of new attempts to articulate pro-LGBT with antiracist struggles, in 2011, Ana, Sandy, myself and a group of others decided to build a cross-movement coalition called *La migration*, which I discuss in the following section. We came together following Audre Lorde's intuition that it is not difference that divides us but our failure to recognise, accept and celebrate difference:

> Being women together was not enough. We were different. Being gay-girls together was not enough. We were different. Being Black together was not enough. We were different. Being Black women together was not enough. We were different. Being Black dykes together was not enough. We were different. Each of us had our own needs and pursuits, and many different alliances.
>
> (Lorde 1986: 197)

E IU CA SUGNU BEDDA UN M'AIU AMMUCCIÀ[9]: CHALLENGING OUR CLANDESTINE CONDITION

Bystydzienski and Schacht (2001) have proposed a new analytical apparatus to capture the ways in which contemporary movements for social change are formed and act. They believe that the structural opportunities, leadership and ideological and organisational networks of resource mobilisation theory are now incapable of explaining how and why people act in solidarity with others. While these approaches were useful in understanding previous social movements, they become inadequate 'when trying to understand the formation of radical alliances whose goals often are in direct opposition to the mainstream conceptualisations of what is or should be a successful social movement' (Bystydzienski and Schacht 2001: 4).

The two authors focus on the politics of coalition or the dynamic and fluid alliances which under certain circumstances bring together different sorts of people who are capable of giving value to their difference not on the

122 *Maria Livia Alga*

basis of shared social identities but of shared values, principles and intentions. This shift occurs when activists are aware that their subjectivity is marked by multiplicity, contradiction and mutual conditioning rather than viewing their identities as fixed and immutable. Activists share an awareness that their relationships with other activists are situational and contextual (Barvosa-Carter 2001: 22–23). This awareness, together with Busarello's call to put social action in its political and cultural context, is key to understanding *La migration*'s role in giving voice to a group of women and its innovative spirit in the context of social activism in Palermo. The group grew out of the analysis of the particular circumstances that different social movements were going through in Palermo around 2009–2011.

At that time, the city witnessed strong antiracist protests against the systematic abuse of migrants (for example, abusive behaviour by the municipal police towards migrant street vendors, episodes of violence towards Nigerian prostitutes). Most important of all, however, was the extraordinary influx of migrants to the Sicilian island of Lampedusa, many of whom were fleeing war-torn Libya. On different occasions, antiracist activists were alerted to the fact that transsexual people from the Maghreb had arrived at border centres and that some gay men were applying for asylum on the grounds of sexual orientation. Crucially, at the same time Palermo's LGBT movement was renewing its activities after two decades of relative silence, organising various initiatives, including a yearly Pride parade attended by more than twenty thousand people. People like Ana, who were interested in both of these struggles, embodied the integration of struggles previously articulated separately. They became aware of the need to create a space of discussion among those who had strong links with the migrant community in Palermo, based on belonging, solidarity and collaboration, and to voice the experiences of people with non-heteronormative sexual practices and lifestyles.

La migration's first initiative was to make contact with the LGBT Network and a number of so-called cultural mediators,[10] who were invited to get involved regardless of their sexual orientation or gender identity. While it has been argued that the intervention of cultural mediators often risks reifying cultural difference and homogenising the experience of migration (Salih 2003), their participation in *La migration* demonstrated how at least some of them show a nuanced understanding of migrant cultures. This call for collaboration was not based on binary notions of identity (heterosexual vs. non-heterosexual, migrant vs. 'native'), and cooperation shows that the group situated its politics outside the confines of single issue identity politics. This political stance originated in a historicised and fluid understanding of difference. While the group recognised that migrant non-heterosexual people may experience multiple levels of discrimination, these were not simply viewed as 'adding up', in order to avoid pathologising supposedly marginalised subjectivities.

This is illustrated by a point made by Sandy during a meeting:

> I should be considered the weakest subject, the unluckiest of all, right? I'm lesbian, black, poor, *extracomunitaria*[11]. I'm an extra-terrestrial!

Activism through Identities 123

When you open a help centre you don't necessarily have to call the psychologist, the doctor and the lawyer.

Sandy summarised one of the key concerns of the group: question the categories we use to think about and nominate oppressions but also imagine new paths towards freedom. The group thus reflected on how to name subjectivities marked by multiple axes of difference in dynamic relation with each other, without becoming victims of normative (heteronormative, ethnocentric) understandings of 'difference'. The risk that Sandy referred to was that of positioning oneself through a pathologising demand for protection, a problem which remains only partially resolved.

While Sandy expressed a desire to free acts of resistance from the (implicitly normative) language of oppression, another member of *La migration*, a cultural mediator of Libyan origin called Yara, expressed a different yet complementary approach:

> *Extracomunitaria* isn't necessarily an insult for me. I consider it a strictly geographical definition. I think we have to embody change first of all in ourselves, even in the smallest things. So sometimes it's useful not to react immediately by thinking about the media reports, with all their racist stereotypes. We should pause and maybe teach a little geography. We should take back our lives with our own words. Of course, it's true that the word [*extracomunitaria*] is used negatively, but I use it to describe myself and react to all the racism I perceive around me, to mark my own difference.

Yara thus favoured the ironic appropriation of racist language, believing this can be empowering and subversive.

Discussing the epistemological and political use of the categories of sex and 'race', Elsa Dorlin (2005: 95) has warned that 'these permanent efforts at turning hurtful contents around, at taking back stigmatised identities, form part of struggles that are strictly determined by the material conditions of power relations'. She thus suggests that 'this subversive dimension is limited and could actually turn out to be threatening if it bypassed or avoided the strategies of the dominant rationality, by using new frameworks'. Yara's positive reappropriation of stigmatised identities would be ineffectual if it implied a narrow emphasis on a fixed identity. However, through this reappropriation, she strived to reconsider her activism and alliances. She believes that lived experiences of violence can become the basis to participate in struggles against forms of discrimination that one does not experience directly:

> The other mediators often ask me: 'Why do you go to the Pride if you're not lesbian?' I tell them: 'I'm black and *extracomunitaria*. You think I don't appreciate the right of people to be respected, to be recognised as human beings in their own lives?'

124   *Maria Livia Alga*

Yara's words were echoed by a Palermo-born lesbian activist:

> The point is to carry out a strong, extreme, but necessary political action, if the conditions require it. One's sexual orientation becomes a marginal aspect from this point of view. Participation is by its very nature inclusive. If you take part in something, you don't necessarily have to be represented, because you are there with all your specificities.

The idea of interconnecting struggles suggested by these words, however, cannot be reduced to fighting *for* someone else or to helping someone else's cause. *La migration* did not have a single cause; although we immediately linked up with lawyers who could help us with asylum requests, we were keen to take part in cultural and political initiatives, as well as providing legal support. The group brought together Italy-born activists with first and second-generation migrants, migrant mothers and lesbian daughters, migrant lesbian mothers, queer-identified individuals, migrant heterosexual women, cultural mediators, interpreters and educators.[12] At first glance, nothing made us similar to one another, not a single identity or a shared story.

Barta-Smith argues that 'solidarity based in a shared identity and interests is an abstract standpoint' (2001: 50). She thus proposes an organic solidarity that brings together perception and action and recognises a common embodiment. 'In perception the "origins" of action lie in presence, proximity and synchrony, not essence, distance and the chronology of a linear, operational paradigm' (Barta-Smith 2001: 54). We are dealing here with a model of coalition politics that is grounded 'not in effective action but affect—which does not mean less effective' (ibid.: 49). The people from *La migration* met on the basis of mutual recognition, friendship and proximity of a shared perception of violence, rage and marginalisation, of empathy and erotic attraction.

In the remainder of this section, I will discuss the practice of representing oneself as *clandestino* and of being represented as such by others. The adjective 'clandestine' has multiple meanings in Italian. It can indicate a migrant's undocumented or illegal status, as well as gay people's condition of 'being in the closet'. Both instances go beyond a lack of rights, implicating a wider condition of invisibility caused by constant stigmatisation. I will show how a cross-cutting political strategy that is not based on identity can unravel facile dichotomies and generate a transformation of the social context.

In 2011, during a football tournament organised as part of an antiracist festival, one of the banners of a mixed team of Italy-born and migrant women read: 'I am beautiful and I don't have to hide anymore. We are all clandestine!' This declaration was not simply a means of denouncing discrimination, but of sharing a condition in order to give new value to it. Corina and I had taken the first half of the team's slogan ('I am beautiful and I don't have to hide anymore') from a poster created for the 2011 Palermo

Activism through Identities 125

Pride parade.[13] The poster depicted a group of people sitting in a living room, which had been set up for the occasion in the middle of Palermo's main square. The aim of the slogan was to underline that LGBT people's lives have the same worth as everyone else's but that these lives are usually relegated to the private space of their homes. The core message of the campaign makes the presence of LGBT people publicly visible.

The banner had three meanings: worth (beauty), encouragement and (il) legality. However, the message aimed to subvert the usual interpretation of these meanings. Not hiding did not stem from legal recognition but from the need to show one's worth and that of one's relationships. Claiming to be clandestine was a way of communicating the revolutionary act of existing despite a complete lack of recognition. Corina, a Romanian, argued for the positive and empowering side of her 'clandestine' status. In her words:

> Being clandestine is by necessity a revolutionary condition. You become a revolutionary because the law itself forces you to break the law. What can you do? Stop living because you're an illegal immigrant? Stop working, stop leaving your home, stop eating? You're forced to live outside the rules. When I didn't have my permit, I never stayed hidden. And I don't hide my relationship with Manola, even though it's a clandestine one.

Here Corina compares migrants' 'clandestine' legal status to the invisibility of her lesbian relationship, which also enjoys no social or legal recognition.

Drawing on similar ideas, *La migration* reflected on the clandestine condition as a starting point to stop hiding and instead to meet and take care of each other in a political space. Working on the definition of *clandestinità*, the group realised the need for each activist to elaborate their positionality in terms of their own life histories. This work also allowed us to recognise the stereotypes we all held and to learn to see the context we lived in, in its true complexity. We agreed on the need to construct new representations in which the dichotomy between a 'European' sexual emancipation and the 'backwardness' of other cultures (especially African and Muslim ones) lost meaning.

The first outcome of this process was to bring into the open how the Italy-born activists in the group were not subject to violent immigration laws. The group discussed numerous examples of racism. Sandy, for example, recollected how 'after all these years people still call me "coloured" [*ragazza di colore*]. Coloured? What "colour"? When my sister was a child, they used to tell her she was the colour of shit'. What also became apparent was that Europe's alleged respect for diversity belonged more to the realm of desire than to the reality of migrants' experiences in Italy. Sandy and I eventually agreed that Italy and Europe cannot be triumphantly described as a place where rights and differences are universally respected, a point on which we had originally disagreed.

126 *Maria Livia Alga*

Openly discussing racist episodes helped us to understand our differences but also our shared positionalities, upon which we could build in the future. This led us to challenge the very notion of 'sexual democracy'. The respect and freedom that migrants like Sandy experienced were due to their particular life trajectories rather than to the values of their host country. They had managed to turn migration into an opportunity for both material and affective well-being. Sandy's mother did not respect her because they were in Europe but because she loved her, valued her choices and had built a relationship with her that was based on respect.

At the same time, it was undeniable that migrant women felt considerably less constrained than Italy-born ones in living their sexuality openly. They experienced their sexual orientation in a less oppressive way. In a mixed lesbian couple, the migrant woman felt more at ease with her family and the wider context than her Italy-born partner. Some migrant families, therefore, were seen as bearers of non-homophobic domestic models and became examples that other group members looked up to. For some of the Italian lesbian and queer activists in the group, me included, this kind of example helped to uncover the ignorance and racist stereotypes that made us think no non-white woman could live her non-heterosexual sexuality freely in Palermo. This was particularly important given Sicilians' self-representations as a less racist people than others. Still, the risk that many non-heterosexual migrant subjects face is of finding themselves marginalised within migrant and LGBT communities alike. As well as experiencing racism, non-heterosexual migrants often self-exclude from their fellow nationals. The gender awareness campaigns of the LGBT movement aimed at Palermo's citizenry and its migrant communities can support non-heterosexual migrants without them having to take on the burden of potential conflicts on their own.

This shared reflection on clandestine life revealed the complexity of the social context in which we fought our struggles. It revealed both the need to live in transcultural communities and to make alliances as a (pre)condition for effective political action.

CONCLUSIONS

Recently, the normative use of the concept of sexual democracy has revealed its limits in Europe, as the struggle for LGBT rights has acquired nationalist and racist undertones. In Italy there are currently two different models for the dis/articulation of antiracism and antihomophobia: a competitive one based on a nationalist paradigm and one that juxtaposes the two struggles, determining a false alternative between sexual democracy and multiculturalism. However, the fact that LGBT subjects and migrants share a clandestine condition, a lack of rights and experiences of discrimination, creates the possibility for a third model: mobilising towards cross-alliances. This

Activism through Identities 127

can take place through a simple form of support, with the LGBT movement endorsing the antiracist cause without problematising its whiteness. Alternatively, alliances can be built between the antihomophobic and antiracist struggles; instead of focusing exclusively on claims to formal rights, these alternative alliances emphasise the importance of building non-oppressive communities of solidarity.

The example of *La migration* shows how processes of authentic and complex social change can be initiated and how solidarity coalitions can be forged. Within *La migration*, three strategies were used to build radical alliances between migrant women and lesbian and queer ones. The first strategy was to find a category with multiple meanings through which all the women in the group could recognise (parts of) themselves, without minimising or denying privileges and power relations; this category was the condition of *clandestinità*. The second strategy involved creating a space in which to talk openly about the experiences of racism and the legal problems faced by the migrant women in the group. This was especially important in terms of questioning the dominant whiteness of LGBT spaces in Palermo. The third strategy was to frame the life experiences of group members within the specific historical and cultural context of Palermo, a Southern Italian city. This allowed the group to construct a different, more complex and meaningful narrative which challenged simplistic notions of sexual democracy. It was this narrative that made it possible to join forces on the ground and each fight for our own causes, but also for those of the others.

ACKNOWLEDGEMENTS

Special thanks go to Ana, Corina and all the other friends with whom in 2011 I shared the struggles and research that changed my life. I would also like to thank Giovanni Orlando for his comments on the draft and his irreplaceable presence. I dedicate this chapter to the memory of my grandmother, *Nonna*.

NOTES

1   The name is a pseudonym.
2   The term action research refers to a set of methodological tools that allow involving research participants from the initial design of the project, through data gathering and analysis, to the conclusions and actions arising out of the research (Foot White 1991).
3   Literally 'stowaways, clandestine people'.
4   This definition was used at the conference In and Out of Sexual Democracies, held in Rome in 2011 by *Facciamo Breccia*, an LGBT group that fights against the Vatican's intervention in Italian public life.
5   *Clandestinità* (literally, the condition of being clandestine) can be interpreted in a strictly legal manner, i.e. an undocumented, illegal or simply

128 *Maria Livia Alga*

unrecognised status, or in a more general one, i.e. a status that is negatively valued or considered unacceptable according to dominant social norms.

6 'I am also Italy'.

7 It should be noted that the use of signifiers of tradition in LGBT struggles does not necessarily express homonationalist values. Parts of the LGBT movement are seeking to rewrite certain regional traditions by subverting them in ironic ways.

8 In Italy, the offspring of migrant couples have the same legal status of their parents, regardless of the fact that they have been born in the country.

9 Sicilian for 'I am beautiful and I don't have to hide anymore'.

10 *Mediatori culturali* (cultural mediators) specialise in intercultural communication. They are often bilingual and their role is to facilitate migrant communities' participation in public life and access to services. Their task is to make social, educational and juridical services more attuned to cultural difference, translating across languages and cultures (Cima 2005). The role of cultural mediators as a professional role was formalised during the mid-1990s as Italy, traditionally a country of emigration, became an immigrant-receiving society.

11 *Extracomunitaria* literally refers to people from non-EU countries, but in practice it is used as a pejorative racialised term to refer to all non-white migrants from the Global South.

12 The age of participants ranged from 17 to 60. They were mostly people with precarious livelihoods (educators, caretakers, cleaners, cultural mediators, social workers, students). Apart from a few native Italians, the other members were from Africa (Eritrea, Uganda, Madagascar, Mauritius, Congo, Lybia, Tunisia) and Eastern Europe (Romania, Ukraine).

13 The campaign was designed by ideadestroyingmuros and laboucherie. It can be accessed via the following link: www.palermopride.it/2011/279. HTM# more-279.

BIBLIOGRAPHY

Arci. (2008) *IO. Immigrazione e Omosessualità, Ministero del Lavoro, della Salute e delle Politiche Sociali*. Available at http://www.arcigay.it/wp-content/uploads/2008-Immigrazione-IO-Broqure-ITA.pdf, last accessed 28 February 2014.

Banfield, E. (1958) *The Moral Basis of a Backward Society*. London: Free Press.

Barta-Smith, N. (2001) 'From Mere Solidarity to Mirror Solidarity: Building Alliances on Perceptual Ground', in Bystydzienski, J. and Schacht, S. (eds.) *Forging Radical Alliances across Difference* Oxford: Rowman & Littlefield, 49–62.

Bartoli, C. (2010) *Esilio/Asilo. Donne Migranti e Richiedenti Asilo in Sicilia*. Palermo: Due Punti.

Barvosa-Carter, E. (2001) 'Multiple Identity and Coalition Building: How Identity Differences within Us Enable Radical Alliances among Us', in Bystydzienski, J. and Schacht, S. (eds.) *Forging Radical Alliances across Difference*. Oxford: Rowman & Littlefield, 21–34.

Bystydzienski, J. and Schacht, S. (eds.) (2001) *Forging Radical Alliances Across Difference*. Oxford: Rowman & Littlefield.

Bonfiglioli, C. (2010) 'Intersections of Racism and Sexism in Contemporary Italy: A Critical Cartography of Recent Feminist Debates'. *Darkmatter*, 6. Available at http://www.darkmatter101.org/site/2010/10/10/intersections-of-racism-and-sexism-in-contemporary-italy-a-critical-cartography-of-recent-feminist-debates/, last accessed 28 February 2014.

Busarello, R. (2011) *In and Out Sexual Democracies*. Audio recording. Available at http://www.inventati.org/scarph/porcoiddio/sexdem/cittadinanza/introduzione.mp3.

Activism through Identities 129

Carnassale, D. (2013) 'La Diversità Imprevista. Negoziazioni della Maschilità, Fluttuazioni Identitarie e Traiettorie Alternative di Migranti Africani in Italia', *Mondi Migranti* 3: 67–94.

Casa Pound (2013) *Unioni Civili: Diritti e Doveri*. Available at http://www.casa pounditaliapadova.org/2013/02/05/93/, last accessed 28 February 2014.

Cersosismo, D. and Donzelli C. (2000) *Mezzo Giorno: Realtà, Rappresentazioni e Tendenze del Cambiamento Meridionale*. Roma: Donzelli Editore.

Chabram, A. (1990) 'Chicana/o Studies as Oppositional Ethonography', *Cultural studies* 4(3): 228–247.

Chang H. (2008) *Autoethonography as Method*. California: Left Coast press.

Cima, R. (2005) *Abitare le Diversità. Pratiche di Mediazione Culturale: un Percorso fra Territorio e Istituzioni*. Roma: Carocci Editore.

Coia, L. and Taylor, M. (2009) 'Co/Autoethnography: Exploring our Teaching Selves Collaboratively', in Tidwell, D., Heston, M. and Fitzgerald, L. (eds.) *Research Methods for the Self-study of Practice*. Dordrecht: Springer, 3–16.

Cole, J. (1997) *The New Racism in Europe: A Sicilian Ethnography*. Cambridge: University Press.

Cole, J. and Booth, S. (2007) *Dirty Work: Immigrats in Domestic Services, Agriculture and Prostitution in Sicily*. Plymouth: Lexington Books.

Cole, J. and Booth, S. (2007) *Dirty Work: Immigrants in Domestic Services, Agriculture and Prostitution in Sicily*. Plymouth: Lexington Books.

De Vivo, B. (2012) 'Omonazionalismo. Civiltà Prodotto Tipico Italiano?', in Marchetti, S., Mascat, J. and Perilli, V. (eds.) *Femministe a Parole. Grovigli da Districare*. Roma: Ediesse, 203–209.

Dorlin, E. (2005) 'De l'usage Épistémologique et Politique des Catégories de «Sexe» et de «Race» dans les Etudes sur le Genre', *Cahiers du Genre* 39: 83–105.

Esteban, M. L. (2004) *Antropología del Cuerpo. Género, Itinerarios Corporales, Identidad y Cambio*. Barcelona : Edicions Bellaterra.

Esteban, M. L. (2011) *Critica al Pensamiento Amoroso*. Madrid: Bellaterra.

Fassin, E. (2006) 'La Démocratie Sexuelle et le Conflit des Civilisations', *Multitudes* 3(26): 123–131.

Feinberg, L. (2006) 'Anti-Iran Protest Misdirects LGBT Struggle', *Workers World*. Available at http://www.workers.org/2006/us/anti-iran-0720/index.html, last accessed 28 February 2014.

Floridia, A. and Ramella, F. (1995) 'Fare Cultura in Città: le Associazioni di Firenze e Palermo a confronto', *Meridiana* 22/23: 155–184.

Foot White, W. (1991) *Participatory Action Research*. London: Sage Publications.

Guazzo, P. (2010) 'Casa Pound', *Quaderni Viola: Orgoglio e Pregiudizio* 3: 16–20.

Haraway, D. (1988) 'Situated Knowledge: The Science Question in Feminism and the Privilege of Partial Perspective', *Feminist Studies* 14(3): 575–599.

Haritaworn, J., Tauquir, T. and Erdem, E. (2008) 'Gay Imperialism. Gender and Sexuality Discourse in the «War on terror » ', in Kunstman, A. and Miyake, E. (eds.) *Out of Place. Interrogating Silence in Queerness/Raciality*. York: Raw Nerve Books, 9–33.

Ibry, H. (2012) *Donne Migranti tra Perù e Italia: Genere e Orientamento Sessuale nel Farsi dell'Esperienza*. Unpublished Ph.D. thesis, University of Verona.

ILGA (2014) *Lesbian and Gay Rights in the World*. Available at http://old.ilga. org/Statehomophobia/ILGA_Map_2014_ENG.pdf, last accessed 28 February 2014.

Jaunait, A., Le Renard, A. and Marteu, E. (2013) 'Nationalismes Sexuels?', *Raisons Politiques* 49: 5–23.

Lelleri, R. and Pozzoli, L. (2009) 'Essere Giovani Gay nella Migrazione. Evidenze e Considerazioni Iniziali', in Napolitano, E. M. and Visconti, L. M. (eds.) *Cross Generation Marketing*. Milano: Egea, 357–378.

Lorde, A. (1986) *Our Dead Behind Us*. New York: Norton.

130   *Maria Livia Alga*

Puar, J.K. (2007) *Terrorist Assemblages: Homonationalism in Queer Times.* Durham: Duke University Press.

Puar, J. K. (2008) 'Q&A with Jasbir Puar', *Darkmatter* 3. Available at http://www.darkmatter101.org/site/2008/05/02/qa-with-jasbir-puar/, last accessed 28 February 2014.

Putnam R. (1993) *Making Democracy Work: Civic Traditions in Modern Italy.* Princeton, NJ: Princeton University Press.

Rebucini, G. (2013) 'Homonationalisme et Impérialisme Sexuel: Politiques Néolibérales de l'Hégémonie', *Raisons Politiques* 49: 75–93.

Sabsay, L. (2012) 'The Emergence of the Other Sexual Citizen. Orientalism and the Modernisation of Sexuality', *Citizenship Studies* 16(5/6): 605–623.

Salih, R. (2003) *Gender in Transnationalism. Home, Longing and Belonging among Moroccan Migrant Women.* London: Routledge.

Trigilia, C. (1995) 'La Ricerca dell'Imes sull'Associazionismo Culturale nel Mezzogiorno', *Meridiana* 22/23: 97–120.

Ticktin, M. (2011) *Casualties of Care: Immigration and the Politics of Humanitarianism in France.* London: University of California Press.

7 What Does a 'Genuine Lesbian' Look Like?

Intersections of Sexuality and 'Race' in Manchester's Gay Village and in the UK Asylum System

Nina Held

INTRODUCTION

This chapter explores the 'racialisation of sexuality', whilst also acknowledging the intersections of sexuality and gender. The intersections of 'race' and sexuality are explored by using material from different projects: ethnographic research conducted in Manchester's Gay Village and examples from grassroots activism gathered through my involvement as a volunteer for the Lesbian Immigration Support Group (LISG) in Manchester. Since the late 1970s, black feminists have stressed the importance of acknowledging that different social identities intersect. In their 'Black Feminist Statement', first published in 1978, the Combahee River Collective, a Boston-based, black, lesbian feminist group, argued:

> The most general statement of our politics at the present time would be that we are actively committed to struggling against racial, sexual, heterosexual, and class oppression and see as our particular task the development of integrated analysis and practice based upon the fact that the major systems of oppression are interlocking.
>
> (1982: 13)

Intersectionality, a concept coined by American legal scholar Kimberlé Crenshaw (1989), has become a buzzword in feminist scholarship (see Davis 2008). In her work, Audre Lorde showed vividly how these intersecting forms of oppression work together and illustrated their psychological impact on black women (Lorde 1984a, 1984b; see also Nayak 2015). She also wrote about the damage that is caused by having to neglect and reconcile different parts of one's identity as a black lesbian. In *Zami*, for instance, Lorde (1984b) describes her difficulties when socialising in predominantly white lesbian environments in New York in the 1950s. Some authors have argued that the identity categories 'lesbian' and 'gay' are coded as white (Creet 1995; Fuller 1999). And indeed, to follow truly intersectional analysis, it seems that the category 'sexuality' itself needs to be interrogated to discover how it might be racialised.

132 *Nina Held*

Geographers of sexualities have researched the development of lesbian and gay spaces in urban areas, or 'gay villages', over the last thirty years. Within this literature, some authors have argued that these spaces produce normativities and exclusion, a certain form of *homonormativity*, a term coined by Lisa Duggan (2003), that is young, able-bodied, male, white and middle class (see, for instance, Bell and Binnie 2004; Casey 2004, 2007; Rooke 2007; Taylor 2008; Brown 2013). However, less attention has been given to how homonormative identities produced in the gay villages are racialised.

The first part of this chapter draws on ethnographic fieldwork conducted in 2006/2007 as part of my PhD research on 'Racialised Lesbian Spaces', which aimed to understand the relationship between sexuality, 'race' and space within the context of urban night-time leisure spaces for women (Held 2011). During the 12 months of fieldwork, I conducted participant observation, primarily in the Gay Village's two lesbian bars Jaguars and Milk,[1] and interviewed 19 women, most of whom regularly visited those spaces. The women who participated in my research variously identified as white (11), mixed-race (4), black (3) and East Asian (1). Most women identified as lesbian, except one woman who identified as bisexual. The participants' ages ranged from 19 to 61; seven women identified as working class, or having a working-class background, and eight as middle class; the remaining four women did not identify in terms of class. I met most of the women who participated in my research in the two lesbian bars. A few women were found through snowballing. In addition, I interviewed the organiser of Black Angel, a women's club night that usually attracts a more racially mixed clientele than any other women's night in Manchester. By drawing on this material, I explore how a certain 'somatic norm' (Puwar 2004) is produced in the Gay Village through representations/images, door policies and other racialising practices that determine which bodies are recognised as unproblematically 'lesbian'.

The second part of the chapter explores how assumptions about the 'genuine' lesbian body, which is produced on 'the scene', can also be found in a very different territory, namely in the asylum process, where women have to 'prove' that they are lesbian (or bisexual) when they claim asylum on grounds of sexuality. Here I draw on examples that have arisen through my work with LISG for which I have been a volunteer since 2009. LISG is a support group for bisexual and lesbian asylum seekers and refugees who come from countries such as Pakistan, Jamaica, Cameroon, Nigeria, Trinidad and Tobago, Afghanistan, Uganda, Saudi Arabia, Kenya and South Africa. The sensitivity of these cases and the need to protect the women's identities means that when I discuss decisions on their cases, I do not refer to the country of origin, nor provide any other details about the claimant. By focusing on issues around 'relocation' and 'credibility', I show that for asylum claims to be successful, the claimant must conform to homonormative notions that are racialised and constructed around a Western model of sexuality that is 'out and proud'.

What Does a 'Genuine Lesbian' Look Like? 133

BEING A 'GENUINE LESBIAN' IN THE GAY VILLAGE

Manchester's Gay Village is one of the most popular sexualised spaces in the UK and was featured in the popular Channel 4 series, *Queer as Folk* (and more recently in *Cucumber* [Channel 4] and *Banana* [E 4]). It consists of more than 50 venues, including bars and clubs, a sex shop, a sauna, a hairdresser and several takeaways. Since 1991, the area around Canal Street is officially recognised as 'gay space' and marked as Gay Village on city maps. The Gay Village thus plays an important role in Manchester's night-time leisure economy. In contrast to other spaces, which are unmarked yet still implicitly (hetero)sexualised, the Gay Village is purposefully constituted as a sexualised space.

Geographers of sexualities in the UK have shown since the 1990s that sexuality and space are interconnected. Lesbian and gay or queer geography look at 'the ways in which space is sexed and sex is spaced, or in other words, the ways in which the spatial and the sexual constitute each other' (Taylor 1997: 3). A focus of the sexual geography literature has been on the development of lesbian and gay spaces in urban areas. As Michael Brown (2013: 1) argues, 'the gayborhood has become a touchstone of sexuality and space studies'. In this literature, especially over the last decade, sexual geographers have shown that within these spaces, exclusions are produced on grounds of identifiers other than sexuality. In that respect, it has been argued that homonormative lesbian and gay identities are constructed in gay villages (see Bell and Binnie 2004; Casey 2004, 2007; Rooke 2007; Taylor 2008; Brown 2013).

However, whilst in this respect, sexuality, gender (appearance), age, class and able-bodiedness have been researched as markers of inclusion and exclusion (see, for instance, Casey 2004, 2007; Cefai 2004; Rooke 2007; McLean 2008; Taylor 2008), 'race' and the racialisation of lesbian and gay spaces in the UK have only been marginally explored. The existing studies in the UK have mainly been conducted in London (Mason-John and Khambatta 1993; GALOP 2001; Kawale 2003, 2004). Research that has been conducted in Manchester's Gay Village (Hindle 1994; Whittle 1994; Quilley 1997; Pritchard et al. 2002; Binnie and Skeggs 2004; Skeggs et al. 2004) has not investigated the importance of 'race' in structuring these spaces, although this has been shown in studies conducted elsewhere (Mason-John and Khambatta 1993; GALOP 2001; Kawale 2003, 2004; Nero 2005; Caluya 2008).

This chapter aims to contribute to the geographies of sexualities literature but also to research that explores the relationship between 'race' and space in the way that space is racialised and 'race' is spatialised (see Knowles 2003; Puwar 2004; Sullivan 2006). As critical 'race' theorists have shown, 'race' is a historical and social construct, but it is also a social practice; it is in process and continuously in the making through everyday interactions (see, for instance, Ahmed 1997; Byrne 2006; Lewis 2007). The connection

134 Nina Held

between 'race' and space is not always apparent and becomes most recognisable when a particular racialisation of space is disrupted, such as when racialised bodies are 'out of place' in certain spaces (Puwar 2004; Sullivan 2006). In her book *Space Invaders*, Nirmal Puwar (2004: 8) argues that in certain spaces:

> Some bodies are deemed as having the right to belong, while others are marked out as trespassers, who are, in accordance with how both spaces and bodies are imagined (politically, historically and conceptually), circumscribed as being "out of place". Not being the somatic norm, they are space invaders.

In the Gay Village, some bodies are perceived and constructed as the 'somatic norm' whilst others are (made) 'out of place'. This norm is produced through representations, door policies and other spatial practices described in the following section.

A Lesbian Image

Most of the participants of my study talked about a certain lesbian image that exists in the Gay Village, especially in the two lesbian bars Jaguars and Milk. For instance, when I asked Joanne (mixed-race, British, 29) if she thinks something like 'lesbian knowledge' or 'lesbian culture' exists, she replied:

> Lesbian knowledge or lesbian culture? Yeah of course. Go to Milk [laughs], yeah there's definitely lesbian knowledge and culture, stuff I didn't know, I had to learn about, yeah [laughs]. I still don't know about, flipping hell. [. . .] I can't identify it, but there is a lesbian culture in terms of, like, Milk, where you've got butch lesbians, lipstick lesbians, you know what I mean, ehm, a certain look, an attitude, a way to speak, actions, mannerism, and things like that . . ., ehm . . . [. . .] Everybody has a Tony and Guy haircut, with the gel and the flip on it and they've got their boxer shorts, their Calvin Klein boxer shorts, showing over their jeans and stuff, a few tattoos, some piercings.

Joanne experiences the Gay Village as a white space. In defining Milk as an example of lesbian culture, Joanne includes dress, hairstyles and a general 'habitus' in her description. Her portrayal seems to reflect what Alison Rooke (2007) calls 'lesbian habitus'. Rooke argues that a sense of belonging in lesbian spaces is only achievable if the 'lesbian habitus' is successfully generated through specific ways of walking, holding a drink, expressing and talking about sexuality and wearing hair, clothes and accessories. Some participants of my research argued that many women adopt or copy a certain style in order to be part of 'the scene'. For instance, Lesley (mixed-race,

British, 30) said that 'there's something that's comfy' about putting a certain lesbian image on, which she described as jeans, a vest and trendy hair. The comfort, she said, is produced through being desirable and would be an image that women fancy, 'what they like to look at'. In order to be desirable, Tania (mixed-race/black, Southern European, 29), changed her style entirely. She told me that when she first went to the Gay Village, she was 'a total hippie', she was wearing 'hippie flair trouser' and had 'a bit of a like a hippie hair, bit of a dreads, on the side and I was wearing hippie clothes, you know a jumper, and stuff like that'. She felt that she was not 'welcomed' in Milk but that the women in there were staring at her at first when she came in but then ignored her. It made her so uncomfortable that she decided to change her style so that she looked more like them to be accepted. Alice (white, Central European, 31) argued that because of the homophobia many women experience outside of lesbian spaces, 'you make more effort to adapt yourself to the gay scene and to become one of them because that's where you feel comfortable and that's where you want to be part of' (see Held 2015).

What the dominant somatic norm in lesbian and gay spaces is becomes also apparent through imagery that is displayed in magazines and flyers displayed in venues across the Gay Village. The organiser of Black Angel, a women's night held at different venues in Manchester, told me that one of her motivations for starting the club night was that when she was growing up she never saw any images of black gay people:

> And then once I came out and I go around the village, all the imagery was of white men . . ., predominantly, there would be white women, but it would be predominantly white men, so there's never anything that I could identify with and the music they played, it wasn't, you know, it's not what I [like] . . .

She stressed two important issues to create a more inclusive space: the imagery and the music. According to her, Black Angel was the first event in the Gay Village that played R&B and Bhangra music. She told me that when she and the co-organiser of Black Angel started the club night (more than ten years ago), they did not want the flyers to specifically say that the event was for black and Asian women, because then other people would feel excluded. Instead, they decided to use the name in combination with the imagery to indicate that the club night was addressed to black and Asian women:

> Well, I tell you what's really interesting. It's like if you look at flyers and they have a white person on it, I don't look at that flyer and think I can't go to their nights, whereas we get white people and they see the flyer and they have black and Asian women on them and they're "alright, we didn't think we could come". It's interesting how people's minds work.

136   Nina Held

They don't see the reverse and think about the imagery they're putting on, then what that says to people and they don't realize how important imagery is.

Although the imagery has arguably changed slightly over the last years, it is still predominantly white. As Rani Kawale (2003: 183) argues, '[a] group or commercial venue does not need to specify that "white" people are welcome: this is assumed because the term "lesbian" is racialised and usually refers to "white" lesbians'. Conversely, events like Black Angel are imagined to be (solely) for black lesbians.

Exclusionary Door Policies

VIGNETTE 1

It was very busy in Jaguars. We were on the dance floor. When I looked at my mobile phone, I saw that Qooz had tried to call me and had also sent me a text message saying, 'They won't let us in. Please come out to get us'. Wondering how I could help them to come in, I went to the entrance. I was still inside, Qooz and Juan were standing outside and the door man represented a border between us. Qooz told me that he did not believe that she and Juan were not a heterosexual couple. I tried to negotiate and told him that we were all 'regulars'. But he misused his power by telling them that they should come back later, when it would not be as busy, and that he might let them in then. My stomach hurt when I saw Qooz begging him to let them in later. Standing there, *inside*, I had the strange feeling that my body had more right to be in that space than theirs.

The few studies that illustrate the racialisation of (white) lesbian and gay spaces in the UK highlight door policies as one of the racist practices experienced by black and Asian LGBT people (Mason-John and Khambatta 1993; GALOP 2001; Kawale 2003, 2004). Whilst during my research, I never witnessed any of my white participants or friends being turned away at the door of a bar in the Gay Village, I heard of and observed various incidents where black and Asian women and men had difficulties in accessing these bars. Most bars and clubs in Manchester's city centre have bouncers at the door, especially on Friday and Saturday nights, so this practice is not specific to the venues in the Gay Village. The Gay Village, however, is a space created for a marginalised group and therefore the boundaries of these spaces seem to require protection. Heterosexuals are often perceived as a threat in lesbian and gay spaces (see Skeggs 1999; Pritchard et al. 2002; Skeggs et al. 2004; Casey 2004, 2007) and therefore, in contrast to those other spaces, bouncers in the Gay Village might specifically look for people they perceive to be heterosexual and not let them in. But how do they 'judge'

What Does a 'Genuine Lesbian' Look Like?   137

whether someone is gay (or bisexual) or not? In the example presented earlier, the bouncer's perceptions were wrong when he decided that Qooz, an East Asian lesbian and Juan, a Latin American gay man, were a heterosexual couple. Unlike them, that night, as well as on any other, I had no difficulties gaining access to the bars and clubs of the Gay Village. I seemed to be easily recognisable as a lesbian, being a white woman with short hair, usually wearing jeans and T-shirt/shirt when going out and having adapted a 'lesbian habitus' (Rooke 2007). I seemed to have a more legitimate claim on lesbian space.

Whilst it is often not easy for *one* black or Asian person to access a gay venue, gaining access seems to be even more difficult when coming in a *group*. Joanne facilitates a black LGBT support group at a local charity. She told me that her group members had reported difficulties in getting into lesbian and gay venues in the Gay Village when coming in a group of more than three or four. The organiser of Black Angel said that she thinks one of the reasons is that some of the club managers are racially prejudiced, and when they see 'more than two black people [together] in the place they think it's a gang and [that] there's gonna be trouble'. One night, after their monthly meeting, Joanne and members of the black LGBT group joined me in a bar on Canal Street where I was sitting with a group of friends and participants. I was the only white woman in the group. It was a warm evening and we were sitting on the bar's balcony, talking and laughing. Suddenly the bar's bouncer came out and told us, in a quite aggressive manner, that we should be quieter. Our racialised group, or members of it, was somehow perceived as 'loud'. We disturbed the place not only visually but also aurally. Joanne then told us that the bouncer had been reluctant to let them in to begin with. It is quite disturbing that a LGBT support group, which is part of the biggest lesbian and gay organisation in the Northwest of England, where they had just been to their monthly meeting, had almost been refused permission to enter a space that has been purposefully created for LGBT people. Inside those spaces, however, there are other practices at work that make some bodies 'out of place' and establish white bodies as the somatic norm.

'Looking' and Other Racialising Practices

In Jaguars and Milk, looking is a key spatial practice. It is a form of addressing someone and is often used as a first step in a flirtatious encounter in the hope that the other woman looks back. Studies on sexuality and space have shown how 'looking' practices contribute to the sexualisation of bodies and spaces (Munt 1995; Valentine 1995; Rooke 2007). Whilst most of these studies have focused on the heteronormative gaze or the pleasurable look constructing lesbian identities, 'the look' described by some of my participants is quite different.[2] All of the black participants of my study gave accounts of receiving certain looks in Jaguars and Milk, which they defined as forms of racism experienced in those spaces.

138   *Nina Held*

For Joanne, 'the look' signals dislike, even hate and disgust. She said that 'sometimes it's just the way that someone looks at you and you can tell by the way that they look at you that they are racist. They look at you like an insect that wants to be squashed'. Echoing Frantz Fanon (1967) and Lorde (1984a), Joanne's metaphor suggests the black body is seen as non-human by the white looker (Lorde uses the analogy of a cockroach). Natasha (32, British, black) received 'the look' by a white woman during her first and only visit to Jaguars. She described it as a 'piercing' look, as a 'what are you doing here?' look. It was not just a matter of looking at her but that it 'felt as though [the woman] was trying to tell me something with that look, which felt like she was questioning my presence in the room'. Hope (42, British, black) described the forms of racism she experiences in the Gay Village as more subtle. It was not blatantly spelled out, she told me, 'but it will be a look or there'd be somebody make an offhand remark and I probably never heard it but somebody else has heard it'. One night when we were in Jaguars together she asked me why they all (the white clientele) look at her when she comes in as if they had never seen a black woman before. 'What are their *fears*?' she asked. During the interview, conducted a few months after that night in Jaguars, I asked her to explain 'the look' further. She said, 'I don't know people's perception of black people. They find us intimidating, sometimes threatening [. . .] I think they're just scared of the unknown, that's what it is, they're just scared.' Hope speaks powerfully of the relationship between 'the look' and what Bridget Byrne (2006) has called 'perceptual practices'. Byrne argues that 'race' is discursively produced through the repetitive use of perceptual practices, through ways of seeing difference; that is, how we see or do not see 'race' actually produces what we think we see (here the 'threatening black body').

In my study, these perceptual practices did not only become apparent through 'the look'. There were other racialising practices, such as comments and assumptions being made about 'ethnic others' or defining sexual attractiveness in terms of 'race' (e.g. 'black women are/are not my type') (see also Mason-John and Khambatta 1993; GALOP 2001; Kawale 2003, 2004; Caluya 2008). One of the racialising practices that were described by black women was white women wanting to touch black women's hair. As a racial signifier, hair has been historically inscribed with social and symbolic meaning. In the era of scientific racism and colonialism, hairstyle was used as a signifier of European superiority and African inferiority, constructing whiteness as the measure of beauty (see also chapters by Robinson and Reynolds in this volume). As Kobena Mercer (1994: 101) argues, 'black people's hair has been historically *devalued* as the most visible stigmata of blackness, second only to skin'. The desire to touch hair carries an element of exotification.

These examples indicate that the lesbian norm that is constructed and confirmed in the Gay Village through representations, door policies and other spatial practices is centred on a white lesbian image and body.

What Does a 'Genuine Lesbian' Look Like? 139

BEING A 'GENUINE LESBIAN' IN THE ASYLUM SYSTEM

VIGNETTE 2

I go outside for my lunch break and check my phone—one missed call, I don't recognise the number. The caller left a message on my voicemail. I listen to it. It's a female voice. She says that her name is Hope and that she wants to join the Lesbian Immigration Support Group (LISG). She asks me to please call her back. When I get home in the evening, I give her a ring. We introduce ourselves, she sounds distressed. She tells me that she does not live in Manchester but in Sheffield and that there is no group for lesbian asylum seekers in Sheffield. After just a short moment of conversation she says, 'Can you explain something to me? They [Home Office officials] say that they don't believe that I am a *genuine lesbian*, what does that mean? I don't understand. How should I prove it?'

Hope comes from one of the 78 countries (which makes 40 per cent of all countries in the world) where legislation is in place that criminalises same-sex consensual acts between adults.[3] In some of these countries, these acts are even punishable by death. If Hope is not able to 'prove' to Home Office officials and the courts that she is a 'genuine' lesbian, then it will be seen as 'safe' to remove her from the UK.

Article 1A(2) of the 1951 Geneva Convention Relating to the Status of Refugees defines a refugee as a person who

> owing to well-founded fear of being persecuted for reasons of race, religion, nationality, *membership of a particular social group* or political opinion, is outside the country of his nationality and is unable or, owing to such fear, unwilling to avail himself of the protection of that country.[4]

All asylum claimants need to prove that they have a well-founded fear of being persecuted for a Convention reason and that the state is unable or unwilling to protect them. Asylum claimants need to provide evidence of political activity, for instance, ethnicity and so on, and in lesbian and gay asylum claims, evidence of persecution or fear of persecution because of sexuality. The existence of laws that criminalise same-sex consensual acts between adults itself is not enough for asylums claims to be successful. It is only since 1999 that gender and sexual identity are recognised as a ground to claim asylum in the UK, since then it has been accepted that women and lesbians and gay men can form a 'particular social group' (Shah and Islam vs. SSHD).

For an asylum claim based on sexuality to be successful, the asylum seeker has to prove that he/she is lesbian or gay and needs to show a well-founded fear of persecution. This seems to be difficult, as the low percentage of

140 Nina Held

accepted lesbian and gay asylum claims indicates. A report from 2010 by the UK Lesbian and Gay Immigration Group (UKLGIG) based in London suggested that whilst on average between 60 and 70 per cent of all initial asylum claims are refused by the Home Office, with regard to claims based on sexuality, it is 98 per cent (UKLGIG 2010). Since this first report was published, there have been some positive changes in UK asylum law, in particular through a ruling by the Supreme Court which has affected how decisions on asylum claims based on sexuality are made, as indicated by a seconded report by UKLGIG (2013). However, especially issues around relocation and credibility still seem to be problematic.

Relocation and 'Being Out'

Before July 2010, based on case law, lesbian and gay asylum seekers could be returned to their countries of origin if 'safely' relocated to an area where their sexuality was not known. The assumption was that they would be safe as long as they lived discreetly: the case law implied that they can be reasonably expected to be 'discreet' about their sexuality in order to avoid persecution. In their 2010 report, UKLGIG identified that in 68 per cent of the cases they looked at, case workers cited the ability to relocate as the basis of refusal of the claim and often argued that the situation of LGBT people is not 'that bad'. In these cases, Home Office officials often relied on outdated or ill-informed sources such as the *Spartacus Guide* or *Gay Times*, magazines that are designed for the white, middle-class, Western gay traveller and describe the situation of LGBT people in different countries, including information about gay venues (if there are any). In some of the decisions of asylum claims from LISG women, these magazines were used as resources for country evidence by Home Office officials and in the courts (in one case even by a High Court judge). In other cases it was argued that the country of origin is large and therefore women would be able to relocate to a different part where nobody knows about their sexuality.

In one case of a LISG member who comes from a small African country where homosexuality is illegal and punishable by death, the Home Office used the relocation argument stating that only people from her village would know that she is a lesbian but that her country of origin has a population of *1.7 million* people and that 'it is therefore considered that the country is large enough for you to relocate to another area'. When she appealed against the decision, in the appeal hearing in January 2010, the immigration judge agreed with the Home Office and argued that she could move to an alternative area:

> It is considered that in this alternative area you could commence and develop future relationships with women in a discrete manner which would not bring you to the attention of either the general public or the police. It is concluded that expecting you to continue any future

What Does a 'Genuine Lesbian' Look Like? 141

relationships with women in a discreet manner would not place you in a situation of persecution.

(IJ, First-tier tribunal, January 2010)

As Toni Johnson (2011: 61) writes, with such decisions, the UK courts 'were effectively perpetuating the silencing of sexuality in the home state' and forcing people back into the closet. Moreover, this often meant forcing women into heterosexual relationships.

On 7 July 2010, the case law on which such decisions were based (HJ Iran 2009) and another case law (HT Cameroon) were challenged by the UK Supreme Court. The five judges who looked at these two case laws decided that the test used in them was incompatible with the purposes of the Refugee Convention. In his decision, one of the Supreme Court judges, Lord Hope, argued:

> The group [particular social group] is defined by the immutable characteristic of its members' sexual orientation or sexuality. This is a characteristic that may be revealed, to a greater or lesser degree, by the way the members of this group behave. In that sense, because it manifests itself in behaviour, it is less immediately visible than a person's race. But, unlike a person's religion or political opinion, it is incapable of being changed. To pretend that it does not exist, or that the behaviour by which it manifests itself can be suppressed, is to deny the members of this group their fundamental right to be what they are—of the right to do simple, everyday things with others of the same orientation such as living or spending time together or expressing their affection for each other in public.
>
> (HJ (Iran) and HT (Cameroon) vs. Secretary of State for the Home Department [2010] UKSC 31)

The Supreme Court decision has had an impact on the ways in which decisions on asylum claims based on sexuality are made. Because of this judgement, it is now much more difficult for Home Office officials and judges to argue that claimants can go back and live their sexuality in secret, without openly claiming a sexual identity, as it had been argued in the earlier example. However, as Janna Weßels (2013) points out, the new test that is proposed to be followed by tribunals in order to establish whether a claimant lives in fear is problematic. This test asks to first establish that the claimant is gay (or would be treated as gay) and whether gay people who lived openly in the claimant's country of origin would be likely to be persecuted. The test then requires identifying how openly the claimant would live his or her sexuality if returned. If he or she lived his or her sexuality openly, the fear of persecution would be well-founded. If he or she did not live his or her sexuality openly, then the tribunal would need to ask why they would live their sexuality discreetly. Here the test then distinguishes between those

142   *Nina Held*

who would be discreet because they chose to do so, or because of social pressures (family, friends), and those who would live discreetly because of the fear of persecution (Weßels 2013).

I want to illustrate this with an example, a LISG case that was heard in court in June 2011. In their decision, the tribunal made the following findings:

> The appellant has since been dispersed by NASS to Wigan. She does not feel at risk there or indeed anywhere in the United Kingdom, because there is legal and police support here. She finds it rather dull and tends to meet her girlfriend in London rather than Wigan, where they go to bars, out to dinner, and dancing together and with other friends. She stays in with her girlfriend too, just watching television and being *normal*. She meets their families and has no difficulty being accepted for who she is.
>
> (IJ, Upper Tribunal, June 2011)

The tribunal did not question the fact that the appellant was a lesbian. It did, however, discuss whether she would be persecuted if she lived her sexuality openly and whether she would in fact live her sexuality discreetly if returned. It should be noted here that her account, summarised by the judge, was given in response to particular questions that aimed at identifying whether she lives an openly gay lifestyle in the UK (including her account of being a member of a couple of lesbian and gay groups and having attended Gay Pride events). After her 'gay lifestyle' was established, further questioning then centred on the level of openness:

> The appellant was asked in cross-examination whether she would be discreet if she were on a brief holiday in Saudi Arabia [not her country of origin] with a girlfriend (though why she might contemplate going there was unclear), or walking on a beach in the United Kingdom where there had recently been a homophobic attack. In both cases, the appellant stated that she would still behave openly, mentioning the sufficiency of protection in the United Kingdom in relation to walking on a beach where there had been a recent homophobic attack.
>
> (IJ, Upper Tribunal)

Satisfied with this (rather exaggerated) answer, the court concluded that the appellant would not live her sexuality discreetly if returned, or if she would, then only because of the fear of persecution rather than social pressures. Therefore, her asylum claim was successful.

Hence the 'discretion requirement' is still alive in this new test. There are a few pitfalls in this reasoning (see Weßels 2013). The Supreme Court test divides the social group of gay people into two categories, those living their sexuality openly and those living it discreetly. It is, however, rather paradoxical to assume that in a country where homosexuality is illegal and/ or heavily stigmatised, where it is likely to be sanctioned through violence, rape, torture or death, LGB people would even 'try' to live their sexuality openly. For instance, most asylum seekers and refugees supported by LISG were not open about their sexuality before coming to the UK, but it took only one incident for someone to find out (for instance, when forgetting to lock door when being sexually intimate and a family member coming in). In these cases it did not matter whether the person tried to conceal their sexuality or not: they were subjected to persecution regardless.

The Supreme Court ruling has been praised as progressive change (see Spijkerboer and Jansen 2011) and there is some indication of better decision making since July 2010 (see UKLGIG 2013). In contrast to other areas of law, in asylum claims there is often not much evidence provided, and as Jane Herlihy et al. (2010: 364) argue, 'decisions are inevitably based on assumptions about the content and quality of the information presented. These assumptions draw on subjective understandings of human interaction and behaviour.' The example discussed earlier indicates that the Supreme Court decision is based on a particular understanding of sexuality, namely one that is 'out and proud'. This 'type' of sexuality seems to represent a stereotypical white, male, middle-class gay identity (see Morgan 2006).[5] This understanding of sexuality draws on a Western model of sexuality, whereby gay identity and homosexual conduct are interchangeable and 'which presumes clarity of boundaries between heterosexual and homosexual identity and requires public expression of private and sexual behaviour' (Morgan 2006: 151–152). Public expression of sexual behaviour is especially difficult for LGBT asylum seekers, who come from countries where such expression would have caused homophobic violence and potentially imprisonment.

Credibility—The 'Not Lesbian Enough' Asylum Seeker

The assumption of an 'out and proud' sexuality is not only relevant in asylum cases where relocation is considered. Unlike the earlier example, in most of the asylum cases based on sexuality it is not even accepted that the claimant is lesbian or gay. Negative decisions on the grounds of 'credibility' seem to have increased since the Supreme Court decision (UKLGIG 2013). The UKLGIG found that whilst before 2010 the majority of claims were refused by the Home Office with the argument that the person can go back to his or her country of origin and live his or her sexuality discreetly (UKLGIG 2010), in the majority of negative decisions made between 2010 and 2013, the claimant was not believed to be gay (though that does not mean that it was necessarily believed that the person was gay when the 'relocation argument' was used) (UKLGIG 2013).

With regard to the US asylum system, Deborah A. Morgan (2006: 136) argues that decisions are based on racialised sexual stereotypes and culturally specific norms of sexuality and that 'it is not good enough for an asylum

144 *Nina Held*

applicant simply to be attracted to people of the same sex; the applicant must be "gay enough" for the government to find that they have met their burden of proof'. This seems to be similar in the UK. For instance, Claire Bennett and Felicity Thomas (2013: 26–27) argue that it is not only the claimant's sexual narrative that is taken as the basis for the decision making but also her appearance in the court and whether she conforms to Western stereotypes. The authors conclude:

> Clearly, decisions regarding someone's claim to be a lesbian were frequently based on the extent to which they conformed to Western stereotypes. Failure to meet these preconceived ideas often resulted in asylum claims being refused and women's individual credibility being questioned.

The asylum system asks for membership of a particular social group and therefore focuses on fixed social identities. The system requires evidence for an 'out' sexuality: having a relationship, adopting a gay lifestyle, including participating in lesbian and gay groups and Gay Prides and visiting the Gay Village, can form part of that proof that is expected to be produced (see Morgan 2006: 147; Bennett and Thomas 2013: 26). It is also often assumed that once LGBT people found 'liberation' and can live an openly gay lifestyle in the UK, they would do so. There is an assumption that they would 'immediately' start sexual relationships and if they do not so then this damages their credibility (O'Leary 2008: 90). Living a 'Western' sexual lifestyle is difficult for LGBT people who have been persecuted and/or prosecuted in their countries of origin. They often experience internalised homophobia and a fear of talking about their sexuality. Women often come from cultures where they have learned not to talk about sexuality in general. In addition, the terms 'gay' or 'lesbian' often do not exist in these countries, where constructions of gender and sexuality might be different, and therefore it is difficult for asylum claimants to identify as such when they come to the UK (see O'Leary 2008; Berger 2009).

CONCLUSION

This chapter explored the intersections of 'race' and sexuality by drawing on two different territories of contestation of what it means to be a 'genuine lesbian'. In the Gay Village some bodies that do not conform to the genuine lesbian norm are out of place and are made out of place. The dominant racialised image of the 'genuine lesbian' is performed through a certain habitus and is visible on 'the scene'. Racist door policies include some and exclude others. Racialising practices such as 'the look', touching hair and racialised desire constitute the lesbian somatic norm.

What Does a 'Genuine Lesbian' Look Like? 145

The question of who counts as a 'genuine lesbian' becomes apparent most dramatically in the asylum process where women have to 'prove' that they are indeed lesbian if they claim asylum on grounds of sexuality. The country evidence that is used by Home Office officials and judges often draws on information that has been created for white, middle-class, gay travellers. The Supreme Court ruling is in some ways progressive, in other ways problematic. By dividing the group of gay and lesbian asylum seekers into two categories, those who live their sexuality openly and those who do not, it draws on a Western model of sexuality that requires public expression of sexual behaviour. A lesbian or gay asylum seeker needs to conform to racial and sexual stereotypes in order to be credible and to get the claim accepted. Part of this is to produce evidence of a (white) gay lifestyle.

In the asylum system, proof of 'belonging to a particular social group' is based on normative and racialised notions of the 'genuine lesbian' and so does belonging to the spaces of the Gay Village. As this chapter has demonstrated, whiteness seems to structure this normative sexual identity.

NOTES

1 I use pseudonyms for these two bars as well as for all of the participants of my study.
2 It is important to note here that 'the look' is not only experienced in lesbian spaces. Critical 'race' scholars have written about experiencing 'the look' in various times and places (see for instance Fanon 1967; Ahmed 1997; Lorde 1984a; Lewis 2004).
3 See www.ilga.org.
4 The emphasis is mine.
5 For instance, in his judgement, Lord Hope also drew on stereotypical images of gay men going to Kylie concerts and drinking 'exotically coloured cocktails'.

BIBLIOGRAPHY

Ahmed, S. (1997) ' "It's a Suntan, Isn't It": Auto-Biography as an Identificatory Practice', in Mirza, H. S. (eds.) *Black British Feminism: A Reader*. London and New York: Routledge, 153–167.
Bennett, C. and Thomas, F. (2013) 'Seeking Asylum in the UK: Lesbian Perspectives', *Forced Migration Review* 42: 25–28.
Bell, D. and Binnie, J. (2004) 'Authenticating Queer Space: Citizenship, Urbanism and Governance', *Urban Studies* 41(9): 1807–1820.
Berger, S. A. (2009) 'Production and Reproduction of Gender and Sexuality in Legal Discourses of Asylum in the United States', *Signs* 34(3): 659–685.
Binnie, J. and Skeggs, B. (2004) 'Cosmopolitan Knowledge and the Production and Consumption of Sexualised Space: Manchester's Gay Village', *The Sociological Review* 52(1): 39–61.
Brown, M. (2013) 'Gender and Sexuality II: There Goes the Gayborhood?', *Progress in Human Geography* 38: 1–9.

146 Nina Held

Byrne, B. (2006) *White Lives: The Interplay of 'Race', Class and Gender in Everyday Life*. London and New York: Routledge.

Caluya, G. (2008) ' "The Rice Steamer": Race, Desire and Affect in Sydney's Gay Scene', *Australian Geographer* 39(3): 283–292.

Casey, M. E. (2004) 'De-Dyking Queer Space(s): Heterosexual Female Visibility in Gay and Lesbian Spaces', *Sexualities* 7(4): 446–461.

Casey, M. E. (2007) 'The Queer Unwanted and Their Undesirable "Otherness" ', in Browne, K., Lim, J. and Brown, G. (eds.) *Geographies of Sexualities: Theory, Practices and Politics*. Aldershot and Burlington: Ashgate, 125–136.

Cefai, S. (2004) 'Negotiating Silences, Disavowing Femininity and the Construction of Lesbian Identities', in Women Geography Study Group (eds.) *Gender and Geography Reconsidered*, Glasgow: Women in Geography Study Group, 108–112.

Combahee River Collective. (1982) 'A Black Feminist Statement', in Hull, G. T., Scott P. B. and Smith, B. (eds.) *All the Women Are White, All the Blacks Are Men, But Some of Us Are Brave: Black Women's Studies*. New York: The Feminist Press, 13–22.

Creet, J. (1995) 'Anxieties of Identity: Coming Out and Coming Undone', in Dorenkamp, M. and Henke, R. (eds.) *Negotiating Lesbian and Gay Subjects*. London: Routledge, 179–200.

Crenshaw, K. (1989) 'Demarginalizing the Intersection of Race and Sex: A Black Feminist Critique of Antidiscrimination Doctrine, Feminist Theory, and Antiracist Politics', *University of Chicago Legal Forum* 14: 538–554.

Davis, K. (2008) 'Intersectionality as Buzzword: A Sociology of Science Perspective on What Makes a Feminist Theory Successful', *Feminist Theory* 9(1): 67–85.

Duggan, L. (2003) *The Twilight of Equality: Neoliberalism, Cultural Politics, and the Attack on Democracy*. Boston: Beacon Press.

Fanon, F. (1967) 'The Fact of Blackness', in *Black Skin, White Masks*. New York: Grove Press: 109–140.

Fuller, L. (1999) ' "Whitie" and "Dyke": Constructions of Identities in the Classroom', in Cuomo, C. J. and Hall, K. Q. (eds.) *Whiteness: Feminist Philosophical Reflections*. Oxford: Rowman & Littlefield, 63–74.

GALOP. (2001) *The Low Down: Black Lesbians, Gay Men and Bisexual People Talk about Their Experiences and Needs*. GALOP: London. Available at http://www.galop.org.uk/wp-content/uploads/2009/05/the_low_down.pdf, last accessed 05/11/2012.

Held, N. (2015) 'Comfortable and Safe Spaces? Gender, Sexuality and "Race" in Night-Time Leisure Spaces', *Emotion, Space and Society* 14: 33–42.

Held, N. (2011) *Racialised Lesbian Spaces: A Mancunian Ethnography*. Unpublished PhD thesis. Lancaster: Lancaster University.

Herlihy, J., Kate G. and Turner, S. (2010) 'What Assumptions about Human Behaviour Underlie Asylum Judgements?', *International Journal of Refugee Law* 22(3): 351–366.

Hindle, P. (1994) 'Gay Communities and Gay Space in the City', in Whittle, S. (ed.) *The Margins of the City: Gay Men's Urban Lives*. Aldershot: Ashgate, 7–25.

Johnson, T. (2011) 'On Silence, Sexuality and Skeletons: Reconceptualizing Narrative in Asylum Hearings', *Social and Legal Studies* 20(1): 57–78.

Kawale, R. (2003) 'A Kiss Is Just a Kiss . . . Or Is It? South Asian Lesbian and Bisexual Women and the Construction of Space', in Puwar, N. and Raghuram, P (eds.) *South Asian Women in the Diaspora*. Oxford and New York: Berg, 181–199.

Kawale, R. (2004) 'Inequalities of the Heart: The Performance of Emotion Work by Lesbian and Bisexual Women in London, England', *Social & Cultural Geography* 5(4): 565–581.

What Does a 'Genuine Lesbian' Look Like? 147

Knowles, C. (2003) 'The Place of Space', in Knowles, C. (ed.) *Race and Social Analysis*. London: Sage, 77–107.

Lewis, G. (2007) 'Racialising Culture Is Ordinary', *Cultural Studies* 21(6): 866–886.

Lewis, G. (2004) 'Racialising Culture Is Ordinary', in Silva, E. B. and Bennett, T. (eds.) *Contemporary Culture and Everyday Life*. Durham: Sociology Press, 11–129.

Lorde, A. (1984a) *Sister Outsider. Essays and Speeches*. Trumansberg and New York: Crossing.

Lorde, A. (1984b) *Zami: A New Spelling of My Name*. London: Sheba Feminist Publishers.

Mason-John, V. and Khambatta, A. (1993) *Lesbians Talk Making Black Waves*. London: Scarlet Press.

McLean, K. (2008) ' "Coming Out, Again": Boundaries, Identities and Spaces of Belonging', *Australian Geographer* 39(3): 303–313.

Mercer, K. (1994) 'Black Hair/ Style Politics', in *Welcome to the Jungle: New Positions in Black Cultural Studies*. London and New York: Routledge, 97–128.

Morgan, D. (2006) 'Not Gay Enough for the Government: Racial and Sexual Stereotypes in Sexual Orientation Asylum Cases', *Law & Sexuality: A Review of Lesbian, Gay, Bisexual, and Transgender Legal Issues* 15: 135–162.

Munt, S. (1995) 'The Lesbian Flaneur', in Bell, D. and Valentine, G. (eds.), *Mapping Desire*. New York: Routledge, 114–125.

Nayak, S. (2015) *Race, Gender and the Activism of Black Feminist Theory: Working with Audre Lorde*. Hove: Routledge.

Nero, C. I. (2005) 'Why Are the Gay Ghettos White?', in Johnson, E. P. and Henderson, M. G. (eds.) *Black Queer Studies*. Durham, NC: Duke University Press, 228–245.

O'Leary, B. (2008) ' "We Cannot Claim Any Particular Knowledge of the Ways of Homosexuals, Still Less of Iranian Homosexuals . . . ": The Particular Problems Facing Those Who Seek Asylum on the Basis of Their Sexual Identity', *Feminist Legal Studies* 16(1): 87–95.

Pritchard, A., Nigel, M. and Diane, S. (2002) 'In Search of Lesbian Space? The Experience of Manchester's Gay Village', *Leisure Studies* 21(2): 105–123.

Puwar, N. (2004) *Space Invaders: Race, Gender and Bodies out of place*. Oxford and New York: Berg.

Quilley, S. (1997) 'Constructing Manchester's "New Urban Village": Gay Space in the Entrepreneurial City', in Ingram, G. B., Bouthillette, A.-M. and Retter, Y. (eds.) *Queers in Space: Communities, Public Places, Sites of Resistance*. Seattle: Bay Press, 275–292.

Rooke, A. (2007) 'Navigating Embodied Lesbian Cultural Space: Toward a Lesbian Habitus', *Space and Culture* 10(2): 231–252.

Skeggs, B. (1999) 'Matter Out of Place: Visibility and Sexualities in Leisure Spaces', *Leisure Studies* 18(3): 213–232.

Skeggs, B., Moran, L., Tyrer, P. and Corteen, K. (2004) *Sexuality and the Politics of Violence and Safety*. London and New York: Routledge.

Spijkerboer, T. and Jansen, S. (2011) *Fleeing Homophobia: Asylum Claims Related to Sexual Orientation and Gender Identity in the EU*. Amsterdam: VU University.

Sullivan, S. (2006) *Revealing Whiteness: The Unconscious Habits of Racial Privilege*. Bloomington and Indianapolis: Indiana University Press.

Taylor, A. (1997) 'A Queer Geography', in Medhurst, A. and Munt, S. (eds.) *Lesbian and Gay Studies: A Critical Introduction*. London: Cassell, 3–16.

Taylor, Y. (2008) ' "That's Not Really My Scene": Working-Class Lesbians in (and out of) Place', *Sexualities* 11(5): 523–546.

UK Lesbian and Gay Immigration Group (UKLGIG). (2010) *Failing the Grade*. UKLGIG: London. Available at http://uklgig.org.uk/wp-content/uploads/2014/04/Failing-the-Grade.pdf, last accessed 08/04/2015.

UK Lesbian and Gay Immigration Group (UKLGIG). (2013) *Missing the Grade.* UKLGIG: London. Available at http://www.uklgig.org.uk/wp-content/uploads/2014/02/Missing-the-Mark.pdf, last accessed 08/04/2015.

Valentine, G. (1995) 'Creating Transgressive Space: The Music of kd lang', *Transactions of the Institute of British Geography* 20(4): 474–485.

Weβels, J. (2013) '*HJ(Iran) and HT (Cameroon)*—Reflections on a New Test for Sexuality-based Asylum Claims in Britain', *International Journal of Refugee Law* 24(4): 815–839.

Whittle, S. (1994) 'Consuming Differences: The Collaboration of the Gay Body with the Cultural State', in Whittle, S. (ed.) *The Margins of the City: Gay Men's Urban Lives*. Aldershot: Arena, 27–40.

8 'Time After Time'[1]
Gay Conditionality, Colonial Temporality and *Āzādī*

Tara Atluri

INTRODUCTION

While there is often a common sense understanding of sexual 'progress' as being tied to legal rights and secularism, this chapter questions the relationship between narratives of Western secular feminism and queer theory by examining the embodied politics of feminist and queer movements in India and the articulations of sexual politics outside of Orientalist and colonial categories of citizenship. Understandings of political subjectivity rooted in Orientalist thought fail to apprehend the divergent ways in which sexual politics are articulated outside the grammars of the Western polis. One should perhaps consider a larger political context that produces what Puar terms homonationalism, a discourse within which sexual politics coincide with the aims of postcolonial Western powers (Puar 2007).

I discuss three interrelated moments within contemporary sexual political struggles: the 2013 decision to uphold Section 377, India's colonial sodomy law, by the Supreme Court of India; the street protests following the high profile 2012 Delhi gang rape case; and the 2011 proposal made by British prime minister David Cameron to slash foreign aid to countries with a poor record on LGBT rights. These three examples are connected through genealogies of colonial history and Orientalist discourse. All of these moments highlight the ways in which contemporary sexual politics in the Global South continue to be informed by the history of imperial domination and challenged by the ongoing resilience of postcolonial publics through localised protest. I place the 2013 decision to uphold Section 377, India's colonial sodomy law, and the 2012 Delhi gang rape protests in the context of global sexual politics. This chapter suggests that the embodied resilience of feminists and queers in India should be considered in relation to neocolonial imperatives to speak on behalf of people in the Global South, within the heart of the former imperial power. Rather than apprehending sexual politics in India through the narratives of state power, I argue that one should pay attention to contemporary feminist and queer protests that emerge in the real time of the Indian street. I suggest that contemporary political struggles happening on the streets of India should be considered

150 *Tara Atluri*

in relation to contemporary bids on the part of political leaders in Europe to utilise the lives of queer people and women in the Global South to suit their economic and political interests. I connect neocolonial posturing on the part of Western leaders of former colonial powers such as Great Britain to colonial history.

This chapter discusses the continued legacies of colonialism that define contemporary queer politics in the Global South, drawing upon fieldwork conducted in Delhi[2] between 2012 and 2014. Having taken part in the 2013 protests that followed the decision made by the Supreme Court of India to criminalise same-sex desire, as well as the 2012 Delhi gang rape protests, I interviewed activists, academics and those who attended the many protests, panels and public events that were part of new feminist and queer movements in the Indian subcontinent.

The chapter does not offer a linear narrative of sequential 'progress' which imagines countries in the Global South to be 'progressing' beyond colonial history. Rather, it suggests that sexual politics are still caught within neocolonial temporalities, which are further exacerbated by global capitalism. First, I discuss queer and feminist struggles that challenge Orientalist images of submissive and passive sexual subjects in India, marked as feminised in relation to the masculinist authorial image of white European colonial power. Second, I challenge homonationalist discourses that imagine idealised Western capitalist subjects to be sexually free. Finally, I challenge colonial constructions of feminist and queer politics as grounded in claims to legal rights, discussing how India remains tied to colonial laws and processes of governance that utilise old colonial laws to criminalise sexualities as occurred throughout history. Against the push and pull of law and capital, people within the Indian subcontinent are enacting new forms of sexual citizenship that perhaps cannot be fully translated into Western secular temporalities and the English language. I begin by contextualising this discussion in relation to key political struggles and legal decisions pertaining to sexual politics in India and in regards to global sexual politics. I then utilise fieldwork to discuss the resilience of those feminist and queer movements which defy colonial and state law. I offer a theoretical reading of these moments, utilising contemporary philosophy and postcolonial discourse.

CONTEXTUALISING SEXUAL POLITICS IN INDIA

In 2009, the Naz Foundation, a queer rights organisation based in Delhi, petitioned the Delhi High Court to challenge the use of Section 377, a colonial law dating back to 1860 that criminalised broadly defined 'unnatural acts', including same-sex intercourse. After a lengthy campaign by the Naz Foundation and activists in Delhi who were part of Voices against Section 377, the Delhi High Court made a landmark decision regarding

'Time After Time' 151

Section 377 of the Indian penal code. Section 377 was read down to exclude adult consensual sex from its remit but not repealed altogether. As journalist Akila(2014) states, 'the effect of the decision was that though homosexual intercourse was no longer illegal, Section 377 would remain in the statue books and could be used to prosecute other unnatural sex acts'(Akila 2014). The decision of the Delhi High Court was striking in the history of queer rights in the Indian subcontinent. However, the decision made by the Delhi High Court was not upheld by the Supreme Court of India, with the Supreme Court choosing in 2013 to overrule the judgement made by the Delhi High Court in 2009 and to uphold the constitutionality of Section 377, once again criminalising queers.

In 2011, David Cameron suggested that British aid to countries in the Global South should be dependent on their respect of LGBTI rights. A letter drafted by several African activists suggested that Cameron's comments smacked of neocolonialism. Keeping in mind Cameron's 'gay conditionality' proposals, I ask how trans-national political solidarity is possible when considered in relation to gender and sexual politics in contexts such as India. Rahul Rao (2012) discusses critiques levelled against Cameron as follows:

> Warning that the refusal of aid on LGBT rights grounds could provoke a backlash against queers who would be scapegoated for reduced aid flows, the critics have pointed out the insidious ways in which such initiatives could drive a wedge between queers and a broader civil society in recipient countries, besides reinforcing perceptions of the westernness of homosexuality as well as the imperial dynamics already prevailing between donor and recipient countries.
>
> (Rao 2012)

From the perspective of neocolonial power and Hindu nationalist rhetoric, feminist and queer bodies in the Indian subcontinent are constructed as an affront to essentialist ideas of Indian 'culture' and tradition, at odds with an image of 'Hindustan' imbued with a biopolitical rhetoric of 'purity'. The irony being that Cameron's 'gay conditionality' proposals support the rhetoric of mainstream political and religious leaders in the Global South who also assume that queer and feminist politics are 'foreign' to the nation and its political history. For example, one can consider the violent assaults of women by Hindu nationalists in the 2009 Bangalore pub attacks, in which women sitting in pubs were beaten on the streets by Hindu nationalists for defying ideas of feminine 'purity' and sexual propriety. One can also consider the outrage generated by the release of the film *Fire* in India, which depicted a queer relationship between women. Hindu nationalists set fire to theatres where the film was being released. These public spectacles of violence are newsworthy items that draw attention to the microcosms of everyday forms of disciplinary power enacted against feminist and queer bodies in India by state power and those using religion as an alibi for gender-based violence.

152 Tara Atluri

However, as with the political protests that followed the 2012 Delhi gang rape case and the queer activist movements that have politicised Section 377 of the Indian penal code, these events of state violence were met with dissent. The Pink Chaadi campaign followed the Bangalore pub attacks and involved women sending pink underwear to the Hindu nationalist groups responsible for these attacks, writing messages of defiance and mockery on the underwear (Varughese 2014). Queer and feminist activists in Delhi and throughout India also protested the attempt to censor the film *Fire*, offering evidence of the vitality of queer and feminist lives in India, against efforts by conservative politicians in the former empire and the postcolonial world to make their lives and work invisible[3] (Bacchetta 2001; Gopinath 2005). Similarly, following the Delhi gang rape case of 2012 and the 2013 decision regarding Section 377, many people engaged in a process of 'world making', attempting to redefine forms of juridical and state, familial and colonial classification (Atluri 2013)' Bourdieu (1989) states that,

> to change the world, one has to change the ways of world-making, that is, the vision of the world and the practical operations by which groups are produced and reproduced.
>
> (Bourdieu 1989: 23)

He further suggests that, '[t]he power to impose upon other minds a vision, old or new, of social divisions depends on the social authority acquired in previous struggles' (Bourdieu 1989:23). The queer movement in India has gained social authority from previous campaigns in 2009 that were successful in their contribution to the decision to amend the usage of Section 377 by the Delhi High Court (Narrain and Gupta 2011). While this activism can be, and has been, challenged at the level of law, a certain form of symbolic authority still informs how queer people and allies continue acts of 'world making' that work towards altering universal understandings of desire and nation (Bhan and Narrain 2005).

Protests movements calling for freedom from patriarchal colonial law, freedom from heteronormative familial narratives and challenging the right of patriarchal fathers to own daughters unite contemporary feminist and queer struggles in India. Following the Delhi gang rape protests of 2012, the government of India made the decision to legally sanction marital rape despite recommendations from the Verma Committee, a judiciary review board appointed to review rape law in the Indian subcontinent. The Committee 'included retired Justice J. S. Verma, retired Justice Leila Seth and Solicitor General Gopal Subramanian' and 'was constituted on December 23, 2012, to look into the possible amendments in the criminal laws related to sexual violence against women' (The *Hindu* 2013).

The decision was justified on the basis that criminalising marital rape would 'threaten the Indian family' (Menon 2013) and a recent 2014 court ruling only further confirmed the legal sanction of rape. The judiciary ruled that a man who allegedly drugged a woman, forced her to marry him and raped her was not legally culpable of any crime. The presiding judge stated that owing to their married status, 'the sexual intercourse between the two, even if forcible, is not rape and no culpability can be fastened upon the accused' (Zimmerman 2014). There is a parallel between husbands owning women's bodies as property and the ownership of land, which turns rape into a legally sanctioned act imbued with nationalist power.

ĀZĀDĪ: BAD TRANSLATIONS IN THE STREETS

In this section, I reflect upon fieldwork done in the Indian subcontinent, which was largely carried out at protests following the 2013 decision to criminalise same-sex desire and the 2012 Delhi gang rape case. There was a momentum to these protests that cannot be fully captured in text. In the streets of Delhi, one could hear the constant refrain from protestors of 'Āzādī', a Persian word meaning 'freedom' that was used as a popular chant during anticolonial struggles. *Āzādī* is now of common use in Farsi, Kurdish, Pashto, Urdu and Hindi. Interestingly, the word as a protest chant was popular in anticolonial rebellions in South Asia (Kishwar 2010). The cry of *Āzādī* could also be heard in Delhi when just one year after the Delhi gang rape case, in 2013, the Supreme Court of India made the decision to uphold Section 377.

In *The Year of Dreaming Dangerously*, Slavoj Žižek (2012) discusses two French words, both meaning 'future': *futur* and *avenir*. He writes,

> [f]utur stands for 'future' as the continuation of the present, as the full actualization of tendencies already in existence; while *avenir* points towards a radical break, a discontinuity with the present—*avenir* is what is to come (*a venir*), not just what is to be.
>
> (Žižek 2012: 134)

He suggests that to envision an *avenir*, or what is to come, one must grasp what he terms 'signs from the future' (Žižek 2012: 134). Žižek (2012) discusses the possibility of a radical openness towards the future, foretold in what appear as outbursts within our political moment. He states that, '[w]e should fully accept this openness, guiding ourselves on nothing more than ambiguous signs from the future' (Žižek 2012: 134). Through Cameron's 'gay conditionality' proposals, what is to come for queers in the Global South remains bound to a *futur*, a continuation of Indian history that remains connected to a colonial past and a colonial empire. An *avenir*, a radical break with the contemporary neocolonial present in India, gestures to what may come, an unpredictable anticolonial queer form of politics that cannot be foretold. The casting of Cameron as a paternal authority who uses queer people in the Global South as an alibi for economic aims continues the legacy of colonial rule. And yet, as I go on to explore through an analysis of contemporary political protests in India pertaining to gender and sexuality, one can look to these moments of revolt as 'signs from the future', as radical breaks from the temporalities of colonial modernity, as signs of a possible openness that might offer alternatives to cycles of colonial exploitation, imposition and civilising missions. The eruption of the masses onto the streets gestured to a gendered and sexual politics not accounted for by state institutions. In beginning with this moment, an optimistic 'sign from the future' (Žižek 2012: 134) becomes visible; one that speaks to the power of people to collectively organise and articulate desire outside of colonial temporalities and spaces.

While David Cameron's 'gay conditionality' proposal imagined the queer body in the Global South as non-existent or 'lagging behind', and the Indian state transforms queers into criminals and women into property, many people continue to engage in their own world making. One queer activist in Delhi stated at a protest following the 2013 Supreme Court decision to criminalise queer desire:

> For a feminist and for people who want social change and who are fighting for a more egalitarian society, we thought that the country is changing; we thought that the people in power are changing. But it was quite a regressive judgment and very unexpected. But yesterday we saw (at the demonstration in Delhi) a lot of the community is stressing that the judgment may have arrived but we are not going to step back. Whatever we have achieved so far, the awareness we've been able to raise, the change we've made. We're not going to step back. It doesn't matter. From now on it's going to be more and more people coming forward talking about more and more issues.
>
> (Interview n. 1)

The activist I spoke with went on to challenge the symbolic power of state authority in their judicially sanctioned representation of the 'common sense' of the nation. When asked what they thought could explain the decision made by the Supreme Court regarding Section 377, they stated:

> If you really look at the judgment and reflect on the judgment, there is no logic to it. There is no logic to that judgment. They just didn't want to deal with it. They didn't have the courage to deal with such an issue. They just wanted to pass it on to others. No one had the courage to really take a stand. So, let me just pass it on to the other governing body, the executive . . . It's not as though the people from Voices against 377 did not have enough evidence to show how crucial the situation is. It's just about the attitude in the Supreme Court. They wouldn't delve into the issue. Instead, they relied on a very regressive politics of the West and the East divide. It just reflects how inept the Supreme Court is in dealing with these issues.
>
> (Interview n. 1)

'Time After Time' 155

We further discussed the many feminist and queer spaces in the city that have gained strength since the 2009 decision by the Delhi High Court to read down Section 377. Bourdieu states that symbolic capital functions as a form of credit, as 'it is the power granted to those who have obtained sufficient recognition to be in a position to impose recognition' (Bourdieu 1989: 20). Feminists and queers in the region recognise their own symbolic authority in the act of 'world making', using the global recognition they have gained to remake social spaces, imposing new understandings of the world onto the consciousness of the Indian public and also trans-nationally. When asked what the impact of the decision made by the Supreme Court would be, another queer activist stated:

> In some ways, it really doesn't matter. Does law impact on my daily activity and everything I do? No it really doesn't. But is there a threat? Is there a threat looming over me because of the existence of this law? Yes, there is. So, one can't give a clear idea of how the law impacts on my life. But there is a threat that looms there. The fact that a law like 377 exists means that there is a threat that looms in my head. It effects upon your psyche, your liberty, your dignity. In one way it doesn't really change. I'm queer and I'm proud and I'm out. So, does a law really change that? No. There are enough spaces that I reclaim for myself.
>
> (Interview n. 2)

As one feminist and queer activist said, commenting on the 2013 decision by the Supreme Court of India to criminalise same-sex desire, almost laughing, 'I'm sorry, but that one is just ridiculous. We all know same-sex couples, we all know same-sex couples with families who are very settled in India and have been for some time' (Interview n. 3). At protests commemorating the 2012 Delhi gang rape, another woman whom I spoke to stated that since this case,

> there are changes. Because now people start to raise questions, especially women. Many women never stood against this kind of thing. There was a fear to speak. Now they are speaking out.
>
> (Interview n. 4)

We discussed changes she feels need to be put in place with regards to gendered violence in India and why gendered violence is rampant. She gestured to the need for education beyond the space of formal institutions:

> It's a matter of education. And not only formal education. It's a matter of value education. Somehow understanding and instruction in the most basic values has been lost. I don't know why this has happened. Or maybe this has always been the case but only now we see how bad things are.
>
> (Interview n. 4)

156   *Tara Atluri*

She challenged the perception of 'progress' put forth by the neo-liberal rhetoric of 'India shining', in which betterment is seen to come from economic growth and secular English-language education. Furthermore, a logic of universal 'progress', in which Indian women and queers are seen to be in need of salvation from the West, was also challenged through the active resilience of women and their reference to a long feminist genealogy in India. She further commented, 'the women's movement has been here for a long time. Longer than I think anyone remembers. What we are doing here is not against India, it is India' (Interview n. 4). The 'world making' aspects of symbolic power are clearly illustrated in these declarations in which people make their own classifications regarding the 'common sense' of social space and history, making declarations that gesture to feminist genealogies which challenge the colonial amnesia of Western benevolence and the paternalistic erasures of dissident desire by the Indian state.

MACAULAY'S HAUNTING: NEOCOLONIAL TEMPORALITIES AND UNSEXY GHOSTS

Following the 2013 decision made by the Supreme Court of India to reinstitute the sodomy bill, Cameron arguably remained politically inactive. James Bloodsworth (2013) refers to Cameron as a 'travelling salesmen' of sorts, suggesting that in order to maintain favourable economic trade relations with India, Cameron has foregone any commitment to advocate for queer people. Bloodsworth (2013) discusses Cameron's investments in the weapons trade throughout the Middle East, which he justified by stating that citizens 'have the right to defend themselves' (Bloodsworth 2013). However, queer citizens in India seem not to have the right to defend themselves against the epistemic violence of a neocolonial state. A report issued by the UK Foreign Commissions Office following the decision to reinstate Section 377 argues that, '[t]he actions of India's Supreme Court are a matter for India' (Bloodsworth 2013). And yet Cameron played the transparently self-serving role of knight in shining armour, using queer rights to justify cutting aid budgets to some of the poorest people in the world, who are largely impoverished due to the after-effects of British colonial rule.

Homi Bhabha (1995) draws on Lord Macaulay's writings concerning the East India Tea Company, writing:

> Between the Western sign and its colonial signification there emerges a map of misreading that embarrasses the righteousness of recordation and its certainty of good government. It opens up a space of interpretation and misappropriation that inscribes an ambivalence at the very origins of colonial authority.
>
> (Bhabha 1995: 135)

'Time After Time' 157

This 'map of misreading' could be seen in Cameron's 'gay conditionality' proposals and the Supreme Court of India's reinstitution of the sodomy bill. As Rao writes, '[i]t is unclear what David Cameron was thinking, or if he was thinking' (Rao 2012). When I was conducting fieldwork in Delhi directly after the Supreme Court decision to recriminalise same-sex desire, there was a similar refrain of disbelief regarding the decision of Indian political leaders to criminalise queer desire. Macaulay wrote that the directors of the East India Company,

> [n]ever perceived the gross inconsistency of which they were guilty . . . Whoever examines their letters written at that time, will find there are many just and humane sentiments . . . an admirable code of political ethics . . . Now these instructions, being interpreted, means simply, 'Be the father and the oppressor of the people, be just and unjust, moderate and rapacious.'
>
> (Bhabha 1995: 135)

Rather than reading these writings as signs of the duplicity of colonial rule, Bhabha reads them as a sign of the ambivalence that lay at the heart of colonialism. One can also ask how the ambivalence of colonial civility expresses the inherent contradictions that structure patriarchal power. The 'father and the oppressor' points to the contradictory ways in which gendered authority is utilised by state power, gesturing to the forked tongue of civility and paradoxes of patriarchal heteronormative power. The pleasures of imperialist power turn political governance into cruel forms of imperialist masculinist enjoyment that govern colonised people in much the same ways as a patriarch governs feminised others. Bhabha (1995) continues:

> What is articulated in the doubleness of colonial discourse is not simply the violence of one powerful nation writing out the history of another. 'Be that father and the oppressor . . . just and unjust' is a mode of contradictory utterance that ambivalently reinscribes, across differential power relations, both colonizer and colonized. For it reveals an agonistic uncertainty contained in the incompatibility of empire and nation; it puts on trial the very discourse of civility within which representative government claims its liberty and empire its ethics.
>
> (Bhabha 1995: 136)

Bhabha suggests that once the excess of colonial administrative power is revealed, the civil authority of imperial governance cannot maintain its ethical claims. He suggests that if the passions of colonial authority are political passions,

> we should pose the question of the ambivalence of colonialist authority in the language of the vicissitudes of the narcissistic demand for

158　*Tara Atluri*

> colonial objects, which intervene so powerfully in the nationalist fantasy of boundless, extensive possessions.
>
> (Bhabha 1995: 136)

He discusses the ambivalence of the colonial utterance which lies in the double inscription of its address, 'father and oppressor or, alternatively, the ruled and reviled—which will not be resolved in a dialectical play of power' (Bhabha 1995: 138). The ambivalent contradictions of 'be the father and the oppressor' emerge again in the gap between civility as governance and economic imperatives, in a time of fiscal austerity throughout Europe. In acting as the pied piper of sexual rights and freedoms, Cameron scripts gendered bodies in the Global South as childlike and in need of paternalistic guidance. Bourdieu suggests that official discourses regarding subjectivity and the nation state serve three functions. First, they perform a diagnostic function, classifying and ordering bodies according to universal norms. Second, he suggests that official discourses are prescriptive. Finally, official discourses lay claims to an imagined past through authorised accounts such as state records. In the case of Cameron's 'gay conditionality', a form of classification assumes there to be a universal 'gay' subject, as a bearer of sexual rights. Those who do not live up to the standard embodied by the universal 'gay' subject are forced to aspire to this ideal. This Western state-led discourse of sexuality prescribes what sexual minorities and women in the Global South should do. Finally, there is an act of fabricating the past, one that implies what has or has not occurred with regards to sexual politics in the Global South. Using Bourdieu's analysis one can see that the discourse of the universal 'rights bearing' sexual minority is connected to an imagining of the European and of European history as the benchmark of civility. This Eurocentric epistemology obscures diverse enactments of gender/sex in contexts such as India and throughout the Global South, in which sexual politics are marked by diverse religious, cultural and colonial histories and by lived realities shaped by local contexts that defy universalisation.

The symbolic power vested in neocolonial authority both misinterprets and attempts to govern the social spaces of former colonies through forms of constructed 'common sense' that perceive the place of 'the European'[4] to be at the centre of world history. The act of naming queer bodies in the Global South as victims simultaneously labels 'the West' as a homogenous space of sexual freedom and its leaders as knights in shining neocolonial armour, coming to the rescue of third world women and queers. This act of naming obscures the displacement of minorities out of Western spaces of sociality through border security and the continued impoverishment of the Global South through neocolonial processes of global capitalist exploitation. It also trivialises ongoing forms of sexual violence towards queers and women in Western nations. Universal 'sexual rights' discourse obscures the position of the European polis as just another place within which reality is not given but is instead perceived through a certain historical, political and psychosocial lens.

CONCLUSION

In this chapter, I have discussed the colonial legacies that haunt sexual politics in contemporary India, emerging through a homonationalist discourse. I suggest that contemporary homonationalism imagines feminist and queer 'progress' to be universally born out of the inculcation of countries in the Global South such as India into secular Western capitalism and neo-liberal forms of globalisation. This universal assumption supports neocolonial imperatives, as evinced in David Cameron's 'gay conditionality' rhetoric and obscures the impassioned struggles of queers and feminists in India, as expressed in the street protests described in this chapter. Drawing on fieldwork done in the Indian subcontinent, I suggest that 'progress' cannot be equated with legal inclusion. I contextualise contemporary sexual politics in India through the rhetoric of a globalisation of 'sexual rights' which informs David Cameron's 'gay conditionality' proposals. In classifying 'sexual freedom' through allegedly universal, English-language categories, authority is placed once again in the hands of old colonial powers. The overarching point that I am making in this chapter is that sexual politics in India should be understood through the political movements of the masses emerging on the streets of India. Just as anticolonial political struggles attempted to challenge the imposition of Western power that was forced onto the Indian subcontinent through an ongoing colonial rape script, new generations of feminists and queers are not waiting to be 'saved' by Western powers.

To name the world is not simply to know it. To name the world is to make certain forms of knowledge possible. To name and rename the world is to make certain lives liveable. In the streets of the Indian subcontinent, there is a constant act of 'world making' that draws its strength from struggles of the past. In the streets of Delhi, capital city of a postcolonial nation of infinitely impure origins, and a beautifully queer place, perhaps beyond English translation and the linear scales and calculators of Western temporality, I stand in the streets with so many others and cry out,

Āzādī.

The spirit of the people in the streets is perhaps beyond translation.

NOTES

1 Whilst not wanting to make light of the serious political and ideological consequences and implications of Cameron's 'gay conditionality' proposals, in the spirit of sly civility see: Cyndi Lauper, *Time After Time: The Cindi Lauper Collection*. Sony Music. May 11, 2009.
2 Delhi refers to both New Delhi and Old Delhi. The city of Delhi is the capital of the Indian subcontinent and encompasses both the New and Old districts of the urban metropolis.

160 *Tara Atluri*

3 Bacchetta (2001) discusses the controversy that arose following the release of the film *Fire*. Against neocolonial and Hindu nationalist wills to construct feminism and queerness as being 'foreign' to India, the author suggests that the film's release was opposed by right-wing Hindu fundamentalists who do not express the sensibilities of the general population and the active cultures and histories of feminist, queer and leftist politics in the subcontinent. The massive demonstrations staged by multiple factions of activists in India are demonstrative of a vibrant civil society: feminist and queer communities do not need benevolent forms of salvation, masking neocolonial imperatives, from political leaders such as David Cameron. As Bacchetta states,

> After winning awards internationally, the film opened on November 13, 1998, in forty two theaters in urban India, and, for the first few weeks, though it played to wide audiences, it caused no great uproar. After the initial peace, Hindu nationalists stepped in, and organized protests, damaging several theaters. In statements to the press, Hindu nationalists, the RSS, and the Hindu Shiv Sena (hereafter HSS) alike argued that the film was an assault on Hindu civilization and Hindu 'tradition . . . 'approximately two hundred members of the HSS had trashed two theaters in Mumbai while *Fire* was being viewed, breaking window glass, destroying a ticket counter, and burning posters of the film. As news about the cinema thrashings spread, they aroused widespread protest, some of which aimed against censorship (mainly from the film industry) and some against the exiling of lesbians (by lesbian, women's, left, and anti communal groups . . . As news of the cinema thrashings spread, lesbian and women's group's mobilized energetically against them. On December 7, lesbians, artists, and women's groups along with *Fire* producer Deepa Mehta, held a candlelight vigil in front of a previously thrashed theater in Delhi (Regal Cinema), photos of which appeared throughout the press, including the Hindu nationalist press. One of the most visible vigil banners read 'Indian and Lesbian' (thereby countering the HSS claim that lesbianism is not Indian.
> (Bacchetta 2001: 236–238)

4 What also emerge in this 'act of forgetting' in relation to the imagined 'freedom' of Europe are ongoing forms of oppression within Europe. In playing the role of benevolent knight in shining armour to queers in the Global South, Western leaders obscure the colonial dynamics of contemporary Europe which often determine who is rich and poor, who lives and who dies in the supposed 'free' West (Haritaworn 1997; Binnie 2004).

BIBLIOGRAPHY

Akila, R.S. (2014) 'Section 377: The Way Forward', *The Hindu*, 1 March 2014. Available at http://www.thehindu.com/features/magazine/section-377-the-way-forward/article5740242.ece. Last accessed 5 March 2015.

Atluri, T. (2013) 'The Young and the Restless: Gender, "Youth", and the Delhi Gang Rape Case of 2012', *Sikh Formations: Religion, Culture, Theory* 9(3): 361–369.

Bacchetta, P. (2001) 'Extraordinary Alliances in Crisis Situations: Women against Hindu Nationalism in India', in Blee, K. and Twine, F. (eds.) *Feminism and Antiracism: International Struggles for Justice*. New York: New York University Press, 220–250.

Bhabha, H. (1995) *The Location of Culture*. London: Routledge.

'Time After Time' 161

Bhan, G. and Narrain, A. (2005) *Because I Have a Voice: Queer Politics in India*. New Delhi: Yoda Press.

Binnie, J. (2004) *The Globalization of Sexuality*. London: Sage.

Bloodsworth, J. (2013) 'Is the British Government Ignoring Gay Rights in India for Trade?' Available at http://www.leftfootforward.org/2013/12/is-the-british-government-ignoring-gay-rights-in-india-for-trade/, last accessed 2 March 2014.

Bourdieu, P. (1989) 'Social Space and Symbolic Power', *Sociological Theory* 7(1): 14–25.

Gopinath, G. (2005) *Impossible Desires: Queer Diasporas and South Asian Public Cultures*. Durham: Duke University Press.

Haritaworn, J. (1997) 'Queer Anti-Racist Activism and Strategies of Critique: A Roundtable Discussion', *Feminist Legal Studies* 19(2): 169–191.

The Hindu. (2013) 'Full Text of Justice Verma's Report', *The Hindu*, 24 January 2013. Available at http://www.thehindu.com/news/resources/full-text-of-justice-vermas-report-pdf/article4339457.ece, last accessed 6 June 2015.

Kishwar, M.P. (2010) "The Many Meanings of Azadi." *The Times of India*, 20 September 2010. Available at http://timesofindia.indiatimes.com/edit-page/The-Many-Meanings-Of-Azadi/articleshow/6585789.cms, last accessed 22 June 2015.

Lauper, C. (2009) *Time After Time: The Cindy Lauper Collection*. Sony Music.

Narrain, A. and Gupta, A. (2011) *Law Like Love: Queer Perspectives on Law*. New Delhi: Yoda Press.

Menon, N. (2013) 'The Impunity of Every Citadel Is Intact"—the Taming of the Verma Committee Report, and Some Troubling Doubts', *Kafila*, 3 February 2013. Available at http://kafila.org/2013/02/03/the-impunity-of-every-citadel-is-intact-the-taming-of-the-verma-committee-report-and-some-troubling-doubts/, last accessed 22 June 2015.

Puar, J. (2007) *Terrorist Assemblages: Homonationalism in Queer Times*. Durham: Duke University Press.

Rao, R. (2012) 'On "Gay Conditionality", Imperial Power and Queer Liberation', *Kafila*, 1 January 2012. Available at. http://kafila.org/2012/01/01/on-gay-conditionality-imperial-power-and-queer-liberation-rahul-rao/, last accessed 23 June 2015.

Varughese, A. (2014) 'Globalization and Culture Wars: The Case of India', in Sandbrook, R. and Güven, A.B. (eds.) *Civilizing Globalization: A Survival Guide*. New York: Suny Press, 93–109.

Žižek, S. (2012) *The Year of Dreaming Dangerously*. London: Verso.

Zimmerman, J. 'Marital Rape Is Officially Legal in India', *Salon Magazine*, 15 May 2014. Available at http://www.salon.com/2014/05/15/marital_rape_is_officially_legal_in_india_partner/, last accessed 17 September 2015.

Part III

Sexuality, Religion and Belonging

9 Creating Citizens, Constructing Religion, Configuring Gender

Intersectional Sites, Scripts and Sticking Points

Yvette Taylor and Ria Snowdon

INTRODUCTION: MAKING, MODELLING AND MIMICKING SPACE

This chapter is a case study exploration of Christianity and sexuality in the lives of young lesbians in the UK based on a subset of data involving 16[1] young lesbian women who variously identify as Christian. Religion matters as a personal and political force, but secularising trends arguably obscure its influence upon the complex convergence and intersection of personal, political, familial and institutional realms. Representations of 'sexual citizenship' are still positioned as separate from and indeed negated by religious rights and some religions are (mis)positioned as more hostile, tolerating and welcoming than others. These collisions have been apparent in recent UK debates on the Civil Partnership Act (2004), the Equality Act (2006) and the Marriage Act (Same Sex Couples) 2013. All have generated significant controversies, frequently positing Christian backlash against more integrative calls for inclusion. Whilst the 'question of homosexuality' has been a central focus in much discussion, highlighting around the presumed discontinuity between sexual identity and Christian identity (O'Brien 2004), there is still a gap in terms of locating first-hand narratives of self-identified young 'queer' Christians.

Rather than assuming that these are separate and divergent paths (Wilcox 2003, 2006), this chapter explores intersectional convergences and divergences, illustrating how religious participation can convey (de)legitimation within family, community and society. Such (de)legitimation is revealed in unpacking scripts of inclusion and exclusion (Taylor and Snowdon 2014), which are (re)circulated via 'hetero-homo normative' ideals, and perpetuated and contested in the context of intersectional Equalities legislation (Monro 2010). Here we examine the highly gendered and heteronormative 'role models', 'mentors' and (familial) mediations experienced by young lesbian Christians as intersecting public-private domains in the production of queer religious subjectivity and disidentification.

Christian stances on 'homosexuality' have been vigorously debated. Into this often highly intense social milieu, young LGBT Christians try to find

166   *Yvette Taylor and Ria Snowdon*

a sense of belonging, and it is within this context that our overall research project stands. Empirical data is taken from wider research, 'Making Space for Queer-Identifying Religious Youth' (2011–2013), funded by the Economic and Social Research Council (ESRC), which explores youth cultures, queer community and religious groups. Overall, the intention is to offer insight into the management of excluded identity positions, building on a growing body of literature (Thumma 1991; Yip 2002; Wilcox 2003, 2006; O'Brien 2004, 2005). Young people's voices are particularly marginalised within writings on religion, often positioned as obvious absences given the assumed dichotomy and mutual disinterest between 'youth' and 'religion'. Queer-identified youth are further negated within this sweep and, as such, their (dis)comforts and (dis)investments are mostly absent. This negation also occurs within LGBTQ 'friendly' religious organisations, practices and spaces, which are often still demonstrably of and for older adults.

These absences emerge in considering sexualised and gendered 'role modes' and 'mentors' for young lesbian Christians, mediated by intersecting public-private domains which produce *and* queer religious subjectivity and disidentification. Alongside the passing of Equalities legislation[2] sits the arguably contradictory and uncomfortable fact of continued male-dominated presences and church hierarchies, impacting on the 'making' of religious and queer space as both gendered and sexualised. The nuclear family, combined with traditional gender roles, is still a foundational pillar of many religions, contested by participation in congregations, levels of ordination and specific sacraments (such as marriage) (see Machacek and Wilcox 2003). Such 'heteronormativity' is still the pervasive context into which young lesbians (re)frame their religious participation, from the public political-policy level to the more intimate-everyday level, where the language of familialism (dis)allows and (re)circulates heteronormativity and, in the context of same-sex rights, certain 'homonormativities' (Duggan 2003; Puar 2007).

Here we explore young people's understanding of religion as fields which they enter, negotiate, participate in and withdraw from, at times searching for and rejecting the role of models and mentors provided in 'making space'; frequently younger (single) adults were welcomed into churches through an implicit—and sometimes explicit—*familial* framing of community, care, grouping and identity. 'Space' is not simply theirs, or there for the taking, rather it is created through processes, actions and policies, including those which contest the place of women in church leadership roles (exemplified in current tensions around the ordination of women bishops in the Church of England). *Gendered* exclusions operate alongside and intersect with *sexualised* exclusions, and thus the purpose of this chapter is to unpack scripts of inclusion and exclusion in relation to young lesbians in church (O'Brien 2014). The aim is to adopt an intersectional lens, both theoretically and methodologically, also uncovering the salience of multiple social divisions and identities in young lesbian lives. Using such a model is relevant

Creating Citizens, Constructing Religion, Configuring Gender 167

where this largely theoretical position is often not fully embedded within empirical studies. Beyond the recognisable material spaces of religion (e.g. in the sacralisation of space and the construction of places of worship, see Gorman-Murray and Nash 2014), religion infiltrates the everyday, intimate and political spaces of family, community and identity.

This chapter first considers the literature on sexuality, religion and youth, making a case for the potential (and perhaps failure) of 'intersectionality' as an *effort* in bringing connecting social divisions to the forefront through specific empirical examples. Using key studies, we consider the place of heteronormativity in shaping religious subjectivity and disidentification before outlining the project's methodology. Subsequent sections pursue connected themes of 'Finding the (Lesbian) Women in Leadership: "Diversity Role Models"' and 'Scary Church Parents: Locating Young Lesbian in Church', leading to a concluding section.

INTERSECTIONAL ABSENCES: REVIEWING SEXUALITY, RELIGION AND YOUTH

Intersectional Anxieties[3] and Enduring Capacities

Much sociological and feminist literature applies a conceptual lens of 'intersectionality' in exploring, theorising and debating social divisions of sexuality, gender, race and class (Anthias 2001; Taylor et al. 2010). Rather than portraying intersectionality as a list to be constructed and completed, whereby inequalities are rated and ranked, others have pointed instead to ongoing complexity and multiplicity, so that inequalities cannot simply be marked onto each other mechanically. Whilst 'intersection' is now a common trope in discussions of social dynamics and identities, there is still immense worth and salience in this concept. Arguably, 'understanding complexities posed by intersections of different axes of differentiation is as pressing today as it has always been' (Brah and Phoenix 2004: 75). Yet, as with Brown's (2012) 'anxious' commentary on the potentiality of 'intersectionality, painful feelings of being failed by the neglect of particular intersections can be experienced (Taylor 2007a, 2007b; 2009).

Few studies have explored the ways that Christian religious identities shape and are shaped by their intersections and interactions with other social identities (although see Yip 2002 on Muslim identities). Yet 'intersectionality' allows for an exploration of the relations between various *social* categories and experiences, between the everyday, ordinary—even contradictory—spaces of (sexual/religious) citizenship (Yip 2003). Inclusions do not necessarily result in resolutions, as 'intersectionality' cannot be simply seen as settled, instead involving enduring efforts and even failures, in the attempt to 'keep trying' (Haschemi Yekani et al. 2010; Taylor et al. 2010).[4]

168 Yvette Taylor and Ria Snowdon

Heteronomativities? Institutionalised Scripts and Individualised Inclusion

Intersectionality as a social frame avoids the pitfalls of more psychologised frames that speak of 'cognitive dissonance' or resolving 'double stigma', where the site of examination is often the individual rather than the social context. As O'Brien (2004) demonstrates, her investigation into the strategies used by LGBTQ Christians to 'integrate' conflicting identities was quickly dismissed in foregrounding the multiple identities held in 'workable tension' (Thumma 1991). Several studies have shown how queer-identified members of Christian churches have developed strategies of adaptation and resistance, reworking scripts of inclusion and exclusion, 'coming out' (or not) and stretching heteronormative theologies of sexuality (O'Brien 2004, 2005, 2014; Wilcox 2006).

Heelas and Woodhead's subjectivisation thesis posits a decrease of participation in and adherence to 'life-as' religions—understood as subordinating to and conforming of individual life to divine life—and an increased interest in holistic 'subjective-life' spiritualities. The latter involves living in tune with *individual* subjectivities as a legitimate form of spiritual living. Current empirical studies amongst LGB Christians support the latter position, with Yip (2003) suggesting that non-heterosexual Christians utilise aspects of detraditionalisation and individualism, whereby senses of 'self' function as ' . . . the ultimate point of reference in the individual's life course' (135). Such privatisation is seen to characterise religious faith today more than external authority structures. There are, however, enduring tensions between 'self-cultivation' in religious subjectivisation and life-as demand where gendered and sexualised scripts recirculate certain sources of authority. 'Queer religion' occurs within intersections of personal, familial, organisational and cultural domains, informing enduring exclusions and questionable inclusions.

'Heteronormativity' is central here, understood as a set of institutional practices that systematically legitimise and naturalise heterosexuality as the norm for sexual and, broader, *social* relations. Heterosexuality becomes the everywhere and nowhere 'organising principle of social life' (Hockey et al. 2007), and the assumption that structures social relations (Weeks et al. 2001) and moral boundaries (Ahmed 2006). Rahman and Jackson (2010) argue that heteronomativity is often an invisible and silent, yet pervasive and entrenched structure, as 'the assemblage of regulatory practices, which produces intelligible genders within a heterosexual matrix that insists upon the coherence of sex/gender/desire' (Chambers 2007: 667). Highly gendered and heteronormative 'role models', 'mentors' and (familial) mediations are experienced by young lesbian Christians. These intersect public-private domains in the production of queer religious subjectivity and disidentification. In bringing such domains to light, Macke (2014) offers 'que(e)rying' as a distinct model of research that integrates ethnographic methods with queer theory and praxis. Such 'que(e)rying' becomes a methodological

Creating Citizens, Constructing Religion, Configuring Gender   169

strategy oriented towards the dialectical relationship between sex, gender, sexualities and religious practices, organisations and cultures.

METHODS

This chapter is based on a subset of data, involving 16 young lesbian women who variously identify as Christian from Manchester, Newcastle and London. Participants were recruited through our website[5] and closed Facebook group (Queer Religious Youth) and also through inclusive churches, university LGBT societies, LGBT youth groups, support services and publications. Snowballing was used with limited success: whilst espoused by researchers of difficult-to-access and marginalised groups (Fish 2000), most respondents did not have an extensive network of young lesbian Christians that researchers could access. As one participant exclaimed in her interview: 'Yeah I would be surprised if I met a gay Christian; I would definitely want to talk to them' (Susan, 19, Newcastle).

A mixed-method research design was adopted, consisting of individual semi-structured face-to-face interviews, diaries and a social mapping exercise. The latter two were employed as participant-led methodologies, generating both textual and visual data to complement the oral stories. Using diaries, participants were invited to keep them for a month after the interview to record their reflections on their everyday lives, events and thoughts relating to the interview themes. Using mind maps, participants were asked to think about the spaces they inhabit on a day-to-day basis and where they felt (un)comfortable to express their religious and sexual identities. This information was visually mapped onto a blank piece of paper with participants choosing different, creative and often colourful ways to express themselves and 'display' their identities, including keywords in the centre of the page with ideas, concept, and pictures radiating from them; graphs; Venn diagrams; lists; and Mandalas. The purpose was to offer insight into identities in a format alternative to the interviews and to represent different intersecting components of lived experiences.

Most of the participants from our sample of 16 young lesbians considered themselves to be white British, with only one identifying as white Other (Welsh). Two participants had disabilities (one used an electronic wheelchair and one claimed Disability Living Allowance because of her specific disabilities). In the overall research project, young people were broadly defined as under 35 years, with the youngest respondent in our subsample of lesbians, discussed in this article, being 19 and the oldest being 30 (the mean age of respondents was 25 years old). 'Youth' is a contested term: it can signify a very wide age range, and the experiences and meanings associated with it are socially constituted, varying both cross-culturally and historically. Some participants identified with the denomination of their church: Church of England (two participants), and Methodist (one). One participant identified as Unitarian but with Pagan and Buddhist leanings. Where churches were

170 *Yvette Taylor and Ria Snowdon*

non-denominational, such as the Metropolitan Community Church (MCC) (nine participants), some participants also identified with the denomination within which they had been brought up (Church of England, two participants, and Catholic, one). Three other participants did not attend a church or attended a non-denominational church (other than MCC).

FINDING THE (LESBIAN) WOMEN IN LEADERSHIP: 'DIVERSITY ROLE MODELS'

Women Bishops and the 'Elders' Wife'

On the 21 November 2012 the Church of England's governing body, the General Synod, voted against allowing women to become bishops (The *Guardian*, 21 November 2012). The young women participating in our project were incensed. What re-emerged in these public controversies was a revisitation and recirculation of traditional gender and religious roles (and 'role models'), whereby leadership and public presences were legitimised, in official votes at least, as specifically male. This questions the 'coming forward' of young lesbian Christians in making queer religious space, a constraint which sat alongside continued gendered, familial and heteronormative roles/spaces more generally. Andrea (24, Newcastle) was writing in her project diary when news of the vote was broadcast live; she interrupted her entry with the following:

> *Wait—I've just been watching the BBC News live news feed from the CofE general synod and just heard that they have rejected the introduction of women bishops. I cannot believe it. What makes even less sense is that the House of Laity voted against it whilst the Bishops and the Clergy were overwhelmingly in favour. I've just looked at the stats apparently a 2/3 majority is needed and the laity voted 132 for and 74 against if another 6 had voted the other way we'd be looking at a world with women bishops in the CofE! I can't quite believe it. I'm worried now the CofE will look even more irrelevant and I think it will really struggle to justify it's [sic] union with the State now. If we can't even have women bishops what's the hope for same-sex marriage?
>
> (Andrea, 24, Newcastle)

Andrea was in the process of reconciling both her sexual and religious identity but felt this ruling undermined the progress she had made and would alienate friends who might see her Christian faith as archaic and irrelevant, further reflecting in her diary: 'it is entirely possible to be young queer and Christian. Sometimes it is easier than others (e.g. it will be embarrassing to be a Christian within my social groups following the rejection of women bishops—hopefully this will ease).'

Evelyn (26, Manchester) returned her diary with thoughts of leaving the church in protest against the General Synod's announcement: 'I don't know

Creating Citizens, Constructing Religion, Configuring Gender 171

how many House of Bishops statements that would take'. She recounted a conversation she had with a work colleague about Diversity Role Models, a charity aimed at helping schools eradicate homophobic bullying: 'they send normal people into schools to go "I'm gay, I'm normal, feel free to ask your questions" (as a side note which just occurred whilst working on this—maybe the House of Bishops need to meet a Diversity Role Model).' Here Evelyn was voicing frustration at a lack not only of women but non-heterosexual role models in the church.

The number of women in leadership roles, regardless of denomination, was a common concern amongst participants. At one end of this extreme, Kelly (26, London) complained in her interview that there were too many women in leadership at her MCC church:

> There are more men in the congregation, always has been, but our leadership team is almost entirely women, which is just as bad. Actually it's almost worse because if there were more men in the congregation there should be more men in leadership to reflect the congregation. (Kelly, 26, London)

Similarly, Claire (24, Newcastle) acknowledged that there were also more women 'in charge' in her local MCC, arguing that this was important to disrupt *traditional heteronormative* leadership structures, which still arguably persist beyond a numerical 'diversity count' (Ahmed 2012):

> . . . people are used to seeing 70% men and 30% women standing at the front of a church, when it's the other way round, they perceive it as a huge problem. Even if it's 50:50, they think because it's more women than they're used to seeing, they think of it as a problem. We had one person complain that there weren't enough men in leadership and I just felt like saying, "If it was the other way round and there were more men than women, you wouldn't even notice because that's normal." '
> (Claire, 24, Newcastle)

Participants also spoke of witnessing negative reactions from congregants towards authority figures because of their gender. Debbie (30, London) attended a Pentecostal church when she was younger, where a woman was discouraged from becoming a priest: 'there was a female person in charge who was involved in the church and it was before female priests and she was so hated because she wanted to be a priest! I thought that was awful. She has become a priest now but she's still getting negative connotations for being there'. Claire (24, Newcastle) attended an Anglican service near to her university and commended the female curate: 'she has a PhD in Theology and she preached really, really well and she preached about women in leadership. And she obviously had a positive view on that being a female curate standing up there.' However, Claire noted a hostile reaction to the curate for positioning herself outside of traditional biblical gender norms: 'afterwards,

172   *Yvette Taylor and Ria Snowdon*

she had a queue of 18 year old undergraduates, men mostly, going up to her telling her how she was wrong because the bible says women should stay quiet. And I just thought, 'How dare you?!'

Within Helen's (20, Newcastle) Charismatic church, an overt message of equality between the sexes was preached: 'men and women are equal, they just have their different strengths'. Helen agrees with this in principle: 'of course only women can have babies, yes, that's obvious'. However, she has begun to rally against this dictate as she realised the restrictions it placed on women and the hypocrisy of the leadership structure:

> . . . the restrictions tended to apply more to women than to men, even though, you know, these perceptions that women can do the kids' stuff but men can also do that if they want, however the elders of the church are men and, 'No, women can't do that', and just this dichotomy and sort of inequality which most people are saying, 'No, no! What are you talking about? Men and women are equal' but then you look at the structure there and think, 'No, that's not true at all'.
>
> (Helen, 20, Newcastle)

As these accounts show, there are persistent gendered and heteronormative scripts which shape the boundaries of inclusion and exclusion evident in public debates and congregational conversations (and challenges); thus the (lesbian) leader can be limited in the, often bracketed and cordoned off, space that she can take up.

'Nudge, Nudge, Wink, Wink': Leading Lesbians?

Where men dominated, some participants, like Helen, spoke of the informal leadership roles women could take, particularly as wives to (male) authority figures, with women's access to authority formulated through heterosexual marriage:

> They have the authority role as elder's wife, which is like elder but it is not elder because they are the elder's wives, if you know what I mean. I think they have as much influence in the church as the actual elders, but the official authority is that of the elders; that's how it works.
>
> (Helen, 20, Newcastle)

Female leaders, however, represented a more inclusive, liberal church to participants. Estelle (25, Manchester) described her local Anglican church in these terms:

> . . . it's quite diverse and it's a woman vicar, which I've found to mean that they are more liberal and do actually dare to talk about things like gay stuff and race and stuff. So that's cool . . . the vicar there, she openly

Creating Citizens, Constructing Religion, Configuring Gender   173

talked about LGBT stuff and women's stuff in sermons, and that's made me want to go back.

(Estelle, 25, Manchester)

At least four participants had aspirations, were in the process or were already acting as lay or ordained ministers of their churches. Claire (24 years old) would consider ordination and has made tentative plans with her wife to 'plant' a new church in Wales. Kelly (26, London) is training on a non-stipendiary basis for ordination with MCC and is considering a chaplaincy career for the future. Andrea (24 years old) has acted as a lay minister in the past and Kirsty (30, Manchester) qualified as a youth minister. Kirsty's story, however, highlights that women's aspirations and trajectories within the church are not always straightforward, particularly amongst those who identify as lesbian.

Kirsty (30, Manchester) studied at university for a degree in Youth Work and Ministry. She got married to a man when she was 19. At 22, whilst on university placement as a youth worker at her church (where her husband was a worship leader), she developed feelings for a close female friend. When she realised her feelings were reciprocated, Kirsty left her husband despite pressure from their mutual friends from church to stay together:

So a 'friend' of ours came round with him (her estranged husband) and said to me, and I was always quite close to her, she was a little bit older than me and had a family and stuff and said how disappointed she was and how sinful it was and how bad I was behaving and didn't know what I was doing and really upset me.

(Kirsty, 30, Manchester)

Suspecting that her church leaders, and placement mentors, would not support her new relationship, initially she kept it from them. However, when she came under increasing pressure from her church colleagues to apply for her placement position as a youth worker and minister to become permanent, she felt compelled to disclose her non-heterosexuality in the interests of honesty:

'Nudge, nudge, wink, wink, you'll get it if you apply, you really should apply . . .' and I tried to fob them off with, 'No, I think it's time to move on and look at new things' but in the end I just had to say, 'Look, I'm gay' and the Minister backtracked a heck of a lot, suddenly it wasn't so certain I would get it and he'd have to speak to the Bishop and get some advice and they didn't think he could support me and a lot of families would leave the church if I were to be there, and all of this business.

(Kirsty, 30, Manchester)

Kirsty's placement subsequently broke down as the church grappled with her sexuality. She felt she had no choice but to leave university, qualifying

174 *Yvette Taylor and Ria Snowdon*

with a diploma rather than graduating with a degree: 'he [the priest and placement mentor] said, "Well I don't think I could support your way of life if you were to stay here with the youth Minister and I think it's incompatible with what the Bible says." ' As a result, Kirsty aspires to work in leadership and ministry but has accepted that

> it's not really likely . . . There aren't a lot of churches that are accepting of gay people really, or if they are accepting then you've got to stay celibate and you can't be in a relationship, and I think that's absolute rubbish.

Kirsty now worships at a Fresh Expressions church, which works with a broad range of denominations and traditions (Anglicanism in Kirsty's case) to encourage them to form new congregations alongside more traditional churches, primarily for the benefit of people who are not yet members of any church or have left in the past. Thus they differ markedly from mainstream churches, often worshipping in unconventional space and creating unique approaches to service. Here Kirsty, alongside her girlfriend, is able to lead worship as congregants take it in turns following a more democratised system. Of the congregation, she says, 'The church I go to has got a lot of gay people . . . It's not a very big church and I think, statistically, it's one in ten people are gay then our church should have about 300 people in it. (Laughter)'.

On the whole, participants were often supportive and sometimes proactive in making space for (lesbian) women in church, but they did so within a policy context which reinforced an institutional glass ceiling for women, creating disillusionment and dismay amongst respondents who feared for the church's future and sometimes their own role within it. Such fears and frustrations persisted in negotiating a place in church as 'God's family'.

'SCARY CHURCH PARENTS': LOCATING YOUNG LESBIAN LIVES IN CHURCH

One of Many: Fitting into God's (Family) Home

Participants often spoke of 'familial' links: it was important to '[feel] home somewhere, feel comfortable' (Claire, 24, Newcastle). 'I get to spend time with my extended family, getting to see people, getting encouraged and spending time with God in a space that's God's space' (Nicola, 21, Newcastle). 'It's an abode, a home' (Sandra, 24, Newcastle). Whilst Claire and Nicola had been excommunicated from earlier churches because of their sexuality, Sandra had left her Catholic church (along with her mother) because of their views on homosexuality. Thus all three young women sought out a spiritual home after being, or feeling, rejected by the churches they had grown up in. Sandra found this in the Metropolitan Community Church (MCC), an inclusive church founded in and for the LGBT community. It was a space

Creating Citizens, Constructing Religion, Configuring Gender 175

that shielded her from the vitriol she had experienced in Catholicism: 'MCC to me is security and warmth and a shelter from the storm'.

Strong adherence to religious ethos can shape the degree of acceptability exhibited towards nonconforming gender and sexual expressions, and whilst Sandra experiences 'shelter', Sally is troubled by her 'scary church parents': 'Go visit the scary church parents tonight and my whole beautiful gay Christian world could be turned on its head . . . ' (Sally, 20, Newcastle). In her diary, Sally judged this visit to be a success as she 'didn't come back angry or wanting to cry'. Her 'scary church parents' are a married couple who 'adopted' her from an Anglican Evangelical church she had previously attended. There, married couples were encouraged to forge these links with young people in the congregation, to provide personal moral and religious guidance and support. Sally left the church (and joined the Methodists) when she realised that she fundamentally disagreed with their views, including those on abortion, 'fornication' and sexuality. LGBT religious participation is tolerated (even encouraged through this familial framing) as long as the 'sinner' (child) remembers her place:

> . . . I have sat in a sermon from that church and they have said, everybody here has sinned, there is probably at least one girl here who has had an abortion, there are people here who have slept with people before marriage, there is a girl who is looking at another girl in the wrong way and it's like, 'What are you saying?' I just find it a bit creepy.
> (Sally, 20, Newcastle)

The queering of religion insists upon a shift away from 'sin' and 'abomination' in the religious script of homosexuality but here we find evidence of their persistent scripting (Wilcox 2006), alongside the questioning/queering of religiosity.

Sally maintained a relationship with the couple, meeting for regular dinners, despite them labelling her a 'sinner' when she told them she had a girlfriend and giving her a book for Christmas which 'suggested I was just going through a phase'. She reflected in her diary that '#comingout [sic] to people who 'adopted' you is harder than coming out to your mother'. But Sally is fond of the couple, she believes they are 'both brainwashed' and hopes she can help reshape their views through example. When talking about her Methodist discussion group at university, Sally told the couple that their talking point had been 'why does God hate gay people?'

> When telling the scary church parents this (her 'mother') automatically answered "but he doesn't!" Which whatever your view on gay people and God is true because God loves everyone but considering they view me having a girlfriend as sinning (which inherently isn't bad, because *they* view everyone as a sinner) . . . it was quite nice to jump on it.
> (Sally, 20, Newcastle)

176 *Yvette Taylor and Ria Snowdon*

Here Sally disrupts the traditional parental authority they assume over her as a young person by gently trying to expose the flaws in their own arguments. However, a more successful example of this 'parental' relationship is represented by Helen (20, Newcastle) and her 'mentor'. Within their Charismatic church, older people are encouraged to mentor students in the congregation:

> . . . I am sort of mentored by an older woman at church who is married and had a family and we have a coffee every now and again and I found I was able to sort of discuss my feelings on sexuality and sort of where I felt I sat and my perspective on what the church was doing and how I related to that. So that, I think, was very valuable to me that I could, there was someone that I could discuss that with, someone who was a Christian and in the church who got that and so I found that very helpful.
>
> (Helen, 20, Manchester)

Therefore, whilst Sally sought a new denomination (Methodism) because there was *no space* for her as a lesbian in her original church, a troubled relationship with her 'church parents' is maintained in the hope of 'saving' each other. Helen, on the other hand, has a more equitable relationship with her church 'mentor', and whilst she also disagrees with her church's views on sexuality (she continues to conceal her own from the congregation at large), her continued membership in their Charismatic church is forged by this outlet where she can discuss and debate freely her views in a one-to-one environment with someone she respects.

Confessing and 'Coming Out' (Or Not)

Not all participants, however, felt this 'anchoring' and belonging within their churches. Evelyn (26, Manchester) has been attending an Anglican church for four years but continues to feel isolated: 'it's a very big congregation and there are a few people I kind of smile to and say hello but I sit on my own'. In her diary, Evelyn wonders if this is because the heteronormative, family-oriented church does not know how to embrace a single lesbian:

> . . . at the 'all talk to your neighbour while the kids head off to their Sunday school groups' bit I spoke to no-one—partly me being shy I guess. I'm not convinced its [sic] actually anything about LGBT, I think they'd struggle with a straight, single young person who isn't that outgoing too. But I wonder sometimes.
>
> (Evelyn, 26, Manchester)

During the service at Evelyn's church, they have a 'This Time Tomorrow' slot where a congregant talks about who they are, what they do during the

Creating Citizens, Constructing Religion, Configuring Gender 177

week, the good parts and challenges and what they would like the congregation to pray for. Perhaps sensing Evelyn's isolation, the curate asked her to speak in this slot at a forthcoming service but Evelyn declined:

> I think I'd struggle to be honest, I haven't yet heard anyone stand up and say 'I live by myself' and to be honest I'd probably want prayer for a welcoming church space for LGBT Christians—but I can't imagine standing at the front of 300 Christians who barely know me and saying that.
>
> (Evelyn, 26, Manchester)

Intimidated by her 'minority' status, Evelyn felt unable to raise the issue of LGBT Christians and welcoming inclusive spaces, despite the fact that she was 'out' to the curate and vicar but not to the wider congregation ('I've never had that conversation, why would I?'). Evelyn does sometimes supplement her regular church worship with an additional LGBT service once a month and a bimonthly Lesbian and Gay Christian Meeting (LGCM). However, she questions the efficacy of carving out that sort of specific space: 'I'd prefer just to know that I'm accepted in any church'.

Some participants did not know their church's stance on LGBT issues but continued to attend regularly despite the potential for prejudice and antigay sentiments (Yip 2002). Andrea (24, Newcastle) is not 'out' to her parents' church, 'because everybody would gossip about it, and probably there'd be a few people who'd definitely raise their eyebrows, but I really don't know in terms of theologically what their stance would be'. Similarly, Lucy (19, Newcastle) has not disclosed her non-heterosexuality to her congregation but has surmised that they 'seem' accepting, if not overtly inclusive. 'I know there's definitely two lesbians there. They are more out than I am and the church always seems to be quite accepting to them, so I would say it is quite inclusive.' Others, like Helen, know their church is not inclusive but it fulfils their spiritual needs first and foremost:

> . . . I have often thought about thinking, 'Well what would it be like if I attended a church that was completely inclusive?' and I think I would really enjoy it and I think it would be a load off my mind, but at the same time, because I'm quite attached to my own church as it is and I have friends, a lot of support there, I find it really . . . It meets my needs in terms of sort of prayer and worship, so I'd much rather feel that, as part of that community . . .
>
> (Helen, 20, Newcastle)

Scripts of inclusion are stretched, queried and desired, evident in public-private debate on same-sex marriage as a lead into—or step away from—the 'straight and narrow' hetero-homonormative family (Taylor 2009).

178 Yvette Taylor and Ria Snowdon

'Doing It in the Eyes of God': Leading into 'Family'

Often participants did not want to explicitly test the institutional, and grassroots, (in)tolerance of their churches. Susan (19, Newcastle), for example, left her Evangelical church not because of their views against non-heterosexuality but because she disagreed with God's perspective and did not believe she could continue to worship him under any denomination:

> . . . I say 'I believe in God but I don't worship him', that's a kind of simple way of putting it. And whether you want to call that a Christian or not I don't know. I would probably say I'm not a Christian because I don't think I'm going to Heaven. That sounds a bit odd, I think I'm probably going to Hell because I'm not a Christian. Basically, God gave me the choice: he says 'you can either stay with your girlfriend . . . and sort of outwardly gay and act like that or you can kind of push that part of you out and take me in, make space for me and in that case you would be very Christian'. And I said 'no, I love my girlfriend and I want to be with her and if that means I'm not going to do what you think's right so be it'. I don't think it's wrong but I understand that he thinks it's wrong. Basically, I disagree with God which is a very weird thing.
>
> (Susan, 19, Newcastle)

Whilst Susan has a deep belief in God, she does not attend a church or identify as a Christian, highlighting the ruptures that were felt by some participants between the intersecting identities of religion and sexuality. Some participants reconciled incompatible scripts between sexuality/religion by invoking what O'Brien (2005) calls a 'bigger God' who stretches out supposed 'natural law' through equal love. Same-sex marriage was a significant setting upon which participants tried and tested ideas of a 'bigger God'. Susan was unique in opposing same-sex marriage and civil partnerships:

> I can see why gay people are fighting for it to be marriage because they want equality . . . Really I think it's not marriage because marriage is a Christian thing. A unity not just between you and your partner but a unity between you and your partner and God. God isn't going to unite in a gay relationship so it shouldn't be a marriage really. I'm not going to march against gay people and civil partnerships but I'd probably—if I met someone who was really passionate about gay marriage, I would question them, I would challenge them.
>
> (Susan, 19, Newcastle)

More common was the view that even if interviewees themselves disagreed with the institution of marriage, they preferred to have the option and equal access:

> I think there should be marriage equality for those people that want it; I think it should just be 'marriage'. Civil Partnerships annoy me, it's like

Creating Citizens, Constructing Religion, Configuring Gender 179

a second-class marriage, I think it's just horrible and I'd never have one. I'd never get married either but I'd rather that was the option rather than Civil Partnership.

(Estelle, 25, Manchester)

Some participants identified contradictions between church leadership's and grassroots' views on same-sex marriage, again revealing the links between official lines (as articulated by religious leaders) and congregational lives:

Like when the Anglican Church said gay marriage is wrong and homosexuality is a sin and didn't consult anybody, any of their members about what they thought? That's completely rubbish. The leadership pretty much said that and didn't consult anyone.

(Kirsty, 30, Manchester)

Evelyn (26, Manchester) even identified contradiction in what the vicar of her parents' church said in a private and public context. In personal conversations, he had supported equal marriage, but in a service she recently attended, he led prayers on 'supporting marriage and the [heterosexual] family', which Evelyn saw as a direct attack on proposed legislative changes around same-sex marriage:

. . . they prayed for those 'supporting marriage and the family', this is taken from the Mother's Union prayer. The MU are anti-equal marriage. I don't really want to pray for people who are saying that I shouldn't be allowed to get married, and that my relationship wouldn't be worthy of that. Then they were praying for particular relationships, parent to child and husband to wife. Because obviously husband to wife is the only acceptable option.

(Evelyn, 26, Manchester)

Evelyn was concerned for those who might have attended the church for the first time and would not realise that it was actually an 'ok space' for lesbian (and GBT) Christians. Participants were mostly in favour of religious same-sex marriage and two of our participants were in civil partnerships (Claire, 24 and Stephanie, 29, both of Newcastle) and both received a blessing at their MCC church. But as a site of 'coming forward' as now included, many championed seemingly homonormative ideals as a good 'fit': 'I want to get married, I want to get married in a church, I want to get married in my church' (Sally, 20, Newcastle); 'I want to get married and have a family' (Lola, 25, London); 'the really important bit [is] getting everyone together and doing it in the eyes of God' (Claire, 24, Newcastle). When 'getting everyone together', certain gendered and heteronormative scripts re-emerge which stretch, query and sometimes reinforce the boundaries of inclusion and exclusion in attempting to 'make' space, as a retention, rejection or religious affirmation.

180 *Yvette Taylor and Ria Snowdon*

CONCLUSION

The young lesbian respondents in this project participated in 'queering religion' at a crucial time when the intersecting tensions between the ordination of female bishops and religious same-sex marriage debates were at the forefront of the UK public imagination. Our participants spoke about the discrimination and marginalisation they felt as a result of their age, sexuality and gender within heteronormative church space. Importantly, in exploring young lesbians' connections with Christianity, we have been able to disrupt an *automatic* association of non-heterosexuality with secularism and an assumed disconnect between 'youth' and 'religion' (Yip 1997; Kubicek et al. 2009; Gross and Yip 2010; Jordan 2011). We have attempted a fuller, 'intersectional' understanding of contemporary dynamics in the queering of religion. Religion matters for our 'queer religious youth' as a site of significant self-identification, situated within a changing landscape and political climate.

These public-private intersections are also bases for determining inclusion and exclusion across families, communities, networks and organisations. Heteronormativity, based on 'natural law' and traditional gender-binary role, can expand to include homonormativity as a certain 'fit' into religious-sexual space; this form of inclusivity often reaffirms certain cultural values even as it stretches the terms and conditions (as made, 'modelled' and/or 'mimicked'). Religious participation conveys (de)legitimation within family, community and society, as apparent in scripts of inclusion and exclusion (O'Brien 2014). Highly gendered and heteronormative 'role models', 'mentors' and (familial) mediations experienced by young lesbian Christians show that queer religious subjectivity is complexly negotiated via intersectional experiences, combining institutional 'official lines' with everyday intimate realities and disidentifications. Intersectional sites, scripts and sticking points converge as young lesbians 'make space' in conversation, contrast and convergence with institutionalised scripts.

NOTES

1 This number increases to 21 if bisexual (four) and asexual (one) participants were to be included.
2 In the UK context, this includes the raft of legislation enacted by the previous UK New Labour government, such as the Civil Partnership Act, 2004; the Gender Recognition Act, 2004; and the Equality Act, 2010. The Conservative-Liberal coalition government have introduced the Marriage (Same-Sex Couples) Act in 2013. Some of these provisions are included and extended through European Union (EU) legislation (see Monro and Richardson 2010).
3 See Brown, M. (2011) 'Gender and Sexuality I: Intersectional Anxieties', *Progress in Human Geography* 36(4) 541–550.
4 To 'queer' often signals a challenging to dualistic frameworks that limit and methodologically marginalize; there are tensions between the naming of identity but there are also links between queer theory and anticategorical approaches to the intersectionality (Haschemi Yekani et al. 2010).
5 http://queerreligiousyouth.wordpress.com/.

BIBLIOGRAPHY

Ahmed, S. (2006) *Queer Phenomenology. Orientations, Objects, Others*. Durham, NC: Duke University Press.

Ahmed, S. (2012) 'Diversity: Problems and Paradoxes for Black Feminists', in Taylor, Y. (ed.) (2012) *Educational Diversity: The Subject of Difference and Different Subjects*. Basingstoke: Palgrave Macmillan, 203–218.

Anthias, F. (2001) 'The Concept of 'Social Division' and Theorising Social Stratification: Looking at Ethnicity and Class', *Sociology* 35(4): 835–854.

Brah, A. and Phoenix, A. (2004) 'Ain't I a Woman? Revisiting Intersectionality', *Journal of International Women's Studies* 5(3): 75–86.

Brown, M. (2012) 'Gender and Sexuality I: intersectional Anxieties', *Progress in Human Geography* 36(4): 541–550.

Chambers, D. (2006) *New Social Ties: Contemporary Connections in a Fragmented Society*. Basingstoke: Palgrave Macmillan.

Duggan, L. (2003) *The Twilight of Equality: Neoliberalism, Cultural Politics, and the Attack on Democracy*. New York: Beacon Press.

Fish, J. (2000) 'Sampling Lesbians: How to Get 1000 Lesbians to Complete a Questionnaire', *Feminism and Psychology* 1(2): 32–38.

Gorman-Murray, A. and Nash, C. J. (2014) 'Queering Religion, Religious Queers: A Geographical Commentary', in Taylor, Y. and Snowdon, R. (eds.) *Queering Religion, Religious Queers*. London: Routledge, xxiii–xxxvi.

Gross, M. and Yip, A. (2010) 'Living Spirituality and Sexuality: A Comparison of Lesbian, Gay and Bisexual Christians in France and Britain', *Social Compass* 57(1): 40–59.

The Guardian. (2012) 'Women Bishops: Church of England Votes No—as It Happened', *The Guardian*, 23 November 2012. Available at http://www.guardian.co.uk/world/2012/nov/20/women-bishops-church-england-vote-live, last accessed 30 April 2015.

Haschemi Yekani, E., Michaelis, B., and Dietze, G. (2010) ' "Try Again. Fail Again. Fail Better." Queer Interdependencies as Corrective Methodologies', in Taylor, Y., Hines, S. and Casey, M. (eds.) *Theorizing Intersectionality and Sexuality: Genders and Sexualities in the Social Sciences*. Basingstoke: Palgrave Macmillan.

Hockey, J., Meah, A. and Robinson, V. (2007) *Mundane Heterosexualities: From Theory to Practices*. Basingstoke: Palgrave Macmillan.

Jordan, M. D. (2011) *Recruiting Young Love: How Christians Talk About Sexuality*. Chicago and London: The University of Chicago Press.

Kubicek, K. B., McDavitt, B., Carpineto, J., Weiss, G., Iverson, E. F. and Kipke, M. D. (2009) ' "God Made Me Gay for a Reason": Young Men Who Have Sex with Men's Resiliency in Resolving Internalized Homophobia From Religious Sources', *Journal of Adolescent Research* 24: 601–633.

Machacek, D. and Wilcox, M. (eds.) (2003) *Sexuality and the World's Religions*. Santa Barbara: ABC-Clio.

Macke, K. (2014) 'Que(e)rying Methodology to Study Church-Based Activism: Conversations in Culture, Power, and Change', in Taylor, Y. and Snowdon, R. (eds.) *Queering Religion, Religious Queers*. London: Routledge, 13–30.

McCormack, M. (2012) 'The Positive Experiences of Openly Gay, Lesbian, Bisexual and Transgendered Students in a Christian Sixth Form College', *Sociological Research Online* 17(3) [Not paginated].

McDermott, E. (2010) ' "I Wanted to be Totally True to Myself": Class and the Making of the Sexual Self', in Taylor, Y. (ed.), *Classed Intersections: Spaces, Selves, Knowledges*. Farnham: Ashgate, 199–216.

Monro, S. (2010) 'Sexuality, Space and Intersectionality: The Case of Lesbian, Gay, and Bisexual Equalities Initiatives in UK Local Government', *Sociology* 44(5): 996–1010.

182   Yvette Taylor and Ria Snowdon

O'Brien, J. (2004) 'Wrestling the Angel of Contradiction: Queer Christian Identities', *Culture and Religion* 5: 179–202.

O'Brien, J. (2005) 'How Big Is Your God? Queer Christian Social Movements', in Breen, M. S. and Peters, F. (eds.) *Genealogies of Identity: Interdisciplinary Readings on Sex and Sexuality*. Amsterdam: Rodopi, 237–236.

O'Brien, J. (2014) 'Outing Religion in LGBT Studies', in Taylor, Y. and Snowdon, R. (eds.) *Queering Religion, Religious Queers*. London: Routledge: xi–xxii.

Puar, J. (2007) *Terrorist Assemblages: Homonationalism in Queer Times*. Durham, NY: Duke University Press.

Rahman, M. and Jackson, S. (2010) *Gender and Sexuality: Sociological Approaches*. Cambridge: Polity Press.

Regnerus, M. (2007) *Forbidden Fruit: Sex and Religion in the lives of American Teenagers*. New York and Oxford: Oxford University Press.

Rogers, S. (2012) 'Mapped: Britain's Young Adults Still Living at Home', *The Guardian*, 1 June 2012. Available at http://www.guardian.co.uk/news/datablog/interactive/2012/jun/01/young-people-living-home-map, last accessed 30 April 2015.

Taylor, Y. (2004) 'Hidden in the Small Ads: Researching Working-Class Lesbians', *Graduate Journal of Social Sciences* 1(2): 253–277.

Taylor, Y. (2007a) 'Going Up without Going Away? Working-Class Women in Higher Education', *Youth and Policy* 94: 35–50.

Taylor, Y. (2007b) *Working-Class Lesbian Life: Classed Outsiders*. Basingstoke: Palgrave Macmillan.

Taylor, Y. (2009) *Lesbian and Gay Parenting: Securing Social and Educational Capital*. Basingstoke: Palgrave Macmillan.

Taylor, Y. (ed.) (2010) *Classed Intersections: Spaces, Selves, Knowledges*. Farnham: Ashgate.

Taylor, Y., Hines, S. and Casey, M. (eds.) (2010) *Theorizing Intersectionality and Sexuality*. Basingstoke: Palgrave Macmillan.

Taylor, Y. and Snowdon, R. (2014) *Queering Religion, Religious Queers*. London: Routledge.

Thumma, S. (1991) 'Negotiating a Religious Identity: The Case of the Gay Evangelical', *Sociological Analysis* 52(4): 335.

Weeks, J., Heaphy, B. and Donovan, C. (2001) *Same Sex Intimacies: Families of Choice and Other Life Experiments*. London and New York: Routledge.

Wilcox, M. (2003) *Coming Out in Christianity: Religion, Identity, and Community*. Bloomington: Indiana University Press.

Wilcox, M. (2006) 'Outlaws or Inlaws?', *Journal of Homosexuality* 52: 73–100.

Yip, A. (1997) 'Attacking the Attacker: Gay Christians talk back', *The British Journal of Sociology* 48(1): 113–127.

Yip, A. (2002) 'The Persistence of Faith among Non-heterosexual Christians: Evidence for the Neosecularization Thesis of Religious Transformation', *Journal for the Scientific Study of Religion* 41(2): 199–212.

Yip, A. (2003) 'The Self as the Basis of Religious Faith: Spirituality of Gay, Lesbian and Bisexual Christians', in Grace, D., Heelas, P. and Woodhead, L. (eds.) *Predicting Religion: Christian, Secular and Alternative Futures*. Aldershot: Ashgate, 135–146.

Yip, A., Keenan, M. and Page, S. (2011) *Religion, Youth and Sexuality: Selected Key Findings from a Multi-Faith Exploration*. Research Report. Nottingham: University of Nottingham.

Yip, A. and Page, S.-J. (2013) *Religion and Sexual Identities: A Multi-faith Exploration of Young Adults*. Aldershot: Ashgate.

10 Changing Churches
Sexuality, Difference, Power

Savitri Hensman

Late on a Saturday afternoon in May 2014, at the end of a busy conference, participants gathered for a closing act of worship. It was the annual gathering of an organisation striving for greater inclusion of lesbian, gay, bisexual and trans* Christians in church and society. For me, and I think other participants, weariness melted away as a mainly Ugandan choir led the singing of the final hymn and a sense of joy and connectedness filled the imposingly built venue, Bloomsbury Baptist Church in central London.

Its founders in the mid-nineteenth century carefully situated the building between smart squares and grim slums, and it has continued to seek to bridge gaps of various kinds. US civil rights leader Martin Luther King Jr., a Baptist minister, preached there in the 1960s (Bowers 2012). It is one of a number of local churches which perceive hospitality and concern for justice as integral to Christian spirituality. Such inclusive churches have provided safe spaces for LGBTQI (lesbian, gay, bisexual, trans*, queer/questioning and intersex) Christian individuals and groups, sometimes coming under pressure as a result, and helped to influence attitudes in the wider church.

Over the years, I had attended many previous gatherings of the Lesbian and Gay Christian Movement, which was meeting that day, and of other organisations seeking greater justice and inclusivity in church and society. I was there not as a dispassionate observer but rather as a long-standing churchgoer and LGBTQI activist who regards loving committed partnerships as fully compatible with faith, while wishing to remain in fellowship with friends and fellow worshippers who take a different view. However, unusually, this conference took place against a backdrop of intensive change.

Several churches in the UK had formally acknowledged that there was no consensus among their members on sexual ethics and moreover that it was important to listen attentively to LGBTQI members in deciding what stance to adopt and were engaged in discussing this at their assemblies. As a writer as well as participant, I have followed with interest various processes of change in my own and other denominations; these can be painfully slow but, at a certain point, take on greater momentum.

In the Midlands, the Baptist Union Assembly was meeting that weekend and agreed to move forward significantly on sexuality, as did the Methodist

184   *Savitri Hensman*

Conference a few weeks later and the Kirk. So did the United Reformed Church General Assembly in Cardiff that summer, though full equality remained some distance away in all these denominations. In the course of the year, several churches in Britain were involved in, or planning, formal discussions on sexuality, reflecting growing recognition of the strength of the case for acceptance of committed, self-giving relationships.

There was also strong resistance to change. The punishment of a Church of England priest for marrying a same-sex partner (Siddique 2014) gained wide media coverage and highlighted internal divisions, echoed in several other churches. Some smaller denominations were still a long way from even discussing the possibility that same-sex partnerships might be acceptable. However, the introduction of marriage equality in law meant that Quakers and the Metropolitan Community Church in England and Wales were enjoying the freedom they had sought formally to marry same-sex as well as opposite-sex couples; and this would be extended to Scotland by the end of the year.

Discussion processes on sexuality and faith (Warnock 2014; Methodist Church in Britain 2014; United Reformed Church 2014; Gledhill 2015) have in some instances been criticised for failing to create a sufficiently safe space for all participants and adequately involve those with the greatest stake in the outcome (Holdsworth 2014). Ministers and elders in particular still sometimes risk being removed if publicly known to be in noncelibate, same-sex partnerships; and even today, some church leaders are authoritarian and intolerant of open dissent. Nevertheless, the visibility of, and diversity among, LGBTQI Christians in mainstream churches today, and range of voices heard in debates about faith and sexuality, would have been hard to predict 30 years, let alone a century, ago.[1]

Openly LGBTQI people and parents with children who identify as such have often spoken in formal assemblies at the national and regional level rather than simply being objects of discussion. At the same time, those opposed to greater inclusion have become better organised and their views too have been articulated.

This chapter focuses on whether, and how, different voices are represented in discussions on acceptance of LGBTQI people and same-sex partnerships in faith-based communities and institutions, looking in particular at recent developments in churches in Britain. This will include looking critically at notions about identity and authority within faith communities and may help to illuminate processes of contestation and change around sexuality and gender identity.

SOME CONSIDERATIONS IN APPROACHING THIS TOPIC

As others have pointed out, reflexivity is important, not least when examining the experience of non-heterosexual people of faith (Yip 2008). I write from an 'insider' perspective in that I am a Christian (specifically a member of the Church of England) who has been involved in debates on faith and sexuality at the local and, increasingly, the national level over the past thirty-odd years, and from the standpoint of a lesbian who has been active in organisations seeking greater equality for LGBTQI people in church and society. I have also written extensively on developments in this area, in particular for Ekklesia, which focuses on the changing role of beliefs, values and faith (or its absence) in public life and seeks to move beyond unjust, 'top-down' models of church and society (Hensman 1991, 2014, 2015).

In certain other senses, I am an 'outsider': my perceptions of what happens in non-Anglican churches are as a non-member, and I have never been a member of a formal church hierarchy (for instance a minister of religion, staff member or representative on a regional or national synod or assembly). Moreover, I am a minority ethnic woman, Sri Lankan by birth and descent, which makes me markedly different from a sizeable majority of members of most inclusive Christian organisations as well as denominational leaders.

However objective I might seek to be, inevitably my own hopes, fears and perceptions of key players and developments will colour my understanding of what has been taking place, even if I take care to compare these with others' understandings. I may take for granted attitudes and behaviours which are familiar to me but could usefully be probed more deeply. At the same time, I have access to insights which might otherwise be unavailable.

At the same time, the notion of a division between 'insiders' and 'outsiders', if taken too far, risks reinforcing a simplistic concept of identity. If, for instance, someone is of Jamaican descent, lesbian and Methodist, these are not discrete aspects of who she is: being a heterosexual woman and Pentecostalist might mean that 'Jamaicanness' would be experienced in a somewhat different way. In addition, understandings of nationhood, ethnicity, gender, sexual orientation and so forth, while possessing some continuity, are not static.

Gurminder K. Bhambra (2006: 36) has suggested that understandings of culture are often unhelpfully 'conceived of along absolutist lines and, as such, fix identities and people in space and time', taking for granted a gap between 'us' and 'them'. Both modernist and postmodernist approaches can fall into this trap:

> Whereas modernist thought is based on conceptual abstractions and ideas of a scientific history that exists outside of particular histories and thus is seen to transcend location, postmodernism projects location as relativism and uses 'others' to deconstruct modernism's categories. In both, however, 'others' are either known in the terms of the discourse (modernism) or, used as tools of deconstruction (postmodernism). In neither is knowledge of the 'other' seen as the basis for the *reconstruction* of received knowledge and traditions . . . the question of the 'other' is not solved by simply adding 'them' to 'us'—it has to be recognised

186   *Savitri Hensman*

that the 'adding to' fundamentally alters the initial paradigm in which there was an 'us' and an 'other'.

(Bhambra 2006: 38–39)

More specifically, there are various interpretations of what it means to be a Christian (or person of faith more generally) in twenty-first century Britain. As has been frequently pointed out, 'belonging' and 'believing' do not always go together and there are various shades of both (Davie 2006). While some people attend church primarily because it offers a sense of social connection, I have also encountered quite a number of LGBTQI people and some heterosexual people committed to greater inclusion who have a deep faith but are no longer regular churchgoers because they have experienced (or are afraid of) rejection. The term 'Christian' is here used to refer to people who self-define as such, whether on the basis of believing some or all of the tenets of faith set out in the historical creeds, trying to live by what they regard as Christian values, formally or informally belonging to a congregation or a sense of cultural heritage.

In addition, especially for LGBTQI church leaders, there can be a tension between their role, especially with regard to promoting unity, and other aspects of their identity. So, for example, even if a bishop or senior elder is comfortable about being gay and is discreetly partnered, he may be reluctant to let more than a handful of people know, not only because he fears being personally condemned by others but also in case this gets in the way of his ministry, though others may regard this as cowardly or hypocritical. Moreover, any yearning he may have for an official shift towards full acceptance may be balanced by apprehension at the thought of possible rifts within his church if it advances towards equality. For participants in church discussions on sexuality, different roles or aspects of identity may come to the fore at different times.

Hence I am aware that some Christians privately affirming of same-sex partnerships face certain risks, which I do not, if they state this openly. Paradoxically, having less overt 'power' in faith communities can sometimes make it easier to argue for what one actually believes.

DISCUSSING ETHICS AND CHANGE IN 'THE CHURCH'

Ordinarily, in Christian discourse, the term 'church' (if not used of a building) tends to refer to a universal fellowship made up of people who may be in smaller churches based on location and/or denomination. The notion of church as institution is secondary.

For example, according to the World Council of Churches, "As instrument of God's plan the Church is the community of people called by God and sent as Christ's disciples to proclaim the Good News in word and deed" (World Council of Churches 2005). A 1979 Anglican/Roman Catholic

International Commission (ARCIC) report stated that "The Church is a community which consciously seeks to submit to Jesus Christ . . . The perception of God's will for his Church does not belong only to the ordained ministry but is shared by all its members" (Anglican/Roman Catholic International Commission 1976). So, for instance, if it is the case that 'the church' should do more about poverty, this is a challenge not just for senior clergy and synods but also for me, my congregation and others in the neighbourhood, Christian friends and acquaintances to whom the church is 'we' rather than 'they' or 'it'.

Confusingly, however, in official statements on sexuality, church leaders sometimes refer to the church as if it were solely an institution, rendering the majority of members invisible. For example, in a response in June 2012 by the Catholic bishops to a government consultation on introducing equal marriage in England and Wales, they stated:

> There is a common and instinctive understanding of the meaning of marriage, shared by people of any religion and none . . . as the voluntary union for life of one man and one woman to the exclusion of all others . . . It is an understanding which the Church believes is still of vital importance for the common good of society today.
> (Catholic Bishops' Conference of England and Wales 2012)

Likewise, the official Church of England response stated that, 'The Church of England cannot support the proposal to enable all couples, regardless of their gender, to have a civil marriage ceremony' (Church of England 2012). It added, 'It is well known that there is a continuing debate within the Church of England about its declared view of sexually active homosexual relationships' but reasserted that 'we believe that the inherited understanding of marriage contributes a vast amount to the common good'.

Yet Linda Woodhead found in early 2013 that half of all religious people in Britain were in favour of marriage equality and those who identified as Anglican, Catholic and Presbyterian supported it by a small margin. Among active churchgoers, the level of support was slightly lower but still considerable: 40 per cent of Anglicans and 42 per cent of Catholics were in favour and 47 per cent of Anglicans and 48 per cent of Catholics opposed, while 54 per cent of Church of Scotland members were for and 37 per cent against. On the different but related question of whether marriage of same-sex couples is right, support was lower but still substantial: 36 per cent of Catholics, 37 per cent of Presbyterians and 38 per cent of Anglicans thought it right, while 44 per cent of Catholics and Presbyterians and 44 per cent of Anglicans thought it wrong (AHRC/ESRC Religion and Society Research Programme 2013).

The apparent confidence among leaders that their own views expressed that of 'the church' (or at least their own denomination) as a whole, despite widespread disagreement among church members, might have arisen from

188 *Savitri Hensman*

a sense that they reflected the 'true', faith-based perspective whereas their 'flock' might have been diverted from the correct path by the influence of 'secular' culture. A paper prepared for the July 2014 General Synod of the Church of England stated that a process of structured conversations on sexuality aimed 'to enable the Church of England to reflect, in the light of scripture, on the implications of the immense cultural change that has been taking place. It is common ground that social attitudes have changed extremely rapidly . . . Clarifying how we can most effectively be a missionary church in a changing culture around sexuality is a key objective'.

Yet members of that and other churches, impelled in part by religious conviction, together with people of other religions and none, have played an important part in this process of cultural change. Even in the early twentieth century, when the dominant view was that same-sex relationships were psychologically and socially defective as well as immoral, Christians as well as people of other faiths and none were beginning to question this apparent consensus. Occasionally this erupted into public controversy.

Fiction (then as now) could offer ways of enabling imaginative readers to cross barriers and enter worlds previously unknown to them; however, those lesbian, gay and bisexual artists who had explored sexuality and gender had generally done so obliquely or in work not aimed at a broad public. But prize-winning novelist Radclyffe Hall, herself a lesbian, set out to write a novel in which the hero was unequivocally lesbian (or perhaps transgender) and which sympathetically depicted the experience of those identified as 'inverts' or members of a 'third sex'. The furore over *The Well of Loneliness*, published by London publisher Jonathan Cape in 1928, reflected differences of opinion not only within society but also within the church, inasmuch as Christians seeking to act in line with their faith found themselves disagreeing vociferously with one another.

James Douglas, then editor of the *Sunday Express*, was outraged and condemned the book as 'a seductive and insidious piece of special pleading designed to display perverted decadence as a martyrdom inflicted upon these outcasts by a cruel society'. He declared that 'I would rather give a healthy boy or a healthy girl a phial of prussic acid than this novel. Poison kills the body, but moral poison kills the soul' (Souhami 2012). The book was banned, though copies circulated overseas and eventually a UK edition was permitted.

The strength of this reaction was probably linked with the religious imagery which suffused the novel and its willingness to address pious objections to same-sex relationships head-on: LGBT people were portrayed as no less part of God's creation than their heterosexual counterparts and as capable of honourable and self-giving love. Douglas was devoutly religious and so was Hall: a Roman Catholic, she approached her work in the light of a religious tradition, albeit interpreted in the light of a certain experience. It is also possible that the spiritual practices undertaken within religious settings, while instilling guilt in some or a sense of obligation to defend the status quo, inspired others to defend the marginalised and promote equality. Both the novelist and the journalist pitched their arguments at a broad range of readers, of various faiths and none, but with religious overtones.

Hence arguments among Christians about the morality of same-sex partnerships, and of legally and socially protecting or penalising those in—or affirming of—such relationships, have not taken place only in institutional settings. These also happen in the domestic and public sphere and help to shape broader cultural attitudes and practices, which in turn provided the context in which subsequent generations of Christians conducted their moral reasoning. While the contribution of non-Christians to creating a more just society should not be downplayed, the relationship between 'the church' and 'secular' developments is not straightforward.

Even if 'Christian' discussions on same-sex partnerships and gender identity are defined more narrowly, these are by no means a new development. Theology might be described as the study of God (if God exists) and God's relationship with the universe, including humankind, and theologians as people who undertake this in a focused way and discuss their findings with one another and the wider community. There are Jewish and Muslim as well as Christian theologians. However, Christian theology is a particularly widespread field of study, including in universities. Unsurprisingly, explicitly theological writings as well as the work of artists and other scholars have played a critical part in the development of Christian thinking on sexuality and gender identity. By the early 1940s, churches in Britain were increasingly accepting the validity of contraception under certain circumstances and hence moving away from the notion that having sex was intrinsically linked with procreation. Anglican theologian Kenneth Ingram, who was himself gay, shocked many people by proposing that, whether partners were of the opposite or same sex, the morality of relationships depends on the presence or absence of love, not in the sense of infatuation but rather a deeper bond that treats the other as a person not an object (Ingram and Hensman 2014).

This was far too radical for most Christians at the time but subsequently growing numbers of theologians, as well as churchgoers more generally, came to believe that same-sex partnerships were not necessarily wrong. By the 1970s, the Church of England had begun to convene working parties to study the issues and weigh up evidence for and against affirmation of same-sex partnerships, and other churches would also later organise formal processes of a similar kind.

Formal and informal processes of discussion among Christians on sexuality and gender identity are intertwined, though church leaders may sometimes downplay the diversity of views within the wider communities which they purport to represent. Certainly a huge shift in thinking (Crockett and Voas 2003) in the pews, among parish clergy and chaplains and in academia has made it harder for senior clergy and spokespeople to behave as if the matter were settled.

190 *Savitri Hensman*

The revisiting of seemingly established norms on gender and sexuality has taken place against a broader backdrop. Pragmatically, the church has had to contend with declining membership and loss of prestige (Gledhill 2014), while also facing the perpetual challenge of maintaining what is of greatest worth in its heritage, while moving away from attitudes and practices arising from ignorance or insensitivity. On other issues, such as the treatment of women, disabled people, ethnic minorities and those who are economically disadvantaged too, numerous Christians have come to believe that there are shortcomings which need to be rectified if the church is to be credible in its claim to seek to treat everyone lovingly. However, there has also been a backlash from people who fear that core religious truths are being called into question or who feel threatened by rapid social change on multiple fronts and, in Britain (Lodge 2014; Clements 2014) and internationally (Kaoma 2009–2010), conflict over diversity within faith-based communities has sometimes taken on broader political dimensions. The questioning of past assumptions in faith communities is by no means new. However, the era of mass communication and, over the past couple of decades, widespread use of the Internet have influenced the ways in which discussions on ethical issues and organisational policies take place. For example, in February 2014, I was able to listen to the Church of England's General Synod talking about a report on sexuality while sitting at my computer and likewise, in July, watch the live streaming of relevant debates at the United Reformed Church General Assembly. An archbishop's intervention forcing the cancellation of a lecture by a progressive theologian (Coday 2014) and a different archbishop's response to questions by pupils in Birmingham about same-sex relationships (Selby 2015) may be reported and analysed in depth in regional, national, international and social media.

A RANGE OF VOICES

Written or spoken accounts of 'coming out' by Christians often touch on the reactions of those who share the same faith within families, friendship networks, congregations or youth groups. Likewise a sermon, article in a parish magazine or casual remark after watching a drama together at home or in the cinema can serve as a cue to exchange views and experiences. Such conversations are critically important in enabling the church, as a community, to reflect on how it does, and should, respond to diversity of sexual orientation and gender diversity.

However, there are various sets of participants in church discussions on acceptance of LGBTQI people and same-sex partnerships that play particularly prominent roles. There are some similarities to discussions of the same topics in other Western countries and, to a lesser extent, debates within smaller faith communities in Britain. Some categories are outlined in the following section, though it should be noted that these are not necessarily

Changing Churches 191

mutually exclusive: for example, a bishop may be a blogger, and a theologian may belong to a group campaigning for, or against, celebrating same-sex partnerships.

Groups Seeking Greater Acceptance, Including of Partnered LGBTQI People

LGCM (initially the Gay Christian Movement) was launched in 1976 for all who believed 'that human sexuality in all its richness is a gift of God gladly to be accepted, enjoyed and honoured as a way of both expressing and growing in love' and 'it is entirely compatible with the Christian faith not only to love another person of the same sex but also to express that love fully in a personal sexual relationship'. A Clergy Consultation for gay clergy, which has continued to foster mutual support, was also founded at that time, as was Quest, a group for lesbian and gay Catholics.

Since then, various organisations and subgroups have been formed which support those facing exclusion by church or society because of sexual orientation or gender identity and encourage churches to recognise and celebrate loving and faithful partnerships regardless of gender. Some have a particular focus: for instance, Changing Attitude works for full inclusion within the Anglican Communion, Affirm is Baptist, Outcome is Methodist, Affirmation Scotland focuses on the Church of Scotland and other Scottish churches, the Sibyls is for transgender people and their supporters and Diverse Church is a supportive community of young LGBTQI people mainly from evangelical churches. Some concentrate on support, for instance, Two: 23, while others are more active in advocacy and campaigning, though there is not a rigid division and many combine aspects of both. Some have a wide remit, such as Inclusive Church, which works for full inclusion in the Church of England and beyond for women, LGBTQI people and people facing exclusion on grounds of ethnicity, disability, mental health or poverty. Accepting Evangelicals brings together affirming Christians and others not convinced that same-sex partnerships should be celebrated but who uphold others' right to act in line with their consciences. These sometimes work together but the range of groups reflects something of the diversity among LGBTQI Christians and their friends, from older people talking about the wording of resolutions to young people talking about Jesus, devotees of the Virgin Mary to enthusiasts for Christian rock music.

The contribution of such groups includes empowering LGBTQI and other affirming Christians to express their views and share their experiences where appropriate, publicising religious arguments for acceptance (sometimes arranging talks by, and publishing the work of, theologians and church historians) and communicating formally and informally with church leaders and other members. Sharing videos and written accounts of life stories which highlight the damage resulting from exclusion and positive consequences of inclusion, responding to media inquiries, preparing submissions

192 Savitri Hensman

to working parties, having stalls at events and liaising with senior clergy and staff in the institutional church are just some of the activities.

Groups Opposing Affirmation of Same-Sex Partnerships

There are a number of groups opposed to full acceptance of LGBTQI people on equal terms, including celebration of partnerships. Many of these cover a range of issues and are generally concerned about what they regard as an erosion of obedience to what they believe the Bible teaches or adherence to 'tradition'. Some of these are careful to stress that all people should be treated with respect regardless of sexual orientation and gender identity, while others are more extreme.

Perhaps the most prominent is the Evangelical Alliance UK, which has many organisational and individual members. Others include Methodist Evangelicals Together, Forward Together (focusing on the Church of Scotland) and Reform (within the Church of England).

These too sometimes get involved in denominational and other debates and encourage their members to do so, promote their views through the news and social media and produce materials which outline a theological case for the 'traditional' view of what family life should be. While some are averse to dialogue, fearing that this might imply that alternative perspectives might be valid, some have been involved in bridge-building initiatives started by one 'side' or other or by other Christian organisations, which have had some success in maintaining fellowship or at least promoting mutual understanding amidst often heated disagreement.

A few are made up largely of people who are gay, lesbian or bisexual in orientation—or, in the language often used, 'same-sex attracted'—though these are usually encouraged to stay celibate unless they happen to fall in love with a member of the opposite sex. These include the True Freedom Trust and Living Out. There used to be more 'ex-gay' ministries who claimed to be able to 'heal' people of feelings of romantic love and desire for members of the same sex, but this approach has been largely discredited (Arana 2012), though a few still practice this and have in some cases promoted such approaches in other parts of the world.

Senior Church Leaders in Britain

Archbishops or presiding bishops, moderators, general secretaries and others at the most senior level in denominations active in England, Scotland and/or Wales not only have authority to make certain decisions but can also help to set the tone in which contentious matters are more widely discussed. Their voices are also amplified by the media. To a lesser extent, this applies to regional leaders such as other bishops, superintendents and so forth. However, they may also experience various constraints, for instance, in voicing their own views if these are not identical with the official stance of

Changing Churches 193

the church they lead, especially since their pronouncements may be widely reported and analysed.

Senior Church Leaders Overseas

Some denominations active in Britain have their headquarters abroad, including some of the African-led Lutheran and Orthodox churches and the Roman Catholic Church. In addition, many other churches are part of international networks such as the Anglican Communion or active in ecumenical circles, where pressure can be brought to bear. For example, some overseas Anglican leaders have threatened a split if the Church of England is too affirming. Moreover, some minority ethnic Christians have links with churches in their countries of origin. At the same time, there appear to be increasing numbers of refugees and asylum seekers from countries where anti-LGBTQI repression has been backed by churches, who to some extent counterbalance the impact of church leaders whose moral authority consists of willingness to condone violence against LGBTQI people and human rights defenders.

Representatives in Church Assemblies and Committees

Members of national assemblies which help to determine policy in particular churches can exert considerable influence, for instance, by putting forward, speaking for or against and voting on resolutions on sexual and gender identity or that which might affect the ability of their church to move forward towards greater inclusion. Regional assemblies may also play a significant part; for example, diocesan synods in the Church of England helped to defeat (at least for the time being) an attempt to introduce a Covenant which might have obstructed moves towards greater inclusion at some point in the future. Not surprisingly, different factions sometimes campaign to get more people sharing their convictions elected or onto key committees.

Theologians

Theologians (many, though by no means all, of whom work in academic settings or for churches, including as clergy) help to influence wider views on sexuality, especially if they are highly thought of in at least some church circles or can come up with clear and persuasive arguments. Many write in ways, and are published in books and journals, which are inaccessible to most Christians without a formal theological education and access to specialist libraries, but others are skilled at articulating their views to reach a wider audience, sometimes using social and other media. Theological discussions often cross national borders, so theologians based overseas can have an impact on sexuality debates in Britain.

Christians with a High Public Profile

Christians prominent in certain church circles or who are public figures can also sometimes be notable participants in discussions on sexuality. This includes pastors of large churches, popular speakers or worship leaders at major Christian festivals, such as New Wine, and frequent participants in programmes talking about religious issues. For example, when Vicky Beeching, a singer-songwriter, broadcaster and theologian with a following largely among young evangelicals, declared her support for affirming same-sex partnerships then came out as lesbian in 2014 (Ormerod 2014), this triggered widespread media coverage and lively discussion.

There are also people well known for their achievements in society who are openly Christian and have spoken out for or against celebrating same-sex partnerships. For example, during parliamentary debates on marriage equality, several MPs and peers shared their own faith-related reflections and experiences which had led them to support or oppose the proposed legislation. This may in part be because these resonate with, and help validate, attitudes and experiences which others hold but might not previously have been articulated or shared.

Broadcasters and Other Journalists

Broadcasters and other journalists who speak or write about Christianity (or commission work by others) sometimes contribute to discussions on LGBTQI inclusion, whether through expression of their own views or through their framing of the debate or choice of those to whom they offer a platform. They may work for mainstream publications and channels, explicitly Christian media such as Premier Radio or stations broadcast solely via satellite or cable, which may target particular ethnic and cultural communities. Nowadays some publishers and broadcasters also allow online comments, which can lead to a vigorous exchange of views, even when moderated to remove overtly offensive posts (and different people have different views on what constitutes offence).

Bloggers and Others with a High Social Media Profile

While some blogs are read by very few people, others are viewed by sizeable numbers of Christians, though the weight these carry varies. Users of Twitter and other social media, including people who post videos on YouTube or elsewhere also sometimes have a significant number of followers who take note of their views and the links they promote. Some people, both for and against wider affirmation of same-sex partnerships and acceptance of gender diversity, make skilful use of social media.

Writers, Musicians and Others Involved in the Arts

The arts can offer important ways of exploring issues and related feelings and encourage empathy or revulsion. Books, plays, films, paintings, television dramas and so forth which touch on issues of faith and sexuality or gender identity can have a substantial impact. For example, in 2015, an actor who plays a gay vicar on the soap opera *Coronation Street* described strong reactions to his character from viewers incensed by the storyline (Crawford 2015). Meanwhile, large numbers watched a powerful video by pop star Sam Smith, to accompany one of his songs, depicting two men being married in church to the joy of well-wishers (Denham 2015). This eloquently expressed the similarities between same-sex and opposite-sex love and the spiritual dimension of the yearning for a church wedding and reached Christians unlikely to read a theological treatise or attend a conference to debate the pros and cons of celebrating partnerships.

CONCLUSION

Churches (and other faith bodies) are sometimes referred to as if they were monolithic institutions in which power is concentrated in the hands of a few. For example, while Anne Jenichen and Shahra Razavi (2010) are right to draw attention to the risks which dominance by faith leaders can pose to women's rights, more questionably they seem to view religious influence in society as wholly set apart from the expression of women's own opinions and yearnings. 'Religious authorities commonly insist on regulating relationships in the private domain, including sexuality,' based on 'transcendental principles' which 'are steeped in patriarchal and hetero-normative assumptions,' they suggest. 'Some of the more insidious and lasting changes that religious actors introduce concern practices and meanings that reshape mindsets and become unquestioned social norms', though 'religious impositions can also elicit resistance when they run counter to existing social practices'.

Yet while there are indeed power imbalances in faith communities and attempts are sometimes made to exercise centralised control, these may be vigorously contested not simply because of outside influences. Members may feel that 'transcendental influences' lead them to seek greater equality and affirmation within religious institutions and wider society, appealing to aspects of tradition and faith-based values.

There are diverse participants in current church discussions on sexuality and gender identity. This polyphony of voices (which may sometimes be discordant or even a cacophony) includes LGBTQI people, despite ongoing discrimination and fear of victimisation and the persistent reluctance of some church leaders to acknowledge how many of their members now support greater equality.

Campaigners for and against affirmation of same-sex partnerships and gender diversity, local, national and international church leaders, representatives on assemblies and committees, public figures known to be Christian and people involved in the media (including social media) and arts are among those who contribute to complex processes of deliberation and change in institutions and the wider Christian community. Those who have

196 *Savitri Hensman*

been marginalised have sometimes found creative ways to express themselves, engage with their co-religionists and neighbours and form alliances to bring about change.

NOTE

1 While some intersex people prefer not to be grouped with others at risk of exclusion on grounds of sexuality or gender identity, others take a different position, and the UK Intersex Association is a member of an LGBTI Anglican Coalition seeking change in the church. In addition, in recent years, many of the religious arguments heard against celebrating same-sex partnerships seem based in part on a rigidly binary view of sex and gender: despite the significant differences among those who might be described as LGBTQI, there is some commonality.

BIBLIOGRAPHY

AHRC/ESRC Religion and Society Research Programme. (2013) 'Do Christians Really Oppose Gay Marriage?', Press Release, 18 April. Available at http://www.religionandsociety.org.uk/events/programme_events/show/press_release_do_christians_really_oppose_gay_marriage, last accessed 18 March 2015.

Anglican/Roman Catholic International Commission. (1976) *Authority in the Church I.* Available at http://www.vatican.va/roman_curia/pontifical_councils/chrstuni/angl-comm-docs/rc_pc_chrstuni_doc_197609_authority-church-i_en.html, last accessed 17 March 2015.

Arana, G. (2012) 'My So-Called Ex-Gay life', *American Prospect* [online], April. Available at http://prospect.org/article/my-so-called-ex-gay-life, last accessed 18 March 2015.

Bhambra, G. K. (2006) 'Culture, Identity and Rights: Challenging Contemporary Discourses of Belonging,' in Yuval-Davis, N., Kannabiran, K. and Vieten, U. (eds.) *The Situated Politics of Belonging.* London: Sage, 32–41.

Bishop of Sheffield. (2014) 'GS Misc 1083: Shared Conversations on Sexuality, Scripture and Mission'. Available at https://www.churchofengland.org/media/2015811/gs%20misc%201083%20-%20shared%20conversations%20on%20sexuality,%20scripture%20and%20mission.pdf, last accessed 2 August 2014.

Bowers, F. (2012) 'Engaging with the Past to Inform the Present'. Available at http://www.open.ac.uk/blogs/boh/wp-content/uploads/2012/10/Faith-Bowers-Building-on-Bloomsburys-past.pdf, last accessed 29 July 2014.

Catholic Bishops' Conference of England and Wales. (2012) 'Response to the Government Consultation on "Equal Civil Marriage"'. Available at http://www.catholic-ew.org.uk/content/download/29644/206517/file/CBCEW-response-equal-civil-marriage-consultation-June-2012.pdf, last accessed 18 March 2015.

Church of England. (2012) 'A Response to the Government Equalities Office Consultation—"Equal Civil Marriage"'. Available at https://www.churchofengland.org/media/1475149/s-s%20marriage.pdf, last accessed 18 March 2015.

Clements, B. (2014) 'The British Election Study 2015: Religious Affiliation and Attitudes', 17 October. http://www.brin.ac.uk/news/2014/the-british-election-study-2015-religious-affiliation-and-attitudes/, last accessed 18 March 2015.

Coday, D. (2014) 'British Theologian (again) Disinvited from Lecture', *National Catholic Reporter* [online], 26 September. Available at http://ncronline.org/blogs/ncr-today/british-theologian-again-disinvited-lecture, last accessed 18 March 2015.

Crawford, S. (2015) 'Coronation Street's Gay Vicar Faces Backlash from Fans and Churchgoers over Role', *Mirror* [online], 15 March. Available at http://www.mirror.co.uk/tv/tv-news/coronation-streets-gay-vicar-faces-5337255, last accessed 18 March 2015.

Crockett, A. and Voas, D. (2003) 'A Divergence of Views: Attitude Change and the Religious Crisis over Homosexuality', *Sociological Research Online* 8(4). Available at http://www.socresonline.org.uk/8/4/crockett.html, last accessed 5 August 2014.

Davie, G. (2006) 'Religion in Europe in the 21st Century: The Factors to Take into Account', *European Journal of Sociology* 47(2): 271–296. Available at https://ore.exeter.ac.uk/repository/bitstream/handle/10036/86938/Davie_EJS.pdf?sequence=1, last accessed 30 July 2014.

Denham, J. (2015) 'Sam Smith New Music Video for "Lay Me Down" Makes Moving Pro-Gay Marriage Statement', *Independent* [online], 5 February. Available at http://www.independent.co.uk/arts-entertainment/music/news/sam-smith-makes-moving-progay-marriage-statement-in-new-music-video-for-lay-me-down-10026535.html, last accessed 18 March 2015.

Gledhill, R. (2014) 'Exclusive: New Figures Reveal Massive Decline in Religious Affiliation', *Christian Today* [online], 17 October. Available at http://www.christiantoday.com/article/exclusive.new.figures.reveal.massive.decline.in.religious.affiliation/41799.htm, last accessed 18 March 2015.

Gledhill, R. (2015) 'Church of England to Begin Sexuality "Conversations"', *Christian Today* [online], 14 February. http://www.christiantoday.com/article/church.of.england.to.begin.sexuality.conversations/48126.htm, last accessed 7 April 2015.

Hensman, S. (1991) 'Pulpits, Courts and Scandal', in Kaufmann, T. and Lincoln, P. (eds.) *High Risk Lives*. Bridport: Prism Press, 210–220.

Hensman, S. (2014) 'Blessed Companionship: A Church's Journey', *Modern Believing* 55(2): 97–113.

Hensman, S. (2015) *Sexuality, Struggle and Saintliness: Same-Sex Love and the Church*, London: Ekklesia.

Holdsworth, K. (2014) 'How Not to Have a Synodical Discussion', What's in Kelvin's Head (blog), 13 June. http://thurible.net/2014/06/13/synodical-discussion/, last accessed 7 April 2015.

Ingram, K. and Hensman, S. (2014) 'Christianity and Sexual Morality Revisited', *Modern Believing* 55(2): 141–147.

Jenichen, A. and Razavi, S. (2010) 'The Unhappy Marriage of Religion and Politics', *Open Democracy*, 30 November. Available at https://www.opendemocracy.net/5050/anne-jenichen-shahra-razavi/unhappy-marriage-of-religion-and-politics, last accessed 8 April 2015.

Kaoma, K. (2009–2010) 'The US Christian Right and the Attack on Gays in Africa', *Public Eye*, Winter 09/Spring 10. Available at http://www.publiceye.org/magazine/v24n4/us-christian-right-attack-on-gays-in-africa.html, last accessed 5 August 2014.

Lodge, C. (2014) 'How Far-Right Party Britain First Is Gaining Traction Through 'Christian' Ideology', *Christian Today*, 22 November. Available at http://www.christiantoday.com/article/how.far.right.party.britain.first.is.gaining.traction.through.christian.ideology/43380.htm, last accessed 18 March 2015.

Methodist Church in Britain (2014) 'Methodist Conference Receives Report on Same-sex Marriage'. Press Release, 2 July. Available at http://www.methodist.org.uk/news-and-events/news-releases/methodist-conference-receives-report-on-same-sex-marriage, last accessed 19 September 2015.

Ormerod, P. (2014) 'Why Vicky Beeching Coming Out Matters', *Guardian* [online], 18 August. Available at http://www.theguardian.com/commentisfree/2014/aug/18/vicky-beeching-coming-out-matters-christians, last accessed 18 March 2015.

198 Savitri Hensman

Selby, J. (2015) 'Archbishop of Canterbury Justin Welby Discusses Gay Rights with Muslim Students: "Who am I to Judge them for their Sins?"', *Independent*, 24 February. Available at http://www.independent.co.uk/news/people/archbishop-of-canterbury-justin-welby-discusses-gay-rights-with-muslim-students-who-am-i-to-judge-them-for-their-sins-10066774.html, last accessed 19 September 2015.

Siddique, H. (2014) 'Chaplain Accuses Church of England of Homophobia', *Guardian* [online], 9 July. Available at http://www.theguardian.com/world/2014/jul/09/chaplain-accuses-church-england-homophobia, last accessed 7 April 2015.

Souhami, D. (2012) *The Trials of Radclyffe Hall*. Hachette, England.

United Reformed Church. (2014) 'The United Reformed Church General Assembly Journeys Together Towards a Decision on Same-Sex Marriage', News Release, 8 July. Available at http://www.urc.org.uk/media-news/1456-the-united-reformed-church-general-assembly-journeys-together.html, last accessed 7 April 2015.

Warnock, A. (2014) 'The Baptist Union to Allow Differences on Same Sex Marriage', *Patheos*, 14 May. Available at http://www.patheos.com/blogs/adrian warnock/2014/05/the-baptist-union-to-allow-differences-on-same-sex-marriage/, last accessed 7 April 2015.

World Council of Churches. (2005) 'The Nature and Mission of the Church—a Stage on the Way to a Common Statement'. Available at http://www.oikoumene. org/en/resources/documents/commissions/faith-and-order/i-unity-the-church-and-its-mission/the-nature-and-mission-of-the-church-a-stage-on-the-way-to-a-common-statement, last accessed 17 March 2015.

Yip, A. K. T. (2008), 'Researching Lesbian, Gay, and Bisexual Christians and Muslims: Some Thematic Reflections', *Sociological Research Online* 13(1): 5. Available at http://www.socresonline.org.uk/13/1/5.html, last accessed 15 March 2015.

11 Counter-Normative Identities
Religious Young Adults Subverting Sexual Norms

Sarah-Jane Page

INTRODUCTION

The twenty-first century is often invoked as a period of greater sexual freedom, with restraint and traditionalism partitioned to the past. The new rights accorded to LGBTQ groups and women have cemented such a perception. But whilst some theorists (e.g. Weeks 2007) remain optimistic about the step-changes that have occurred, others proceed more cautiously, instead focusing on the regulatory mechanisms remaining (Jackson and Scott 2004; Klesse 2007). Religious young adults are perceived as something of an oxymoron in this environment, seemingly unable to participate in these new liberatory sexualities because religion is often inscribed with traditionalism and religious (un)freedom.

This chapter will map the attitudes and choices of religious young adults who were situated both within 'secular' and religious discourses on sexuality. Attention will be given to those contexts where young people seemed to be out of synch, not only with contemporary youth culture but also, on occasion, with their religious traditions. How did these counter-normative choices come about, and how did young adults make sense of them in negotiating their sexuality? Two issues will be the focus: young adults who promoted and practised celibacy and those who endorsed non-monogamous relationships. Such identities subvert normative sexualities and can in turn help illuminate remaining regulatory frameworks.

Youth Culture, Sexualisation and Religion

Recent research has explored contemporary sexual cultures (Attwood 2006, 2009; Nikunen and Saarenmaa 2007; Rossi 2007; Weeks 2007), with Terry (2012: 872) noting, 'Sex has, to a large degree, become seen as an imperative to the basic function of a mature individual's identity, without which a person is deemed incomplete'. This sexual imperative becomes linked to youth culture, as sexuality becomes commodified through mediums such as music videos, advertisements, magazines and the Internet (Attwood 2006, 2009; Nikunen 2007; Plummer 2003). At the level of sexual practice, reports

200 Sarah-Jane Page

suggest that some young people are stalling engaging in couple-relationships, instead privileging casual relationships, underscored by a university campus 'hook-up' culture (Freitas 2008; Heldman and Wade 2010). In this process, stable relationships are problematised, replaced with pleasure-seeking hedonism (Attwood 2006; Boynton 2009), epitomised through new terminology such as 'friends with benefits' (Anapol 2010).

Despite these shifts, researchers still highlight the centrality of traditional values, such as monogamous relationships. Rather than relationships disappearing, they instead come to take on new forms (Weeks 2007). 'Playing the field' may no longer be solely the preserve of men, but casual relationships are not constructed as a meaningful strategy for long-term happiness and fulfilment—instead this remains concentrated in monogamous, long-term partnerships (Weeks 2007; Wellings et al. 2001). Casualised sexual relationships are understood as immature practices from which individuals will progress (Klesse 2007). Marriage remains an ideal in young people's 'imagined futures' (Hall 2006; Carroll et al. 2007; Page et al. 2012). Equally, fidelity remains important to young people (Johansson 2007), highlighting that although new ways of negotiating sexuality may have arisen, this does not mean a total displacement of older discursive frames.

Meanwhile, religion has been invoked as a sexually illiberal sphere; religious rules and edicts are seen as negatively determining sexual practices. In this invocation, sexual liberation is seen as overcoming the religious shackles of the past. But some argue that the 'religious' and the 'secular' cannot be simplistically pitted against each other, for

> the disciplinary regime of Christendom is the forerunner, not the opposition, to today's disciplinary regime of sex, where modern subjects are left to believe that they must explore, and manage, every tiny tremor of erotic affect if they want to be sufficiently free.
>
> (Alcoff and Caputo 2011: 6)

Following this Foucauldian vein, Jordan (2011) adds that the death of God leaves a space to be filled, but regulation remains at the heart of the contemporary discourse on sexuality, despite the veneer of liberation.

Celibacy—Sacred or Secular?

Celibacy can be variously defined, from temporarily refraining from sex (Fahs 2010) to longer-term abstinence. Imtoual and Hussein (2009) link celibacy to a stage in the life course prior to marriage. Others view celibacy as a more permanent arrangement (Cornwall 2013). Abbott argues that celibacy is a multifaceted phenomenon, existing in various forms in different times and places; thus a broad, rather than narrow, conceptualisation is needed. She argues that making clear distinctions between parallel terms such as chastity and virginity is 'unhelpful' (2001:17), for being too rigid and pedantic. Rather, she advocates for a more encompassing and inclusive definition, due to the various ways in which celibacy has been lived and experienced over time. Thatcher (2011) encourages more precise definitions, especially in the religious context, as there are large differences between asserting virginity for a short period, to taking a lifelong religious vow. These distinctions are paramount in the ways the religious young adults in this project related to this terminology. Whilst a high number were supportive of virginity until marriage (Yip and Page 2013), as we shall see, support for chastity was lukewarm at best. Clearly, our religious adherents meant something different between virginity and celibacy, and this meaning was understood as a more permanent status of nonsexual contact.

In a highly sexualised culture, there is little support for celibacy (Terry 2012); instead, celibacy is situated as an unhealthy practice, connected to sex abuse scandals in the Roman Catholic Church (Cavendish 2003). It is within religious contexts that celibacy is most associated (although see Abbott 2001 and Fahs 2010 for celibacy in secular contexts), but religions are diverse in their approaches. Broadly speaking, some religious traditions strongly discourage celibacy, whilst others allow limited room for its practice. For example, Islam, Judaism and Sikhism prioritise heterosexual sexuality and eschew celibacy (Hidayatullah 2003; Mernissi 2003; Rait 2005; Imtoual and Hussein 2009; Dialmy 2010). In other religious traditions, limited space is made for celibacy; within Hinduism, celibacy is seen as a stage in the life cycle, before one embarks on a sexual relationship and parenthood (Abbott 2001; Lidke 2003). Christianity has strong historical ties to celibacy, with early Christianity endorsing the celibate path (Clark 1995; Abbott 2001; Price 2006). In more recent years, whilst Catholicism has continued to make space for celibacy, in Protestant Christianity, it is married sexuality which is usually privileged (Jordan 2011; Cornwall 2013). Hence, for many Christian communities, celibacy is out of synch with current theology. Meanwhile, Buddhism can be deemed pro-celibacy; celibacy is a prerequisite for those ordained as a monk or a nun, and more generally, celibacy is understood as a means of avoiding craving (Wilson 2003; Powers 2008). More commonly, religions may promote periods of sexual abstinence, such as prior to marriage. But this is not celibacy in the longer-term sense.

Non-Monogamy

In the broader context of the liberalisation of sexual relationships, monogamy remains a cornerstone principle, with its desirability intensifying in recent years (Jackson and Scott 2004). For example, monogamy has been endorsed by some LGBTQ individuals as a means of displaying 'good' sexual citizenship (Jakobsen and Pellegrini 2003; Richardson 2005; Klesse 2007). Although support for the notion of one lifelong partner has waned, contemporary relationships are associated with serial monogamy (Anapol 2010). Meanwhile, engaging in concurrent sexual relationships is seen as

202   Sarah-Jane Page

extremely problematic (Jackson and Scott 2004; Ritchie and Barker 2006). Attitudinal research indicates strong support for monogamous relationships, whereby 'the UK public are [sic] firmly in favour of sexual exclusivity . . . [with] near universal condemnation of sexual relationships outside of regular ones, which the vast majority of both men and women believe to be wrong' (Wellings et al. 2001: 18). Non-monogamy is associated with infidelity and harmful relationships (Jackson and Scott 2004; Ritchie and Barker 2006) and is rarely considered an ethical practice.

Similar to celibacy, it is not possible to crystallise the religious diversity on monogamy, either cross-culturally or historically. Even within a singular tradition, there is not necessarily one narrative operating; individual traditions have varied over time in their approach. For example, Islam is popularly associated with non-monogamy (specifically polygamy) due to Qur'anic verses that are interpreted as allowing a man to marry up to four wives. This measure was originally instituted as a means of providing support to dispossessed women but has more recently been condemned as a negative practice that benefits men's sexual access to women's bodies (Mernissi 2003). Polygamy has also been used by dominant populations to stereotype and govern minority Muslim communities (Fetzer and Soper 2003; Selby 2014). Indeed, the reality is more complex, with its practice being culturally contingent (Mahmood 2005). In the Western European context, it is not widely practised (Field 2011; Selby 2014). Meanwhile, Christianity is strongly associated with monogamous relationship practices (Yip 1997; Robinson 2012), but there have been examples of non-monogamy in certain times and places. Price (2006) documents the sexual communism advocated by the theologian Epiphanes in early Christianity, based on the ideal of sharing everything as a Christian community. Meanwhile, in modernity, the Church of Jesus Christ of Latter Day Saints is popularly associated with polygamy, despite the fact that polygamy was officially abandoned by the group in 1890 (Campbell 2014). However, offshoot movements such as the Fundamentalist Church of Jesus Christ of Latter Day Saints continue to practise polygamy. They view it as a biblical practice endorsed by patriarchs, such as Abraham, and believe that acceptance into the highest heavenly realm after death depends on a man taking more than one wife (Campbell 2014). Despite these theological commitments, in practice, Campbell's research with a Canadian FLDS community revealed that polygamy was a minority practice. What these cases indicate is that there is theological potential within Christianity to support non-monogamy; indeed, some contemporary theologies have connected Christianity specifically with polyamory (see the following section), which is ethically grounded around love and friendship (Goss 2004, Klesse 2006, Klesse 2007; Anapol 2010).

Many religious traditions endorse monogamy, especially monogamy connected to marriage (Rait 2005; Meirowitz 2009). Meirowitz describes her Jewish upbringing, whereby 'The structures of monogamy, marriage, and procreation are what move and motivate social interactions in both the

Counter-Normative Identities 203

traditional and less traditional Jewish world' (2009:173–174). In Protestant Christianity, marriage is elevated to special status; sexual relationships beyond this partnership are routinely condemned (DeRogatis 2003). An exception to unilateral support for monogamy can be seen in some Buddhist traditions. Avoiding sexual misconduct is one of the five precepts, but what constitutes sexual misconduct has been varyingly interpreted (Wilson 2003; Powers 2008; Keele 2012). Whilst some traditional Buddhist understandings assert that sexual expression in anything other than a heterosexual marriage is harmful, other Buddhists posit that any relationship (including monogamous heterosexual ones) has the potential to cultivate harm, if it is premised on negative forces such as coercion or lust (Keele 2012). Instead, in order for sexual practice to be deemed ethical, it has to be constituted through values such as love, commitment and longevity. Whilst non-monogamous practices such as 'casual sex, lying, cheating' (Keele 2012: 167) are condemned, this does give potential for non-monogamous relationships to be positively endorsed within a Buddhist framework, so long as they are premised on ethical principles such as honesty and truth (Anapol 2010).

Some have argued that a turn to polyamory (which Sheff [2006: 621] describes as those who 'openly engage in romantic, sexual, and/or affective relationships with multiple people simultaneously') has spiritual roots in subcultures such as Paganism and the New Age (Klesse 2007; Anapol 2010). Polyamory is but one of a range of non-monogamous practices, but polyamorists often distance themselves from seemingly unethical practices, such as casual sex and swinging (Sheff 2006; Klesse 2007). Instead, the etymology of polyamory—taken from the Latin word for love (*amore*) and the Greek word for many (*poly*)—downplays sexuality and the negative connotations of 'promiscuous' sex. In addition, polyamory tends to be underpinned by ethical values such as honesty, emotional connection, friendship and intimacy, over shallow and fleeting encounters (Klesse 2007; Anapol 2010). Some, however, have argued that this creates a hierarchy of ethics, where those who do choose to be promiscuous are denied a space. In addition, the primacy of love elevates it to an uncritical status. Research has revealed how the discourse of 'love' can endorse gender inequalities (Jackson 1993; Evans 2003; Johnson 2005; Klesse 2006, 2007). As Evans (2003: 85) argues, 'Western society continues to regulate love, romance and sexuality in terms of the interests and perceptions of men rather than women', with Jackson (1993) noting the way in which the discourse of love is utilised as a means of perpetuating the unequal division of labour in heterosexual relationships.

THE PROJECT

The project, entitled *Religion, Youth and Sexuality: A Multi-faith Exploration*[1], researched young adults aged 18 to 25 of diverse religious and sexual

204 *Sarah-Jane Page*

self-identifications living in the United Kingdom. The aims were to examine young adults' religious and sexual identities, the factors informing the construction of such identities and the strategies employed to navigate these identities in everyday life.

Mixed-methods were deployed, including online questionnaires, interviews and video diaries. The questionnaire, completed by 693 participants, asked a range of questions from demographic information, religious involvement, attitudes to religion, sexuality, gender and living in a secular society (see Yip and Page 2013).

Participation was based on being aged between 18 and 25 and identifying with one of six religious traditions (Buddhist, Christian, Hindu, Jewish, Muslim, Sikh) or a combination of these. Participants were recruited through various means: publicity posters/postcards/emails to a diverse number of groups such as university societies, LGBTQ support groups, advertisements in media and *Facebook*. This constituted purposive sampling (Spencer and Pahl 2006), producing a study that is not representative or generalisable. However, the project's substantial sample size and the generation of in-depth qualitative data offer an important contribution into the meanings and practices of young adults negotiating their religious and sexual identities.

A number of participants who completed the questionnaire (61) were selected to participate in an in-depth interview. This selection was based on obtaining a diverse sample around demographics such as religious identification, sexual identification, gender and religious community engagement. Meanwhile, 24 interviewees undertook a video diary, whereby participants recorded over the course of a week their reflections and experiences in relation to the project's themes (see Yip and Page 2013). Fieldwork was conducted between May 2009 and November 2010. Unless otherwise stated, quotes were taken from the interviews. Pseudonyms have been used throughout.

CELIBACY: SUPPORT AND AMBIVALENCE

Most participants were negative about celibacy. In questionnaire responses, only 29.9 per cent agreed or strongly agreed that celibacy could be fulfilling to one's sexual health [n:652]. Isma, a heterosexual Muslim, saw celibacy as interfering with a Muslim's ability to enact God's chosen path of marriage and reproduction:

> I completely disagree with [celibacy] because my religion teaches us that celibacy is unnatural . . . [People] need to fulfil their desires and satisfy themselves; that is why they have the whole marriage thing . . . What is the point of celibacy? You can't procreate; you can't have children.

Isha, a heterosexual Hindu, said 'I just don't see how that would be fulfilling . . . sex is a natural thing'. Meanwhile, Jacob, a homosexual Jew said that 'human beings are sexual creatures', and although he supported

Counter-Normative Identities 205

anyone's personal choice to be celibate, he said 'what I'm negative about is the idea that it's in some way virtuous', critiquing the moralising stance he felt some celibates made in asserting it as the 'better' state. Buddhist participants from more pro-celibacy traditions could also be negative, such as Rosie, who said 'I've got this view [that] you'd be repressing [your sexuality]'. Jenny, a heterosexual Christian, said, 'I don't think [celibacy] is healthy at all. It is not so much the sexual aspect; it is the non-relational aspect'.

Similarly, Amelia, a heterosexual Christian woman, discussed in her video diary the difficulties she encountered relating to a celibate Jesus and how the *Da Vinci Code* (by Dan Brown), implying Jesus's sexuality, was refreshing:

> I loved the idea of Jesus having a family. It suddenly made it much more accessible to me . . . sexuality is very much part of being fully human . . . within the Christian tradition really it is Jesus and Mary who are the male and female icons . . . they have both been de-sexualised . . . [Mary] didn't stay a virgin, but we call her the Virgin Mary. And those are the male and female icons. Role models even. How good is that?

These narratives highlight a number of dimensions to the negativity around celibacy. For some, it was derided because it challenged seemingly God-ordained rules for humanity, where heterosexuality and procreation were prioritised. Even those who did not invoke God still supported a view that there was something unnatural about celibacy, in repressing something essential about one's humanity. Another dimension was the personal cost assumed by living out a celibate life, epitomised by unhappiness and lack of companionship (Terry 2012). A third dimension was the value system invoked, particularly when celibacy is endorsed as a worthier path; this links to the privileging of the mind over the body and a sense in which those who 'succumb' to the sexual body are in some way inferior. This mind-body dualism has traditionally been deployed in Christian discourse (Furlong 1988; Althaus-Reid and Isherwood 2008; Douglas 2011). Some narratives hinted at the gendering of this, with desexualised codes being damaging to women, such as the problematic invocation of the Virgin Mary as both mother and virgin, something that ordinary women cannot replicate (Byrne 1990). Women have historically been invoked in Christian discourse as the embodiment of sexuality and carnality, over men's links to spirituality and sacredness (King 1989; Furlong 1988; Isherwood and Stuart 1998).

Despite this negativity, some participants, principally from Christian and Buddhist traditions, endorsed celibacy. Here I am defining celibacy as an ongoing choice; this excludes those individuals who were abstaining from sex until marriage. In other words, celibacy is seen as a long-term commitment, and is not a short-term management strategy. All were drawing on elements of their religious tradition, which endorsed celibacy; so although broadly religious communities could be more negative about celibate lifestyles, religion was still utilised as a resource to draw upon.

206   Sarah-Jane Page

Alex, a Buddhist, identified as asexual (defined as those 'who do not experience sexual attraction or desire'—Scherrer 2008: 621) and was struggling to articulate his celibate identity in broader culture. Alex wanted to practise celibacy but also maintain intimate nonsexual relationships with people, but in sexualised contexts, his intentions were often misconstrued as sexual flirting:

> It's part of the sexual world we live in because I can hardly hug someone or say something without making them think of what I want with them. So if I was completely celibate and I practise celibacy then it would put this barrier or wall between physical contact with people.

Alex wanted to maintain emotional connections with people, as well as display tactile modes of behaviour, including hugging. But such behaviour was routinely sexualised. His intentions were misunderstood, meaning that it was difficult to live out a celibate lifestyle in the way that he envisaged—close relationships without genital contact.

Whilst Alex was struggling for his celibacy to be understood in broader friendship networks, it was Craig's experience of broader youth culture which made celibacy a preferred option:

> I always thought the idea of celibacy as a very positive thing . . . I've always thought of sex as sort of like something that ruins things . . . the idea of celibacy [is] the ability to like tame and control sexual desire . . . which is probably another one of the reasons why I became a Buddhist because I want to have this control of myself

Aged 18, Craig was one of our youngest participants and was still in school studying for his A-levels when we interviewed him. His experience of sexualised youth cultures was intense, and included friends engaging in hook-up sex. Craig felt that sex permeated every moment of his life, and he felt bombarded. Celibacy was a means of asserting control over this situation, bucking the broader trend within his friendship circles. The age participants were impacted on the spaces with which they engaged. Craig's life was very much mediated through the experiences of school; this structured many of his encounters around sexuality (indeed, he talked about his friends having hook-up sex on the school premises—see Page and Yip 2012). Participants who were older were able to engage with a broader range of spaces and enact more choice regarding the spaces that they chose to participate. For example, participants often framed university as a time of finding more affirming spaces (Yip and Page 2013). Therefore, Craig's engagement with the culture of school became totalising. This impacted on his response to the situation—unable to escape this environment, celibacy (and control of the body, rather than control of the space in which he was situated) was cultivated as a form of resistance.

Counter-Normative Identities 207

For Kyle, a bisexual Christian, his decision to be celibate was influenced through his commitment to two distinct friendship networks: the LGBTQ group and the Evangelical Christians. He discussed this in his video diary:

> I have made the decision to be celibate. I agree with the biblical rules on when and where sex is allowed within the context of male and female marriage. And I am fine with that . . . I still get involved in LGBT stuff where I live . . . People in my [LGBT] group know that I am Christian but they don't know, for example, that I am celibate. They assume I am single because I haven't found the right guy yet, or girl yet because I am bisexual. Though I think they would prefer me to go out with a guy . . . [then they] could treat me as gay. Rather than embarrassingly turning up to a gay club with a girl; too much straightness there . . . On the other hand though, the Evangelicals . . . don't know that I am bisexual. I was thinking of telling them [But] I found out [the rules of the] Christian camp . . . if any [participants] are gay or bisexual, they can't stay overnight. That made me a little bit nervous about coming out . . . I want them to treat me as a fellow Christian, not because of my sexuality.

Kyle was managing the tensions of being connected to two friendship networks with radically different views on sexual relationships. As far as his LGBTQ friendship network was concerned, his bisexuality and his Christianity was tolerated, but hierarchies were invoked—Kyle understood that if he embarked on a relationship with a woman, this would be coded as 'too heterosexual' for the group. To be accepted within this community, one has to eschew everything heterosexual (Rambukkana 2004). Bisexuals fails to be incorporated because they are in a liminal space, in a situation where sexuality is coded in a binary fashion (Daniels 2012). Meanwhile, Kyle also understood the predicament that would ensue were he to fully disclose his bisexuality to his Christian friendship group, in a context where same-sex relationships (and, implied in this exchange, same-sex orientation) is problematised. Celibacy allowed Kyle to situate himself securely within both groups concurrently. Whilst more broadly, celibacy is out of synch within both his Christian network and his LGBTQ network, celibacy is at least tolerated (in a way that a heterosexual relationship would not be tolerated by the LGBTQ network, and a gay relationship would not be tolerated by the Evangelical Christian network). Kyle's celibacy operates as a means of fitting into both cultures, without being excluded from either.

The aforementioned participants were able to draw on celibacy narratives appropriated from their religious traditions to solve the dilemmas they were currently facing. But celibacy was not just followed for the benefits derived. Indeed, for some, the religious injunction to be celibate *was* the starting point, instituted as something that needed to be followed for religious reasons. Whilst Kyle gained practical benefit from celibacy through

208 *Sarah-Jane Page*

maintaining various friendship networks, his celibacy was also adopted as a God-given mandate. His interpretation of the Bible was such that for him, celibacy was a necessary identity in accommodating his religion and sexuality.

Similarly, Ryan, a gay Christian, discussed the need to 'reconcile my sexuality and faith' in a Christian context where homosexuality was not encouraged. His relationship with God was the focus of this endeavour, premised on advocating a 'godly celibate relationship' with a fellow gay Christian.

> I have accepted that I am gay and I have these feelings and have accepted that there are ways of being able to live with those feelings and live as Christian whilst being real about what the Bible says about homosexuals . . . this is who God made me to be. [But] the dynamics of [a godly celibate relationship] would be interesting because a lot of people would say, 'Where are you going to draw the line?' . . . 'Would you share a bed with someone?' And you have to be aware of the temptations . . . People would expect if you live and sleep in the same bed, society's expectations are that you are having a sexual relationship . . . I don't think anything genital is appropriate . . . I think it is appropriate to share in some physical intimacy but that doesn't involve the sexual bits.

Ryan did not want to foreclose intimacy, even as he asserted sexual celibacy. In this way, he was circumventing many negative assumptions around celibacy (such as lack of intimacy). But he anticipated that this relationship would be interpreted as sexual due to current preoccupations where bed sharing is equated with sexual activity (Klesse 2007; Donnelly and Burgess 2008). In navigating this, Ryan termed this as a *godly* celibate relationship, highlighting its sacred (and God-ordained) nature. This invoking of the divine made managing potential negativity possible.

Meanwhile, other participants had inherited a religious injunction to be celibate and were not entirely reconciled with this. Robert, a gay man, wanted to become a Buddhist monk. But this would entail celibacy.

> I don't feel like I can go around saying 'I'm going to be a monk'. People would just think it's bizarre . . . I have told my mum, I've told my two best friends and my boyfriend is aware of it as well but I don't think any of them understand it . . . [my boyfriend] doesn't really respond very well to [the idea] but I said that nothing is set in stone and I certainly don't have the intention to just end the relationship and go in the monastery or anything.

Robert was acutely aware of the unpopularity of the path he envisioned. He had told very few people of his intentions, and he did not think those he had told had fully understood or supported his decision. This negativity meant that Robert stalled the decision making around this intended path and instead located the enactment of his dream to some unspecified future point (Page et al. 2012). This was a means of containing this decision, deemed so out of synch with mainstream norms; and in the meantime, Robert continued his relationship with his boyfriend.

Similarly, Stephen, a gay Christian, wanted to be an Anglican priest but believed that this would only be possible if he were to be celibate, in order for him to be 'pastorally acceptable'. He was aware of priests who were in gay relationships and who hid this from parishioners and the church hierarchy (see Keenan 2009), but Stephen endorsed potential celibacy in a religious context where gay relationships are discouraged:

> [I]f I do end up single for the rest of my life I'm not worried, as long as I'm happy . . . if I was to choose celibacy, for me it would be about being able to identify with those people in the parish who are for whatever reason single . . . [I]f I don't meet anybody then I'll be happy enough. If I meet somebody then I will have to decide.

Stephen was utilising celibacy as a potential future option, even if at the same time he continued to explore the possibilities of engaging in a relationship with someone. There was a level of ambivalence towards celibacy, with a question mark hanging over whether he could be happy living a celibate life; he envisaged tough choices to be made in the future, if the Church of England did not alter its view of gay priests.

For some, celibacy was a strategy utilised in living out one's sexual and religious principles in a supposedly sex-saturated society. For others, celibacy was envisioned as part of their future life plans, and there was less commitment to celibacy in the present moment. Some had done a lot of theological thinking and research to endorse a celibate life path, whilst others were ambivalent about celibacy, even as they endorsed it, leading to uncertainty regarding whether celibacy would be lived out in the future.

No women in the study endorsed celibacy, and this may be a result of the research sample. But even though some women were not engaging in sexual relationships in the current moment, most of the heterosexual women were envisioning a future life with marriage and children at its heart; lesbian participants often did not foreclose the possibilities of future motherhood. This could point to the way celibacy disrupts expectations of women's sexual identities, far more than men's, because motherhood remains valorised and is a normative identity for women (Letherby 1994; Forna 1998). It therefore could be one step too far for women to renege on a future involving motherhood.

NON-MONOGAMY, POLYAMORY AND CENSURE

Across the sample, there was enormous support for monogamous relationships, with 83.2 per cent either agreeing or strongly agreeing with the

210   *Sarah-Jane Page*

statement, 'Monogamy should be the ideal for a partnered relationship' [N: 666]. Monogamy, however, was varyingly interpreted. For some, support for monogamy was understood as being faithful. Having an affair, and the associated deception and lying, was condemned, as Abby and Heather narrate:

> I do believe that if you're in a relationship you should be in a relationship . . . [But] I have messed up on that.
>
> (Abby, Jewish lesbian)

> In past relationships . . . I wasn't faithful and I didn't, I don't like myself for doing it and regret [it] . . . [Now I'm] fiercely monogamous.
>
> (Heather, heterosexual Christian)

At another level, non-monogamy was equated with (one-off) sexual encounters with more than one person, popularised in the notion of the 'threesome'. Again, participants tended to have a very negative view of this:

> A relationship has to be built on commitment and trust . . . if you get any more than one party involved it can get very awkward indeed . . . we were talking about threesomes in the pub the other night; this is with the un-Churched friends as it happens [laughs] and they were like, 'Wouldn't you?' and I said 'No actually' . . . They couldn't believe my dislike of it; they were all like, 'I'd be up for that'.
>
> (Adam, heterosexual Christian)

Certain forms of non-monogamy, such as threesomes, are coded as sexually adventurous, titillating and associated with male heterosexual fantasy (Pallotta-Chiarolli and Martin 2009). As Harper discusses, women willing to have sex with another woman in front of a man are coded as 'hot' (2012: 206) by their male partners, and in the process their identities are fetishised.

Meanwhile, a third group shifted the definition of non-monogamy from one-off sexual encounters to ongoing non-monogamous relationships. Charlotte, a Buddhist who did not define her sexuality, was critical of long-term relationships involving more than one person and whether equity was ever possible:

> I don't think that open relationships actually work in the long run; it's just one person having to put up with something that they probably don't want, just to keep that relationship, so yeah, monogamy probably is important to me.

Therefore at every level, whether non-monogamy was invoked in terms of extra-relationship affairs, one-off multipartnered sexual encounters, or longer-term multipartnered relationships, participants tended to be very negative.

Counter-Normative Identities 211

Meanwhile, a minority were either theoretically supportive of the idea of non-monogamy, or had engaged in non-monogamous relationships. For example, Tamara, a Buddhist bisexual, critiqued the primacy given to monogamy, and if no harm was induced, non-monogamy was seen as ethically sustainable:

> I'm completely monogamous; I wouldn't cheat on him or anything like that . . . but I don't think I'd particularly be that bothered if there were, like, say three people in our relationship.

Tamara supported non-monogamy in theory, whilst she did not enact this in practice. Indeed, she was quick to stress that she herself conformed to normative monogamy and was a 'good' sexual citizen (Richardson 2005; Klesse 2007), but she recognised the future potential for non-monogamy. Therefore, the strength of Tamara's tangible commitment to non-monogamy remains untested.

Alan initially defined himself as a heteroflexible Buddhist, but in his video diary, some months later, he had started to explore Quakerism. His attitudes to sexuality were complex, mediated through his experiences of being celibate for some years. He was fundamentally opposed to monogamy on the grounds that it involved the

> Exclusive possession of the person . . . I really can't stand the idea of making exclusive possession the defining characteristic of a relationship.

He felt this possessiveness garnered unequal relationships. He therefore had embarked on relationships which were open to non-monogamy but underpinned by honesty. For example, his girlfriend had just started dating another man, but this was currently being negotiated, as Alan was not clear to what extent his girlfriend had informed her new lover of Alan's status. He therefore refused to engage in genital contact with her until he was clear that his girlfriend had been honest with her new lover, and instead they were cultivating an intimate relationship through cuddling.

Meanwhile, Ellie defined herself as a polyamorous bisexual Quaker-Buddhist-Pagan, arguing that polyamory was an ethical sexual practice which

> Is very much in favour of people having full agency of everybody communicating properly. Of everybody being properly honest with each other.

Ellie had previously engaged in two concurrent relationships: one involving online cybersex, whilst the other was based on emotional and sexual intimacy. Having relationships in different spaces allowed Ellie to clarify the boundaries between relationships and avoided any potential conflicts

212 *Sarah-Jane Page*

between lovers, but the cybersex encounter was specifically empowering for Ellie, a sufferer of vulvodynia (a condition making vaginal sex very painful), as it allowed her to explore sexual pleasure beyond the narrow confines of vaginal penetration.

Both John and Ellie were drawing on similar theological scripts in advocating their commitment to polyamorous relationships, for as previously articulated, Buddhist sexual ethics are premised on the likelihood of harm; practices which would be readily endorsed in other religious traditions (e.g. heterosexual marriage) could be questioned in this ethical schema, and equally, practices which would be rendered suspicious, could find an ethical base (Keele 2012).

Meanwhile, the UK Religious Society of Friends (Quakers) has traditionally disrupted the sexual ethics promoted by other Christian denominations, affirming as early as 1963 that homosexuality should not be considered 'morally worse' than heterosexuality (Munt 2010: 60). As Pilgrim argues, Quakers promote 'alternate ordering' (2003: 151); they envision new possibilities, other ways of living, while at the same time prioritising inclusivity. This gives space for creative sexual ethics to emerge. Therefore, both Quakerism and Buddhism gave Ellie and John suitable resources to cultivate polyamorous identities.

Despite a theological congruence, however, Ellie still specified difficulties in how polyamory was perceived by those around her, not from her religious community (indeed, her Quaker parents had polyamorous friends), but from one partner's circle of friends:

> [O]ne of my partners at the time did get some quite negative stuff from his friends about you know, 'She's just trying to string you along' and 'You should drop that whore'.

The most injurious and harmful reaction to her relationships emerged from the nonreligious sphere. It is also prudent to examine the gendering of this, in the specific hate speech (Butler 1997) reported. In the context of a relationship which outwardly appeared to be conventionally heterosexual, here was a woman taking explicit control of her relationships, eschewing the idea that a heterosexual relationship ties her solely to one man. This sexual independence and assertiveness contradicts the norms expected of women in a hegemonically masculine economy, where men are expected to own the love of one woman and act territorially and possessively if this is undermined (Sheff 2006). Meanwhile, feminists have highlighted that the use of the world 'whore' has played 'a central role in controlling and policing women's sexual behaviour . . . [such] labels . . . function as an attack on women's reputations' (Klesse 2007: 79–80). Therefore, the resistance to Ellie's relationship choices in the secular sphere could be understood within this gendered framework. Meanwhile, John did not highlight any negativity relating to his own non-monogamous practices.

CONCLUSION

Choices around sexuality continue to be lived out in regulatory frames. For religious young adults, they are situated within a number of discourses pertaining to sexuality, both secular and religious. This can instil greater constraints, as well as opportunities for forging new practices. Indeed, in some instances, religious perceptions on sexuality were utilised as a means of exerting control over sexualised youth cultures, where some individuals felt out of step. This returns to the point made by Alcoff and Caputo (2011) that religious and secular scripts have the potential to regulate and sexual regulation should not solely be associated with religious frameworks. Although religion is popularly perceived as the repository of repressed, unhealthy and unfree sexuality, the reality is that *both* religious and secular frames can offer constraint as well as opportunity.

Indeed, the fact that the young adults in this study had available to them a broader range of sexual scripts allowed a minority to cultivate new ways of living out their lives. This was usually out of synch with dominant youth culture. Both celibacy and non-monogamy are generally condemned in broader culture, despite the reputed loosening up of sexual attitudes and practices. Relationships may be more fluid, evidenced in the forging of new ways of doing relationships (e.g. 'hook-up sex' and 'friends with benefits'), but fidelity remains a cornerstone value (Johansson 2007); non-monogamy is perceived as a disruption to this. Meanwhile, celibacy is out of synch with broader values where fulfilment is underpinned by sexual relationships (Terry 2012). Those who choose not to have sex are seen as repressed; to be truly complete, it is envisaged that one should seek out a sexual partner. Indeed, both celibacy and non-monogamy disrupt cherished sexuality binaries. Despite increased acceptance of gay and lesbian relationships, and the normalisation of having premarital sex, sexuality still operates on dualistic lines, premised on the gender divide. This is why bisexuals and trans individuals continue to experience negativity (Rambukkana 2004; Daniels 2012; Cornwall 2013). They operate in the liminal space between categorisations and disrupt the binary divide. Non-monogamous individuals also disrupt this dualism by advocating multiple concurrent relationships rather than dualistic pairings. Celibates, too, by insisting that they can 'go it alone' and be happy and fulfilled, are negating the ideal of partnerships. The idea that an individual can be celibate and fulfilled remains anathema.

Those within the *Religion, Youth and Sexuality* project endorsing celibacy or non-monogamy were in a minority; they did not constitute a large group, for the majority were opposed to both celibacy and non-monogamy. But within particular contexts, some young adults were able to cultivate innovative sexual identities out of the available scripts. More often than not, religion was utilised as a resource in enabling these different ways of living, despite the fact that the practices that the young people advocated could be out of synch with their broader religious tradition as well. But

214 Sarah-Jane Page

religions are complex repositories of ideas about sexuality. Their history, breadth and depth allow for multiple meanings to be generated. Religion could be a source of constraint as well as an opportunity for new sexual ethics to be promoted. Therefore, we cannot assume *a priori* that religion will be censuring in relation to sexuality. But it was also evident that even as these young adults bravely cultivated new ways of living out their sexuality, opprobrium could be experienced both within their religious traditions, as well as from secular networks; significantly, gender played a part in this, with women's bodies being more tightly regulated than men's. The title of this chapter posits these participants as 'counter-normative', and indeed they are. But as Klesse (2007) rightly points out, the existence of counter-normative and transgressive sexual practices do not, on their own, challenge well-established norms and power relationships—indeed, the regulatory mechanisms experienced by our participants highlights that contemporary sexual cultures are entrenched and hard to dislodge. As Johansson (2007: 40) asserts, 'Although the liberal view on sexuality has a strong influence on young people's attitudes and actions, this does not mean "anything goes" '. Religious and secular frameworks are simultaneously regulatory as well as offering potentiality.

NOTE

1 The project was funded by the Arts and Humanities Research Council and the Economic and Social Research Council under the Religion and Society Programme (Award no. AH/G014051/1). The research team consisted of Prof. Andrew Kam-Tuck Yip (Principal Investigator), Dr. Michael Keenan (Co-investigator) and Dr. Sarah-Jane Page (Research Fellow). The research team is grateful for the funding, as well as the invaluable contribution from the respondents, individuals and groups who helped with the recruitment of the sample and the members of the advisory committee.

REFERENCES

Abbott, E. (2001) *A History of Celibacy.* Cambridge, MA: Da Capo Press.
Alcoff, L. M. and Caputo, J. D. (2011) 'Introduction', in Alcoff, L. M. and Caputo, J. D. (eds.) *Feminism, Sexuality, and the Return of Religion.* Bloomington: Indiana University Press, 1–16.
Althaus-Reid, M. and Isherwood, L. (2008) 'Slicing Women's Bodies', in Althaus-Reid, M. and Isherwood, L. (eds.) *Controversies in Body Theology.* London: SCM Press, 1–6.
Anapol, D. (2010) *Polyamory in the 21st Century.* Lanham: Rowman and Littlefield Publishers.
Attwood, F. (2006) 'Sexed Up: Theorizing the Sexualization of Culture', *Sexualities* 9(1): 77–94.
Attwood, F. (2009) 'Introduction', in Attwood, F. (ed.) *Mainstreaming Sex.* London: I. B. Tauris, xiii–xxiv.
Boynton, P. (2009) 'Whatever Happened to Cathy and Claire?', in Attwood, F. (ed.) *Mainstreaming Sex.* London: I. B. Tauris, 111–125.

Counter-Normative Identities 215

Butler, J. (1997) *Excitable Speech*. London: Routledge.

Byrne, L. (1990) 'Apart from or a Part of: The Place of Celibacy', in Joseph, A. (ed.) *Through the Devil's Gateway*. London: SPCK, 97–106.

Campbell, A. (2014) 'Plus Ça Change?', in Calder, G. and Beaman, L. G. (eds.) *Polygamy's Rights and Wrongs*. Vancouver: UBC Press, 21–45.

Carroll, J. S., Willoughby, B. Badger, S., Nelson, L. J., Barry, C. M. and Madsen, S. D. (2007) 'So Close, Yet So Far Away: The Impact of Varying Marital Horizons on Emerging Adulthood', *Journal of Adolescent Research* 22: 219–247.

Cavendish, J. C. (2003) 'The Vatican and the Laity', in Machacek, D. W. and Wilcox, M. M. (eds.) *Sexuality and the World's Religions*. Santa Barbara: ABC-CLIO, 203–229.

Clark, E. A. (1995) 'Antifamilial Tendencies in Ancient Christianity', *Journal of the History of Sexuality* 5: 356–380.

Cornwall, S. (2013) *Theology and Sexuality*. Norwich: SCM Press.

Daniels, M. (2012) 'Not Even on the Page', in Hutchins, L. and Williams, H. S. (eds.) *Sexuality, Religion and the Sacred*. Abingdon: Routledge, 12–21.

DeRogatis, A. (2003) 'Varieties of Interpretations', in Machacek, D. W. and Wilcox, M. M. (eds.) *Sexuality and the World's Religions*. Santa Barbara: ABC-CLIO, 231–254.

Dialmy, A. (2010) 'Sexuality and Islam', *The European Journal of Contraception and Reproductive Health Care* 15: 160–168.

Donnelly, D. A. and Burgess, E. O. (2008) 'The Decision to Remain in an Involuntary Celibate Relationship', *Journal of Marriage and Family* 70(2): 519–535.

Douglas, K. B. (2011) 'It's All about the Blues', in Alcoff, L. M. and Caputo, J. D. (eds.) *Feminism, Sexuality, and the Return of Religion*. Bloomington: Indiana University Press, 103–123.

Evans, M. (2003) *Love: An Unromantic Discussion*. Cambridge: Polity Press.

Fahs, B. (2010) 'Radical Refusals: On the Anarchist Politics of Women Choosing Asexuality', *Sexualities* 13(4): 445–461.

Fetzer, J. S. and Soper, J. C. (2003) 'The Roots of Public Attitudes Toward State Accommodation of European Muslims' Religious Practices Before and After September 11', *Journal for the Scientific Study of Religion* 42(2): 247–258.

Field, C. D. (2011) 'Young British Muslims since 9/11: A Composite Attitudinal Profile', *Religion, State and Society* 39(2–3): 159–175.

Forna, A. (1998) *Mother of All Myths*. London: HarperCollins.

Freitas, D. (2008) *Sex and the Soul*. Oxford: Oxford University Press.

Furlong, M. (1988) 'Introduction', in Furlong, M. (ed.) *Mirror to the Church*. London: SPCK, 1–16.

Goss, R. E. (2004) 'Proleptic Sexual Love: God's Promiscuity Reflected in Christian Polyamory', *Theology and Sexuality* 11: 52–63.

Hall, S. S. (2006) 'Marital Meaning: Exploring Young Adults' Belief Systems about Marriage', *Journal of Family Issues* 27: 1437–1458.

Harper, S. (2012) ' "All Cool Women Should be Bisexual" ', in Hutchins, L. and Williams, H. S. (eds.) *Sexuality, Religion and the Sacred*. Abingdon: Routledge, 187–215.

Heldman, C. and Wade, L. (2010) 'Hook-Up Culture: Setting a New Research Agenda', *Sexuality Research and Social Policy* 7(4): 323–333.

Hidayatullah, A. (2003) 'Islamic Conceptions of Sexuality', in Machacek, D. W. and Wilcox, M. M. (eds.) *Sexuality and the World's Religions*. Santa Barbara: ABC-CLIO, 255–292.

Imtoual, A. and Hussein, S. (2009) 'Challenging the Myth of the Happy Celibate: Muslim Women Negotiating Contemporary Relationships', *Contemporary Islam* 3: 25–39.

Isherwood, L. and Stuart, E. (1998) *Introducing Body Theology*. Sheffield: Sheffield Academic Press.

216 Sarah-Jane Page

Jackson, S. (1993) 'Even Sociologists Fall in Love: An Exploration in the Sociology of Emotions' *Sociology* 27(2): 201–220.

Jackson, S. and Scott, S. (2004) 'The Personal Is Still Political: Heterosexuality, Feminism and Monogamy', *Feminism and Psychology* 14(1): 151–157.

Jakobsen, J. R. and Pellegrini, A. (2003) *Love the Sin*. Boston: Beacon Press.

Johansson, T. (2007) *The Transformation of Sexuality*. Aldershot: Ashgate.

Johnson, P. (2005) *Love, Heterosexuality and Society*. London: Routledge.

Jordan, M. D. (2011) 'The Return of Religion during the Reign of Sexuality' in Alcoff, L. M. and Caputo, J. D. (eds.) *Feminism, Sexuality, and the Return of Religion*. Bloomington: Indiana University Press, 19–54.

Keele, L. (2012) 'The Third Precept', in Hutchins, L. and Williams, H. S. (eds.) *Sexuality, Religion and the Sacred*. Abingdon: Routledge, 159–170.

Keenan, M. (2009) 'The Gift(?) That Dare not Speak its Name', in Hunt, S. (ed.) *Contemporary Christianity and LGBT Sexualities*. Farnham: Ashgate, 23–37.

King, U. (1989) *Women and Spirituality*. Basingstoke: Macmillan Education.

Klesse, C. (2006) 'Polyamory and Its "Others": Contesting the Terms of Non-Monogamy', *Sexualities* 9(5): 565–583.

Klesse, C. (2007) *The Spectre of Promiscuity*. Aldershot: Ashgate.

Letherby, G. (1994) 'Mother or Not, Mother or What? Problems of Definition and Identity', *Women's Studies International Forum* 17(5): 525–532.

Lidke, J. S. (2003) 'A Union of Fire and Water', in Machacek, D. W. and Wilcox, M. M. (eds.) *Sexuality and the World's Religions*. Santa Barbara: ABC-CLIO, 101–132.

Mahmood, S. (2005) *Politics of Piety*. Princeton: Princeton University Press.

Meirowitz, S. N. S. (2009) 'Not Like a Virgin', in Ruttenberg, D. (ed.) *The Passionate Torah*. New York: New York University Press, 169–181.

Mernissi, F. (2003) *Beyond the Veil*. London: Saqi Books.

Munt, S. R. (2010) 'Quakers: Post-Christian Selfhoods within the Liberal Sphere', in Browne, K., Munt, S. R. and Yip, A. K. T. (eds.) *Queer Spiritual Spaces*. Farnham: Ashgate, 51–79.

Nikunen, K. (2007) 'Cosmo Girls Talk: Blurring Boundaries of Porn and Sex', in Paasonen, S., Nikunen, K. and Saarenmaa, L. (eds.) *Pornification*. Oxford: Berg, 73–85.

Nikunen, K. and Saarenmaa, L. (2007) 'Pornification and the Education of Desire', in Paasonen, S., Nikunen, K. and Saarenmaa, L. (eds.) *Pornification*. Oxford: Berg, 1–20.

Page, S. and Yip, A. K. T. (2012) 'Religious Young Adults Recounting the Past', *Journal of Beliefs and Values* 33(3): 405–415.

Page, S., Yip, A. K. T. and Keenan, M. (2012) 'Risk and the Imagined Future', in Hunt, S. and Yip, A. K. T. (eds.) *The Ashgate Research Companion to Contemporary Religion and Sexuality*. Farnham: Ashgate, 255–270.

Pallotta-Chiarolli, M. and Martin, E. (2009) ' "Which Sexuality? Which Service?": Bisexual Young People's Experiences with Youth, Queer and Mental Health Services in Australia', *Journal of LGBT Youth* 6(2–3): 199–222.

Pilgrim, G. (2003) 'The Quakers: Towards an Alternative Ordering', in Davie, D., Heelas, P. and Woodhead, L. (eds.), *Predicting Religion*. Aldershot: Ashgate, 147–158.

Plummer, K. (2003) *Intimate Citizenship*. Montreal: McGill-Queen's University Press.

Powers, J. (2008) 'Celibacy in Indian and Tibetan Buddhism', in Olson, C. (ed.), *Celibacy and Religious Traditions*. Oxford: Oxford University Press, 201–224.

Price, R. M. (2006) 'Celibacy and Free Love in Early Christianity', *Theology and Sexuality* 12: 121–141.

Rait, S. K. (2005) *Sikh Women in England*. Stoke on Trent: Trentham Books.

Rambukkana, N. P. (2004) 'Uncomfortable Bridges', in Anderlini-D'Onofrio, S. (ed.) *Plural Loves*. Binghampton, NY: Harrington Park Press, 141–154.

Richardson, D. (2005) 'Claiming Citizenship?' in Ingraham, C. (ed.) *Thinking Straight*. London: Routledge, 63–83.

Ritchie, A. and Barker, M. (2006) ' "There Aren't Words for What We Do or How We Feel So We Have To Make Them Up": Constructing Polyamorous Languages in a Culture of Compulsory Monogamy', *Sexualities* 9(5): 584–601.

Robinson, M. (2012) 'Reading Althaus-Reid', in Hutchins, L. and Williams, H. S. (eds.) *Sexuality, Religion and the Sacred*. Abingdon: Routledge, 102–114.

Rossi, L. (2007) 'Outdoor Pornification', in Paasonen, S., Nikunen, K. and Saarenmaa, L. (eds.) *Pornification*. Oxford: Berg, 127–138.

Scherrer, K. S. (2008) 'Coming to an Asexual Identity: Negotiating Identity, Negotiating Desire', *Sexualities* 11(5): 621–641.

Selby, J. A. (2014) 'Polygamy in the Parisian Banlieues', in Calder, G. and Beaman, L. G. (eds.) *Polygamy's Rights and Wrongs*. Vancouver: UBC Press, 120–141.

Sheff, E. (2006) 'Poly-Hegemonic Masculinities', *Sexualities* 9(5): 621–642.

Spencer, L. and Pahl, R. (2006) *Rethinking Friendship*. Princeton, NJ: Princeton University Press.

Terry, G. (2012) ' "I'm Putting a Lid on that Desire": Celibacy, Choice and Control', *Sexualities* 15(7): 871–889.

Thatcher, A. (2011) *God, Sex, and Gender*. Chichester: Wiley Blackwell.

Weeks, J. (2007) *The World We Have Won*, Abingdon: Routledge.

Wellings, K., Nanchahal, K., Macdowall, W., McManus, S., Erens, B., Mercer, C. H., Johnson, A. M., Copas, A. J., Korovessis, C., Fenton, K. A. and Field, J. (2001) 'Sexual Behaviour in Britain: Early Heterosexual Experience', *Lancet* 358: 1843–1850.

Wilson, L. (2003) 'Buddhist Views on Gender and Desire', in Machacek, D. W. and Wilcox, M. M. (eds.) *Sexuality and the World's Religions*. Santa Barbara: ABC-CLIO, 133–175.

Yip, A. K. T. (1997) 'Gay Male Christian Couples and Sexual Exclusivity', *Sociology* 31(2): 289–306.

Yip, A. K. T. and Page, S. (2013) *Religious and Sexual Identities*. Farnham: Ashgate.

12 Angels and the Dragon King's Daughter
Gender and Sexuality in Western Buddhist New Religious Movements

Sally R. Munt and Sharon E. Smith

INTRODUCTION

Buddhism is gaining an increasing profile in Western popular culture. Its adherents (including a significant number of converts) have developed new religious movements (NRMs) in the West (Wallis 1976; Barker 1990, 1998). 'NRM' is the more academic definition of what are some- times popularly and pejoratively labelled 'cults'. Murray Rubinstein, Professor of History at Baruch College, defines them in the Encyclopaedia Britannica concisely as follows:

> [NRM]s offer innovative religious responses to the conditions of the modern world, despite the fact that most NRMs represent themselves as rooted in ancient traditions. NRMs are also usually regarded as 'coun- ter- cultural'; that is, they are perceived (by others and by themselves) to be alternatives to the mainstream religions of Western society, especially Christianity in its normative forms. These movements are often highly eclectic, pluralistic, and syncretistic; they freely combine doctrines and practices from diverse sources within their belief systems.
>
> (Rubinstein 2011)

This paper examines the construction of gender norms within two such NRMs, drawing on our empirical work developed from 2003–2009 within new and alternative religious spaces. We debate gender heteronormativity following interviews within two Buddhist organisations, exploring how respondents construct gender and sexuality also informed by their intersec-tionality with queerness (lesbian, gay, bisexual, transgendered, questioning and intersex or LGBTQI) and, less so, with ethnicity and race.

There is a limited amount of literature already on gender, sexuality and NRMs. Catherine Wessinger's collection (1993) found that marginal reli-gions in the United States have been supportive of women taking leadership roles at least since the nineteenth century. Puttick, on the other hand (2003), observed the sex/gender conservatism endemic to most groups, even though there were signs of potential variation from these norms. Susan Palmer's

Angels and the Dragon King's Daughter   219

work on women's experience of NRMs stressed the diversity of roles open to women who often engage with them for short periods of time in order to explore alternative renditions of selfhood. Palmer offered three distinct models of gender: sex complementarity, sex polarity and sex unity, arguing that 'members appear to undergo a self-imposed psychological metamorphosis, or "cocoon work," which in many ways resembles the ritual process found in feminine rites in traditional societies' (2003: 250).

Our exploration starts by outlining the main approaches to gender and sexuality by various Buddhist traditions, noting that in the West, the academic literature on these matters tends to focus primarily on normatively sexed women or homosexual men (Cabezon and Anderson 1994). Focusing on two of the largest Buddhist groups in the UK, which are the Triratna Buddhist Community (TBC, formerly the Friends of the Western Buddhist Order or FWBO) and the Nichiren group Sōka-Gakkai International-UK (SGI-UK), we describe their history and key practices (Waterhouse 1999; Bluck 2006). In our exploration of gender norms for each movement, we then deploy our adapted version of Linda Woodhead's (2007) model as an analytical framework.

Gender and sexuality within Buddhist traditions has generated much critical comment (see for example Cabezón 1992; Gross 1993; Faure 1998, 2003; Leyland 1998, 2000; Gyatso 2003; Harvey 2000). Most of this discussion focuses on the status of women, although in explorations of Buddhism and male sexuality, homosexuality predominates. The consensus is that the Buddhist tradition sees male monasticism as the most efficacious form of practice; although both sexes can realise Enlightenment, normatively sexed male bodies are advantageous. The ethical guidelines to monks and nuns prohibit same-sex practices; however, unlike some other faiths, they do not single out homosexual acts *qua* heterosexual ones, as it is sexual activity that is seen as problematic rather than the gender of the partner (although women are understood to be a particular potentially strong distraction to monks).

The ethical guidelines for laypeople prohibit 'sexual misconduct', but as there is no agreement on sexual morality, it is open to each tradition to determine what this means in practice. Homoeroticism is largely ignored, although commentators from some traditions (especially some Tibetan Buddhist schools and schools dating from early Buddhism) have made negative remarks about homosexual practices. In terms of people who fall outside the 'male'/'female' binary (e.g. intersex people), early Buddhism debarred them from entering the monastic community, and this continues to be the case throughout the Buddhist world.

Traditionally, in some contexts, Buddhism has been able to accommodate gender variation and (particularly male) homosexuality (see Coleman et al. 1992; Peletz 2006), in Thailand (Jackson 1998, 2000) and in thirteenth-to fourteenth-century Japan (Schalow 1998a, 1998b; see further Yip and Smith 2010). Within Buddhism, sex and gender are largely seen as operating

220 Sally R. Munt and Sharon E. Smith

within a heterosexual economy, masculine and normatively sexed bodies typically being privileged (Butler 1993, 1999). Karma Lekshe Tsomo's work has outlined the historical inequalities between monks and nuns in Buddhism (1999, 2000, 2004a, 2004b, 2004c). This continues to place the status of women and gender minorities under question, and where Buddhism has gained a following, there are tendencies to androcentrism and imbrications with heteropatriarchal regimes. The spread of Buddhism to the West leads to speculation as to what gender norms might emerge.

OUR RESEARCH CONTEXT: QUEER METHODOLOGIES, INTERSECTIONALITY AND 'FISH IN WATER'

The data in this paper comes from two research projects using the same fieldworker, Smith, a Black British lesbian who is a member of one of the case study movements, Triratna Buddhist Order. The first project, which was her doctoral ethnographic research that focused primarily on race and class in Western Buddhism, also examined the intersectionality of gender and sexuality in Western Buddhism as an integral part of the thesis (Smith 2008). The second project comprised a set of discrete individual and group interviews for the AHRC/ESRC-funded Queer Spiritual Spaces project for which Munt, the co-author, a white former working-class lesbian Unitarian was principal investigator (Browne, Munt and Yip 2010). Smith was employed as a post-doctoral researcher.[1] In both cases, our insider status in terms of 'queerness' was of utility in recruiting participants and gave us considerable insights into our empirical material. The fieldworkers' familiarity with UK Buddhism worked to the advantage of both studies in terms of access.

We were concerned to elucidate participants' meanings in terms of which social categories they felt best reflected them. This meant, for instance, in terms of race and class we did not use UK census categories but invited participants to define themselves using their own terminology. We felt especially concerned to maintain this practice in terms of definitions of gender and sexuality rather than impose a definition of 'queer' on participants. In this way we sought to move away from the potential danger of essentialising the category 'queer', which after all is meant to be a non-normalising 'identity without an essence' (Halperin 1995: 62). We consider our reluctance to have a fixed definition of queer in this paper, preferring to mainly use the term LGBTQI to be in keeping with the spirit of queer theory (see 'Introduction' and 'Conclusion', Browne, Munt and Yip 2010).

As part of our concern with research ethics, we were committed to respecting the anonymity of participants. Because of the minoritisation of LGBTQI people of colour within Buddhism, it has meant that it is not always possible to give full descriptions of the demographic details of participants, as these would lead to some being recognised all too easily in

Angels and the Dragon King's Daughter 221

print. Some participants, however, saw this as an opportunity to increase the visibility of LGBTQI issues in relation to Buddhism, so these asked not to be anonymised. Participants were invited to give feedback through seeking their comments on interview transcripts and case study summaries for the movement they belonged to. For the QSS study, participants were invited to a project-wide conference in 2009 where our early findings were presented and debated.

Each movement was studied ethnographically through participant observation for four years. A total of 39 interviews were conducted with participants with a range of involvement and leadership positions within each case study. For the Queer Spiritual Spaces project, a total of 18 further interviews were conducted as well as two meetings of a focus group for "women" in one of the case study movements who identified as LGBTQI.

The fieldworker also performed thematic narrative analysis following close readings of each movement's publications and websites in order to identify what discourses of gender and sexuality were hegemonic within the case study movements. In exploring participants' own positionalities, we found the theoretical point Pierre Bourdieu makes about the nature of individuals' *habitus* to the spaces they occupy of utility. This states:

> . . . when habitus encounters a social world of which it is the product, it is like a 'fish in water': it does not feel the weight of the water, and it takes the world about itself for granted.
>
> (Bourdieu and Wacquant 1992: 127)

In other words, the level of ease that someone experiences within a social world will depend on the ways in which that world relates to their socialisation and predispositions around class, sexuality, gender, race and other axes of difference.

Although the intersectionality of gender with other axes of difference is more recognised, there has been little theorisation of how this applies to religion. Linda Woodhead (2007) suggests that gender be understood as a complex and interlocking set of power relations constituted in the historical process that leads to unequal distribution of power and thus a 'gender order'. We found Linda Woodhead's model formed a useful and complementary basis for the analysis of our data. She suggests that religion be considered as 'the social expression of engagement with a source of power that is unique to religion' which she calls 'sacred power'. 'Sacred power' can have independent force but is enhanced through alignment with secular power; these can reinforce or repudiate one another. However, in line with King's (1999) critique of religion as *sui generis*, we would suggest that religion be seen as one of many vectors of power encountered through what Foucault (1997) referred to as 'technologies of the self' (Foucault 1984). Religion is therefore *pace* Foucault a form of governmentality and/or ethics that may have hegemonising and/or emancipatory effects.

222 *Sally R. Munt and Sharon E. Smith*

Anthony Giddens (1991) argues that, within the context of late modernity, the construction of the self becomes a reflexive project in which individuals have to work out their roles for themselves. It is in this context that self-help books and various therapies proliferate and themselves reflexively constitute the issues they explore. Neo-liberalism has given rise to increasing individualisation that led Foucault to suggest not only emancipatory possibilities through ethics but new forms of governmentality through the encouragement of the 'self as enterprise' (McNay 2009), in which individuals are forced to account for themselves, for their 'choices' around gender and sexuality throughout their life course, whilst making little, if any reference to their wider social context (e.g. McRobbie 2004). Therefore, at the current time, *religion functions within a context where individuals increasingly 'govern' themselves*. This affords a synchronicity within the West towards Buddhism, as it has long been perceived as supporting such processes of individualisation (e.g. Sangharakshita 1990; Tweed 1992; Hori 1994). Within these individualising processes, gender appears in flux, yet continues to be organised around heteronormativity.

Woodhead goes on to argue that the interaction of religion and gender can and does occur by way of symbolic and material practices through which religion reinforces or challenges existing gendered distributions. She posits two main variables arising from this: first, religion's *situation* with respect to gender, that is how it relates to existing distributions of secular power, and second, religion's *strategy* in relation to gender, that is how it mobilises in relation to existing distributions of secular power. She suggests this can be expressed diagrammatically as follows:

'Mainstream' religion is integral to the existing distribution of power in society and read as socially respectable. "Marginal" religion is seen as socially deviant by those who accept the dominant distribution of power.

MAINSTREAM

Consolidating	Tactical
CONFIRMATORY	CHALLENGING
Questing	Counter-cultural

Figure 12.1 Religion's positioning in relation to gender from Woodhead (2007: 670, used with permission).

Angels and the Dragon King's Daughter 223

'Confirmatory' religion seeks to legitimate, reinforce and sacralise the existing distribution of power, particularly the 'existing gender order'. 'Challenging' religion seeks to ameliorate, resist or change the 'gender order'. Any one religion may have more than one tendency associated with it due to the differences amongst its adherents even within the same religious movement, leading to them having different positionalities within the same religion.

As can be seen from the diagram, this leads to four "cells" that represent four main positionalities of religious adherents in relation to gender. These are:

1. *Consolidating.* Where religion functions in both a mainstream and confirmatory mode, it is integral to the existing gender order and serves to reproduce and legitimate gender inequality for both its practitioners and those who fall within its penumbra.
2. *Tactical.* Here participants gain access to power from 'inside'. This can be used in ways that subvert the existing gender order to 'strike a bargain with patriarchy'.
3. *Questing* occurs where religion may be marginal to the existing gendered distribution of power but is used to access that power from the outside, without necessarily intending to disrupt its distribution.
4. *Countercultural* religion may be marginal to the gendered distribution of power and used to attempt to contest, disrupt and redistribute that distribution.

We would suggest that this typology need not only apply to individual religious movements as a whole but rather reflects the contested and contesting positionalities of members within particular religious movements. For example, within the Christian Anglican Communion, some members vigorously seek to hegemonise heteronormativity within this institution, representing a *consolidating* position. Others actively counter these efforts through strongly arguing for a more inclusive stance, thus representing a more *countercultural* tendency. Also, it is necessary to consider how factors of 'nation', region and globalisation affect gender norms within religious institutions. So in the case of the Anglican Communion, there has been an appeal through US fundamentalism to parts of the global South to further hegemonise *mainstream* and *confirmatory* positionalities, whilst at the same time some parts of the US Episcopal Church are experiencing contestation for showing *marginal* and *challenging* perspectives.

We would argue, following Pierre Bourdieu, that those involved in 'mainstream', 'confirmatory' and 'consolidating' positionings are like 'fish in water' (Bourdieu and Wacquant 1992: 127). Those in 'challenging', 'tactical' or 'questing' positionings are like 'fresh water fish in sea water'. This expression is used by the black female sociologist Felly Nkweto Simmonds to describe her position within academia: 'In this white world I am a fresh water fish that swims in sea water. I feel the weight of the water . . . on my body' (1997: 227). Finally, 'challenging' and 'countercultural' adherents are like 'fish out of water' who find it hard to swim and breathe.

224 Sally R. Munt and Sharon E. Smith

CASE STUDIES: TWO BUDDHIST NEW RELIGIOUS MOVEMENTS

1. Triratna Buddhist Community (TBC)

The TBC, one of the largest Western Buddhist movements with over 75 public centres and retreats and several businesses in the UK, was founded in 1967 as the Friends of the Western *Sangha* (becoming the FWBO a year later) by a white, working-class Englishman who had been given the name Sangharakshita (1925-) on his ordination. TBC was devised as a new form of Buddhism for a modern society that was 'secularised, and industrialised' (Sangharakshita 1990: 8); it synchronises elements from Nietzsche and psychotherapy with strands of different Buddhisms. A key teaching of Sangharakshita is that his disciples should move from 'group consciousness' towards 'true individuality' (ego-lessness). This has led to a culture of suspicion for 'identity politics' within this movement.

In TBC, there are flexible levels of membership—a possible indication of the need to recruit as widely as possible—and three levels of involvement, the first being *Friend*, the second being *Mitras*, who decide to become more involved but not to fully commit, then *Members* have responsibility for directing the activities of the TBC, following a period of training. From its outset, the TBC has emphasised meditation as a principal technology of the self, and it is the predominant means through which people become involved.

TBC has developed a large network of centres and an international following. It has attracted controversy that has led to considerable debate within the movement and led to several significant changes to its structure and practices. In 2003, the then College of Public Preceptors, whom Sangharakshita had designated as the Head of the Order, relinquished its role on the grounds that the Order was meant to be a 'free association of individuals', leading to a perceived organisational void and lack of coherence. Recently, Sangharakshita is back at TBC's helm and continues to be respected as its founder; it is unclear what this will mean for this movement in the future, especially after he dies. At present, however, there appears to be a concomitant attempt to reassert 'traditional' principles and doctrines. In January 2010, Sangharakshita requested, in somewhat postcolonial mood, that the FWBO's name should change to Triratna (Three Jewels) Buddhist Order (TBO), and following discussion with the European Chairs' meeting, the movement's name should become Triratna Buddhist Community (TBC).

2. Sōka-Gakkai International-UK (SGI-UK)

This international movement, comprising over 450 local groups in the UK with approximately 12,000 committed members, is based on the teachings of the Japanese Buddhist teacher Nichiren (1222–1282) that focus

Angels and the Dragon King's Daughter   225

exclusively on the Lotus Sūtra. Unlike the emphasis in most Western Buddhist movements on meditation practice, the core practices of SGI are:

(a) Faith: Believing in the *Gohonzon*, a sacred scroll to which Nichiren Buddhists chant that is believed to embody the law of life and is meant to be a representation of Buddhahood.
(b) Practice: Chanting *Nam-myoho-renge-kyo* (*daimoku*) a salutation of the title of the Lotus Sūtra) and performing *gongyo*[2] (a twice-daily ritual in which one recites portions of the Lotus Sūtra and prayers). Also sharing Buddhist teachings with others.
(c) Study of the teachings of Nichiren and application of these in daily life.

A fundamental belief of this movement is that all one's experiences and circumstances are due to one's *karma* and that adversities can be overcome through its practices of Nichiren Buddhism. SGI is organised bilaterally into divisions—for adult Men, adult Women, with Young Women joining Lilac, and Young Men joining Sōka (Value Creative) respectively. Members of SGI meet regularly several times a month in various forums. Each has leaders at various regional levels, who coordinate group activities and provide personal counselling ("guidance"). The most basic group activity for members is the monthly discussion meeting (which is mixed in terms of gender) where they can share their experience of practice and offer support and encouragement to others and to which guests are also welcomed.

A key moment in the development of SGI has been the bitter dispute with its former priestly arm, Nichiren Shōshū, which led to a split in 1991. At this time, the priesthood excommunicated all SGI members and advised them to join its new lay division *Hokkeko*. Most of the membership however remained within SGI, which has since emphatically declared itself to be a lay organisation. In the UK, there has been some questioning as to the appropriateness of SGI-UK organisational structures based on the Japanese model. As a result, a reassessment group was established in 1995 under the then general director, Ricky Baines. He observed tensions between traditionalists who were reluctant to see change and modernists who desired new structures based on teamwork rather than designated leaders within the existing stratified hierarchy. Gender roles were also questioned. After a series of consultations between Baines and his leadership team, the Japanese parent organisation and other representatives from Europe, it appears, according to Waterhouse (2002), that only minor changes were made, meaning that the traditionalists largely won.

THE RELEVANCE OF THE WOODHEAD MODEL

Woodhead suggests that where religion is integral to the existing gender order, it can be 'consolidating' and serve to reproduce and legitimate

226   *Sally R. Munt and Sharon E. Smith*

gender inequality for those who practice the religion and those who fall within its penumbra but can be also used in a 'tactical' way to give access to power from 'inside'. This power can be used in ways that subvert the existing gender order to 'strike a bargain with patriarchy'. 'Questing' religion occurs where religion may be marginal to the existing gendered distribution of power but is used to access that power from the outside, without necessarily intending to disrupt its distribution. Finally, religion may be marginal to the gendered distribution of power and used in a 'countercultural' way to attempt to contest, disrupt and redistribute that distribution. We now turn to consider how this might relate to the findings of our empirical research.

Consolidating Approaches in TBC

Sangharakshita had been critical of the view that to be a committed Buddhist practitioner one had to become a monastic and so established the Western Buddhist Order as an institution whose members are 'neither monastic or lay' in which 'commitment [to following the Buddhist path] is primary, lifestyle secondary' (cited in Subhuti 1994: 145–146). Both men and women receive the same ordination and follow the same set of ten ethical precepts, although if a member wishes to be celibate, they follow a different version of the third precept, to become *anagarikas*—a commitment to not engage in sexual activity and have a simpler lifestyle.

Nonetheless, one highly controversial aspect of TBC throughout its history has been its founder's approaches to gender issues, for whilst Sangharakshita asserts the soteriological equality of women with men, and women ordain women into the TBO without reference to men (unlike many parts of the Buddhist world), he sees gender in essentialist terms and regards women and men as fundamentally, biologically different (Subhuti 1995). Women are seen to tend to have more of the 'feminine' qualities of 'softness, compliance and concern for others'. Men, on the other hand, tend to possess more of the 'masculine' qualities of 'strength, initiative and independence' (Subhuti 1994: 165).

Sangharakshita has said that it is important that men and women seek to relate to others as 'individuals', and to move beyond 'exclusive identification with one's biological sex' (Subhuti 1994: 167). However, before that point is reached, it is best for men and women to be as separate as possible on account of an assumed erotic tension between the sexes that also applies to homosexuals as 'the essential differences [are] deeper than sexual orientation' (1994: 164). In what he refers to as his Last Will and Testament to the TBO (Sangharakshita 2009b), he states his continuing belief in single-sex institutions. This is despite many followers living with their partners and forming nuclear families of their own within a 'heterosexual matrix' to use Judith Butler's term (1999). A binarist view of gender also leaves transgendered people largely unplaced, as Sangharakshita has insisted that it is birth,

Angels and the Dragon King's Daughter 227

rather than affect, that determines gender.[3] Perhaps most controversial has been Sangharakshita's polemical assertion that:

> The feminist reading of history as the story of Woman's oppression and exploitation by Man belongs not to history but to mythology, and can be compared with the anti-Semitic reading of history as the story of the world-wide conspiracy on the part of the Jews to concentrate wealth and power in their own hands so as to be able to enslave the Gentiles.
>
> (cited in Subhuti 1995: 11)

Sangharakshita continues to be strongly opposed to the political concepts of patriarchy, 'difference', and the social constructedness of gender. However, his belief in equality, with organisational positions within the TBO and TBC being open to both men and women, also places him within the modernist era of liberal feminism.

At one point an attempt was made to expound Sangharakshita's views on women, men and feminism so as to encourage wider adoption of these throughout this movement. This culminated in the publication of an essay by one of Sangharakshita's most senior male disciples, Subhuti, published as *Women, Men and Angels: An Inquiry Concerning the Relative Spiritual Aptitudes of Men and Women*.

The title alludes to an aphorism by Sangharakshita: 'Angels are to men as men are to women—because they are more human and, there- fore, more divine' (Subhuti 1994: 65). The resulting furore within the TBC was raised by participant Dh. B in his interview for the Queer Spiritual Spaces study:

> [Sangharakshita] gave his blessing to a book called *Women, Men and Angels* which has proved highly controversial within the Order, then within the Movement, and then there was a rather strangled debate about it and then people just voted with their feet, several Buddhist centres refused to have their book in Buddhist centres and I think it's been pulped now . . .

Sangharakshita has recently been more cautious about expressing his views on gender. Although Subhuti's *Sangharakshita: A New Voice in the Buddhist Tradition* was reissued in 2009 without any changes, thus leaving the original assertions about gender intact, in Sangharakshita's Last Will and Testament he says that agreement with these is not essential to discipleship.

In the TBC there has been concern that in recent years men form a minority of newcomers to the movement and seem to have 'lost their way'. The then outreach worker for a London TBC Centre suggested:

> I think we still assume that it's women that have problems in the world and in some places in the world that's very much the case. My own feeling is that at the moment men are having much more problems,

probably especially, probably more black men than white men. But my own experience is meeting a lot of men who don't really know what they're doing. Who don't know what they're supposed to be, what it is to be a man.

Some senior male TBO members argue that men need to discover their 'manhood' and can be undermined or emasculated by too much dependence on women (see for example Devamitra 2001). Some suggest drawing on the mythopoetic Men's Movement. But the functioning of the single-sex principle has led to opportunities and resources for women, as we will see in the next section.

Tactical Approaches in TBC

In its early days, the few female members of TBO took it upon themselves to develop women-only spaces that would make TBC teachings more accessible, encouraging women to develop their friendships with one another and to invest more in their relationships with other Buddhist women. Whilst this reflected the influence of the 'Second Wave' women's movement, this did not mean that what became known as the 'women's wing' had a clear feminist agenda; in fact, it was critical of more radical and separatist sections of the women's movement. Whilst feminism was notionally agreed to be of significance in advancing the social status of women, it is seen as not able to offer the complete emancipation offered by Enlightenment and freedom from egotism (Maitreyi 1997). Also, in keeping with Sangharakshita's teaching that one should be less attached to one's biological sex and also to other markers of identification, women in this group tend to be wary of emphasising their gender identities and the contestations around these as they wished to develop 'true individuality', Sangharakshita's term for what is referred to in Buddhism as the gaining of Insight. As Diana, a black lesbian who had been active in the women's queer and anti-racist movements of the 1980s and 1990s says: 'I've loosened my attachments to my blackness and to my lesbian self and my female self'.

Yet the single-sex practice of TBC has proved attractive for many feminists and lesbians. Alison, a bisexual participant, says:

> I think on the one hand I felt there was quite a bit of misogyny in the Movement and on the other hand I felt you know with the single sex, what was then called principle, that made sense to me, and I was quite happy because it was part of my feminist days . . . that worked for me, so, even though I did feel that there was quite strong elements of misogyny, there were strong elements that came through . . . ethoses [sic] and cultures in which women were particularly valued.

Thus 'tactical' religion is used to create space for women's mutual support.

Angels and the Dragon King's Daughter 229

Where such androcentrism proves problematic, women expressed disagreement with, and de-emphasised these views. As one lesbian interviewee for the Queer Spiritual Spaces project stated:

> Well I just know that when I've read his [Sangharakshita's] seminars and he's doing a seminar with men and suddenly something comes up or there's a comment about you know, 'Oh and you know, the woman is doing the knitting' sort of thing, that it strongly affects me. I feel that there's a kind of stereotyped, I mean this is in the past; these seminars are very old . . . And so those views or comments, I mean they just really irritate me. I just thought, 'They're just typical', kind of typical male, the sort of stereotyped views.

The 'tactical' situation of women in the movement was not lost on some participants; Mike, a black gay man, when describing his response to *Women, Men and Angels* asked rhetorically:

> . . . if Subhuti believes this, not only believes this but wants to also exhibit his belief in this, about the relationship between men and women, what does he think between white people and black people, men, white women and black women?

Mike indicates that questions of gender cannot be so easily separated from discourses around race and were in fact inseparable due to their intersectionality.

Questing Approaches in TBC

In the case of TBC, special events for newcomers who are gay and/or people of colour are organised. A lesbian member of TBO interviewed for the Queer Spiritual Spaces project, described why she was trying to develop spaces for lesbian and bisexual newcomers to TBC:

> I've done workshops for lesbians like on confidence, but using meditation because you know I notice that for some lesbians there is in my own experience a kind of lack of confidence, just to stand your ground and say, 'Well this is how I am' and you know, really come into yourself, and that's not to say that people of all different sexualities might not need meditation for confidence so that's just an interesting answer for me, that it's about empowering and if there has been discrimination or difficulty, you know, for many people there may well be a number of years when one's trying to come out or come to terms with who one is, which then affects your personality to some degree and just to unravel that conditioning, you know, say, always feeling the outsider or that kind of thing.

230 *Sally R. Munt and Sharon E. Smith*

People in this category usually have to make a decision to take part in 'tactical' spiritual spaces, should they wish to engage more fully in TBC. However, for participants of colour, this can present particular challenges because of the ways in which such more 'generic' spaces are racialised. Mike described his experience of the national retreat centre for men Padmaloka in these terms:

> It was unapologetically white male dominated. It . . . had a very similar feeling to . . . Parliament . . . A sense of white male dominance, just unquestioned. Absolutely unquestioned. No concessions to anybody or anything.

If we describe whiteness as Sara Ahmed suggests 'as a bad habit: as a series of actions that are repeated, forgotten and that allow some bodies to take up space by restricting the mobility of others' (2006: 129), we can begin to understand why 'questing' people of colour who are members of TBC may come to limit their involvement with it.

Countercultural Approaches in TBC

In the early days of TBC, Sangharakshita's position vis-à-vis the British Buddhist establishment struck a chord with countercultural enthusiasms of the late 1960s and early 1970s. His approach to sexuality and family orientation was to prove highly contentious. The TBC was quite critical of the nuclear family for what was described as its 'restrictiveness and exclusivity' (Subhuti 1988: 177). This early stance along with the favouring of same-sex institutions as part of the drive to create what was termed the *New Society* attracted many middle-class 'hippies' to the movement. However, the introduction of the 'single-sex principle' in the 1970s was by no means a smooth and easy process, leaving many women feeling marginalised (Suryaprabha 1997), as was also observed by participants in the Queer Spiritual Spaces focus group for LGBTQI 'women' in TBC.

Homosexuality has never been proscribed by the movement. Furthermore, Sangharakshita has said that there should be no discrimination on the grounds of sexual orientation within the movement, but members are encouraged not to "over-identify" with their sexual orientation. Sangharakshita's sexual relations with some of his male disciples have provoked criticism (Bunting 1997, 1998), especially in the context of the ongoing debate about the ethicality of relationships between Buddhist teachers and their students (see for example Gross 1993; Bell 2002; FWBO Files [1999]). In August 2009 on Sangharakshita's website, he published a transcript of a series of interviews he gave to two male senior members of the Order, breaking his long-standing silence on allegations about his sexual practice (Urgyen Sangharakshita 2009b; Mahamati and Subhuti 2009). In his view, these were conducted on an equal and consensual basis so should not be regarded as unethical. Jnanavira (2010), a member of TBO, argues:

> Sangharakshita's sexual activities took place within a countercultural context between the 1960s and 1980s. This involved sexual

experimentation as a means to encourage intimacy between men by overcoming the socially instilled fear that many have of seeming gay or effeminate if they express love or affection for male friends. As part of this, there was a stress on the provisional . . . nature of the categories 'gay' or 'straight' and an emphasis upon a more holistic development of the individual.

This suggests that TBC members seek not to 'over-identify' with their sexual orientation, rather seeing such practices as instrumental in a spiritual objective. This practice can be seen in terms of the Buddhist doctrine of *anatta*, the lack of an essential or 'core' self with which one can totally identify. Conversely, this also could be read as glossing over the potentially abusive sexual relations in which Sangharakshita engaged, indeed some have attacked both his perceived misogyny and his seeming hypocrisy for abandoning celibacy in favour of 'promoting' homosexuality through his preferment of single-sex institutions.[4]

CONSOLIDATING APPROACHES IN SGI-UK

The Buddhist teacher Nichiren did not endorse the traditional Japanese view of women as 'polluting'. Whereas the soteriological status of women has been questioned in some Buddhist schools, he affirmed women's ability to gain Enlightenment through the power of the Lotus Sūtra in several of his writings, saying at one point that female devotees of the sūtra are superior to profane men and that women need not become men in order to become Enlightened (Faure 2003: 91–93). A story from the Lotus Sūtra that is often quoted within SGI is that of the Dragon King's daughter. Despite being female, young and having a non-human form, she suddenly attains Enlightenment to the astonishment of the men around her. When one of the men, Shariputra,[5] questions her attainment, she challenges him to see her attainment of Buddhahood and becomes male. Sarah Norman (2006) suggests that her gender transformation is not a prerequisite for her attainment of Buddhahood but serves some other purpose. Daisaku Ikeda, President of SGI asserts that the story represents: '[a] grand declaration of human rights that refutes, by means of actual proof, ideas and beliefs that discriminate against women' (2006: 93–94).[6]

The strong affirmation of soteriological equality within SGI should not be taken to mean that the gender order within this movement is an equal one. A heteronormative gender order prevails, reflecting the gender culture of modern Japan. Women are expected to be 'good wives, wise mothers' and this continues to be the basic role assigned to members of Sōka Gakkai's (the Japanese branch of SGI) Married Women's Division (McLaughlin 2009). For Japanese men, the hegemonic model of masculinity that arose out of modernity is the 'salaryman' (corporate warrior) figure that in many ways embodied the notion of the Japanese male as the archetypal

Figure 12.2 The Dragon King's daughter. This is clearly an East Asian depiction, since the young woman is standing on the back of a dragon.

heterosexual husband/father and producer/provider (Dasgupta 2003: 594). Haruko Okano expresses the view that Japanese new religious movements such as Sōka Gakkai encourage the husband to assume the role of leader and the wife that of a subordinate (1995: 24).

Angels and the Dragon King's Daughter 233

Figure 12.3 In this image, the Dragon King's daughter offers a jewel to Buddha. Both images are from http://www.gakkaionline.net/mandala/devaDKD.html.

Atsuko Usui has also suggested that 'the structure of the Sōka Gakkai organisation continues to function along gender lines' (2003: 197). Despite this, Abby in her interview envisioned:

> . . . I think it would be really nice in the next twenty years or so to see a Sensei[7] that's female. Now that shouldn't be something that's radical or feel radical but it does. And I'm not angry about the fact that there

234   *Sally R. Munt and Sharon E. Smith*

hasn't been because obviously historically that wouldn't make sense. But I think that the fact that Nichiren all those centuries ago actually said that women could be Buddha is amazing, and testament to his belief that we are all equal, and I think it needs to continue to be pushed and seen.

In SGI-UK, people from the youth divisions can decide to perform duties at larger meetings as part of the 'dedicated groups', and in such capacities wear uniforms. The young men's Sōka (value-creation) duties involve security of the venue and the young women's Lilac duties are giving hospitality by ushering, providing refreshments and ensuring that people at the event are comfortable. This is not to say that this allocation of duties passes without comment,[8] and it has changed in some countries where SGI has a following.

The president of SGI, Daisaku President Ikeda, has also spoken of men having 'hard power' that makes them more likely to start wars, whereas women have the maternal 'soft power' that gives them a specific role to promote nuclear disarmament and world peace. Although this is a classic designation of (predominantly heterosexual) femininity, it has led to a considerable level of international campaigning by women within SGI for peace (Usui 2003), an example of a 'tactical' approach by women to the gender order, and perhaps, of a cultural feminist spirituality akin to that practised in the 1980s at sites such as Greenham Common.[9] Men have a more orthodox 'masculine' role within the organisation, male leaders are slightly more prominent than their female counterparts. Atsuko Usui has also suggested that 'the structure of the Sōka Gakkai organisation continues to function along gender lines' (2003: 197).

Ikeda has suggested in one of his guidelines to the men's division of SGI that it should seek to be the 'golden pillar' of *kōsenrufu*—world peace through propagation of the Lotus Sūtra. At the SGI-UK General Meeting for 2005 in the Royal Albert Hall, Robert Harrap, the Men's Division leader for the UK said that his message for men at the meeting was that in Ikeda's terms they were the 'citadel that provides a happy haven for your family'. Jacqueline Stone argues that SGI's approach to social issues has conservative aspects and cites gender as an example (Stone 2003: 92 n. 41). All this suggests that SGI, like TBC sees gender as a male/female binary operating within a heterosexual matrix (Butler 1993, 1999).

In terms of sexuality and family orientation, a common slogan within SGI is that Buddhism equals daily life (Wilson and Dobbelaere 1994: 57–59). SGI has been more positive towards the nuclear family than TBC and has specific sections for adolescents (Future group), girls (Mimosas) and boys (Young Eagles) as well as organising regular events for families. The first of the "five eternal guidelines" of SGI is *faith for a harmonious family*.

Same-sex relationships are not currently proscribed, although this has not always been the case, at least informally. Due to the recent influence of LGBTQI members, the mood is more tolerant and supportive in keeping with the liberalising of attitudes towards homosexuality in the UK, and President Ikeda has sent positive messages of encouragement to each of the SGI international LGBT conferences that have taken place. Will, a Queer Spiritual Spaces project interviewee, described feeling affirmed by these messages:

> The Americans, SGI-USA set up these LGBT conferences and President Ikeda every year he sends a message to them of encouragement. I mean I just cried the first one I read, because it was just like, "Oh my God, you know if I ever thought that you didn't understand it, you know, I was wrong."

Also, since the passage of the Civil Partnerships Act in 2004 in the UK, same-sex couples can have their relationships celebrated at SGI-UK's headquarters at Taplow Court.

TACTICAL APPROACHES IN SGI-UK

The ethnographer found a much greater depth of emotional sharing at the SGI's women's division meetings than at the mixed district meetings. In terms of how male participants might see the men's divisions, Will questioned the gender divisions but also found it useful that SGI-UK had a space where both gay and 'straight' men could get together:

> Japan's so rigid in its gender structure that, it sort of took me quite a while to understand and probably I still don't understand a little bit, 'cos when I used to see those gender divisions and the kind of expectations for gender, I used to think; "Oh fucking hell, you know, that's so stereotypical, and so rigid." And I couldn't understand it, and . . . we had these divisional meetings and I used to think . . . "Well, why aren't we just homogenous?" And then when I came to realise that, you know, actually I really like the divisional meetings because it really challenged me, to be with men when actually sometimes I was more comfortable with women, or to be with straight men and for straight men to be with me. And then I began to see, actually we're not an organisation that says, "Oh, let's not go near the straight guys, let's not go near the gay guys. At times let's put them together and see what happens and see how they can really transcend their differences."

Leading members of SGI-UK's Women's Division have also reflected on what being female in SGI-UK might mean. Reflecting on the significance of the SGI president describing the twenty-first century as 'The Century of Women', Michele Lamb and Sue Thornton say that twentieth-century

236 *Sally R. Munt and Sharon E. Smith*

women can create 'a future in which women are respected and their contribution to the world is fully valued' (2006: 22). They say that the story of the Dragon King's daughter represents Enlightenment for all life, not just women, and that women contribute to *kōsenrufu* by developing self-esteem and confidence, compassion and wisdom and becoming truly happy irrespective of their circumstances. This state of Buddhahood is seen as a 'greater self'. This suggests several differences from the Married Women's Division of Japan that is very much based on the Japanese hegemonic model of the feminine. For members of the SGI-UK Women's Division, the model presented is on empowering one's self as a woman faced with a range of choices arising out of feminisms and postfeminisms.

As SGI globalises and SGI-UK becomes established, one can observe hybrid gender formations emerging. These norms are seen as 'complementary': for women, the forward focus is on working for a peaceful world through their 'soft power', and for men, they will question what masculinities are required to become 'golden pillars' of SGI, helping their communities and their families to work for *kōsenrufu*.

QUESTING APPROACHES IN SGI-UK

SGI-UK has several groups, for example, for artists, people of African-Caribbean heritage, and people involved in education. These groups, though open to all, are seen as ways of doing outreach. The leadership of SGI-UK were eventually persuaded that an outreach group to present a LGBTQI-friendly face would be valuable. This group (formerly Absolute Freedom) now the Rainbow Committee, attends annual Pride events across the UK and invites festival goers to come to a meeting. There, members of SGI-UK give testimony as to how their practice of Nichiren Buddhism helps them address problems that LBGTQI people specifically face, such as coming out, mending fences with homophobic family members and developing satisfying sexual relationships. As the meeting is open to all, it is seen as an opportunity for non-LGBTQI SGI-UK members to support and develop awareness of LGBTQI issues. This is to encourage LGBTQI 'questers' to enter the mainstream of SGI-UK rather than remain on its fringes. Unity has become a key theme for SGI-UK as it develops; more recently, the leadership of the Rainbow Committee was changed as its activities were deemed too 'separate' from its parent organisation, indicating the organisation's ongoing ambivalence towards identity politics and the politics of difference.

COUNTERCULTURAL APPROACHES IN SGI-UK

Gender norms within SGI have been contested by some, especially during 'SGI-UK's reassessment period' (see Waterhouse 2002). Although as a

Angels and the Dragon King's Daughter 237

lay organisation, SGI is less hierarchical than some other Buddhist movements, strongly asserting the equality of all people's potential for Buddhahood, SGI-UK has proved to be more conservative in other respects. Some participants reported that SGI's approach of methodological individualism is potentially empowering through its advocacy that the individual's environment is a reflection of their karma, which can be transformed through Buddhist practice. However, Jacqueline Stone argues that the wider social structures of discrimination and militarisation remain ignored, despite the rhetoric encouraging people to work for justice and peace. She suggests SGI and other similar Nichirenist movements' mode of social engagement is, 'a style of social engagement that tends to 'work within the system'; it does not issue a direct challenge to existing social structures or attempt fundamentally to transform them' (2003: 76–77). This focus on the individual is in keeping with neo-liberal modes of governmentality that focus on the ways in which individuals make themselves subjects.

CONCLUSION: NEO-LIBERAL INDIVIDUALISM WITHIN WESTERN BUDDHISM

In *Governing the Soul*, Nikolas Rose, following an intellectual tradition including Max Weber, Foucault and others, states how contemporary spiritual pilgrimages can be read as the offspring of medieval systems for the administration of the soul that were fundamental to the modernity of the West. He argues more broadly that:

> ... 'belief systems' concerning the self should not be construed as inhabiting a diffuse field of 'culture,' but as embodied in institutional and technical practices—spiritual, medical, political, economic—through which forms of individuality are specified and governed (1999: 222).

Positing that religious allegiance is now a matter of choice 'from the varieties of belief and practice on offer in a shopping mall of spirituality' (1999: 272), Rose returns religious practice firmly inside the dominant modes of Western individualism.

Our empirical findings suggest that each Western Buddhist NRM is highly heteronormative, yet these norms continue to be contested in a variety of ways by their members, reflecting the contradictory impulses of previous feminist research (Wessinger 1993; Puttick 2003; Palmer 2003). Although linked to Buddhist traditions that tend to privilege the 'masculine', the gender norms and attitudes to feminism within the TBC reflect the habitual androcentrism of Western modernism, primarily liberal feminisms' agenda of equality between the sexes. Those in SGI-UK reflect the hybridity of gender norms developed during modernity in Japan, together with a focus on a liberal, perhaps even postmodern form of feminist individualism

238   *Sally R. Munt and Sharon E. Smith*

or social distinction. Two of the most important traditions within British Buddhism have addressed gender and, to some extent, heteronormativity and queer issues. Of those members minoritised by those norms, some engage 'tactically', others choose to stay on the fringes of these movements as 'questing members', installing acquisitive practises of self. Woodhead's model (2007) can therefore be seen to have analytical purchase and could be enriched when informed by Bourdieu's insights on *habitus*, combined with further reflection on gender's intersections with race, ethnicity, nationality, sexuality—including the ways in which forces such as globalisation and neo-liberalism continue to influence and reinscribe heteronormativities. Participants find the technologies of the self-offered by each movement conducive to self-empowerment and this attracts many women, LGBTQI individuals and people of colour to join. But this very focus on subjectivity, arising out of the reflective and contemplative nature of many Buddhist practices, has paradoxical effects: on the one hand, it reinforces neo-liberal forms of governmentality that privilege the individual subject. On the other hand, it enables dissenting grassroots, particularly female and LGBTQI members, to negotiate hegemonic discourses of gender and sexuality in such a way that they can centre authority on themselves as individual practitioners, endorsing their 'experience' in favour of 'doctrine' or 'tradition'. This is in keeping with other studies of Buddhists in Britain and LGBTQI practitioners of religious/spiritual traditions (Waterhouse 1999; Yip 2005). Whilst TBC hegemonises white middle-class identity positions, SGI-UK is unique amongst British Buddhist movements in its ethnic diversity. SGI-UK stands out in offering spaces where people of colour can be empowered through its technologies of the self (see Smith 2008 for more detail). But in most Buddhist institutions, those who are LGBTQI (particularly those who are not white, middle-class, gay men) and/or racialised as people of colour may find themselves even more marginalised.

So whilst Buddhism might initially appear to offer spaces for those traditionally disempowered on account of their 'difference', women and queer people (especially lesbians, bisexual women, trans and intersex people) may find their passage within its institutions more difficult to negotiate once they have joined. Whilst there remains a seemingly intransigent symbolic pressure within contemporary NRMs for women to be as 'angels', despite this, women, queer people and people of colour are able to create more negotiated (though contingent) spaces of articulation, once inside. Their critical interventions manage to challenge NRM's hegemonising attempts at inscribing traditional and heteronormative gender subjectivities upon their followers. For such members, the queerly symbolic (but still reinscribable) Dragon King's daughter might provide a more amenable mythical figuration in which to invest their faith than the vaunted 'angel'. These symbolic mediations are of considerable continuing significance for Buddhist NRMs and their minority members.

Angels and the Dragon King's Daughter 239

Figure 12.4 Vijayatara/Sharon Smith (1962–2011). To whom this publication is dedicated in respectful and loving memory.

ACKNOWLEDGEMENTS

The authors would like to thank the ESRC/AHRC Religion and Society programme for funding the Queer Spiritual Spaces project and project colleagues for their collective humour, patience and insight in executing this research, in particular Andrew Kam-Tuck Yip. They would also like to thank Sarah Norman of the IOP-UK and Dharmacharini Anaga- rika Parami for their comments on this paper. Sally would like to thank Savi Hensman, Sharon's partner, for kindly providing last minute references from Sharon's books.

Sally R. Munt has revised this article for publication in light of the death of her co-author, Dr Sharon Smith, on 13 March 2011 (see obituaries in the *Guardian* newspaper at http://www.guardian.co.uk/theguardian/2011/apr/11/vijayatara-obituary and at http://www.sussex.ac.uk/sccs/news andevents?id=7497).

NOTES

1 The Queer Spiritual Spaces project was funded by the Religion and Society Programme, jointly financed by the Economic and Social Research Council and the Arts and Humanities Research Council UK. This research ran from 2007–2009 and involved a team of ten researchers; the project explored non-hegemonic LGBTQI faith and religious groups, including Quakers, Buddhists, Muslims, New Age, Michigan Women's Festival and the non-aligned spiritually curious online. The research has been published as Kath A. Browne, Sally R. Munt and Andrew K. T. Yip (2010).
2 Both *gohonzon* and *gongyo* are concepts used by most sects of Japanese Buddhism.

240 *Sally R. Munt and Sharon E. Smith*

3 For more details how some trans people have experienced TBC see Yip and Smith (2010).
4 See the work of Sandy Boucher (1993) on sexual abuse in Buddhist groups in the USA.
5 Shariputra is not simply a 'man'. Shariputra was a revered elder monk in the Buddha's day, noted for his deep understanding and ability to teach the Buddha's doctrines. By the time the Mahayana texts were composed, Shariputra was presented as a foil representing monks who do not really understand the depth of the Buddha's teachings. Shariputra is depicted in this manner in a number of Mahayana scriptures, including the Lotus Sutra.
6 Our description here is purposefully filtered through Soka Gakkai and does not represent broader understandings of the original story in the Lotus Sutra or of the feminist scholarly analysis of this story. In India, where the Lotus Sutra was composed, the reference is to 'the Naga king's daughter'. Nagas in India are described as having a human appearance from the waist up and having tails of serpents from the waist down. They live in the waters. So while Soka Gakkai promotes the interpretation that this is the Dragon King's daughter, the reference is in fact to Nagas. The princess in question was a Naga. The story of the Naga King's daughter is addressing the Buddhist concept that only a person with all the characteristics and marks of a 'superior man', including a non-circumcised penis, can achieve awakening. The Naga King's daughter, who is not named as in so many patriarchal scriptures, is a twelve-year-old girl who teaches the Dharma with brilliance. Shariputra in effect says, if you understand the Dharma so well, why are you still female? She then instantaneously changes herself into a male Bodhisattva or Buddha, sits under a tree and expounds the Dharma. This is not exactly a resounding affirmation of embodied femaleness, although it is the only Mahayana scripture available along these lines to Soka Gakkai due to its sole focus on the Lotus Sutra. A stronger feminist story is found in the Vimalakirti Sutra (Vimilakirtinirdesa Sutra), where a 'goddess' turns Shariputra into her body and herself into Shariputra's body and back again to demonstrate that physical characteristics are impermanent and irrelevant to whether or not one can become awakened. There is also the Srimala Sutra in which Queen Srimala is depicted as a female Buddha. See further the work of Diana Paul, also perhaps Serinity Young. Thank you to Catherine Wessinger for this observation.
7 Sensei is a Japanese term meaning teacher currently used in SGI-UK to refer to President Ikeda.
8 See for example the discussion of an interview with a member of SGI-UK's young women's division in Yip and Smith (2010).
9 Greenham Common Peace Camp was a protest against the US deployment of cruise missiles during the Cold War. For further information see Hipperson (not dated) and Roseneil (2000).

BIBLIOGRAPHY

Ahmed, S. (2006) *Queer Phenomenology: Orientations, Objects, Others*. Durham, NC and London: Duke University Press.
Akashavana (n.d.) www.akashavana.org/
Barker, E. (1990) *New Religious Movements: A Practical Introduction*. London: Bernan Press.
Barker, E. (1998) 'New Religions and New Religiosity', in Barker, E. and Warburg, M. (eds.) *New Religions and New Religiosity*. Aarhus: Aarhus University Press, 10–27.

Angels and the Dragon King's Daughter 241

Bell, S. (2002) 'Scandals in Emerging Western Buddhism', in Prebish, C. S. and Baumann, M. (eds.) *Westward Dharma: Buddhism beyond Asia*. Berkeley, CA: University of California Press, 230–242.

Bluck, R. (2006) *British Buddhism: Teachings, Practice and Development*. London and New York: Routledge.

Boucher, S. (1993) *Turning the Wheel: American Women Creating the New Buddhism*. Boston: Beacon Press.

Bourdieu, P. and Wacquant, L. J. D. (1992) *An Invitation to Reflexive Sociology*. Cambridge: Polity Press.

Browne, K. A., Munt, S. R. and Yip, A. K. T. (2010) *Queer Spiritual Spaces: Sexuality and Sacred Places*. London, Burlington: Ashgate.

Bunting, M. (1997) 'The Dark Side of Enlightenment', *The Guardian*, 27 October.

Bunting, M. (ed.) (1998) *Westward Dharma: Buddhism beyond Asia*. Berkeley, CA: University of California Press.

Butler, J. (1993) *Bodies That Matter: On the Discursive Limits of "Sex."* London: Routledge.

Butler, J. (1999) *Gender Trouble: Feminism and the Subversion of Identity*. London and New York: Routledge, 10th anniversary edition.

Cabezón, J. I. (ed.) (1992) *Buddhism, Sexuality, and Gender*. New York: Suny Press.

Cabezon, J. I. and Anderson, C. (1994) 'Buddhism, Sexuality and Gender', *Journal of the History of Sexuality* 4(3): 469–472.

Coleman, E., Colgan, P. and Gooren, L. (1992) 'Male Cross-Gender Behavior in Myanmar (Burma): A Description of the Acault', in Comstock, G. D. and Henking, S. E. (eds.) *Que(e)rying Religion: A Critical Anthology*. New York: Continuum, 313–321.

Dasgupta, R. (2003) 'Creating Corporate Warriors: The "Salaryman" and Masculinity in Japan', in Louie, K. and Low, M. (eds.) *Asian Masculinities: The Meaning and Practice of Manhood in China and Japan*. New York: Routledge, 118–134.

Dawson, L. L. (2003) *Cults and New Religious Movements*. Oxford: Blackwell.

Devamitra. (2001) 'On Manhood', *Madhyamavani Online*. Available at http://madhyamavani.fwbo.org/5/manhood.html, last accessed 29 January 2010.

Faure, B. (1998) *The Red Thread: Buddhist Approaches to Sexuality*. Princeton, NJ: Princeton University Press.

Faure, B. (2003) *The Power of Denial: Buddhism, Purity, and Gender*. Princeton, NJ: Princeton University Press.

Foucault, M. (1984) *The History of Sexuality, vol. 2*. London: Penguin Books.

Foucault, M. (1997) 'Technologies of the Self', in Rabinow, P. (ed.) *Michel Foucault: Ethics, Subjectivity and Truth*. London: Allen Lane, Penguin, 223–251.

FWBO Files. (1999) Available at http://www.fwbo-files.com/.

Giddens, A. (1991) *Modernity and Self-Identity: Self and Society in the Late Modern Age*. Cambridge: Polity Press.

Gross, R. M. (1993) *Buddhism after Patriarchy: A Feminist History, Analysis, and Reconstruction of Buddhism*. New York: State University of New York Press.

Gyatso, J. (2003) 'One Plus One Makes Three: Buddhist Gender, Monasticism, and the Law of the Non-Excluded Middle', *History of Religions* 43: 89–115.

Halperin, D. (1995) *Saint Foucault: Towards a Gay Hagiography*. New York: Oxford University Press.

Harvey, P. (2000) *An Introduction to Buddhist Ethics: Foundations, Values and Issues*. Cambridge: Cambridge University Press.

Hipperson, S. 'Greenham Common Women's Peace Camp: 1981'. Available at http://www.greenhamwpc.org.uk/, last accessed 21 August 2010.

Hori, I. (1994) *Folk Religion in Japan*. Chicago: Chicago University Press.

Jackson, P. A. (1998) 'Male Homosexuality and Transgenderism in the Thai Buddhist Tradition', in Leyland, W. (ed.) *Queer Dharma: Voices of Gay Buddhists*. San Francisco: Gay Sunshine Press, 55–89.

242 Sally R. Munt and Sharon E. Smith

Jackson, P.A. (2000) 'An Explosion of Thai Identities: Global Queering and Re-imagining Queer Theory', *Culture, Health and Sexuality* 2: 405–424.

Jnanavira. (2010) 'RE: Feminist Review Article on Buddhism, Sexuality and Gender' [Personal Email] S. Smith, 16 February.

Karma Lekshe Tsomo (ed.) (1999) *Buddhist Women across Cultures: Realizations.* Albany, NY: State University of New York Press.

Karma Lekshe Tsomo. (2000) *Innovative Women in Buddhism: Swimming against the Stream.* Surrey, England: Curzon Press.

Karma Lekshe Tsomo. (2004a) *Buddhist Women and Social Justice: Ideals, Challenges, and Achievements.* Albany, NY: State University of New York Press.

Karma Lekshe Tsomo. (2004b) *Discipline and Practice: Buddhist Women Past and Present.* Honolulu: Sakyadita.

Karma Lekshe Tsomo. (2004c) *Bridging Worlds: Buddhist Women's Voices across Generations.* Taipei: Yuan Chuan Press.

King, R. (1999) *Orientalism and Religion: Postcolonial Theory, India and "the Mystic East".* London: Routledge.

Lamb, M., and Thornton. S. (2006) 'A Century of Women', *Art of Living.* Taplow: SGI-UK, 22–23.

Leyland, W. (ed.) (1998) *Queer Dharma: Voices of Gay Buddhists.* San Francisco: Gay Sunshine Press.

Mahamati and Subhuti. (2009) 'Conversations with Sangharakshita'. Available at http://www.sangharakshita.org/interviews/CONVERSATIONS_AUGUST_2009.pdf.

Maitreyi. (1997) 'Feminism and Buddhism', in Kalyanavaca (ed.) *The Moon and Flowers: A Woman's Path to Enlightenment.* Birmingham: Windhorse Publications, 111–120.

Mclaughlin, L. (2009) 'Sōka Gakkai in Japan'. PhD thesis, Princeton, NJ: Princeton University.

McNay, L. (2009) 'Self as Enterprise: Dilemmas of Control and Resistance in Foucault's *The Birth of Biopolitics'*, *Theory, Culture and Society* 26: 55–77.

McRobbie, A. (2004) 'Post-Feminism and Popular Culture', *Feminist Media Studies* 4: 255–264.

Norman, S. (2006) 'Women in the Lotus Sutra', *Art of Living.* Taplow: SGI-UK, 15–16.

Okano, H. (1995) 'Women's Image and Place in Japanese Buddhism', in Fujimura-Fanselow, K. and Kameda, A. (eds.) *Japanese Women: New Feminist Perspectives on the Past, Present and Future.* New York: Feminist Press at the City University of New York, 15–28.

Palmer, S.J. (2003) 'Women's 'Cocoon Work' in New Religious Movements: Sexual Experimentation and Feminine Rites of Passage', in Dawson, L.L. (ed.) *Cults and New Religious Movements.* Oxford: Blackwell, 245–256.

Peletz, M.G. (2006) 'Transgenderism and Gender Pluralism in Southeast Asia since Early Modern Times', *Current Anthropology* 47: 309–340.

Prebish, C.S. and Tanaka, K.T. (eds.) (1998) *The Faces of Buddhism in America.* Berkeley, CA: University of California Press.

Puttick, E. (2003) 'Women in New Religious Movements', in Dawson, L.L. (ed.) *Cults and New Religious Movements.* Oxford: Blackwell, 230–244.

Rose, N. (1999) *Governing the Soul: The Shaping of the Private Self.* London: Free Association Books, 2nd edn.

Roseneil, S. (2000) *Common Women, Uncommon Practices: The Queer Feminisms of Greenham.* New York and London: Continuum.

Rubinstein, M. (2011) 'New Religious Movements', *Encyclopaedia Britannica online.* Available at http:// www.britannica.com/EBchecked/topic/1007307/ New-Religious-Movement- NRM, last accessed 6 February 2011.

Angels and the Dragon King's Daughter 243

Sangharakshita, U. (1990) 'The Individual and the World Today', in Sangharakshita (ed.), *New Currents in Western Buddhism: The Inner Meaning of the Friends of the Western Buddhist Order*. Glasgow: Windhorse Publications, 16–39.

Sangharakshita, U. (2009a) *Conversations with Bhante*. Available at http://www.sangharakshita.org/interviews/CONVERSATIONS_AUGUST_2009.pdf, last accessed 23 January 2010.

Sangrarakshita, U. (2009b) *What Is the Western Buddhist Order? A Message from Urgyen Sangharakshita*. Available at http://www.sangharakshita.org/What_is_the_Western_Buddhist_Order.pdf, last accessed 23 January 2010.

Schalow, P. G. (1998a) 'The Legend of Kukai and the Tradition of Male Love in Japanese Buddhism', in Leyland W. (ed.) *Queer Dharma: Voices of Gay Buddhists*. San Francisco: Gay Sunshine Press, 91–106.

Schalow, P. G. (1998b) 'Spiritual Dimensions of Male Beauty in Japanese Buddhism', in Leyland W. (ed.) *Queer Dharma: Voices of Gay Buddhists*. San Francisco: Gay Sunshine Press, 107–124.

Simmonds, F. N. (1997) 'My Body, Myself: How Does a Black Woman Do Sociology?', in Mirza, H. S. (ed.), *Black British Feminism: A Reader*. London: Routledge, 226–239.

Smith, S. E. (2008) 'Buddhism, Diversity and "Race": Multiculturalism and Western Convert Buddhist Movements in East London—a Qualitative Study'. PhD thesis. Goldsmiths College: University of London.

Stone, J. I. (2003) 'Nichiren's Activist Heirs: Sōka Gakkai, Risshō Kosekai, Nipponzan Myōhōji', in Queen, C. Prebish, C. and Keown, D. (eds.) *Action Dharma: New Studies in Engaged Buddhism*. Curzon, London: Routledge, 63–94.

Subhuti. (1988) *Buddhism for Today: A Portrait of a New Buddhist Movement*. Glasgow: Windhorse Publications.

Subhuti. (1994) *Sangharakshita: A New Voice in the Buddhist Tradition*. Birmingham: Windhorse Publications.

Subhuti. (1995) *Women, Men and Angels: An Inquiry Concerning the Relative Spiritual Aptitudes of Men and Women*. Birmingham: Windhorse Publications.

Suryaprabha (Director) (1997) *Time of Fire: 1975–77*. Video recording. London: Lights in the Sky.

Tweed, T. A. (1992) *The American Encounter with Buddhism 1844–1912: Victorian Culture and the Limits of Dissent*. Bloomington and Indianapolis: Indiana University Press.

Usui, A. (2003) 'The Role of Women in Machacek', in Wilson, D. and Wilson, B. (eds.) *Global Citizens: The Soka Gakkai Movement in the World*. Oxford: Oxford University Press, 153–204.

Wallis, R. (1976) *The Road to Total Freedom: A Sociological Analysis of Scientology*. New York: Columbia University Press.

Waterhouse, H. (1999) 'Who Says So? Legitimacy and Authenticity in British Buddhism', *Scottish Journal of Religious Studies* 20: 19–36.

Waterhouse, H. (2002) 'Soka Gakkai Buddhism as a Global Religious Movement', in Beckerlegge, G. (ed.) *Religion Today: Tradition, Modernity and Change*. Aldershot: Ashgate in association with the Open University, 109–155.

Wessinger, C. (ed.) (1993) *Women's Leadership in Marginal Religions: Explorations Outside the Mainstream*. Chicago: University of Illinois Press.

Wilson, B. R. and Cresswell, J. (eds.) (1999) *New Religious Movements: Challenge and Response*. London: Routledge.

Wilson, B. R. and Dobbelaere, K. (1994) *A Time to Chant: Soka Gakkai Buddhists in Britain*. Oxford: Clarendon.

Woodhead, L. (2007) 'Gender Differences in Religious Practice and Significance', in Beckford, J. A. and Demerath III, N. J. (eds.) *The Sage Handbook of the Sociology of Religion*. London: Sage Publications, 566–586.

244 *Sally R. Munt and Sharon E. Smith*

Yip, A. K. T. (2005) 'Queering Religious Texts: An Exploration of British Non-Heterosexual Christians' and Muslims' Strategy of Constructing Sexuality-Affirming Hermeneutics', *Sociology* 39: 47–65.

Yip, A. K. T. and Smith, S. (2010) 'Queerness and Sangha: Exploring Buddhist Lives', in Browne, K. Munt, S. R. and Yip, A. K. T. (eds.) *Queer Spiritual Spaces: Sexuality and Sacred Places*. Aldershot: Ashgate, 111–138.

Contributors

Maria Livia Alga is a PhD candidate at the Centre d'Etudes Féminines et d'Etudes de Genre, University of Paris 8 and the Department of Educational Sciences, University of Verona. Her work is funded by the Institut Emilie du Chatelet, Ile de France. Her research interests are the study of contemporary social movements and feminist civil society groups in Italy. She is particularly concerned with the articulation of anti-racist and anti-homophobic activism in changing urban contexts. Her work is inspired by a post-exotic, autoethnographic practice closely linked to her political engagement. She currently collaborates with the trans-feminist associations Casa di Ramia and Ideadestroyingmuros. She is also part of a university research team working on conflict resolution and institutional racism in the context of Verona's municipal social services, with a specific focus on Nigerian women. She has published on anti-homophobic and anti-racist activism in Palermo and on the phenomenon of Italy's neo-diaspora.

Tara Atluri is currently a Lecturer at the Ontario College of Art and Design University in Toronto, Canada. She previously worked as a researcher with Oecumene: Citizenship After Orientalism at the Open University in the United Kingdom (http://www.oecumene.eu). As part of her position with Oecumene she conducted research regarding sexual politics and social movements in the Indian subcontinent. She joined Oecumene as part of a postdoctoral project funded by the Social Sciences and Humanities Research Council of Canada.

Calogero Giametta's research focuses on the discourses linking the politics of sexuality/gender and the refugee granting process in the UK and in France. In 2014, he obtained his PhD in Sociology at London Metropolitan University with a thesis based on a long-term ethnography with sexual and gender minority asylum claimants and refugees living in London. Currently, he is a postdoctoral research fellow at Aix-Marseille Université within the research project 'Emborders: Problematising Sexual Humanitarianism through Experimental Filmmaking'. Working between the UK

246　*Contributors*

and France, through the Emborders project, he is exploring the effectiveness and scope of humanitarian practices and discourses by comparing the experiences of two groups of migrants who are addressed as potential 'target victims': migrants working in the sex industry and sexual/gender minority refugees.

Nina Held received her PhD in Women's Studies from the Centre for Gender and Women's Studies at Lancaster University (UK) in 2011. Her PhD thesis, *Racialised Lesbian Spaces*, explored the relationship between sexuality, 'race' and space within the context of urban night-time leisure spaces for women. The ethnographic study carried out in Manchester's Gay Village looked at the role of 'race' in the construction of lesbian bodies and spaces and how sexuality, 'race' and space work together in shaping subjectivities. Her current research interests in sexuality and asylum have developed through her previous role as Centre Coordinator at Freedom from Torture (FfT) and through her voluntary role at the Lesbian Immigration Support Group (LISG) since 2009. Nina currently works as Development Worker at Trafford Rape Crisis.

Savitri Hensman was born in Sri Lanka in 1962 and lives in London. As a Church of England member and lesbian activist seeking greater equality in church and society, she has extensive experience with debates on faith and sexuality at the local, national and international level. She has written extensively on these and other issues, including welfare and human rights, for a wide range of print and online publications, including newspapers, magazines, books and journals. She is also a consultant and works in the voluntary sector on equalities, involvement, health and social care. She is an Ekklesia associate.

Sally R. Munt is Professor of Gender and Cultural Studies at the University of Sussex and Director of the Sussex Centre for Cultural Studies. She is the co-author (with Andrew Yip) of *Cosmopolitan Dharma: 'Race', Gender and Sexuality in Western Buddhism* (forthcoming, Brill, 2016) and is the co-author, with Kath A. Browne and Andrew K.T. Yip, of *Queer Spiritual Spaces: Sexuality and Sacred Places* (Ashgate, 2010). She is the author of many books including *Queer Attachments: The Cultural Politics of Shame* (Ashgate, 2007) and editor (with Olu Jenzen) of *The Ashgate Research Companion to Paranormal Cultures* (Ashgate, 2014). Sally is also a BABCP-accredited cognitive behavioural psychotherapist.

Nadya Nartova is a Research Fellow at the Centre for Youth Studies and a lecturer in the Department of Sociology at the National Research University Higher School of Economics (HSE) in Saint Petersburg, Russia. Her research interests lie in the sociology of motherhood, age, the body and sexuality. She has published several articles and book chapters and is the co-editor of two edited collections on the sociology of the body: *Pro Telo: Molodezhnyi Kontekst* (2013) and *V Teni Tela* (2008).

Sarah-Jane Page is Lecturer in Sociology at Aston University, Birmingham, UK. Her research interests include religion and gender, sexuality and feminism. She has undertaken projects looking at religion, youth and sexuality, Anglican women priests and gender and clergy family life. She has published in journals such as *Feminist Review*, *Gender Work and Organization* and *Feminist Theology*, and she has co-authored (with Andrew Kam-Tuck Yip) a book entitled *Religious and Sexual Identities: A Multi-faith Exploration of Young Adults* (Ashgate, 2013).

Tracey Reynolds is Professor of Social Sciences at the University of Greenwich. Tracey's research interests focus on trans-national families and kinship networks, constructions of motherhood, parenting and childrearing. She has conducted extensive empirical research in the UK across a range of social issues, including black and minority families living in disadvantaged communities. Previous publications include 'Exploring the Absent/ Present Dilemma: Black Fathers, Family Relationships and Social Capital in Britain', *The Annals of the American Academy of Political and Social Science* (2009). She is also the author of *Caribbean Mothers: Identity and Experience in the UK* (published by Tufnell Press, 2005); *Transnational Families: Ethnicities, Identities and Social Capital*, with Harry Goulbourne, John Solomos and Elisabetta Zontini (published by Routledge, 2010) and Guest Editor of Special Issues 'Young People, Ethnicity and Social Capital' (*Ethnic and Racial Studies*, May 2010) and 'Transnational and Diasporic Youth Identities: Exploring Conceptual Themes and Future Research Agendas' (*Identities: Global Studies in Power and Culture*, April 2015, with Elisabetta Zontini).

Antoine Rogers is a Principal Lecturer in Sociology at London Southbank University. Antoine's main areas of academic research include sexuality, the voluntary sector and qualitative research methods. His research and teaching has been greatly informed by his professional experiences as a qualified social worker and as a political activist. Antoine is a Chicago native and his work critically reflected on national and local identity and the role of personal experiences as a source of knowledge and understanding. In 2007, Antoine embarked on research activities that explore Black British sexual identity. Initially in collaboration with the London based voluntary organisation, the rukus! Federation, he produced the film *In This Our Lives—The Reunion*. The documentary film explores the complex intersection of race, sexuality and social policy within a British context. The film featured in the 2009 London Lesbian and Gay Film Festival. Since 2008, Antoine has facilitated events under the banner of Rage and Desire, a partnership between acclaimed photographer

248 *Contributors*

and cultural producer Ajamu in his capacity as curator for rukus! Black LGBT archives. Rage and Desire includes a programme of themed events, with academic discussions, international speakers, seminars, film screenings and exhibitions exploring Black and Asian LGBT academic and cultural production in the twentieth century. Antoine's most recent publication, 'Crossing Deep Waters: Transatlantic Reflections Black Gay Men and Journeys Influenced by "In the Life" ' is part of the edited collection from Stephens and Fullwood (2015) *Black Genius: Joseph Beam and In the Life*. Antoine also wrote ' "In This Our Lives": Invisibility and Black British Gay Identity' as part of the edited collection from Rivers and Ward (2012) *Out of the Ordinary: Representations of LGBT Lives*. Antoine has also served as Chair of the Board of Trustees for centred, a London based LGBT community development and research charity that provides space and opportunity with and for lesbian, gay, bisexual and transgender people and friends to gain support, grow and affect wider social and strategic change. Antoine is diligently working on his first solo book, *The Evidence of My Existence*, which explores the intersection of race, sexuality and nationality.

Róisín Ryan-Flood is a Senior Lecturer in Sociology and Director of the Centre for Intimate and Sexual Citizenship (CISC) at the University of Essex. Her research interests include gender, sexuality, citizenship, kinship and critical epistemologies. She is the author of *Lesbian Motherhood: Gender, Families and Sexual Citizenship* (Palgrave, 2009) and co-editor of *Secrecy and Silence in the Research Process: Feminist Reflections* (Routledge, 2010), as well as numerous journal articles and book chapters. She is co-editor of the journal *Sexualities: Studies in Culture and Society* (Sage).

Sharon E. Smith was a Research Associate at the Sussex Centre for Cultural Studies. She was a sociologist of religion whose interests were in the ways religious/spiritual spaces and identities are taken up and further inscribed by other axes of 'difference' (particularly 'race', ethnicity, class, gender and sexuality). Her doctoral research at Goldsmiths', University of London, was an ethnography of Western convert Buddhist movements in East London and their interactions with people minoritised due to being people of colour and/or being working class. She was also a postdoctoral research fellow for the AHRC/ESRC funder Queer Spiritual Space(s) project at the University of Sussex. Sharon was a practising Buddhist with the TBO.

Ria Snowdon was previously a Research Associate in Social and Policy Studies at the Weeks Centre for Social and Policy Research, London South Bank University, working alongside Yvette Taylor on the ESRC project

Contributors 249

'Making Space for Queer Identifying Religious Youth'. With Yvette she co-edited *Queering Religion* (Routledge, 2014). Other co-authored publications include 'Sexualities and Religion' (*Sexualities*); 'Making Space for Young Lesbians in Church?' (*Journal of Lesbian Studies*); 'Queer Youth, Facebook, and Faith: Facebook Methodologies and Online Identities' (*New Media and Society*); and 'Sounding Religious, Sounding Queer' (*Journal of Ecclesial Practices*).

Francesca Stella is a Research Fellow in Sociology at the School of Social and Political Sciences, University of Glasgow. Her research interests include sexuality, gender, migration, human rights and activism, state socialism and post-socialism and research epistemologies. Her publications include the monograph *Lesbian Lives in Soviet and Post-Soviet Russia: Post/ Socialism and Gendered Sexualities* (Palgrave, 2014) as well as numerous book chapters and articles, including 'Queer Space, Pride and Shame in Moscow' (*Slavic Review*, 2013) and 'The Politics of In/Visibility: Carving out Queer Space in Ul'yanovsk' (*Europe-Asia Studies*, 2012). She has also co-edited a special issue of *Europe-Asia Studies* on everyday life in provincial Russia (2012). She is lead investigator on the ESRC-funded project 'Intimate Migrations', which explores the experiences of lesbian, gay and bisexual migrants from Eastern Europe and the Former Soviet Union in Scotland (www.intimatemigrations.net). She is a member of GRAMNet, a network bringing together researchers, practitioners and activists working on migration.

Yvette Taylor is Professor of Education at the University of Strathclyde, and was previously Head of the Weeks Centre for Social and Policy Research, LSBU. She was a Fulbright Distinguished Scholar at Rutgers University and has held visiting posts including at the Australian National University and McGill. Her books include *Fitting into Place? Class and Gender Geographies and Temporalities* (2012); *Lesbian and Gay Parenting: Securing Social and Educational Capitals* (2009) and *Working-Class Lesbian Life: Classed Outsiders* (2007). Edited collections include *Critical Consumption* (2015); *Educational Diversity* (2012); *Sexualities: Reflections and Futures* (2012); *Theorizing Intersectionality and Sexuality* (2010) and *Classed Intersections: Spaces, Selves, Knowledges* (2010). Yvette is currently working on an ESRC standard grant 'Making Space for Queer Identifying Religious Youth'.

Matthew Waites is Senior Lecturer in Sociology within the School of Social and Political Sciences at the University of Glasgow. He is author of *The Age of Consent: Young People, Sexuality and Citizenship* (Palgrave Macmillan, 2005) and co-editor of three recent special issues on sociology and human rights, all edited by P. Hynes, M. Lamb, D. Short and M. Waites:

'Sociology and Human Rights: New Engagements', *International Journal of Human Rights*, Vol. 14, no.6, November 2010; 'The Sociology of Human Rights', *Sociology*, Vol. 46, no.5, October 2012; and 'New Directions in the Sociology of Human Rights', *International Journal of Human Rights*, Vol. 16, no.8, December 2012. He is also editor, with Kelly Kollman, of *The Global Politics of LGBT Human Rights*, Special Issue, *Contemporary Politics*, Vol. 15, no.1, March 2009.

Index

activism: antihomophobic 113, 115, 117, 119–21, 126–7; antiracist 96, 122, 124; antiracist and antihomophobic 114–15, 120; feminist 95–111, 112–30, 149–63; Global South, in the, 82–7; in India 149–63; in Italy 112–30; LGBT 74, 79, 81, 113, 131, 151–2, 154–5; networks 118; and privilege 73–93, 97–8, 115, 125; and the state 119, 160; in UK 73–93, 183–98; *see also* homonationalism; femonationalism
Ahmed, Sara 2, 6, 105, 133, 145, 168, 171, 230

belonging: and difference 105; lesbian 134, 145; national 95, 115; and migration 40, 42, 48, 52, 64, 122, 145; and religion 165–6, 176, 186
Binnie, Jon 39, 40, 44
biopolitics 20, 25, 32, 58, 151; *see also* Foucault, M.
biopower 4, 17, 20; *see also* Foucault, M.
borders: biographical 56, 62, 68; and control 3–4, 7, 58, 116, 119, 158, 193; and 'fortress Europe' 3–4, 7, 116; and LGBT migration 39, 66–7, 122; symbolism 116
Butler, Judith 49, 226

citizenship: and inclusion/exclusion 17–36, 70, 100, 108, 113, 121; and queer migration 44, 46; and 'race'/ethnicity 96; and right to asylum 4–5, 7–8, 55–72,

120–2, 124, 132, 139–45; and sexuality 29, 41–2, 47, 48, 49, 51–2, 113, 117–18, 150, 165, 201–2; and undocumented migration 116–17, 124–7; *see also clandestinità*; sexual citizenship
clandestinità 116–17, 124–7; *see also* undocumented migration
class: and capital 59, 69; and migration 47, 117; and privilege 87; and religion 224, 230, 238; and 'race'/ethnicity 105, 114
colonialism 2–3, 6, 8, 41–2, 52, 74–7, 80, 98, 100, 102, 107, 138, 149–63; and anticolonial struggles 153, 159; and postcolonialism 5, 11, 40, 71, 73–4, 86–7, 149–63, 224

demography 17–22, 33n5; and pronatalist policies 25, 32

Fassin, Didier 56, 115
feminism: and activism 95–111, 112–30, 149–63; Black feminism 2, 6–7, 95–7, 99, 101, 106–8, 131–2, 223; and Black feminist theory 2, 6–7, 95–7; and black women 95–109; gender politics 1–2, 6–8; in India 149–63; and intersectionality 2–3, 85–8, 99, 131, 166–8, 180, 218, 220–1, 229; and nationalism 1,18; and religion 8–9, 149, 227–8, 234, 236–7; Western 149, 160; and white privilege 97–8, 115, 125; *see also* femonationalism

252 *Index*

femonationalism 1, 18
Foucault, Michel 4, 17, 20, 56, 221–2

gender: in Buddhism 218–23, 225–9, 231, 233–8; in Christian churches 21–2, 165–6, 168–9, 170–2, 175, 179, 180, 189–96, 205; and colonialism 154–5, 157; and diversity 84, 188, 190, 213; and equality 2–4, 6–7, 9, 17–18, 30, 115, 117, 172, 178–9, 180n1, 223, 226, 231, 237; and human rights 74–80, 86, 151; and the law 22–7, 55–63, 115; and migration 68–70, 120, 139, 144; and national belonging 17, 18–19, 32, 117–18, 126; policing of 212, 214; and 'race'/ethnicity 95–6, 98–100, 102, 104–9; transgender 84
Global North 55, 73–4, 76–7, 95–6, 104
Global South: LGBT movements 73–4, 76–7, 78, 82–3, 87; and migration 95–6, 99, 104, 107–8; and postcolonialism 149–51, 153–4, 158–9; as West's 'irrational' Other 1–3, 63, 71

heteronormativity: in Buddhism 218, 222–3, 231, 237–8; in Christian churches 21–2, 165–6, 168–9, 170–2, 175, 179, 180, 189–96, 176, 180, 205; and citizenship 27–32, 39, 49; and colonialism 107, 152, 157; and migration 52, 114; and nationalism 38; and racism 121; in social theory 43, 48–9
homonationalism 18, 41, 73, 116–18, 120, 149, 150, 159; see also Puar, Jasbir
humanitarianism 4–5, 55–72, 85; sexual humanitarianism 57

identity: counter-normative 199–214; and diaspora 37–8; and disidentification 165–8, 180; display of 169, 206; diversity 83–4, 122–3, 220; European 3–4, 7, 8, 18, 31–2, 112, 113–14; gender identity 77–80; in global context 37, 86–7, 143;

intersectional 131–2, 170, 185; LGBT 38, 41–3, 45–6, 47–8, 57, 65, 74–5, 165, 209–10; and migration 40, 46, 99, 120, 124, 141; national 18–19, 22, 32, 101, 121; and privilege 39, 238; and 'race'/ethnicity 7, 96–7, 107–8, 112, 113–14, 115–16, 125, 158; religious 165, 167, 168, 186, 199–217; and young people 166, 199, 204, 213
identity politics 86, 122, 224, 236
imperialism 42, 74, 116, 157
intersectionality 2–3, 85–8, 99, 131, 166–8, 180, 218, 220–1, 229; see also feminism
Islamophobia 3, 8, 119–21

Lorde, Audre 121, 131

methodology 42, 55–6, 66, 78, 115, 169–70, 204, 220–3
migration: and asylum 4–5, 7–8, 55–72, 120–2, 124, 132, 139–45; costs 39; gendered 104; and inclusion/exclusion 44–6, 58, 61, 66, 69–70, 99, 100–1; LGBT/queer 37–52, 55–9, 68, 120–7, 139–40; and political discourse 61, 69, 116; and 'race'/ethnicity 119–27; rural to urban 39–40, 42; transgender 45–6

nationalism: and diaspora 37–38; and demography 17–22, 33n5; and Europe 4, 17–36; and family norms 17–36; in India 151–2, 160; and nation-state 17, 20, 101, 108, 116, 158; in Russia 17–36; see also homonationalism; sexual democracy; sexual nationalism
neocolonial 149–50, 153, 156, 158–9; see also postcolonialism
new religious movements (NRMs) 218, 224–38
non-governmental organisations (NGOs) 55–6, 73–88

Orientalism 116, 149–50
othering: categorisation 70, 185–6; LGBT 29, 64, 116; migrants 57–8; and racialisation 18, 95, 98, 100, 108, 138

postcolonialism 5, 11, 40, 71 73–4, 80, 86–8, 149–63, 224; see also *neocolonial*

Puar, Jasbir 1, 3, 6–7, 18, 41, 73, 85, 116, 118, 149, 166

'race': and Black feminism 2, 6–7, 95–7, 99, 101, 106–8, 131–2, 223; and Black feminist theory 2, 6–7, 95–7; and black women 95–109; categorisation of 100, 123, 133, 138; and equality 102, 104; and exclusion 39; and gender 96–9, 102, 105, 107, 229, 238; and intersectionality 37, 99; and normativities 6–7, 40, 95–7, 99, 101, 119, 126–7, 131–2, 138, 145, 223, 230; and migration 116, 119; and racialisaiton 18, 95, 98, 100,108, 138; and sexuality 100, 131, 133, 144–5; and space 133–4; and whiteness 6–7, 40, 97, 119, 126–7, 138, 145, 230

religion: and gender 166, 170, 218, 221–38; and intersectionality 167, 178; and national identity 22, 151; and new religious movements (NRMs) 218–38; and reproductive rights 22; and sexual citizenship 165; and sexuality 50, 85, 87, 165–80, 187–91, 194–6, 207–9; and sexual practices 200–3, 205–8; and young people 165–80, 199–214

sexual citizenship 29, 41–2, 47, 48, 49, 51–2, 113, 117–18, 150, 165, 201–2; and civil partnerships 29, 39, 41, 44, 46, 117–18, 165, 178–9, 235; in Commonwealth of Nations 73–93; in India 149–63; in Ireland 37–54; in Italy 112,130; in Russia 17–36; in UK 55–72, 131–48, 183–98; *see also* sexual democracy

sexual democracy 4, 7–8, 30, 32, 115–17, 120, 126–7

sexuality: and citizenship 29, 41–2, 47, 48, 49, 51–2, 113, 117–18, 150, 165, 201–2; diversity 84, 207, 220; and equality 41, 48, 52, 81, 115, 184–7, 189, 194–5; and family 49–51, 112, 166, 173, 174–9, 192, 205, 230, 234; and global aid 84–5, 149, 151, 156, 158; and intersectionality 99–100, 131, 218, 220; and the law 27–9, 39, 55–70, 80, 139–45, 150; and migration 37–8, 40–1, 42–3, 46, 55–70, 114, 132, 139–45; and morality 26; and nationalism 17–20, 41, 73; and 'race'/ethnicity 95–6, 98, 100–3, 106–9, 116, 120, 126, 131–2; and religion 165, 168, 173–80, 184–96, 199–214, 218–38; and reproductive rights 17–32, 115; and space 38–9, 49, 133–4, 137, 140–1, 144–5; and young people 165–80, 199–214; *see also* sexual citizenship

sexual nationalism 1–4, 17–19, 41, 73, 117–18, 149, 159; and Europe 4, 17–36; *see also* femonationalism; homonationalism; sexual democracy

sexual norms: and celibacy 10, 199, 200–1, 204–9, 213, 226, 231; and kinship, 17–36, 170–2, 174–6; and monogamy 10, 199–200, 201–3, 203–6, 210–13; and non-monogamy 10, 201–3, 210–11; and reproduction, 17–36

Weeks, Jeffrey, 1, 2, 51, 168, 199–200

Yip, Andrew Kam-Tuck, 8–9, 166–86, 177, 180, 184, 201–2, 204, 206, 2014, 219–20, 238, 239